Maya® Manual

Springer-Verlag London Ltd.

Dan Lavender

Maya Manual

Springer

Dan Lavender, BA, MA

The publisher would like to acknowledge the support of John Cowell, De Monfort University, Leicester, Series Editor of the Essential series, for which this book was originally proposed.

British Library Cataloguing in Publication Data
  Maya manual. - (Springer professional computing)
  1. Maya (Computer file) 2. Computer animation
  I. Title
  006.6'96
  ISBN 978-1-4471-3924-9   ISBN 978-1-85233-858-9 (eBook)
  DOI 10.1007/978-1-85233-858-9

Library of Congress Cataloging-in-Publication Data
A catalog record for this book is available from the Library of Congress

http://www.springer.co.uk

© Springer-Verlag London 2003
Originally published by Springer-Verlag London Berlin Heidelberg in 2003
Softcover reprint of the hardcover 1st edition 2003

Typeset by Gray Publishing, Tunbridge Wells, UK

34/3830-543210 Printed on acid-free paper SPIN 10865143

For Nicky

Acknowledgements

Thanks go, first of all, to all at the NCCA Bournemouth, past and present, students and staff. This book is a direct result of teaching and being taught there.

Thanks also go to John Cowell, and Rebecca Mowat and Joanne Cooling at Springer, for their suggestions, editing and help.

Finally, thanks are due to my wife, my friends and my family for their support and patience whilst this book was written.

Contents

Basics 1

What Is Maya?

Maya is an integrated collection of tools for creating computer generated (CG) images from Alias|Wavefront. It combines animation, dynamics, modeling and rendering tools that were only available as distinct packages plus some tools that are unique to the package itself. Maya is able to create a fully functioning piece of computer animation, whether as digital characters or visual effects for inclusion in live action footage or in a piece of stand-alone animation. It can be used to create 3D work from start to finish, which means that the user never has to move to another package in order to fulfil the requirements of a production. Maya can also be integrated into any production pipeline because of its flexible scripting mechanisms, open architecture and plug-in development. If many users are creating work with Maya, then many file operations and import tools are available to make sure that a multiple user environment connects together seamlessly. Now in its fourth version and one of the most popular computer animation packages available, Maya is used in every single Oscar winning special effects films that has been released in the last four years and Alias|Wavefront has just been awarded an Oscar for technical achievement.

How Best to Use This Book

Maya is a big package. It has a fairly steep learning curve that starts to level off after a few months of use, but nevertheless, it is a fairly daunting piece of software to learn. This book will be for two types of people: those who have not used a 3D package before and those who have used other 3D packages and are looking at the feature set of Maya. If you are the latter type of reader, then you should not have too much difficulty understanding the concepts and terminology used when we are looking at operations within Maya. Although jumping in and out of chapters is understandable if there are sections that are of no interest, be aware that some of the chapters will use previously created material. This is because the book has been written in a specific order: beginning at the basics that go to making up the heart of Maya, the chapters will then progress through each part of Maya, often using what has been investigated and discovered in previous chapters to add depth to the current chapter. Some chapters may utilize previous examples and demonstrations to illustrate new concepts or tools and some chapters may not. The reason for this is that it is often easier to open up scenes that have been used than start over from the beginning of each chapter. Most of the examples in this book are very simple,

1

as we are looking at how Maya functions and not how to achieve a certain effect using Maya; however, the final chapter will be a look at putting together a relatively complex scene using different tools and techniques.

If you have not used a 3D package before, then there will be a lot of new terms and ideas used here. The scope of this book does not cover the art of animating or how to model a character, because there are a lot of other books that cover the subjects in great depth. Technique is not the driving motivation behind this book, although there will at points be the odd helpful comment, as Maya covers a lot of ground. Animation is a large area of study, as is programming and rendering, so this book will not start to go into the concepts behind lighting models or programming constructs. What is assumed is that the reader will be familiar with the concepts that we will cover; so if we are discussing animation, then familiarity with the basics of keyframing is required. If not, then any of the Springer "Essential" family of books that are concerned with maths for computer graphics and computer animation are excellent resources. In addition to this, all copies of Maya ship with a comprehensive set of online documents and tutorials which should be consulted at any point, as there are details that are beyond the scope of this book and that complement the work presented here. Other useful learning features are built into Maya that will provide further help, such as the help line which will provide usage instructions on tools and actions and small pop-up windows when the cursor is over various interface items. This book has been written to provide the reader with a fundamental understanding of Maya across all of its modules and functions and provides a solid foundation with which to explore the software further through other books, training courses and the many online resources that exist for Maya. What this book will not do is teach how to animate, how to model or how to program; just the solid basics of using Maya and how its architecture fits together as an integrated 3D package.

The Desired Environment

Maya runs best with as fast a processor (or processors) as possible and as much RAM as can be shoehorned into a computer (but Maya can happily run on 256 Mb of RAM). This is true whether the current platform is Windows, Linux, Mac or UNIX based, but choosing the correct graphics card is a whole different kettle of monkeys. The Alias|Wavefront Maya site at www.aw.sgi.com will carry a full list of compatible graphics cards and a full list of compatible computer systems.

Notes and Notation

Because a three-button mouse is essential when using Maya the notation in the book is as follows:

    LMB: left mouse button
    MMB: middle mouse button
    RMB: right mouse button

All of these modes are used to click, drag or hold on interface items in Maya.

Any text that represents code to be entered into text fields in Maya will be displayed as code such as `ball.translateY += 5;`. Any text that is surrounded by ⟨ ⟩ (i.e. ⟨my_name_here.mb⟩) means that the text is variable and has usually been left for you to fill in.

Many of the nodes or attributes that will be used as examples throughout this book are numbered using the suffix "n" such as skinClustern. This notation is used because Maya will either number the nodes in the order that they are created during its use, or because a subscripted attribute should be accessed but it isn't important which is used, i.e. controlCurve[n].

Illustrations in the colour section are a combination of rendered examples from the book, rendered pieces I have created using Maya and images created by students I have taught who "road tested" the portions of the syllabus that became this book and I would especially like to thank Duncan Price, Stefan D'Hont, Unnstein Gudjohnson, Jordan Kirk, Gawain Liddiard, Mohamed Soby, Claire Pakeman, Jessica Groom, Alison Muffit, Mark Hatchard, Seth Dubieniec and Thom Greybe for their help in the production of colour stills for this book.

The Maya Interface

Before we look at any of the workings of Maya, it will be worthwhile explaining the basics of navigating and interacting with the main workings of the software. This chapter will concentrate on getting used to working with Maya from the moment the interface appears: what the interface consists of, moving our point of view about the workspace and some of the interface methods that are unique to this software package. One of the key concepts underlying the interface is the idea of speed and usability. Usually, one has to resign oneself to working in only one fashion: with the interface that was created at the design stage. Although we will be starting with the default interface settings for Maya (how it ships from the "factory floor"), we will be looking at small examples to alter Maya to perhaps enhance some aspect of our workflow throughout the book. But for now, we will start with the basics and get oriented.

Starting Maya is just a question of double-clicking the Maya icon, from the Start menu or Maya from the command line if using. After a loading screen is displayed, the Maya interface will appear. The default display is divided into four screens with a Menu Bar, Shelf and

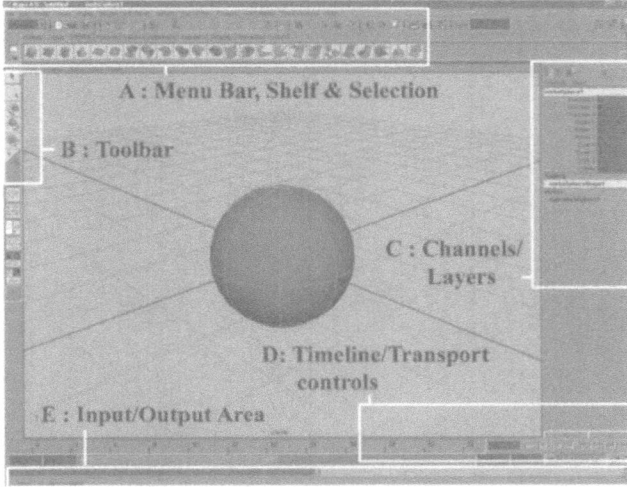

Figure 1.1 The Maya Main Window.

Selection Mask area (A), a Tool Bar (B), a Channel/Attribute display area (C), a Timeline with transport tools (D) and an input/output area (E).

The Camera Views

Within the Maya GUI (graphical user interface) are four views. Each view is a camera and can be manipulated as such, not only in terms of movement (dollying, tracking etc.) but also in terms of taking pictures (rendering) and changing other camera-related attributes such as focal length and depth of field. So for each view we are looking through a separate camera. The views that are represented here can be broken down into two types: *orthographic* and *perspective*. These two types of camera can be differentiated easily by the fact that an orthographic camera does not display its viewpoint in terms of perspective, that is, lines do not vanish to a meeting point on a horizon. These orthographic cameras are aligned in terms of up, front and side views, which allow you to accurately position items in terms of the X, Y, and Z co-ordinates of the universe.

LMB click into the perspective window (the border should turn blue to indicate that it is active). To move your point of view around (in effect move the perspective camera) use the keyboard and mouse in the following combinations:

- Alt+LMB will tumble the camera view around the centre of interest.
- Alt+MMB will track the camera view up/down or left/right from the centre of interest, depending on which way the mouse is moved.

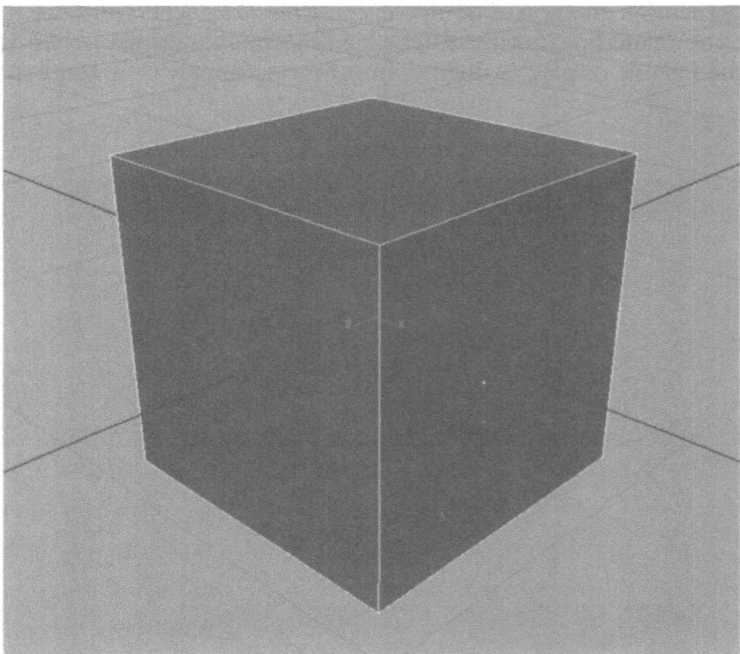

Figure 1.2 A Cube in the Perspective View.

- `Alt+(LMB+MMB)` will dolly the camera view towards or away from the centre of interest, depending on whether the mouse is moved left or right.
- `(Ctrl+Alt)+LMB` will allow you to draw a box around your point of interest and bounding-box dolly the camera view. Draw the box from the left to dolly in and right to dolly out.

As can be seen, Alt is used constantly as the camera viewpoint is changed within the scene. All of the above functions will work in the orthographic camera views with the exception of tumbling (`Alt+LMB`), because the camera position is represented in only two axes. Which brings us to an important part of working with Maya: using the keyboard and mouse in accord. Throughout the examples in this book and further, you will generally need to have one hand on the keyboard and one hand on the mouse in order to navigate through and operate Maya's various features. This makes it harder to eat and work at the same time.

The global axis is displayed in the perspective camera view and is the centre of the Maya 3D world, the origin of all three dimensions and where all new items will be created. Each camera view also has its own viewing axis displayed at the bottom left, which gives the current alignment of the camera. If you want to change the camera being used in each window, the menu bar at the top of each view panel can be utilized. Using `Views|Perspective...` or `Views|Orthographic...` you can either change to an existing camera view or create a brand new one. To the top left of the screen in the toolbox area, there are several icons that can be used to change the views that are displayed. The icon at the top of the list brings the perspective camera view to the foreground, while the icon below it sets the screen back to the default four camera view panels. Below that are four icons controlling various window combinations, but the more useful icon is at the bottom, which will change depending on the number of panels displayed. LMB clicking on each arrow in the icon will open a list of editors/views that the panel may contain.

Hotkeys

As with any program, there will be a number of keyboard shortcuts such as "open" and "save" plus the generic shortcuts for cut, copy and paste (`Ctrl+x`, `Ctrl+c` and `Ctrl+v` respectively). Maya makes full use of these standardized shortcuts: the command to open a file can be made from the menu: `File|Open Scene` or it can be made using the keyboard shortcuts `Alt+f` followed by `o`. `Ctrl+o` is shown alongside this menu item. This is the *hotkey* for this menu item and there are many other hotkeys throughout Maya that allow quicker access to functions. In order to speed up workflow, it's also possible to define custom hotkeys that can be mapped to any command, menu item or user defined commands. For example, it might be a lot more useful to have in your hotkey armoury a hotkey that is mapped to the `File|Save Scene As` command instead of having to use the main menu bar. To define a custom hotkey:

- Open up the hotkey dialog window by using `Windows|Settings/Preferences|Hotkeys...` This window not only shows the available list of currently set hotkeys but also allows you to set up new hotkeys, delete hotkeys or overwrite existing hotkeys.
- Set the `Categories to File` and click on. There should be no currently assigned hotkey.
- In the area labeled `Assign new hotkey`, LMB click in the window, type s and tick the options for Alt and Ctrl.
- Click the Assign button, save the configuration and close the window.

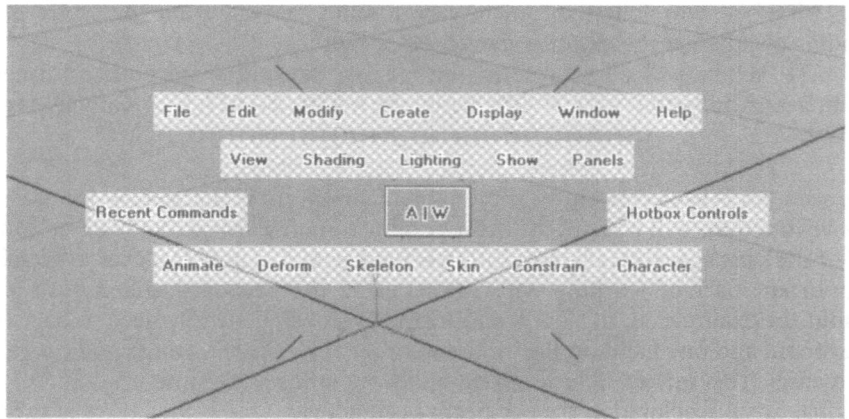

Figure 1.3 The Hotbox and Zones.

Now try out the new hotkey by using Ctrl+Alt+s. The hotkey window can also be used to list all of the currently available hotkeys by clicking the List All... button.

The Spacebar and the Hotbox

When working on items within Maya, it is often necessary to maximize the amount of screen space being used. Being that the screen size available is a finite amount dictated by your monitors (or your wallets) it's going to be a lot easier to focus on various aspects of your work by bringing one camera view to the foreground, known as "popping the view".

Move the mouse cursor into the view panel that you wish to maximize and just press the spacebar quickly. You should see that the view "pops" to the foreground, which gives a lot more visual elbowroom to play with. Pop the view back to the original layout by tapping the spacebar again. So with one hand resting near the spacebar and the Alt and Ctrl key, very rapid view manipulations can be effected. If you didn't press the spacebar quite as quickly as was required, you may notice another function occur instead of the required view popping. Press and hold the spacebar down. This will bring up a floating menu system known as the Hotbox.

The Hotbox will centre itself on the mouse cursor, no matter where it is in the Maya GUI, allowing very rapid selection of menu items and other functions, so that you don't have to move the cursor to a menu item or heading. If you look at the top menu row of the Hotbox, you should see that it mimics the top menu row of the Maya GUI; the Hotbox will also contain any other menu sets that are relevant to the current module in which you are working. While holding the spacebar down to activate the Hotbox, clicking on any of the menu headings will have exactly the same functionality as if you had clicked on them at the top of the main window.

Marking Menus

A marking menu is a context sensitive menu type with varying functions. These functions will depend upon the position in the view from which you invoked the menu, whether you are near an item that can have a marking menu associated with it or whether you were using a hotkey to invoke it. Holding down any of the hotkeys that represent the transform tools (q, w, e) and using the LMB will bring up a marking menu that allows us to change the function of the tool, instead of double clicking on it in the Toolbar area. A context sensitive marking menu we can easily examine is the one activated by holding down the RMB in an empty part of any view. This will allow you to quickly select all items in your workspace by holding the RMB down and moving the cursor over to "select all". When moving the cursor over any part of the Maya GUI or over any part of a window or editor, the cursor icon may change so that it has a small box with it. This indicates that an RMB menu can be brought up. Bring up the Hotbox again and you should see that it is divided into five zones (centre, left, right, top and bottom).

Holding the LMB down in each zone will bring up a different marking menu with a different function (holding down the LMB in the north zone will bring up a different set of menu headings to the south zone). To use these menu items just move the cursor over to the required item – this is known as "rubber banding". So, we have a set of marking menus that are context sensitive (they can be invoked only when the Hotbox is active) and also position sensitive (where the cursor is in the Hotbox). Using the LMB to bring up the marking menu from the centre zone will allow you to change the current view to another. If you are working with the perspective view currently popped forward, you can rapidly change views by holding down the spacebar and selecting another from this centre zone marking menu.

Summary

In this chapter we've seen that we can not only move our point(s) of view about within the 3D workspace, but also create new views. Central to this chapter has been the various different ways of interacting with the many functions and tools that Maya contains. This multiplicity of menu items is presented in the form of pull-down menus, the Hotbox, hotkeys and marking menus and means that we can work using the methodology best suited to us. Core to the design of Maya is the ability to change any aspect of the system. This may be in order to work faster or to work in a manner that suits you, your team and your production, even creating custom interfaces or menus depending on your situation: a unique situation may well require a unique interface.

Objects, Duplicates and Transforms 2

Introduction

Now that you are familiar with moving around in Maya, we can move onto creating some primitives and see how their position and orientation within 3D space are represented and how these attributes can be edited. We call basic objects "primitives" in that they are the basic Maya 3D shapes from which we can model objects – in the same way that molecules are composed of atoms, complex models and characters are composed of sets of primitives.

A Simple Object

To examine how Maya represents objects and their positions we'll show you how to create a NURBS torus (a doughnut-shaped surface) using Create|NURBS Primitives|Torus. In addition to 3D object primitives, Maya also collects curves, lights and camera creation under the Create menu heading – because these are essentially primitives of other types.

Let's pause briefly to examine some of the functionality within the menu items that you've just used:

- *Actions and tools.* All menu items can be classified as either an action or a tool. An action works on currently selected things, whereas a tool requires no selection in order to work.

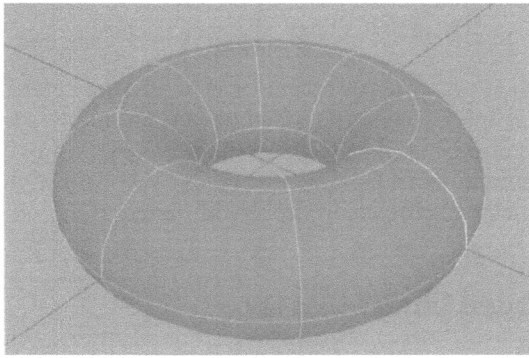

Figure 2.1 A NURBS Torus.

9

A tool will also have some usage instructions that appear in the help area (the NURBS Torus menu item is a tool and not an action).

- *Menu hierarchies.* In Maya there is a menu hierarchy that we will constantly follow: Menu Set|Menu Heading|Menu Item|Options Box.
- *Options box icons.* Beside most menu items there is a small box-like icon. When this icon appears it means that we can open up a dialogue box to change various options concerning how the action or tool will function (such as setting the inner and outer radius of the torus).

Any dialogue options that are changed will not reset to the default when you close the window – so *do* remember if you've changed various attributes as this can cause a fair amount of irritation due to unexpected results caused by "option fiddling". As soon as the torus is created and displayed on screen, several parts of the Maya interface will update to reflect this change to your scene. All of the interface changes that you can see right now will constantly update in relation to your currently selected item or items.

Selection Methods

Using the selection tool you can select single or multiple objects in Maya: selection of a single object can be achieved by LMB clicking on an object or holding down the LMB and dragging a box over it – in any of the views. Use the "f" key to focus the view around the currently selected object and the "a" key to focus the view around all objects in the scene. The selection tool is in the toolbox at the top and can be activated by either clicking on its icon or by using the hotkey "q".

Multiple objects can be selected by dragging a selection box over all of them, using the lasso tool to draw a selection around them, or selected one by one through Shift+LMB clicking on each required object. This method is particularly useful when a tool requires items to be picked in a certain order. Deselecting is a matter of LMB clicking onto an empty area. Note that whenever a new item is created in Maya, either through an action or the use of a tool, it becomes the currently selected item. As more objects are created, it's now going to be useful to have a list of objects (and items) in the scene.

The Outliner

The Outliner enables you to organize your scene by listing all the items that have been created – useful for selection in complex scenes and when objects are hidden. Windows|Outliner will invoke this editor. It can also be used to select items in a scene, using the LMB to click on the desired item. Using combinations of Shift+LMB and Ctrl+LMB multiple item selections can be made (note that the cameras for each view are already listed).

Shaded and Unshaded Object Display

You can change between a shaded and unshaded display mode in each view by pressing "4" for unshaded and "5" for shaded. If you have any NURBS objects in your scene, you can vary the

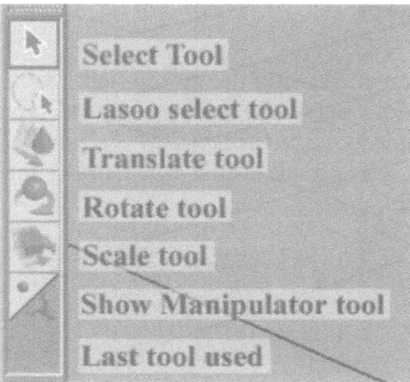

Figure 2.2 The Toolbox.

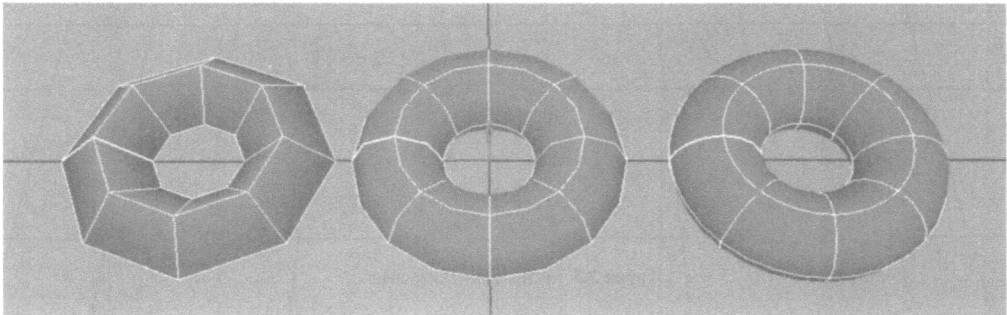

Figure 2.3 The Three Smoothing Modes.

degrees of smoothing by selecting the NURBS object and using keys "1", "2" or "3" to step through the smoothing levels. This allows you to optimize your display to give the best level of interaction. Note that this does not affect how smooth the objects actually are, just how fast your graphics card's interaction with Maya will be.

Transformations

To the right of the Maya screen is the Channels Box. This displays a list of attributes common to the item or items currently selected. For instance, if you were to select the NURBS torus then its name would appear at the top, followed by a list of the keyable attributes that this item possesses; keyable attributes are also known as channels. The first set of channels contains the transformation (or transform) attributes. Transforms come in three flavours – `Translate`, `Rotate` and `Scale` – in the three axes, X, Y and Z. In the same way that complex characters or models are described by collections of primitives, movement is described by concatenations of these transforms. Intriguingly, there is another set of channels below, containing attributes describing the inputs to the shape of the selected item – you may notice that these mirror the choices in the options box for the NURBS torus. We will examine this in greater detail in the following chapters.

Transform Manipulators

Objects can be quickly transformed using the manipulator tools which are in the toolbox at the left-hand side of the window. Below the lasso tool is the Translate manipulator, the Rotate manipulator and the Scale manipulator (hotkeys "w", "e" and "r" respectively). Activation of these tools while an object is selected will display the handles for the manipulator – each one having their own specific form.

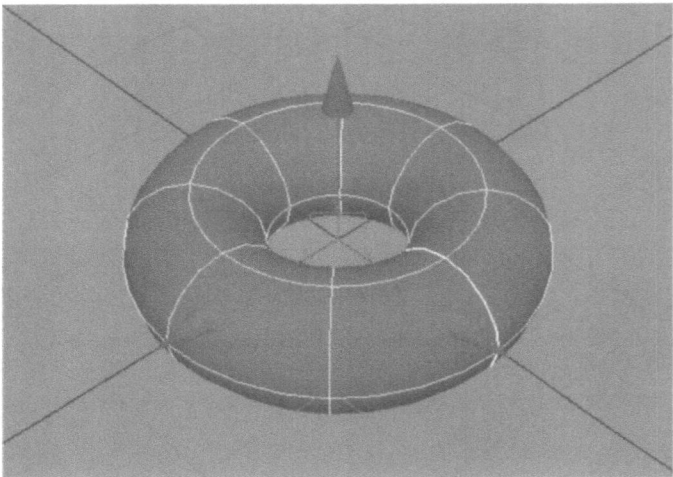

Figure 2.4 The Transform Manipulator.

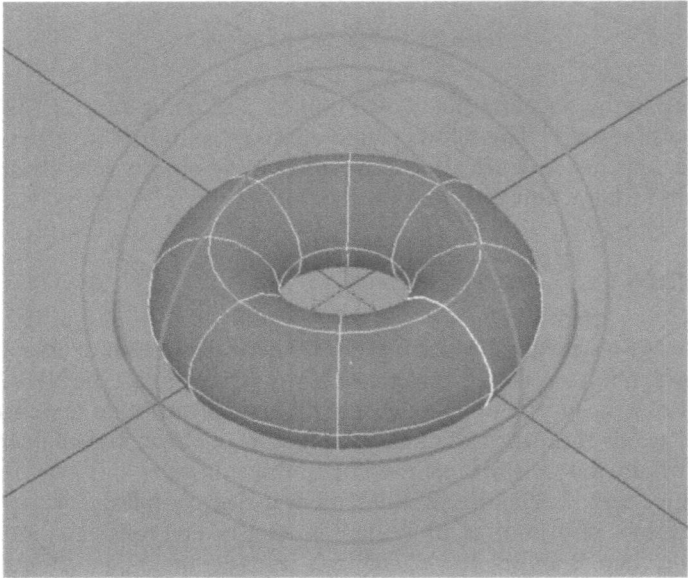

Figure 2.5 The Rotate Manipulator.

Common to all axes and manipulators is a colour coding: red for X, green for Y and blue for Z. This makes it easy to determine which axis is which no matter what you or the handle's orientation is in space when you use the manipulators, so note that the relevant attributes update in the Channels Box. Clicking and dragging on any of the handles with the LMB will activate it – turning it yellow – and will allow you to transform the item. It is also possible to translate, rotate or scale in more than one axis at a time without having to individually click on the handles one after another. For translating, Ctrl+LMB clicking on the X axis handle will move the object in the YZ plane, clicking on the Y axis handle will move the object in the ZX plane and clicking on the Z axis handle will move the object in the XY plane (notice how the centre square changes to align itself with the active plane). If you Ctrl+LMB click on the centre handle, you will return to translating the object relative to your viewing plane (the default). With the rotate handle there is an outer ring that remains perpendicular to your view and selecting that handle will allow you to rotate an object around the view axis. For scaling, click on the centre handle to scale in all axes at once and hold the Ctrl+LMB on a single handle to scale in the plane the other handles form. Additionally, you can transform an object quickly in only one axis by holding down shift and dragging the MMB in the direction of the handle of the currently active handle.

Be careful when translating or rotating items relative to the viewing plane, because the object can sometimes end up in a completely different orientation to the one required (look at the rotate values changing in the Channels Box using the outer rotate manipulator ring). Double LMB clicking on the icons for translate and rotate will bring up an options box allowing you to change the relevant tool's behaviour – for example, double LMB clicking on the translate tool will allow you to define the co-ordinate space that the translation works in and whether the tool will work in discrete units. When using discrete units, relative mode will increment the current position/rotation/scaling by the amount, otherwise all values will be in absolute transforms. This LMB double-clicking method in the toolbar will also bring up options (if available) for any icon displayed in the toolbox area. While a handle is active (yellow), you can still use the MMB to control it by holding it down in a window and dragging the cursor in the direction of the handle.

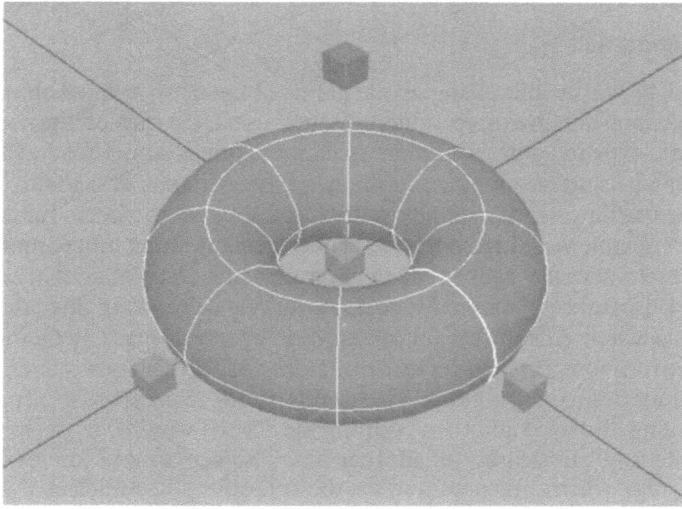

Figure 2.6 The Scale Manipulator.

Using the Channels Box for Transformations

The Channels Box not only displays the keyable attribute values for the currently selected item, but also enables these values to be changed. Some of the channels have attributes, such as visibility, that are represented by different data types like Booleans (yes/no, on/off). LMB clicking on any of the values makes the text field active and you can type any number into it. LMB drag over a series of fields and the value you type into the remaining active field will ripple down into the other highlighted fields. Typing in numbers for the values could quickly become tedious though, if you consider how many times this would have to be done over the course of animation. A greater degree of speed and interaction with the selected item's attributes can be achieved by using the "virtual slider". LMB click an attribute name, hold the MMB down in an adjacent window and drag left and right to see the attribute change value. This can very quickly allow you to sketch in the broad strokes of your transforms before typing in values to give a greater degree of accuracy. This method is pretty useful and is one of the ways that Maya will allow you to work faster. It keeps you focused on the job in hand by not having to move your mouse away from the important areas of the interface, such as trying to click on a manipulator handle for the attribute. This may sound a little like laziness, but if you're working on a large scene day-in day-out, then it's going to save you time – which in the long run equates to finishing your scene on time.

A Simple Stick Character from Primitives

So far, we've covered enough ground that you can make a stickman from a combination of primitives. However, if you are going to use this as a simple character, then there are still a couple of modifications that you will need to make to the primitives that you will use. For this section, the primitives can be either *polygonal* or *NURBS* surfaces.

The head can be made from a sphere, the arms, legs and torso from cylinders. For starters, we will just make the head and torso from a sphere and cylinder.

Renaming and Annotation

At this point it will be worthwhile changing the names of the newly created objects, as the default names are not only long but give no real clue as to their use. LMB click on the name of the objects in the Outliner and type in something more meaningful: Head and Torso. It is a good idea to make a habit of this, because as you start working on more complex scenes with larger collections of items, it will be useful to see at a glance in the Outliner what the item's function is. Also, you might not be the only one working on the scene and there's nothing more annoying than trying to figure out what relevance nurbsSphere136 has from a huge list of names in a scene that you've been given. It may also be useful to pop the current working window (in this case the front) to the foreground, as this will give us the maximum amount of screen space. Remember that you can quickly switch between foreground windows by holding down the Hotbox and LMB dragging in the centre zone to the desired view choice. This avoids having to press the spacebar to return to all of the windows being displayed and then popping the desired window to the foreground.

To make a scene even clearer to another user, object annotation can be used. This creates 3D nametags which are parented to the relevant object. Select the Head and use Create|Annotation to bring up the text input field, enter "head" and press OK. The annotation will appear in the viewport and can be translated so that it doesn't get in the way. The text

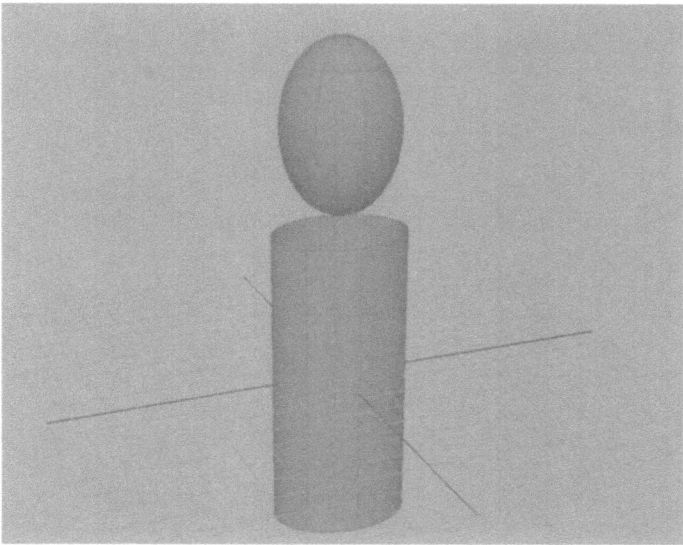

Figure 2.7 The Torso and Head.

can also be changed by selecting the annotation*n* node in the Outliner and opening the Attribute Editor on this node. The text input field will appear at the bottom.

Moving Pivot Positions

One of the changes that need to be made to the objects is the position of their manipulators. For example, if you were to rotate the head object so that the character could look up and down, the position of the rotate manipulator should be at the bottom of the head.

Each manipulator appears at a specific location in the primitive and it is from this location that the calculations for transformations are made. This position is known as the "pivot point" and by default appears at the object's local origin (i.e. at the centre of it). So you need to change the pivot point for the head to allow you to rotate it correctly.

- Select the item in question.
- Click on the transform tool for the pivot you want to change (in this case, the rotate manipulator).
- Press the Insert key – you should notice that the display of the pivot changes. This indicates that its position relative to the object can now be edited.
- Move the pivot to the bottom of the head by dragging with the LMB as you would a standard translate manipulator.
- Press the Insert key again to take the pivot out of edit mode.

Repeat these steps for the torso. Notice that the Insert key is purely a toggle for the editable mode of the selected pivot. Now for the arms:

- Create a cylinder and in the top view scale it in the X and Z axes so that it has the correct proportions.
- Position the arm in the front view so that it is at shoulder height.

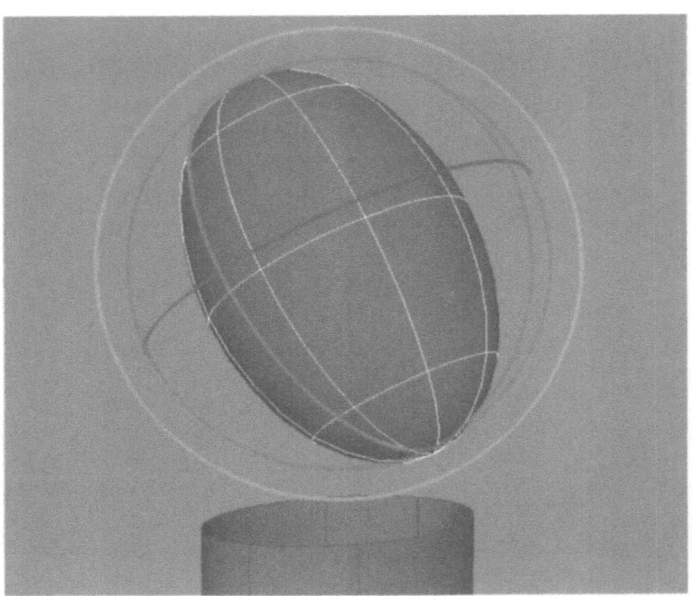

Figure 2.8 Incorrect Pivot Position.

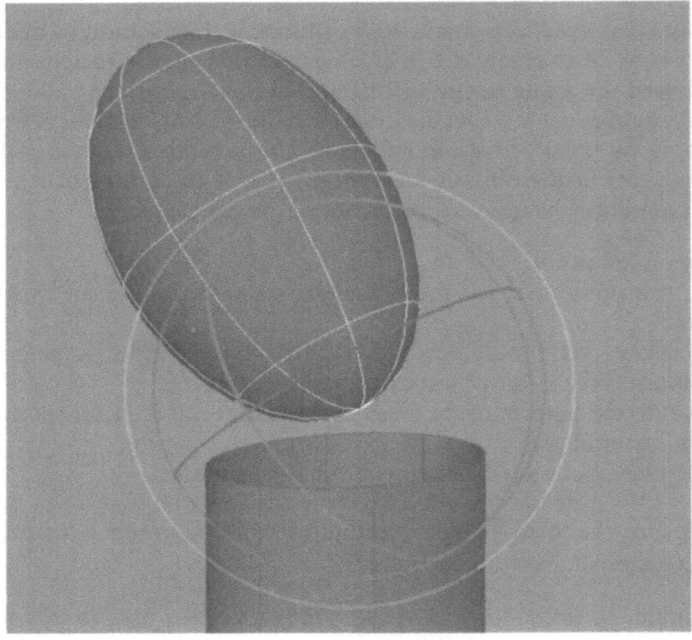

Figure 2.9 Correct Pivot Position.

Figure 2.10 The Pivot in Edit Mode.

- Move the pivot to the top of the arm object.
- Scale the arm down to elbow length.
- Rename the cylinder rightUpperArm.

Duplicating Objects

Now that the cylinder is positioned, you can take a couple of shortcuts by making duplicates of this rightUpperArm object as a starting point for all your other body parts. This is because they all have the same basic shape as the rightUpperArm, but more importantly because they will also need to have their pivots in the same place. Select the rightUpperArm and duplicate it by using Edit|Duplicate. The new object will appear in the same place as the original and as it has just been freshly created, it is the currently selected object. Translate this new object down to the correct position and rename it rightLowerArm. To aid in the positioning of the new object we can use the Snap Together tool (Modify|Snap Align Objects|Snap Together Tool) and the Align Tool (Modify|Snap Align Objects|Align Tool). The Snap Together tool lets us pick the surface of the object we wish to align (marked with an arrow), then pick the surface that we wish to align to (we can drag the arrow marker or just repick the required surface until correct). Pressing enter will then align the two surfaces. This can be used to easily align the lower arm to the upper arm, but won't be as precise as needed. Instead, the Align tool can align one object to another using their bounding box edges:

- Select the Align tool.
- Select rightUpperArm and then shift-select rightLowerArm (or drag across both objects with the tool).
- Press the icon at the bottom edge of the combinedbounding boxes to move and align the two objects.

The Align tool will only turn off if another tool is selected, such as the select tool (hotkey "q"), so the aligning process can be carried out until correct. If more than two objects are selected, the tool will align all selected objects with the last one.

Now that you have one limb for the character, you can use some further functionality of the duplicate command to provide all of the other limb objects.

- Select both upper and lower arms and duplicate again – this time use the hotkey Ctrl+d.
- Translate the new limbs down to leg height and change their scales if required.
- Rename them rightThigh and rightShin.

If you look at the dialogue options for Edit|Duplicate, you can see that it's also possible to reposition the duplicates, without needing to use the manipulators after. But remember that these changes will remain every time you use the action (even if using Ctrl+d) until you reset them.

Freezing Transformations

Looking at the values for translate and scale on any of your selected objects, you can see that these have changed over the course of the manipulations. The next operation will be to "freeze" these transformations. This means that you will be setting these attributes to 0 for Translate and Rotate and 1 for Scaling, without moving them. This is useful in that it allows you to start the transform values from their current position, so that if you were to translate the rightUpperArm to 0,0,0, this will position it at the correct torso position. In effect, you have created a new origin for the object. Select the object you wish to freeze and open the dialogue box under Modify|Freeze Transformations. Turn on Translate, Rotate and Scale, click Apply and close the dialogue box. Freeze the transformations for all of the objects created so far.

Mirroring Objects

We can use the above techniques to quickly mirror the limbs across to the other side of the torso. Mirroring will allow you to copy an item and reflect it across a chosen axis.

- Select the rightUpperArm.
- Select the Translate tool and press Insert.
- In the front view, move the pivot to the middle of the torso (onto the thicker line describing the Y axis).
- Open the options box for Edit|Duplicate.
- Enter a value of -1 in scale X and 1 in scale Y and scale Z; keep all other attributes to 0.
- Click Apply.
- Freeze the transformations of the new arm object and rename it leftUpperArm.

The duplicated object was effectively mirrored by scaling it negatively around its own axis and the transformations were frozen, because having objects with a negative scaling value is not useful – it is better to have all objects with a positive scaling value so that transformations can be applied equally. However, the pivots need to be returned to their correct position. Select all of the new arm objects and use Modify|Centre Pivot to automatically move the pivot points to the centre of each object. Then it is just a case of selecting both objects, pressing Insert and moving both pivots upward to the correct positions so that the arms rotate correctly. Repeat these steps with all of the remaining limbs until you have a full set of arms and legs for your character and because we'll be using this scene in the next chapter, save it as `StickMan.mb` using `File|Save Scene As`.

Hiding, Displaying and Templating

Objects can exist in several display states: shown, hidden, referenced or templated. These different states will be extremely useful during the course of your work. Hidden objects, while they will take up disk space in terms of scene size, won't be considered when viewing or rendering and so won't take up memory. Hiding objects will also make it easier to concentrate on the important parts of your scene by reducing visual mess. For example, if you view your character from the side and wish to work on one of the limbs, you can see that it would be easier to hide all the other objects. Select them in the Outliner and use `Display|Hide`. To unhide them, select and use `Display|Show`. If you wanted to work on one of the arms while having the other objects available for visual reference, it may be useful to template them. A templated object is an object that you can see but cannot select – so you won't accidentally move or change it while working on another aspect of your scene. To template, select the object and use `Display|Object Display|Template`. To untemplate, select the object (you'll have to do this in the Outliner) and use `Display|Object Display|Untemplate`.

Summary

We've now seen how Maya allows you to change transform attributes of primitives in several ways. You can type, use the virtual slider and use the manipulators, giving a variable degree of use and of accuracy. You should also be starting to use Maya with one hand on the keyboard and one hand on the mouse at all times – look at how the transforms and select tools can be selected by "q", "w", "e", "r" and "t". Couple this with constant use of the space bar and combinations of the Alt and Ctrl keys and it gets harder to eat and work at the same time. Get used to the concepts that we've covered such as editing pivot positions, freezing transformations and templating because we are going to be using these ideas heavily in modeling and animation. Try creating a spiral staircase from one polygon cube with some transform options in the duplicate dialogue box. In the next chapter we're going to have to put the stick character together in a more coherent manner so that it's easier to move it around the scene.

Hierarchies, Groups and Nodes

3

Introduction

Because our stickman is created from a large collection of objects, we are going to require a high degree of control over these collections while retaining all of the methods and workflow for transformations that we used in the last chapter to create the stickman. The first method that will be examined will be putting our composite character into a more organized collection, known as a hierarchy. The second method will be concerned with creating groups, which are a more specialized collection of items. It's also time to start looking at some of the inner workings of Maya. The representation of the items in terms of data will become an important issue as you work, enabling you to have specialized access to attributes, troubleshoot problems within your scenes and generally be able to exert more control over items.

Hierarchies

A hierarchy is a relationship between two things. One is the parent and the other is the child. In Maya, transformations (for one) are passed down from parent to child, making these hierarchies extremely useful and extremely powerful. Imagine trying to animate the stick figure we made in the last chapter walking along without using a hierarchy; it would be practically impossible to animate each object individually while making the character appear to move as a cohesive whole. This kind of relationship is quite straightforward if you examine your arm. Your finger moves through space as a function of the movement of your hand, which moves through space as a function of the movement of your forearm, which moves through space etc. In other words: the knee bone's connected to the thighbone, the thighbone's connected to the hipbone. There are several redundant areas in the Maya GUI that could be better used as screen space for camera views. Use `Display|UI Elements|Hide UI Elements` to do this. Open up the Outliner as well, as you are going to be using this to create your hierarchies. Additionally, you might need to undo quite a lot of operations as you work through these examples so you need to set the size of the undo queue. Open up the preferences dialogue with `Windows|Settings/Preferences|Preferences` and in the left-hand side click on Undo. Set the queue size to 50 and click on Save. Although you can set the queue size to infinite, this can start to slow Maya down as memory gets eaten up remembering everything that has gone before.

Create a cone and sphere, rename the sphere `Head` and the cone `Hat`. Move `Hat` to the top of `Head` and freeze `Hat`'s transformations. In the outliner, use the MMB to drag and drop `Hat`

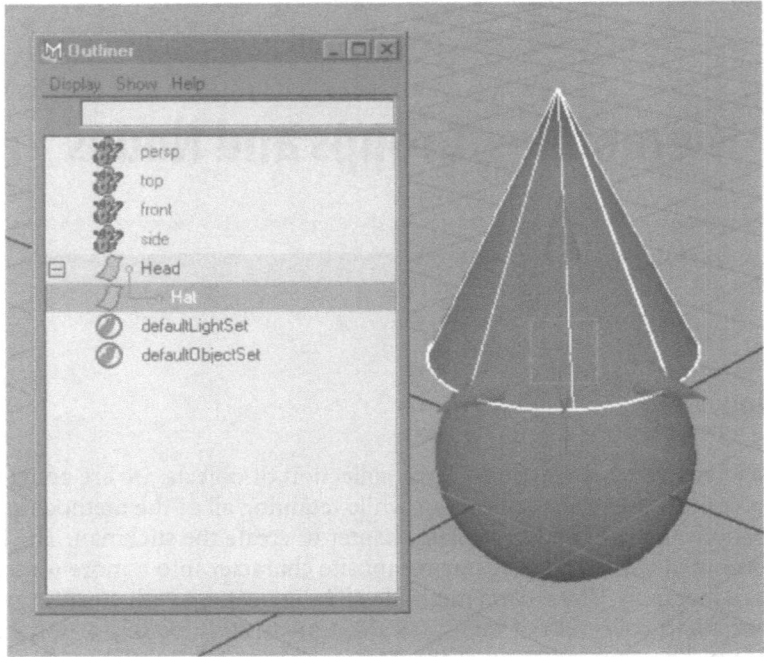

Figure 3.1 The Hat and Head and the Outliner Showing the Hierarchy.

onto Head. Three things should be apparent here:

1. The mouse cursor changes to reflect the operation within the Outliner. You can use the MMB to drag and drop objects into hierarchies, out of hierarchies or even to reorder the list within the outliner. (To reorder the list of objects in the Outliner, just MMB drag an item until a single black line appears between the objects that you wish to place the item.)
2. Head is highlighted in green. You currently have Hat selected. As Hat now lies under a parent in a hierarchy, the higher level of the hierarchy that is visible in the Outliner will turn green to declare the item is below it somewhere.
3. Beside Head, there is a little box with a cross in it. If you click on the box with the cross in it, your hierarchy will unfold showing the parent–child relationship clearly.

Select Head and transform it in the view. Both objects are transforming, but Hat is only moving because the transformations from Head are being passed down the hierarchy from parent to child. If you select Hat on its own, you'll see that in order to keep things simple, the transformations are not represented in the Channels Box. Not only are transformations passed down, but most messages as well. Selecting Head and deleting it will delete all objects below it in the hierarchy. Adding more objects to the hierarchy is just a matter of MMB dragging and dropping in the Outliner. This action is known as "parenting"; you can also use Edit|Parent to create the relationship, but this is an action so you will need to select the parent and then Shift-select the child. If you want to remove item from a hierarchy (unparent) then either MMB drag and drop the selected item outside of the hierarchy or use Edit|Unparent.

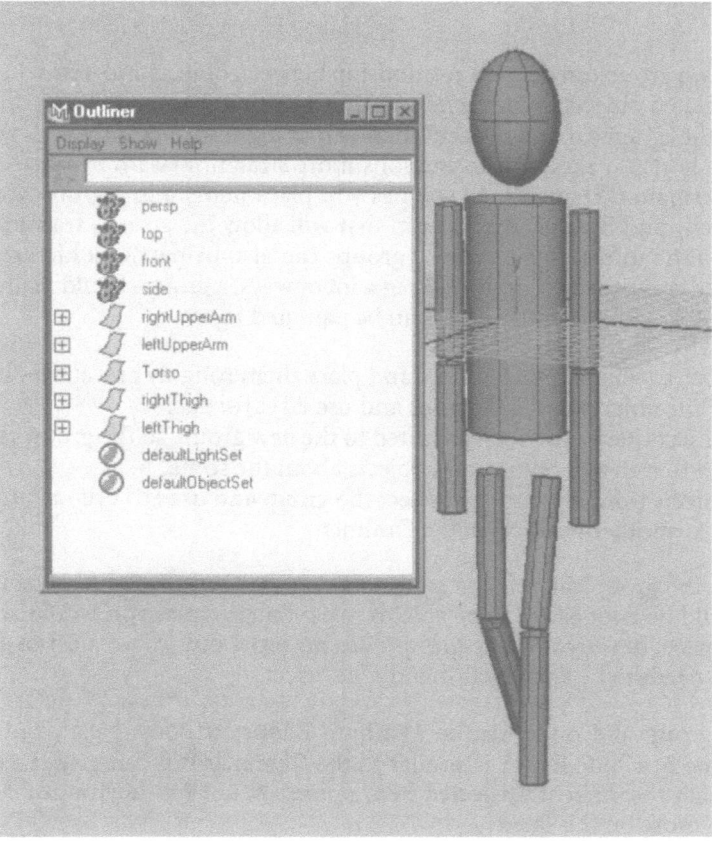

Figure 3.2 The Outliner Showing the Stickman Hierarchies.

Creating a Usable Stickman Hierarchy

We're going to put this into practice with the stickman file we saved, so open up the saved StickMan.mb file. The root of the hierarchy for the character will be the Torso, all other objects will become children of this object.

- In the Outliner, MMB drag the Head onto the Torso to form the first link in the hierarchy. LMB click the fold-out button beside Head to give a clearer indication of the relationships within the scene.
- Build the arms and legs by MMB dragging the child onto the parent so that there are five groups of hierarchies representing the different limbs.
- MMB drag the parents of the limb hierarchies onto the Torso.

There should now be a usable hierarchical character in the workspace that can be posed using rotations for all children of the torso. Save this as StickManHr.mb.

Groups

Like a hierarchy, a group can define a relationship between objects and items. Instead of selecting all of the related objects in the scene and transforming them, it is easier and more logical to place all of these items into a collection known as a group. Not only does this make selection easier, but it also makes transformations more straightforward because each group has its own transformation channels. As soon as you place items into a group you have created another hierarchy and it is this mechanism that will allow the group's transformations to be passed down to the underlying children (groups can also be part of a hierarchy and hierarchies can also be composed of groups). So in a lot of ways, a group should really be thought of as a set of transformation channels that can be parented to.

- Create a cone, a cylinder and a sphere and place them roughly one above the other.
- Select all of the objects in the Outliner and use Edit|Group.
- All of the objects have now been parented to the new group, so the group's transforms can now be used to move all of the child objects about the scene.
- To move objects from a group, just select the group and use Edit|Ungroup or MMB drag the objects to another position in the Outliner.

Unfortunately, the group can only be selected using the Outliner, which is somewhat inconvenient. It would be a lot easier to be able to select the group as you would any other object in your workspace, but because the group does not exist outside of a set of transformation channels there needs to be a physical "handle" to select.

- Select the group and open up the Attribute Editor (Windows|Attribute Editor or Ctrl+a). The Attribute Editor is similar to the Channels Box but gives access to all of the attributes that the currently selected item possesses, not just keyframeable attributes (or channels) – more on this later.
- Fold out the tab labeled Display and tick the box beside Display Handle. You should see a new icon appear at the centre of the group (i.e. where the transform pivot origin is).
- Set the Y component (centre text input box) of the handle to 10.0.
- Close the Attribute Editor.

Now you can select the group by selecting its handle in a view, instead of having to return to the Outliner, which is far more convenient. Using groups can be extremely convenient for purposes of collection and purposes of parenting. Importantly, the use of groups allows you to start encapsulating items within a scene, so that each item only has a couple of tasks to carry out. This method of working allows you to keep scenes simpler and the division of labour more straightforward. For example, if you return to the stickman scene that you previously saved, you can see that the top of the hierarchy for your character is the Torso object. You can move your character about by selecting the Torso and transforming it, but what if you wish to rotate the torso without affecting the other objects?

- Open up the saved StickManHr.mb and unparent the arms, legs and head from the torso.
- Select the torso, the head and the arms. Group them and rename the new group TorGrp.
- Move the pivot for TorGrp down to waist level.
- Select the legs and group these, calling this new group LegsGrp.
- Move the pivot for LegsGrp up to waist level.

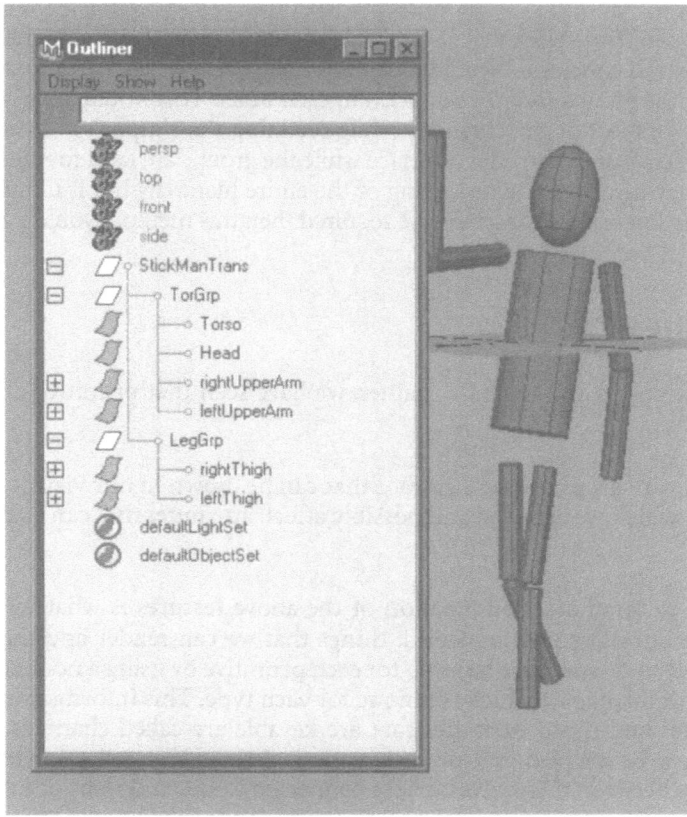

Figure 3.3 The New Hierarchy for the Stickman with Twisting for Different Sections.

So you now have two independent groups allowing you the freedom of movement that would have been difficult to create without parenting the existing objects to new objects. You can now use these groups to pass down new hierarchic transformations to your sub-groups (arms, torso, legs etc.).

These new groups are being used purely for local transformations, so you should create another group to provide explicit global transformations and parent the TorGrp and LegsGrp to it.

- Clear the selection list by LMB clicking in a window.
- Create an empty group with Edit|Group, Create|Empty Group or Ctrl+g and rename it StickManTrans.
- Using the MMB, drag the TorGrp and the LegsGrp onto ManTrans.
- Move the pivot for ManTrans to somewhere useful and display the selection handle.
- Save the scene as StickManGrpd.mb.

Unfolding the hierarchies in the Outliner provides a much clearer picture of the makeup of the stickman hierarchy. This will become a lot more intuitive when you come to animate a character and this sort of preparative work will always yield results later on. Following the idea of division of labour to its logical conclusion would mean grouping every object that the stickman is made of and parenting the groups (not the surfaces) to each other. This would allow you to have total control over every aspect of the character while retaining the simplicity of each item doing a single job (the object purely provides a surface while the groups are used for hierarchic transformations). This may involve some reworking of the entire hierarchy but if ultimate control over every and any portion of the character were required then this method would pay dividends.

Node Structures

In the past two sections and the past chapter, we have seen that primitive objects are represented in two forms:

- That portion which we can see: a surface that can be drawn in our viewport.
- That portion which we can read and possibly affect: attributes that can be displayed in various editors.

It would be fair to say that a combination of the above features is what we want from any primitive within our 3D animated world: things that we can render and that we can transform. Maya is able to divide these tasks up for each primitive by using a node structure. A node is a collection of information which is unique for each type. This information is stored in the form of attributes and those attributes that are keyable are called channels. Each item that exists within Maya, be it a primitive or a character is defined by a collection of nodes that can pass information between themselves. These connected nodes and webs of information manifest themselves within Maya as the actions, animations etc. that are presented to you.

If you create a NURBS sphere, there will be three headings in the Channels Box:

1. nurbsSphere*n*: this is a transform node.
2. nurbsSphereShape*n*: this is a shape node.
3. makeNurbsSphere*n*: this is an input node.

Each node can pass information into other receptive nodes, which will then resolve this data plus its own to produce a new or interpreted action, event or effect.

LMB click on the makeNurbsSphere*n* title to fold out the attributes relevant to that node and change the start sweep value. This affects the shape of the sphere by passing information about the surface through to the shape node, which deals with creating the surface. You cannot see any channels for this node as it contains non-keyable attributes. Any attributes can be displayed using the Attribute Editor, which displays the attributes for all of the nodes that are involved with the currently selected item (or node). Select the sphere and either use Window|Attribute Editor or the hotkey Ctrl+a. You can now see that there is a tab for every node that is relevant in some way to the sphere, even the shading group and colour of the sphere's surface. Open up the input node (makeNurbsSphere1) section that controls the construction of the sphere and you can change the start sweep there instead of in the Channels Box. If the currently selected node is fed into by node X, then it is said to be upstream of node X and is receiving an input connection from node X; node X is downstream of the currently selected node and has an output connection that

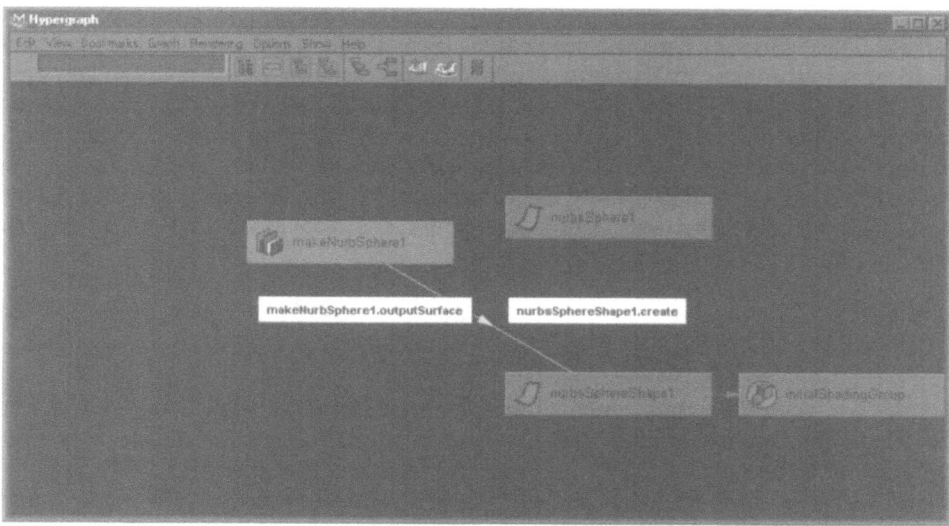

Figure 3.4 Input and Output Connections in the Hypergraph.

feeds into the currently selected node. A note can be saved with each node in the Attribute Editor, so custom uses or "don't delete this!" messages can be stored and displayed easily. These notes at the bottom of the Attribute Editor will also duplicate if the node is copied and can make the propagation of information amongst groups of people on the same project much easier.

This is why the input node is also known as the construction history node. Sometimes it isn't necessary to carry around this construction history so you can either delete this node or turn off construction history while shapes are created. Deleting unused or defunct history nodes is a very useful operation, as each node takes up memory and as we'll see in the next chapter, sometimes history can be a potential hazard.

Select the object in question and use Edit|Delete By Type|History or you can delete the history of everything in your scene by using Edit|Delete All By Type|History. This will "freeze" the appearance of the object in time.

To stop objects being created with an input node, toggle the construction history button to "off". Create a NURBS torus and look at the Attribute Editor – no inputs. This button creates non-undoable actions, so don't forget what its state is. It is often easier to keep the construction history button set to "on" and delete the history/input node manually. The transform node for your object sits atop a hierarchy for your object – in the scene this is the node that must be resolved last as Maya builds the surface and then positions it in 3D space. So we have a situation where the input node feeds information to the shape node, both of these nodes are parented to the transform node. This can be a lot easier to visualize, however, and you can use the Hypergraph to do this. The Hypergraph gives a graphical layout of the scene and also, if required, a visualization of the message passing connections between nodes; Window|Hypergraph will open up this window. Items in the scene will be represented by rectangles with the node's name on it and camera controls (apart from tumble) will work inside this window, as will the Hotbox.

The shape node can be displayed by using Options|Display|Shape Nodes so that the transform node will have the shape node lying below it in a hierarchy. Select the shape node and use Graph|Input and Output Connections to show how message passing is established between these nodes. You can return to the normal scene layout by using Graph|Scene Hierarchy. These functions are also represented by icons and the Hotbox, which changes its menus to suit the context. The Hypergraph allows you to visualize the connection between the nodes that the Attribute Editor presents: a list of linked nodes, each with their own set of traits. Select the node and use the RMB to bring up a floating menu, from which the Attribute Editor can be selected. This is why just duplicating in standard duplicate mode will only duplicate the selected node. If you look back at the stickman, you should see that the original primitives that you created have their own shape nodes, the duplicates do not. Try this while keeping the Hypergraph open to give a better idea of this.

Summary

Hierarchies and groups are undoubtedly useful for any manner of work that you wish to create, from high quality stills to full length feature animation. It is key that the creation, manipulation and implementation of these methods are understood. Experiment with placing the stickman in different hierarchies to see the effect that this would have on the way you work – what tends to make things easier to animate and how much complexity is too much? Consider this if you are going to be creating and setting up characters for other animators to use. The underlying structure and connectionism of Maya is represented using the Hypergraph and the data in each node is represented using the Attribute. As scene complexity grows, the Hypergraph will become the editor that will allow you to see the web of connections between many different nodes and also to troubleshoot your scenes if unexpected things occur. Understanding the fact that nodes not only contain attributes, but that these attributes can be connected is key to using Maya. Although Maya can be used as a 3D animation and rendering package, keeping this idea of connected nodes in the mind's eye will allow you to maximize your input and control over your work and extend your creative abilities.

Modeling and Surface Creation

4

Introduction

The process of modeling is to provide a surface that can be used in many ways – to provide the "skin" of a character, props for a character to use or even provide surfaces for functions that need to reference a position in space. The most basic form of modeling is to use primitives to create an object – the stickman that you created in the last chapter, for example. This can yield good results if the character in question doesn't need to be any more detailed – for instance, to create a character purely for animation purposes.

The next stage is to create a surface by manipulating the primitives at a component level, analogous to modeling with a lump of clay. There will be a point where the required object cannot be made from any of these techniques (a mobile phone or pair of spectacles for example), or will take so long using one of the above methods that it is not a worthwhile use of time. It is at this point that you will have to create surfaces from basic building blocks – curves and components. Whenever attempting any sort of modeling, it is worth having a clear design of the desired object/character available. Designs should be at least in two planar views (front and side) which should be in digital form – either drawn in a paint package or scanned from paper. Try and keep the designs clear so that the important details stand out. You can now load the side and front views into the side and front orthographic cameras within Maya to give the perfect modeling aid.

In the Outliner, select the camera view in which you wish to create the image plane. Open the Attribute Editor, open up the tab labeled `Environment` and click the Create button beside the text entry field labeled `Image Plane`. The Attribute Editor will now change focus to the image plane node. You can load in the image file using the button beside the text field labeled `Image Name` (toggling the `Attached to Camera` or `Fixed` attributes will affect the placement of the image plane in the 3D view). Maya is divided into four menu sets – `Animation`, `Modeling`, `Dynamics` and `Rendering`. It is from these four sets that all of the other menu headings are derived. Change into the `Modeling` menu set by either using the fold-down menu at the top left of the Maya GUI or in any viewport, hold down "h" and the LMB to open a marking menu that allows you to change between menu sets.

Surface Types and Their Components

In Maya we will be working with the three types of surface: NURBS, polygonal and Subdivision. These surfaces already appear as the primitives that we looked at previously and as new user defined surfaces, for when a primitive will not suffice.

29

Create a NURBS sphere and a polygon sphere and place them side by side. The first thing to be seen is that the NURBS sphere tends towards a smooth definition, whereas the polygonal sphere tends to appear more faceted. Now create a subdiv Sphere. The subdivision surface falls somewhere inbetween the other two surfaces, being both rough and smooth with no real definition in terms of faces or curves and because these types of surface are a type that involve aspects of polygon surfaces and NURBS surfaces, we will look at them after these other two surfaces.

NURBS stands for Non Uniform Rational B-Spline, which describes the mathematics that create the curves and these surfaces that are used in Maya. It is the mathematical definition of these curves that make them so useful within Maya; they can be cut, joined and controlled with a great degree of accuracy. Any point along a NURBS curve can be defined as a point in terms of a "U" parameter that defines the length. The position of any point on a NURBS surface can be determined by quantities in two parameters: "U" and "V". These U and V positions are then determined in terms of a 3D global position in Maya to give the normal Cartesian X, Y and Z position.

These U and V parameters are parameterized into values between 0 and 1, which is extremely useful for some modeling operations, but mainly for applying texture maps. All bitmaps are defined in two dimensions so that the co-ordinates from the NURBS surface (two parameters) can be mapped to an XY position in the bitmap giving the colour at that point. A good analogy for a NURBS surface would be a series of wires that have cloth stretched over them – the cloth is a mathematical interpolation of the surface that exists between the curves. This is why there are three smoothness levels for NURBS surfaces, as this describes the interpolation used by the graphics card to speed up display of the surface. A polygon is a series of points that can be connected together to form a polygonal surface. These surfaces are called faces and can be connected together along their edges. A polygon object is described purely in terms of this with no mathematical interpolation of the faces or edges (this is why the polygon sphere appears faceted). The only way to increase the smoothness of the polygon sphere would be to increase the number of faces making up the object, until an approximation of a curved surface is achieved.

The components that these different surfaces are made from will explain why these two objects differ so much in terms of surface description. At one level we have the object – in this case, a sphere. This can be described in terms of size, smoothness, how complete it is, etc. There is another description level that lies beneath this called the component level. The component level describes the underlying nuts and bolts that provide the underpinning for the surface itself. To allow the easy selection of different items and their components, Maya has an *Object Mask mode* and a *Component Mask mode*. These modes mean that you will be able to limit (mask) your selections to only certain items – known as a "pick mask". At the top of the Maya GUI, but just below the menu area is the status line that informs you of the items that you can currently select in the viewports. The F8 key alternates between the object and component modes and will change the available masks on that status line. This can also be toggled using the icon at the side of the status line. As a scene becomes more complex and more items are included it will become harder to consistently pick the item or components that you want to edit. Using pick masks mean that you can keep dragging a selection box over parts of your scene and only select the things you want, allowing you to retain complexity without suffering for it.

- Turn off all object masks by LMB clicking on the leftmost icon in the status line and selecting "all objects off".
- Try to select any of the objects.

- Turn on "all surfaces" by LMB clicking on the surfaces icon.
- Select any of the objects.

Each of the masks in the object or component section can be further divided into sub sections:

- LMB hold on the "all surfaces" icon until a submenu with a series of check boxes appears.
- Uncheck all surface types apart from NURBS.
- Drag a selection box across both types of sphere; you should only be able to select the unmasked surface type (NURBS).

Pick masks also exist for every type of component that exists in Maya. The components for a polygonal surface are vertices, edges, faces and UVs, a NURBS surface has control vertices (CVs), edit points, hulls, normals (shaded mode), patch centres and surface origins. One way to display and select the components that go to make up a type of surface is to use one of the default marking menus. Move the cursor over one of the spheres and hold down the RMB. This will bring up a marking menu showing the selectable components for the surface type, but will not change the current pick mask, just the current objects' pick mask. We can return to object selection mode by selecting the "Object Mode" menu item from the RMB marking menu, without deselecting the component (this marking menu system will work with all surface types).

Most component types can be transformed using the standard transform tools in Maya and will give an indication of how the components make up and will affect a surface.

- Select the NURBS sphere.
- Use F8 to go into component mode and turn off all component masks apart from CVs.
- The CVs should lie in an evenly distributed cloud around the NURBS surface.
- Select a CV and using the translate tool, move it about.

Do the same for the polygon sphere.

The differences in effect between the NURBS components and the polygon components should be obvious straightaway. A CV controls an area of a NURBS patch without actually lying on it while a polygon vertex is explicitly linked to the polygonal shape. This means that a surface with a high degree of smoothness and curvature will have more components if it was made of polygons than if it was made from a NURBS patch. Thus, NURBS surfaces are very good at creating smooth organic shapes whereas polygon surfaces are better suited surfaces with sharp edges and creases or objects that have a large change in topology.

In the last chapter we saw that if the construction history was left on, primitives were composed of several nodes. One important upshot of this is that changing the inputs to the shape node after changing the position of any of the components can create problems. Create a brand new NURBS sphere and select a CV on it using the RMB marking menu. One of the first things you should notice is that the display in the Channels Box will change – no more transform channels. Click on the line that says CVs (click to show) to display the CVs' number and position in X, Y and Z (these values are displayed in object space not world space, so all start at 0,0,0 which is relative to the position of the object's centre). If a transform node were attached to every component, the data structure for a few objects in Maya would be so large as to make the entire program unusable. But this does create a few problems, which will be addressed later, when we want to inquire about or keyframe the positions of these components.

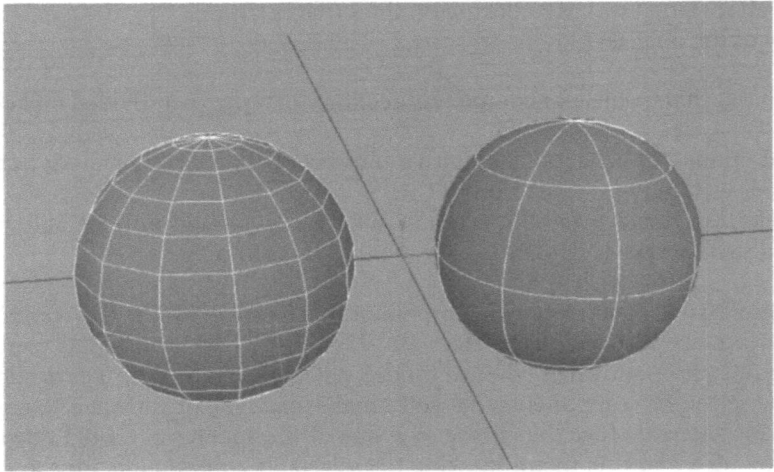

Figure 4.1 A NURBS Sphere and Polygon Sphere.

- Move a couple of the CVs to see the change in the Channels Box.
- Go back into object selection mode with F8.
- Change the number of sections in the inputs section in the Channels Box.

The reason that the object changes shape so drastically is because new information about the shape and number of CVs of the sphere is being fed into the shape node. Beforehand, the shape node had a list of all the CVs on the sphere and using this list, knew which CVs had been transformed. If the number of CVs in the list changes, so does the size of the list. The number in the list that related to the CV and its relative position means that the transformed CVs are in a different place on the sphere. So any information changes that are made to the node of an object can ripple through to the upstream nodes, possibly having an unforeseeable effect on the final description or behaviour of an object. Remember that the top level of an item is dependent on the underlying network of nodes, which will be especially important for the next stage where modeling depends on a series of interlinked operations. There are several other components, which can be displayed, yet cannot be transformed. These components can be used as references because certain operations will require some form of knowledge about them. One of these components are surface normals (these are vectors that are perpendicular to the surface and are normalized to have a length of 1), which are primarily used for shading operations but can also be used for other operations as well. Both polygonal surfaces and NURBS surfaces have surface normals and these can be displayed by using either Display|NURBS Components|Normals or Display|Polygon Components|Normals. NURBS surfaces can also have their surface origins displayed, red for U and green for V allowing you to see where these parameters begin – again more useful for shading and texturing purposes.

NURBS Modeling

One way to create a surface is to start with a primitive that roughly mimics the topology of the object you wish to make, and squash and stretch it into shape. The other modeling method that we will be exploring is concerned with creating NURBS surfaces from NURBS curves. As we further examine NURBS modeling, we will be using and creating many different components, curves and surfaces. This will have the cumulative effect of filling up viewports quickly, not so good when we want to keep work areas clear and uncluttered. One way to avoid this would be to keep hiding and showing convenient groups of items through the Outliner, but this becomes highly repetitive, especially when one considers the other useful operations that will have to be performed, such as templating or creating reference objects. You can greatly speed up these operations, by creating a new type of collection known as a layer. For now we will be using layers in one mode: "display" (the other mode is "render"). Collecting items into a layer allows a convenient grouping without the transform node that is attached to normal groups. Layers allow quick access to the templating and referencing operations, because these layers exist only to control the display of a collected set of items.

If the Layer Editor is not displayed in the Maya GUI, then LMB click on the Show Channel Box/Layer Editor button in the status line to display both panels. For now we will just set up the editor and prepare it for use. LMB click the Create layer button to the right of the panel and the new layer will be visible. With the editor exposed, set the layer type to Display and double LMB click on the layer itself. Change the layer's name to Curves. Within the modeling menu set, there are three menu headings that will be relevant to this section: Edit Curves, Surfaces and Edit NURBS. These concisely describe the workflow for modeling NURBS surfaces: create and edit a curve or curves, create a surface from these curves and then edit the surface until the desired shape is achieved.

Before creating new NURBS surfaces, looking at a few NURBS primitives can illustrate the components that underlie the construction of a NURBS surface. Create a NURBS torus and look at the attributes of the input node in the Channels Box and in the Attribute Editor. Outside of the various shape-related attributes (such as inner radius) that are relevant to the shape of a torus, there are additional attributes that pertain to the NURBS surface itself. Spans and sections will drastically affect the quality of the interpolated surface (you can change these attributes in the Attribute Editor or the Channels Box to see the effects). What these are changing are the number of curves that define the surface; less spans will give less curvature and, thus, surface resolution. At this component level, these construction curves are called *isoparms*. All of the available NURBS primitives are made from a single four-sided patch – four curves to define the edges and curves in between these edges to define the shape of the surface as it is interpolated between these edge curves. For some of the primitives, these patches have to cheat a little: the NURBS sphere, for example, has two edges shrunk to zero length. A modeling oxymoron is the NURBS cube (NURBS patches are by definition curved surfaces: sharp corner edges are not a natural characteristic of a NURBS surface) thus a NURBS cube is simply a collection of six flat patches.

Curves

All of the creation tools for NURBS modeling use combinations of NURBS curves to produce surface patches; as curves are the underlying structures for these surfaces, it is important to understand the methods for creating, manipulating and editing curves. A NURBS curve has a start and an end, a direction, a hull, edit points, curve points and CVs that help define overall shape. Most of these components will also manifest in a NURBS patch.

There are two main tools that you can use to draw a curve: the EP (edit point) Curve Tool and the CV (Control Vertex) curve tool. The EP curve tool allows you to place the start and end

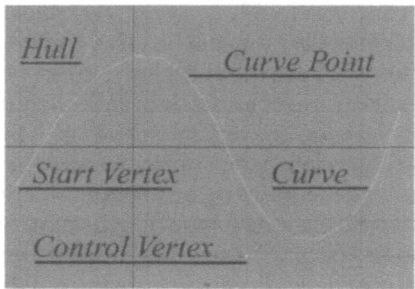

Figure 4.2 NURBS Curve Components.

positions of the curve whereas the CV curve tool gives you more control over the curvature of the curve during creation. Both tools are found under the Create menu heading. Make sure that this is in an orthographic view, as point placement is not particularly precise in the perspective view.

Drawing with the EP tool first, place five or so more CVs (until you release the mouse button the placement of the CV is not finalized) and press Enter to finalize. Now draw with the CV curve tool. The CV curve tool will behave differently to the EP curve tool: you will find that the curve will begin only after four clicks. This demonstrates one of the important details about curves: degree. All curves are NURBS and their curvature is governed by their degree. Effectively this means that (degree + 1) CVs need to be placed before one curve span is created. The higher the degree, the more curvature the curve can possess in each span, but this also means that the control of the curve becomes more complex (more CVs). Experiment with different methods of drawing curves and different degrees of curves. It is generally preferential to use degree 3 curves as they represent a good trade off between complexity and ease of use, but find a happy medium. If you know that a NURBS curve forms a fundamental part of a NURBS surface, then this trade off will be an important one – creating a NURBS surface from a complex set of curves will yield a surface with too many CVs to be useful. Create a NURBS sphere with 30 spans and 30 sections; picking and transforming the CVs should demonstrate that less CVs can generally give the same curvature. Note as well that the pivot for every curve is created at 0,0,0 – this will have more bearing when you start to use the curves to make surfaces.

The EP curve tool will allow a precise placement of points onto the orthographic plane, but there is an aid to help you place and move CVs (and all other items) more accurately. Turn on the display of the grid (if it isn't already displayed) in the window that will be drawn in, with Display|Grid and turn on Snap-to-grid. The snap-to-grid drawing aid will allow you to place CVs only on the grid points, so it's worth using the EP curve tool to draw with. When you have finished, press Return to finalize and then use F8 to go into component mode. You will only be able to translate selected CVs onto grid points so be aware that choosing more than one CV to translate with this aid turned on can be disastrous as they will all snap to the single grid point. Snap-to-grid will affect any object or component that is transformed. Each CV has its own pivot point when picked, and each group of CVs are given an arbitrary pivot point as well, which is placed at the centre of the current selection. This centralized position may not be convenient or correct for the situation; for example, you may want to scale the CVs around a different point, so the pivot can be moved in the normal manner by using the Insert key. This repositioning is only temporary; if you select the same CVs again, the pivot will be re-centralized. You can quickly move your current CV selection up or down a curve by using the left and right arrow keys (for a NURBS surface, the up and down keys will also change to other CV rows).

More complex curves can be created from joining or cutting a series of curves and it is possible to create new curves as a function of the shapes of previous curves. To make things a little more user-friendly, you can save some of the tools that you are going to be using repeatedly (i.e. the EP curve tool) to a shelf. Shelves allow the storage of buttons that represent tools, actions and custom items. Maya ships with two shelves set up already (`shelf1` and `shelf2`), `shelf1` having a set of default tools and icons. Turn on the shelf display tabs by LMB clicking on the Shelf Editor icon at the top left of the shelves, as this will make it easier to select shelves – especially if you are using seven or eight of them. Next, MMB drag the EP curve tool to the trash bin icon (far right side of the shelves) and release to drop it in. Open up the Shelf Editor (either using the Shelf Editor icon or using `Windows|Settings/Preferences|Shelves`) and change the names of the shelves to something more meaningful such as `default` and `curves`, click Save shelves and close the `Editor`. With the `default` shelf in the foreground, MMB drag the remaining CV curve tool icon onto the `curves` tab which will transfer the icon. To place an EP curve tool icon onto the currently visible shelf, hold down `Ctrl+Alt+Shift` and select the EP curve tool from the menu. This will place the menu item onto the shelf which will also save the current options state of the item so any changes to the dialogue will be frozen into the icon's use. This method will not work with the Hotbox, however.

With a curve drawn in the top window, you can now cut it into sections using `Edit Curves|Detach Curves` (if unsure how to use a tool or an action, the appropriate usage will be shown in the help line at the bottom of the Maya GUI). Cutting curves can be useful to trim away useless sections or to set up several sections to join them. This tool requires a curve point to be specified so use the RMB marking menu over the curve and select `curve point`. A curve point is an arbitrary position along the length of a curve. LMB click on any part of the curve to define one (shown as a yellow icon). You can place multiple curve points by holding down Shift to add and can also LMB drag a curve point along the curve until in the correct position. So select a point on the curve and use `Edit Curves|Detach Curves`. Curves can also be cut by, funnily enough, cutting them. In Maya these cuts will occur at the point where two or more curves intersect. Draw two curves that cross each other, select them and use `Edit Curves|Cut Curves`. The options for this action are concerned with criteria for resolving intersection and to determine which curves should be kept. The intersection criteria for this action are inherited from the `Edit Curves|Intersect Curve` action which will place a specialized curve point at intersection points which can, for example, be used with `Cut Curves`.

To attach curves, the action requires either two curves or two curve points to be selected. Draw two curves, but instead of reselecting the curve tool on the shelf, press the "y" key which will activate the last used tool or select its icon on the tool box and place the curve ends close to each other. Select both curves and use `Edit Curves|Attach Curves`. You can change the options afterwards in the Channels Box or Attribute Editor to see their effect. The curves will now be attached and changing attributes, such as the blend/attach method and `reverse1` and `reverse2`, will obviously change the resultant curve. To select two curve points, select one curve and use the RMB marking menu to allow selection of the curve point. Shift-select the other curve, use the RMB marking menu and hold down Shift to place the curve point on the other curve. However, there is an important option that isn't represented in the Channels Box or Attribute Editor – it is set on the tool's use – and this is whether to keep the original two curves or not. Delete this newly attached curve and select both of the old curves again and open up the options for `Attach Curve`. Turn off `Keep originals` and click Attach. The original curves will now have been deleted leaving the new curve, but if you try and transform this new curve only one section of it will be affected.

This weirdness occurs due to the fact that construction history is still on. Open up the Hypergraph and look at the shape node network for the new curve: these are the shape nodes from the original curves feeding into the construction of the new curve. The construction history has overwritten some of the new curves' world position with the world position of only one of the old nodes, creating this problem (notice that the only section that moves is the same part as one of the old curves). So use `Edit|Delete By Type|History` to remove these inputs.

Additionally, curves can also be connected together using fillets. Fillets are curved sections that fit between two selected curves or curve points. Clear the view and draw two more curves that intersect each other; with both curves selected open up the options for `Edit Curves|Curve Fillet`. The important options are whether the fillet will be circular or freeform (circular gives a tighter curve fitted closer to the originals), so to see the differences, copy the two curves and move these new ones to the right. Select the left-hand side curves and use the circular fillet option and use the freeform option for the right-hand side. It is worth using the Attribute Editor to display and change most of the options for the fillet operation, as some of the options, such as Circular or Freeform, are not keyable so they won't appear in the Channels Box. Moving any of the curves will update the fillet curve, because the fillet operation is receiving the continually updated positions of the curves due to the active construction history. The fillet curve turns purple to show that a connection exists from the currently selected item. One way to delete the fillet operation at a node level instead of deleting the fillet curve itself is to use the Attribute Editor to select the current node using the select key at the bottom. Pressing Delete will then delete this current selection.

Another operation that can be accomplished using the fillet action is to trim the curves to create a new curve. Trimming is as it sounds and will remove/trim away the extraneous portions of the curve that the fillet does not touch. Draw two curves that cross each other, select both of them and open up the options for `Edit Curves|Curve Fillet`. Turn on Trim and turn on the `Keep originals` option so the original curves can be referred to for comparison. The option to join will determine whether a single curve or two new curves are created. Again, while construction history is on, the fillet operation can be updated using the Attribute Editor

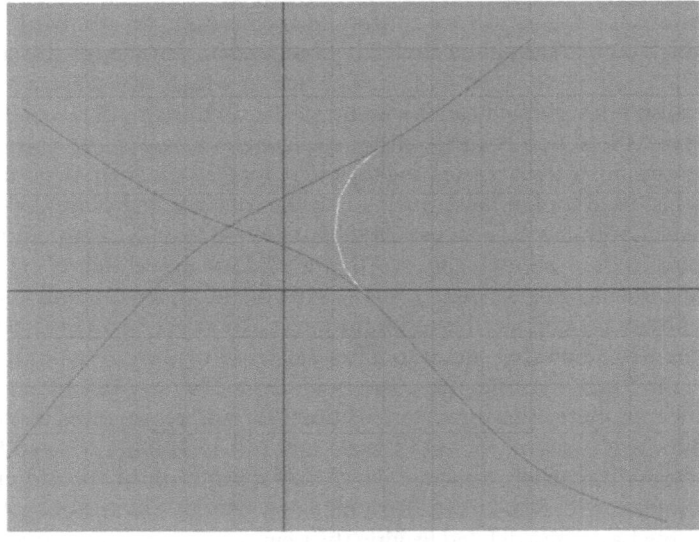

Figure 4.3 Filleted NURBS Curves.

and the Channels Box. The other curve operations under the Edit|Curves menu set are divided into roughly two parts: adding to or changing the shape of curves. Out of the latter, the curve editing tool is a most powerful tool and allows total control over the curve's tangency, direction, scale and position at any position. Rebuild Curve is also extremely useful as it allows the re-parameterizing of a curve. Use this if you would like to keep the curve the same shape but have the CVs and/or spans placed evenly, or would like to reduce/increase the number of CVs or spans while keeping roughly the same shape. This is a useful function when trying to get the trade off between complexity and usability of a curve to work. If you just want to add some local complexity to the curve then Edit Curves|Insert Knot will give you another edit point and corresponding CV when placed at a selected curve point.

There will be a point when a curve is either the correct shape or as good as is required. At this time it is worth shedding the construction history, as keeping this can cause unforeseen errors later on (curves are going to be used as the basis for NURBS surfaces). It also keeps memory use to a minimum, which at this point may seem to be rather picky, but as scenes get larger so will the data sets used to construct it and we are going to want all the available memory we have to manipulate these scenes. Edit|Delete By Type|History will delete all nodes that feed into the currently selected node, "freezing" its shape.

NURBS Surface Tools

Applying a further dimension to the components that we have seen in NURBS curves gives us the components of a NURBS surface. Each NURBS surface contains isoparms, which are the

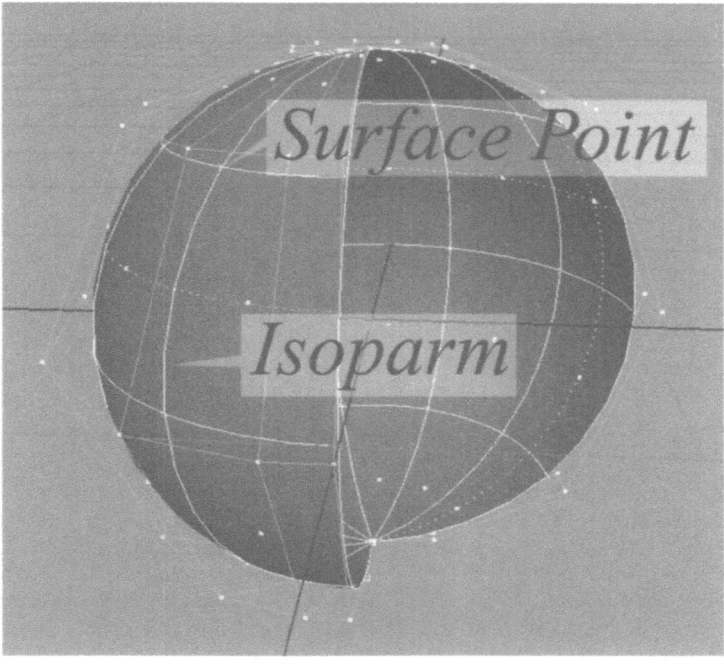

Figure 4.4 NURBS Surface Components.

U and V "flow lines" of the surface and are the construction curves of the surface. Curves contain CVs, so we can expect a row of CVs for each isoparm that lies on the surface (correspondingly, each isoparm has its own hull). Other components are now extended into the next dimension, so that instead of a curve point in U, we now have a surface point in U and V. When working with NURBS components, we can alter the number of CVs selected quickly by using CTRL+RMB over our selection of CVs and selecting shrink CV selection or grow CV selection to increase or decrease the total number of CVs selected on the surface, whilst select CV selection boundary will only select the CVs on the edge of the current selection. The option to select CVs on the surface border will only select CV on the U and V edges (the behaviour of this can also be changed from this marking menu).

Revolve

A real world analogue for a revolved surface would be creating an object using a lathe. All that is required is a single profile curve and an axis of revolution, creating a surface with only one axis of symmetry (wineglasses, vases etc.).

In the side view, draw a profile curve and make sure that Construction History is on. Keep the curve selected and RMB click over the layer curves and select Add Selected Objects – now

Figure 4.5 A Revolved NURBS Surface.

the display of the curve can be controlled by the mode of the layer. With the curve still selected, open up the options dialogue for Surfaces|Revolve. There are a wide range of options concerning the surface definition and surface type but the options concerning the axis of revolution are the important ones for now. Set the axis to "Y", the surface degree to cubic and click the Revolve button. In common with the NURBS primitives we have been looking at, the input node for the surface contains the creation options that you can see in the options dialogue. Changing the axis of revolution will give a fundamentally different surface, as will changing the pivot (the position at which the axis is placed). All of these changes can be effected within the Attribute Editor or the Channels Box giving real-time feedback. This can refine our idea of a node structure now, seeing them as a series of functions providing and/or interpreting data to arrive at a result – in this case a surface. Open up the Hypergraph, select the output surface and use Graph|Input and Output Connections to show how the nodes are connected. Moving the curve itself will also change the output surface. An object's history is the list of nodes with input connections that lie downstream from it.

Create another layer in the Layer Editor, name it Revolve and add the new surface to it; rename the layer called Curves to Rcurves. You can now control how the curve and the surface are displayed – for instance, it may be easier to set the display mode to "T" (template) which means that for now, the surface cannot be selected or changed by the normal methods – only from changing the curve shape. If the viewport gets too cluttered, the layer visibility can always be turned off.

Because the nodes are still connected (due to the construction history) you can further affect the shape of the revolved surface. These connections have the curve shape feeding into the revolve node. The curve is still an independent entity and can still be changed on a component and object level, so experiment with transforming the curve and moving the curve's CVs. The shape of the curve feeds into the revolve function to automatically change the output surface downstream from it. Looking at the CVs for the revolved surface, we can see that the number of CVs corresponds to the meeting points of the vertical (U) and horizontal (V) isoparms. The profile curve gives us the number of isoparms in V (the degree of the curve) and the sections in the revolve options give the isoparms in U. The higher degree of the curve, the more horizontal resolution the resultant surface has and the more CVs on the surface to control it with.

Extrusion

The next order of modeling complexity is the extrusion, which sweeps a cross-section down a curve, similar to using a die or cake icer. Two parts are required for the operation: the profile curve (cross-section) and the path curve. Create another two layers, one called Ecurves and one called Extrusion. Draw the profile curve in the top view (keep it centred about the origin as the profile curve will be swept down the path curve with its pivot on the path curve) and draw the path curve in the side view. Add these curves to the Ecurves layer. The Extrude action will require you to pick two curves, but the order is going to be important – the easiest way to find out is to keep the cursor over the menu item and the relevant information will be given at the bottom in the help area. In this case, the path curve is the item to be picked last.

- Select the profile curve.
- Shift-select the path curve.
- Choose Surfaces|Extrude to create the surface.

The first thing to notice is that although a surface has indeed been created it might not be in the desired position or be the desired shape. This is now the time to look at the creation options. All of these options determine the placement of the profile curve at the path curve and the orientation of this cross-section as it traverses the path, all of which affect the final output surface.

- Style/Extrude Type determines how the profile curve is moved down the path. Distance means that a straight extrusion will be created along a defined axis ignoring the path curve. Flat means that the profile curve will remain in the same orientation at which it was created along the path. Tube will keep the profile curve perpendicular to the path.
- Result Position determines whether the output surface is placed at the path or the profile (in the Channels Box/Attribute Editor this is the Fixed Path toggle). Pivot determines whether the profile curve pivots at each path CV or uses the path end point for the pivot instead. This is Component Pivot in the Channels Box or Attribute Editor.
- Orientation determines whether the profile curve will be swept down the path using the normal of the profile curve or not – use Profile Normal in the Channels Box or Attribute Editor.

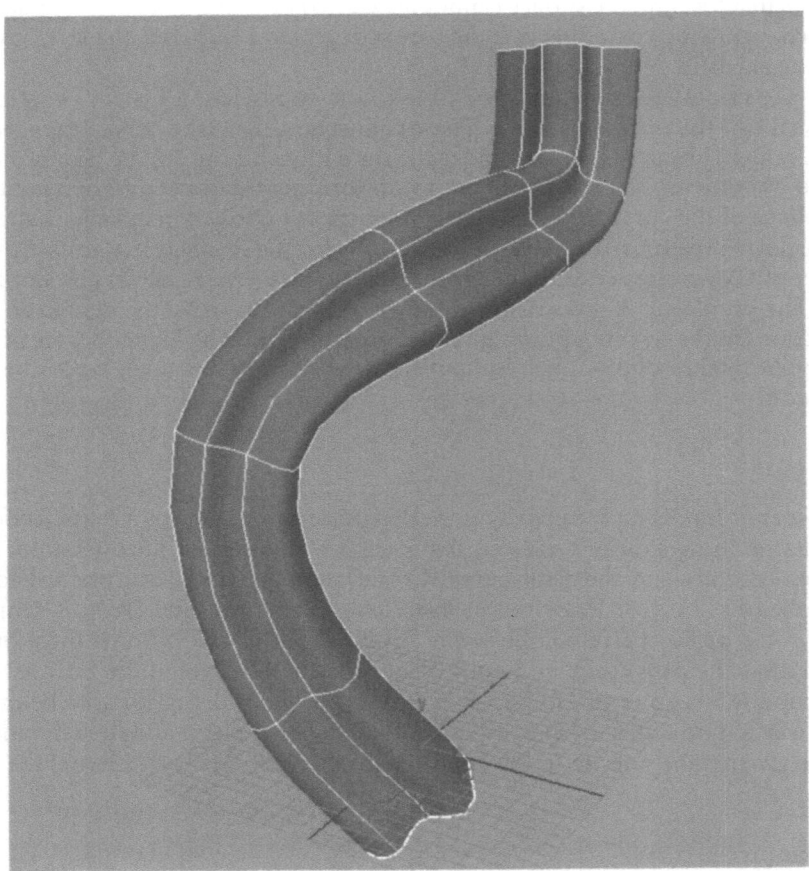

Figure 4.6 An Extruded NURBS Surface.

It is worth having all of the above three attributes turned to "on", as this will create a more expected output surface and position. Additional attributes such as Scale or Rotate will affect the profile curve shape as it moves down the path. The resolution of the output surface is now determined by the number of profile curve CVs multiplied by the number of path curve CVs. Again, place the output surface into the Extrusion layer and hide both of the layer contents.

Loft

A lofted surface is formed from a series of two or more curves, the surface results from these curves forming the underlying cross-section. The term loft comes from shipbuilding where cross-sections of a boat's hull (later on, aeroplanes) were laid out and a wooden, fibreglass or metal skin was laid between them. Any number of curves can be used and although they don't have to have the same number of CVs, it will help as it keeps the surface definition regular. Otherwise Maya will create a best guess surface which means that you won't have total control over the shape and positions of the CVs. Make one more layer for the curves and one more for the output surface. Draw a single curve in the side view, and duplicate it four times. In the Outliner, select each curve in turn and move some of the CVs around so that each curve has a different profile shape and then move the curves in the top view so that there is some distance between them. Selection of the curves is important for this operation, so Shift-select the curves in the order that you would want them to be connected. Once these have been selected, select Surfaces|Loft to create the surface. The options again govern the shape of the resulting surface, with parameterization defining whether the spans (another option concerned with placing additional rows of CVs between the control curves) are equally spaced between the control curves. Surface Degree will change the complexity of the NURBS surface and Close will create a closed (or periodic) NURBS surface. Auto reverse is usually worth

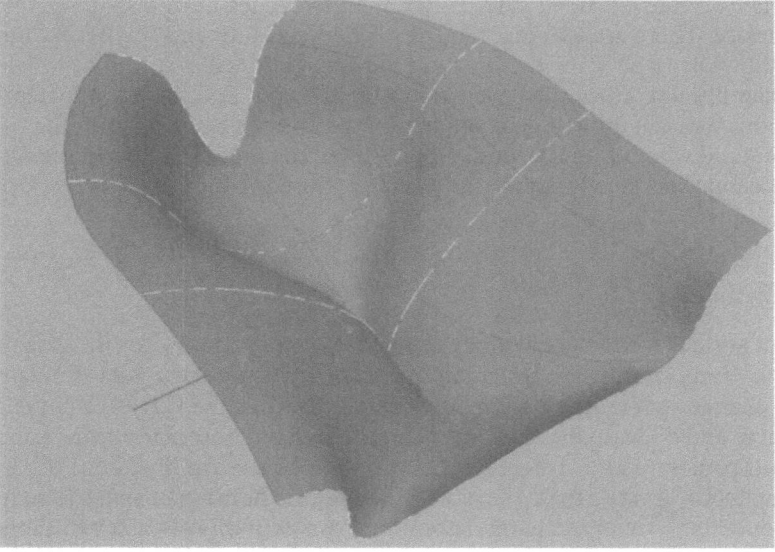

Figure 4.7 A Lofted NURBS Surface.

Figure 4.8 The Bevel and Bevel Plus Output Surfaces.

having turned on as it will automatically keep the start and end points for the curve (its direction) uniform, otherwise twisting could occur – but experiment with changing this in the Attribute Editor.

Bevelling

Bevelling lets us create extruded surfaces with curved edges from a single curve, isoparm or curve on surface. There are two tools for this: The Bevel tool and the Bevel Plus action. The Bevel tool allows us to pick any curve in our viewport and will return a bevelled surface with three blue handles to control the bevel width, bevel height and the extrude depth. The other options for this tool can only be changed within the options box and cover the type of surface that is output and whether to use a full or partial curve range. The Bevel Plus action creates a fully closed, capped surface (as long as the curve is closed) which makes it perfect for creating 3D text.

Additional Methods

If the output surface is too detailed, not detailed enough or hasn't got the isoparms and CVs spaced evenly (important when attaching surfaces) you can use the Rebuild Curve action to effect these changes without redrawing the curves. To space the CVs on a curve more evenly, select the curve and open up the Attribute Editor to find out how many spans the curve is composed from (Spans = CVs − Degree). This can then be used in the Rebuild Curve options box – set the Rebuild Type to Uniform and then set the number of spans as required, but set Keep Ends and Keep Tangents to on. Rebuilding curves in this manner can allow a quick way to evenly parameterize or reparameterize the output surfaces. Use this once an object's history has been deleted or simply duplicate the object and rebuild the new surface instead.

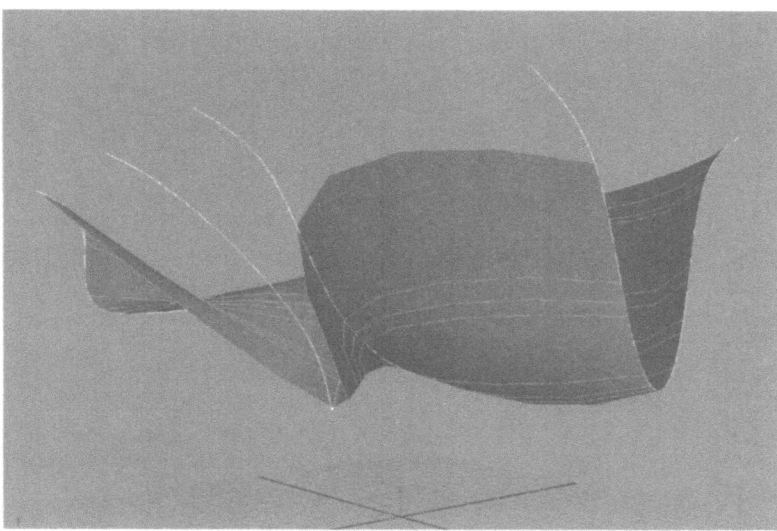

Figure 4.9 Partial Curves in a Lofted NURBS Surface while Construction History Is Active.

We have seen how the construction history can be used to affect the output surfaces by changing a number of inputs and also the shapes of input curves. This makes changes extremely intuitive as the shape of your object updates in front of you. One attribute that is common to all of the above techniques that hasn't been covered is the use of the full or partial curve option. Create a lofted surface from two curves, but in the options box turn on Partial Curve Range – this is an option that cannot be altered after surface creation. Both curves used in the operation are now represented in the inputs area in the Channels Box and Attribute Editor. You can change the positions on each curve that the surface is evaluated from, in terms of 0 to 1 – this is where the U parameterization of a NURBS curve can be useful. Change these values in the Channels Box to see the results. This is possible because the positions on the curve are interpreted by the node subCurven which then passes this information to the extrude operation (which is why the option for this cannot be changed after the operation). So now this node can pass a section of the curve to the loft to the Loft node. Open the Hypergraph window, select the node for the extruded surface and choose Graph|Input and Output Connections to see the node structure for this surface and how these subCurve nodes are utilized. With this window still open, select the two curves and extrude a surface with the Curve Range set to "Complete" and the Hypergraph display will show the differences in construction and node connection (turn off the pick mask for surfaces to allow the easier selection of the curves).

Highlight the subCurven node's name in the Channels Box and activate the Show Manipulator tool. This tool is below the Scale tool icon and allows access to special parameters that can be changed using the usual manipulator methods – you should see two blue diamonds at the start and end of the selected curve. LMB drag one of the diamonds and move it around the curve for a more interactive method of changing the subCurve parameters. At any point during modeling, you can select the output surface and duplicate it. This will create a snapshot of the surface with none of the input nodes. When the surface is finished in terms of using

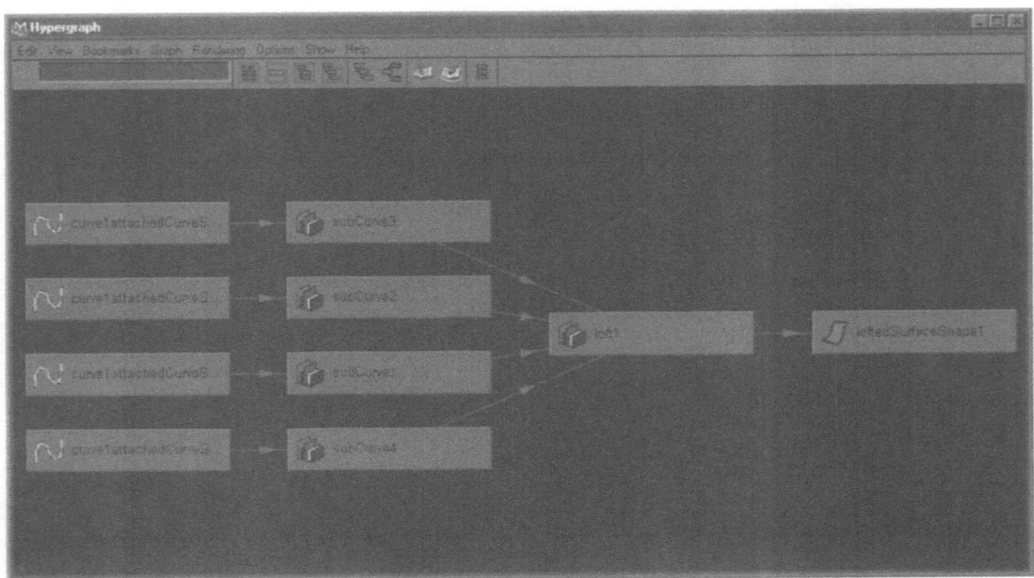

Figure 4.10 Hypergraph Showing the Relationship between Partial Curves and an Output Surface.

curves to define a modeling operation, the construction history for the surface can be deleted by using Edit|Delete By Type|History, which will delete all nodes before the shape node. Again, it's worth creating an icon on the shelf for this action.

Attaching and Detaching Surfaces

Because NURBS surfaces are composed of NURBS curves, it is reasonable to expect that many of the operations that can be performed on curves can be performed on surfaces. NURBS patches can be cut and attached in exactly the same manner as curves but this can only work at parametric co-ordinates. These co-ordinates are defined by the isoparms which exist on a surface and are picked in the same way that a curve point was defined by clicking on a curve (the isoparm is a curve point with an additional dimension – U). Detaching a surface is simply a case of picking an isoparm (or isoparms) in U or V and selecting Edit NURBS|Detach Surfaces to split the surface into parts. Conversely, attaching NURBS patches is a case of selecting either both surfaces (in which case the closest edges will be attached) or two isoparms and using Edit NURBS|Attach Surfaces to connect the surfaces together. Be careful about the Keep originals option when using construction history; any problems can be alleviated by deleting the history of the new surface.

Stitching Surfaces

There are cases when attaching surfaces will not create the continuity that is required, such as when using multiple surfaces or when trying to keep the identity of connected NURBS patches individual. Clear the workspace and delete any old surfaces and layers. Create two NURBS planes with four spans in U and V and position them so that two edges are adjacent.

The Stitch Edges tool requires two isoparms to be selected which are then joined together while allowing positional or tangential continuity (curvature across the surfaces) to be maintained. Use the Stitch Edges tool (`Edit NURBS|Stitch|Stitch Edges Tool`) to pick two edges and press Return when the position of the stitch is acceptable (again, you should see two blue diamonds representing the extent of the stitch across the edges). Move one of the surfaces and the stitch will constantly update, meaning that this technique is especially suited to connecting animated surfaces (i.e. a head joining a neck). More so, because the edges do not require the same amount of CVs.

To stitch multiple surfaces together (for instance, any complex patch model) a global stitch can be used. This looks at the closest edges that are shared among selected surfaces and performs a stitch between all of them. Create four NURBS planes very close to each other, select all of them and then use `Edit NURBS|Stitch|Global Stitch` to connect them (you may have to adjust the `Max Separation` values until the stitch connects). More surfaces can be added to the existing stitched surfaces using the Stitch Edges tool but it is usually best to position all of the surfaces that you want stitched and then use this method in one final pass prior to the next stage of any modeling project. It is important not to delete the surface's history now as the stitch is part of this, so make sure the prospective surfaces are "clean" before stitching.

Trimming Surfaces

So far you have only been able to attach, detach and stitch NURBS surfaces. Although these tools and actions are extremely useful, it means that you can only use parametric positions on the surface. This doesn't give much room for manoeuvre when you start to design complex surfaces, characters and locations, as you are tied to using these boundary edges. Trimming, however, allows you to define a completely custom edge or line on a surface and remove/trim away the remainder. These custom edges are called "curves on surface" and are created when curves have been projected onto a surface, where two surfaces have intersected or where a surface has been drawn on. Once these curves have been defined, the trim operation can be used which creates "trim edges" that also lie on the surface defining the trimmed area. One of the simplest methods is to intersect two surfaces.

Create a NURBS sphere and a NURBS plane and position the plane so that it cuts the sphere diagonally in half. Select both surfaces and use `Edit NURBS|Intersect Surfaces` (make sure that curves are created on both surfaces in the options box).

Again, construction history will update the positions of these curves if you move the objects. To keep the curves where they are, just delete the history of each surface and you can move the surfaces apart. If you select the curve and use the translate manipulator, only two axes will be shown because the curve is defined in terms of the surface it has been created on and thus can only be moved in U and V. Now that there are some curves on the surface, you can use the trim tool (`Edit NURBS|Trim Tool`) which will ask you to pick a surface and then to define the portion of the surface that you want to keep by LMB clicking onto it. The surface, in order to keep a curved edge at the trim position, may well increase in complexity. If you want to reverse this operation, simply select the surface and use `Edit NURBS|Untrim Surfaces`. To draw a curve onto a surface, you can make the surface in question "live" by clicking on the magnet icon at the right of the "Snap To" tools (the display will show the surface in green wireframe). This will then allow any curves drawn over the surface to stick onto it. So select the EP curve tool and draw onto the surface. Press Return to finalize curve creation, use `Edit Curves|Open/Close Curves` to close the curve and click Make Surface Live to return everything to normal (curves have to be closed in order to define a trim surface edge).

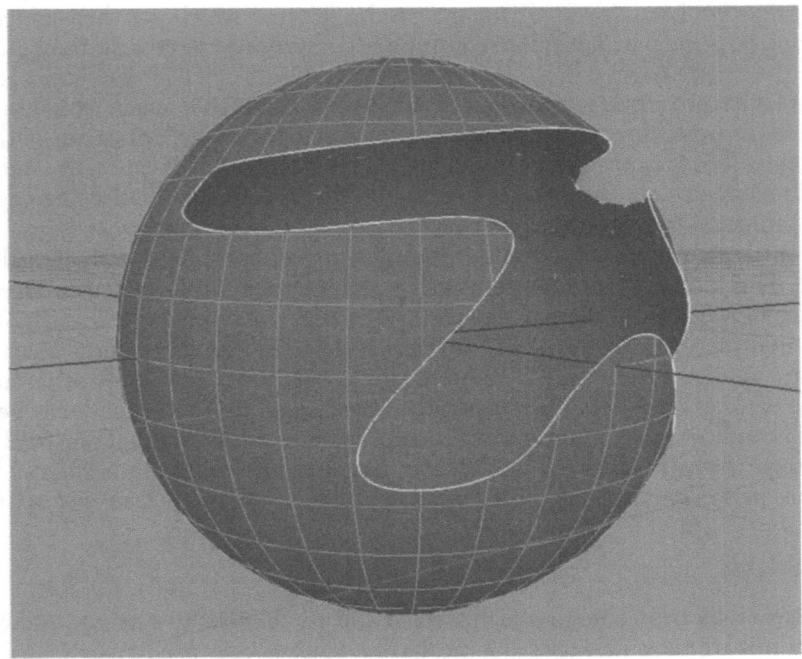

Figure 4.11 A NURBS Sphere with a Trim Edge.

Projection is simply a question of drawing a curve, selecting a surface and using `Edit NURBS|Project Curve on Surface`. The curve will be projected onto the selected surface using a projection plane perpendicular to the currently active viewport.

Create a NURBS sphere, draw a closed curve in the top view that remains within the edges of the object. Select the curve and the surface, and making sure that the top view is currently selected (the safest way is to pop it to the foreground) use `Project curve on surface`. Two curves will be created as the projection only looks at where the curve and the surface intersect in 3D space (front and back). Either of these curves can be selected and deleted if required before trimming. The perspective view can be used with this action to precisely place curves onto a surface. Effectively, a trimmed surface is just not being shown – go into component selection mode and the CVs for the trimmed portion of the surface will still be visible. What trimming is used for is to hide one section of a surface while providing a custom edge (a trim edge visible by bringing up the RMB marking menu) which can be used to provide information for tools like the Fillet Blend tool.

Fillets

This operation is exactly the same as the fillet operation for curves, except that it comes in three flavours. Each variant requires different information to build the fillet blend and the nature of the information provided will decide the situations in which each is used.

Create two spheres and position one above the other. Select both of them and use `Edit NURBS|Surface Fillet|Circular Fillet` creating a smooth surface between them.

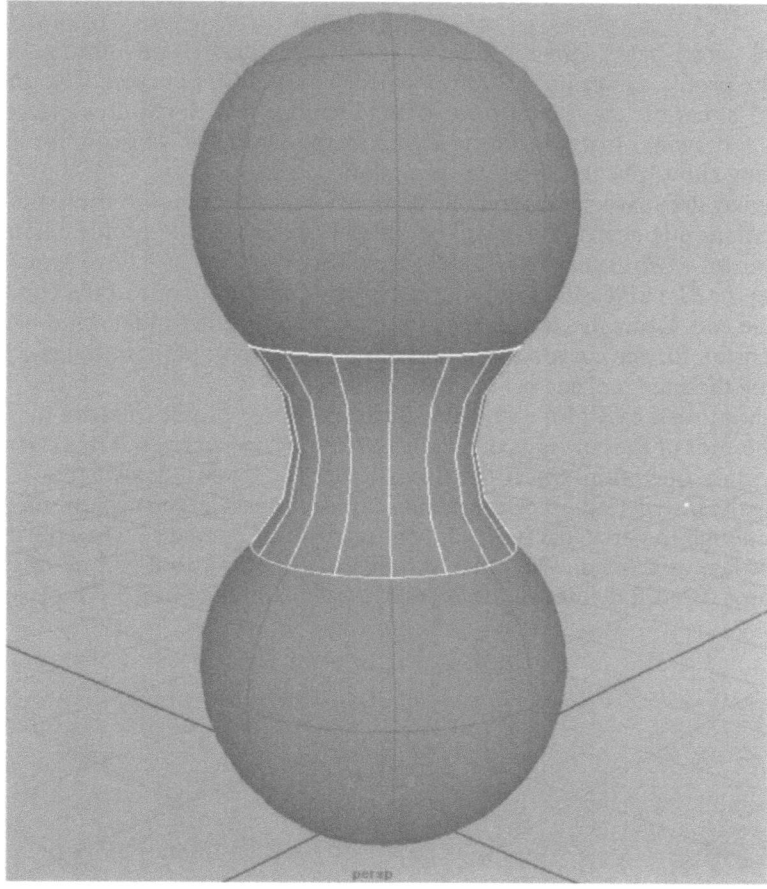

Figure 4.12 A Filleted NURBS Surface.

This fillet is fairly well defined, but if you try and move the surfaces apart, the fillet blend updates extremely slowly. Delete the fillet blend and select a horizontal isoparm on each sphere and use the `Freeform Fillet` action. Again, you get a good rounded fillet, but the update is a little slow as Maya calculates the position in 3D of the surface isoparms to create this freeform surface. Delete the fillet surface. This time, with nothing selected, use the Fillet Blend tool, which will ask for any mixture of isoparms, curves on surface or trim edges. Select an isoparm on each sphere, pressing Enter when prompted in the help line. The Freeform Fillet tool is happy using any combination and any number of pieces of information (curves and trim edges) when creating a left edge to join to a right edge. This means that it can be extremely useful in situations which require the connection of multiple surfaces that cannot be defined by patch edges (otherwise, a global stitch could be used).

It is worth experimenting here with the various different options with each tool/action and the different pieces of surface information that can be used to define the fillet. Remember that the fillet surface only updates while its construction history/input nodes are active. Selecting the blend and deleting its history will create a static piece of geometry.

Birail and Boundary Tools

The Birail tool (which again comes in three flavours) is a sophisticated loft tool. It lets you not only define the profile curves but also the two edge curves (rail curves). The one caveat for using this tool is that the curve ends have to be touching – which requires a large amount of precision when drawing. Instead of a steady hand and good eye, you can use the "snap-to-curve" modeling aid to give the necessary precision.

In the top view draw two curves roughly parallel with each other but move the CVs to give them some variation in shape. These will be the rail curves that the profile curve (or curves) will be swept down – two edges of a NURBS patch. Turn on Snap to curve (or use the hotkey "c") and using the EP curve tool position the first edit point onto one of the curves, dragging it down to one end. Draw the rest of the curve maybe using the other windows to provide another dimension for the curve's shape and place the last edit point at the end of the other rail curve using the snap tool again.

You can now move the CVs for each curve into any desired profile (just not the CVs that are touching at the ends of the curves as they have to remain connected) but this can also be done after the modeling operation. Select the Birail 1 tool (Surfaces|Birail|Birail 1 Tool) and, following the instructions, pick the profile curve followed by the two rail curves. The tool is intelligent enough to know that it will only be using three curves, so when the third curve is picked, the surface is created. The other variants of the Birail tool just allow more profile curves to be used: Birail 2 defines all the edges of a patch and the Birail 3+ tool can give much

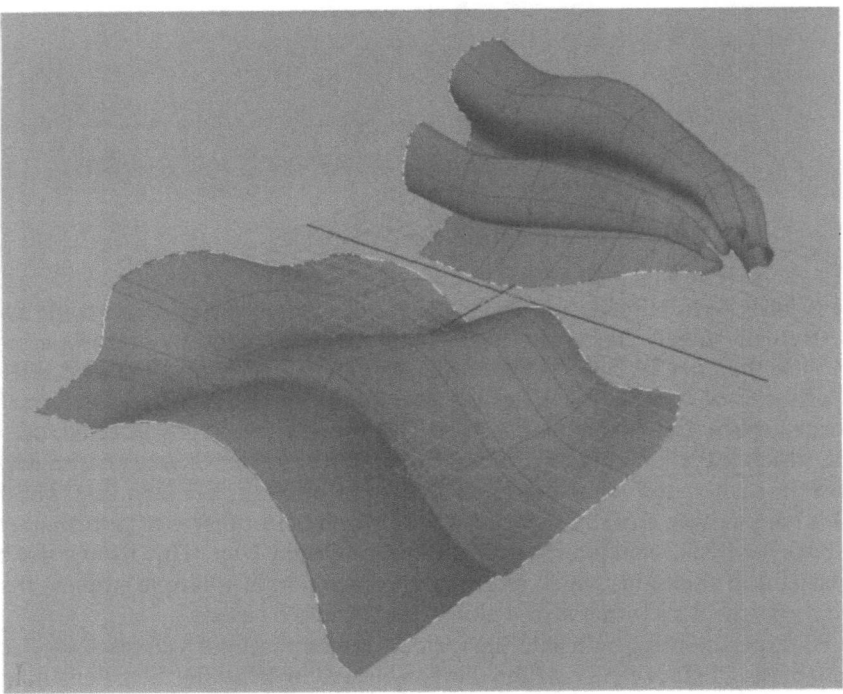

Figure 4.13 A Birail and Boundary Surface.

greater definition over how a surface will be interpolated. The curves for relatively complex surfaces can be easily drawn now and the Birail tool will create the surface. Consider a shirt, for example: if the curves are drawn where the seams are then the front, back and sleeves for the shirt can be reproduced with ease, creating a composite model.

The Boundary action has the same behaviour as the Birail tool, except that it uses three or four curves that form the edges (boundary) of a NURBS patch. So instead of sweeping a set of profile curves over rail curves to form a closed patch, the Boundary tool just uses the supplied edge curves to interpolate a patch between them. This tool is extremely useful when creating a complex surface from many different patches, as we can create new patches from the edge curves of other surrounding patches. Once this boundary surface has been created it can then be stitched or even attached to the surrounding surfaces, as they both share at least one edge curve between them. To create a surface using the boundary action, four or three edge curves need to be created and have their end points touching (use the snap to curve tool when drawing them). Select the curves in order and then use Surfaces|Boundary. The Curve Ordering option will ignore the order in which the curves were selected if set to automatic, while the Common End Points option will resolve the requirement for the end points to touch exactly or whether they can be within a tolerance if set to As Required. Partial or Complete Curves will, like some other surface operations, determine whether you can affect the output surface by changing the proportion of the edge curves used.

Editing the Final Surface

Information can also be taken from a surface to allow modeling decisions to be continually made all the way to the deadline. Isoparms and trim edges can be duplicated into 3D curves so that Maya can use them as components for other modeling operations; usually curves defined in two dimensions (U and V) can only be used in a very limited way. Select an isoparm or trim edge of a surface and use Edit Curves|Duplicate Surface Curves to create an exact copy of the 2D curve in three dimensions. This can be useful when a surface needs to be remodeled using elements from previous surfaces or to provide Birail surfaces with rail and/or profile curves. For example, an extrusion could create the basic shape for a tree trunk but won't give much cross-sectional variation along its length. Duplicating surface curves along the surface length will give a series of cross-section curves that can then be reshaped and then lofted. Another way to quickly re-edit a surface once completed is to rebuild it in just the same way that a curve is rebuilt. Using Edit NURBS|Rebuild Surfaces you can specify the number of spans in U and V to change the curvature of a surface or to even out the positions of the isoparms. This should really be done, however, when the construction history has been deleted.

If additional surface complexity needs to be added, for example if the area around an elbow needs more CVs to help define some bumps, then new isoparms can be inserted onto the NURBS surface. Isoparms are the underlying curves of a NURBS surface and define where rows of CVs exist in either U or V, but because isoparms are the longitude and latitude of a surface patch any new isoparms will run the length of the model. To add a new isoparm, its new position can be defined in the same way that a curve can be defined. Select the surface and select Isoparm from the RMB marking menu and LMB drag an isoparm marker (yellow line) to the required position. With this line now determined use Edit NURBS|Insert Isoparm to add a new isoparm. Multiple isoparms can be inserted by Shift-selecting new positions on the surface (conversely, isoparms can be deleted by just selecting them and pressing delete). However, surface complexity has now increased because isoparms run the length or breadth of a NURBS patch. This means that a surface can very quickly become overly heavy in terms of control points just because some local complexity was required. This is why models that tend to have a lot of varying shapes across their surface will be made up from patches that have been stitched together. A head, for example, won't need as much complexity in the back, the crown and the nose as the areas around the mouth and eyes will.

A NURBS Teapot

One of the important things when starting modeling is to be able to decide how a surface is going to be created. If you are going to be creating something from life, as opposed to a Martian, then it is worth observing the object itself. Several things can be ascertained, such as which method will yield the best basic shape. The modeling process is a process of gradual refinement, so a basic shape from an extrusion or a revolution provides the starting point. Can the basic shape be represented using four-sided patches? Will you need to connect objects together and what will provide the best options for this? Do trims need to be used? And does the object have holes in it? The teapot has a two-hole topology and two additional surfaces will need to be attached to the main body – the handle and the spout. However, you can start with a primitive from which useful shape information can be extracted: a NURBS sphere.

- Create a NURBS sphere, select an isoparm near the top (where the lid would be), detach the surfaces and delete the detached top surface. This now gives a basic starting shape from which you can extract information.
- Select an isoparm at the side of the sphere and duplicate a surface curve from it and delete the sphere. The new curve is going to be revolved because there is some additional detail

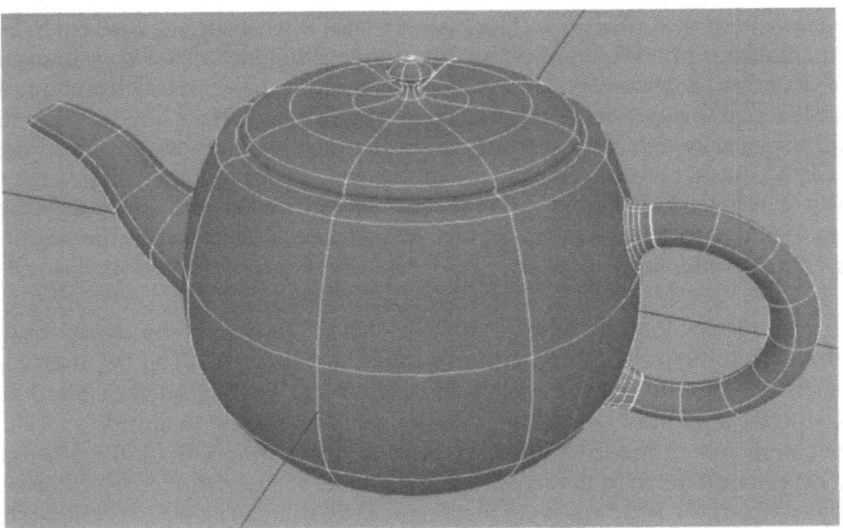

Figure 4.14 A NURBS Teapot.

needed in the teapot body that is easier to implement in a surface of revolution than by trying to build it into an existing 3D surface.

- First you need to add a few more points to the end of the curve as an edge needs to be created in the top hole of the teapot. Select the curve and open up the options for `Edit Curves|Extend|Extend Curve`, and set `Extension Type` to `Extrapolate`, `Extend Curve At` to `End`, turn on `Join to Original` and `Remove Multiple Knots` and turn off `Keep Original`. This will provide a few extra CVs from which you can now fashion a rim.
- Additionally, flatten the bottom and revolve the curve about the Y axis. Edit the shape of the curve until a good "teapot" shape is attained (name it `teapot body`) and then delete the history of the surface.

To create a teapot lid that fits the teapot body there is already existing information in the scene that can be used. Zoom in to the edge of the hole in the side view so that you can see the original curve used for the teapot body. The lid has to fit the rim of the teapot, so you should use the original curve. Select `Curve Point` from the RMB marking menu or component masks and create one where the rim ends on the curve. Detach the curve here. Turn on `Snap to curve` and use the EP curve tool to draw the first vertex at the end of the detached curve portion. Turn off `Snap to curve` and continue drawing the cross-section of the lid. As you are going to create the lid from a revolve, the last vertex should lie exactly on the Y axis, otherwise there will be a minute hole in the top. To place this vertex exactly, you can use the snap-to-grid modeling aid. Select the last vertex of the new curve and move it to a grid point that lies on the Y axis. All you have to do now is turn off the "snap" tool and move the vertex upwards.

If these curves have any history then delete them, as the curves need to be attached and any operations lying downstream might cause untoward problems. Select both curves and open up the options for `Edit Curves|Attach Curves`. Set the attach method to `Connect`, turn on `Keep Multiple Knots` and `Keep Originals` and click Attach. Delete history and now delete the original curves. You can now revolve this curve, and the output surface (name it `lid`) should fit the teapot body exactly, prior to deleting its history. Before creating the handle and the spout, you need to decide where the seam of the teapot should lie. The seam is displayed as the thicker green isoparm and is the line where two of the edges of a NURBS patch meet. One problem that can be thrown up from this is that if creating a curve on surface (for a fillet blend or extrusion) across this seam, the seam will cut the curve where it crosses. If trying to draw on a "live" surface, you will not be able to cross the seam as the curve has to be defined in terms of U and V; the seam is where the U parameter starts and ends (it isn't mathematically continuous). Because you are going to be creating a spout and handle, the seam needs to be placed away from the front or back of the teapot. Select a side isoparm on the teapot and use `Edit NURBS|Move Seam`.

Create a NURBS circle (`Create|NURBS Primitives|Circle`) and transform it in the front view so it is placed where the spout will start on the teapot body. Select the teapot body and the NURBS circle and project the curve onto the surface. Delete the curve at the back of the teapot body and delete the NURBS circle, as they aren't needed any more. This curve on surface will be the starting point for an extrusion that will form the spout. The curve on surface was used because it is wrapped directly onto the teapot body, so the resulting extrusion will have one end that fits the teapot surface. Change to the side view and turn on `Snap to curve`. Using the EP curve tool, position the first vertex along the side profile isoparm of the teapot so that it starts from the centre of the projected curve; draw the rest of the path for the extrusion so that it is roughly spout shaped. Extrude the circle along the path, and change the options of the extrude in the Attribute Editor so that the output surface is in the correct position. You can now change the shape of the path and the profile curve to get the correct spout shape.

Additionally, you need to give the spout an inside edge so that the surface does not appear to be paper-thin. This can be done at the component level. Delete the history of the spout first and then select Hull from the RMB marking menu. A hull is a line that connects a row of CVs together and can allow you to modify whole sections of CVs in one go. You need to edit the row of CVs at the end of the spout, so instead of trying to select them in the usual manner you can change them using the arrow keys. Select a cross-sectional hull anywhere on the spout and use the up or down arrow keys to change the selection to the hull at the end of the spout. Now transform this hull (and any hulls nearby) until an edge is formed. Name this surface Spout.

For the handle, create a NURBS torus and in the side view, rotate and translate it so that it sits where the handle should. Use the channels in the inputs section of the Channels Box to change the shape of the torus so that it looks more like a handle, then delete its history. Select the isoparms at either end of the torus and duplicate them as curves. These curves are going to be projected onto the surface of the teapot body and used for a fillet to make a nice smooth edge. These curves should be scaled before this happens, as the fillet will look better blending from a large shape (projected onto the teapot) to a small shape (the handle edges). Select both curves and use Modify|Centre Pivot because the pivot for these new curves have been created at 0,0,0 which is no good for the scaling operation, and scale each curve up a little. Curve projection uses the current camera view, so change to the perspective view and move the viewpoint around until you are looking down the upper curve and onto the teapot surface. Project the curve and repeat this for the lower curve as well, using a different viewpoint. Again, delete the curves that have been created on the back half of the teapot as they won't be used and delete the other duplicated curves.

To create the fillet, you have to use the Fillet Blend tool because you are mixing the types of curves that you are blending. The tool will ask you to select one edge – the projected curve – press Return and then select the other edge. This other edge is the isoparm at the edge of the handle, so it will make selection a little easier if you change into unshaded mode and make sure that the lowest level of smoothing is on. Once this has been created, you can repeat the process for the other handle. If you retained the history of the handle and the fillet, you can change its position and shape by changing the start and sweep channels of the handle and also by moving the vertices of the curves on surface. Again, when all of the objects have been finished, it is worth putting them into a group for ease of selection and manipulation. However, if you select all of the surfaces and group them, you'll find that a strange translation error will occur if you try and move the group: the fillet blend surface will gain a double transformation. This is because the group is passing down its transformations to the children in its hierarchy. Additionally, the fillet surface is defined by the (transforming) surfaces and edges that form the handle and teapot body. Thus the fillet blend is receiving twice as many transformations. To combat this effect you can either delete the history of the fillet blend surface or keep the blend outside of the hierarchy.

Polygon Modeling

Polygons and polygon surfaces consist of a series of connected points (vertices). The connections are called edges and when these connections form a closed loop, another component called a face is created. Polygonal objects are different from NURBS objects because all of the

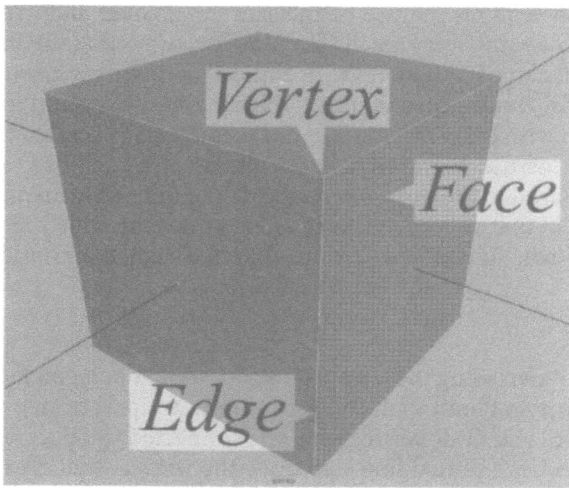

Figure 4.15 A Polygon Face and Its Components.

components lie on the object's surface. Because the points do not have a weighted control over a local area, the definition of a polygonal surface is controlled explicitly by its components. This creates a problem in that a highly curved polygon surface will require an order of magnitude more control points than a highly curved NURBS surface, so changing the surface shape will involve more components being picked and transformed.

An advantage that polygon modeling has over NURBS modeling is that the polygon surface is not defined by parametric equations that require four clearly defined edge curves. Thus a polygon surface can be cut and joined at any place and will not require operations such as trimming and filleting to create a surface with a complex topology such as a hand or one containing multiple holes. A polygon surface can also be built from component definition, so that you can draw the surface directly instead of drawing a series of curves and applying a surfacing operation to them, giving a more direct feedback of how the surface will look. Local complexity can also be added to polygon surfaces, so if a bump needs to be added, then new components can be included that won't affect the definition of the rest of the model. There are only two menu sets concerned with polygon creation and polygon editing (Polygons and Edit Polygons), but it is possible that the main four menu headings in the Modeling menu set may be used in combination as polygon surfaces can be extracted from NURBS patches and NURBS surface operations. Polygons also have their own variant of the CTRL+RMB marking menu which will also shrink and grow the current selection (faces, edges and vertices) but will also convert the selection of one component type to another, so that vertices can be used to select faces or edges that they are part of. This allows rapid selection changes through the entire component range of a polygon surface.

Polygon surfaces can be created through several methods that allow great degrees of flexibility in approach. These approaches can also be interleaved during modeling, giving many different answers to shape problems that can crop up. Creating a polygon from scratch will allow you to see how the basic components function, how they can be manipulated and how these manipulations affect the surface. Delete or hide all the layers that you have used for NURBS modeling and, if you prefer, create a new layer called PolyBuild. Because building polygons from scratch requires the use of the same tools over and over again, it will make sense to keep these tools within easy reach. There are two ways that this can be solved: one way is to create a new shelf, name it `PolyTools` (or similar) and transfer the tools to this shelf. This technique is very useful, but we covered this in NURBS modeling and there also some predefined shelves that ship with Maya, so you can use menu tear-offs instead. If you've hidden the menu bar at the top of the Maya GUI, then display it using `CTRL+m`. LMB click on the `Polygons` menu and scroll to the three bar widget at the top of the menu heading and release, tearing off the menu so that you can place it where you want. This keeps all the menu items and their options available (if you had saved tools to the shelf, their options would be frozen).

Polygons from Scratch

Polygon faces can be drawn using the Create Polygons tool. A polygon face can have any number of sides, so there is no set limit to the object complexity apart from what you need this face to do later on. This tool will draw vertices that are connected by edges – the shape of the face will be shown enclosed by a dotted line – so draw the vertices that create the face in the top view and press Enter to finish. The options for the Create Polygons tool will govern the number of vertices from which the face is created and also the number of vertices that each edge can contain. Set the `Limit Points` option to 3 and use the tool again (if this is set to -1 then the face is only completed when you press Enter). After three vertices have been drawn, the tool will close the face. The other modeling option is to keep the vertices planar or not – but this will be ensured if drawing in an orthographic view. Experiment with different variations of this tool. A hole can be drawn into a polygon face while in the create mode: before finalizing the polygon face, hold down Ctrl and now draw within the face. This will create a three-sided hole within the polygon face. The hole cannot have more than three sides upon construction but if you want it to have more sides, set the subdivisions option in the Create Polygons tool to be greater than one and draw the polygon and the hole. You can now transform the vertices of the hole. If you don't want the additional complexity on the outer edge, simply select the unwanted vertices and press Delete.

Once a face has been drawn, some of the components can be transformed. Edges and vertices can be transformed but transforming faces won't be relevant until the polygon surface consists of more than one face. Generally, you should aim to keep polygons three or four sided as this allows each face to be kept simple. If further complexity or faces are desired then you can add to your existing polygon by using the Append to Polygon tool. This tool will ask you to pick an edge and then to draw the new polygon, which will be connected to the selected edge. The tool has similar options to the Create Polygon tool in terms of vertex limits and subdivisions, and either tool can have the operation of the other by using the checkboxes at the bottom. Select the polygon and use the Append to Polygon tool to select an edge. A purple arrow will appear, indicating the direction that the polygon is to be drawn – the functioning of this tool is the same as the Create Polygons tool but the new polygon will be attached to the selected edge (this is why the two are interchangeable). Using these tools, you can create the faces of a polygon object extremely quickly (use "y" to select the last tool used – its icon is displayed in the Toolbox under the Show Manipulator tool). If you try appending polygons to the surface using another view to start adding dimensionality, make sure that the `Ensure planarity` option is off. This option can be set to "on" when adding polygons in the perspective view and the vertices will be defined on the same plane as the selected edge.

Another quick method to define new polygons based on the edges of existing polygons is to use `Edit Polygons|Extrude Edge`. This will create a new four-sided polygon that is defined

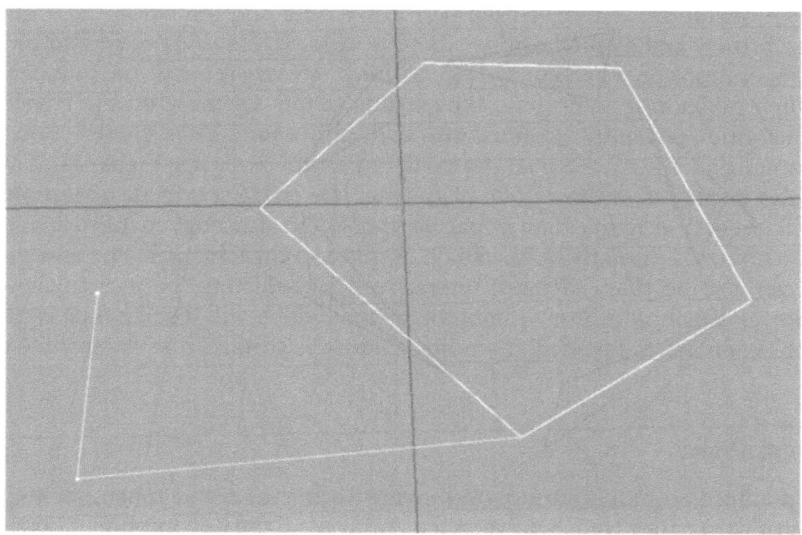

Figure 4.16 Appending to a Polygon with Arrows Defining the Direction of Face Creation.

using the original edge and the newly extruded edge. Select an edge and use the `Edit Polygons|Extrude Edge` and the extrude manipulator should appear. This manipulator is a combination of all of the transform manipulators, but with a difference: its orientation is perpendicular to the new edge. Use the translate manipulator to move this new edge away and place it in the correct position. To continue this process, keep this new edge selected and use the hotkey "g" to repeat the last action or item; this method can be used to very quickly build surfaces from single edge or multiple edge selections. If two or more adjacent edges have been selected to extrude, then you have the choice of whether to keep these newly extruded faces together or apart, planar or non-planar. Check off "keep new faces together" under `Polygons|Tool Options`, select two edges, use the extrude edge tool and translate them. Now check on "keep new faces together" select two edges, use the extrude edge tool and translate them.

The `Polygons|Append to Polygon Tool` won't allow you to connect edges together, however, so the `Edit Polygons|Merge Edge Tool` needs to be used. Using the current polygon, append another face to an edge and position the final vertex so that the last edge is close to another edge on the polygon. To close the "crack" and sew these edges together use `Edit Polygons|Merge Edge Tool`, picking one edge then the other and pressing Enter to complete the action. This method can now be used in conjunction with appending polygons to keep a good surface continuity and to help create surfaces with holes. This method can be used to close a ring of polygons by merging the end edges, and changing the merge options will help define how the polygon surface will be connected. If a hole has been created as a process of polygon modeling, `Edit Polygons|Merge Vertices` and its variant `Edit Polygons|Merge Edges` may not be able to close it. Using `Edit Polygons|Fill Hole` will fill all holes in a polygon surface – this tool does not have any options and acts on all holes. If you need to fill only certain holes in a surface then a combination of appending and merging edges and vertices will have to be used.

All of these operations that have been performed on a polygon will be kept as part of the construction history and as such can be edited or deleted. However, it should be noted that most of the operations on a polygon surface will in some ways change the number of vertices or change their position in the case of the extrude action. Opening up the Hypergraph and looking at the input and output connections will show a long list of these connected operations, so changing an input node operation will impact the node upstream of it. The Attribute Editor will also display all of these nodes. However, selecting the extrude operations and editing them will not have as much of an impact as long as the attributes changed are generally the transform attributes. These attributes can be changed in the Channels Box and the Attribute Editor but can also be changed more interactively by selecting the particular node in the Channels Box and using the Show Manipulator tool which will display the original extrude manipulator. Again, when satisfied at any stage with the surface, it is worthwhile deleting its history.

Modeling from a Solid

Instead of creating a polygonal surface by drawing from scratch and appending to it, it may be a lot more intuitive to start from a polygonal primitive and use its components as a good starting point for the final model. This also means that we can already discern the start object in three dimensions as well. Starting with the correct polygon primitive will help, so choose one whose overall shape is roughly similar in terms of symmetry and shape to the model that's designed. Generally a cube is a good starting point as it has many axes of symmetry and is simple enough to provide a good clean slate to start with.

Two operations, which will probably form the major underpinning to this method of modeling, are extruding faces and splitting polygons. Extruding faces is exactly the same operation as extruding edges and yields the same type of results when combined with the "keep new faces together" toggle. Select the top face of the cube by using the RMB marking menu to change to "faces" and clicking on the pick handle in the middle (the filled blue square), the face should have an orange cast to it marking it as selected. Edit Polygons|Extrude Face will bring up the familiar extrude manipulator, but this one will be orientated perpendicular to the selected face. If "keep faces together" is toggled off, then each face that is extruded will have faces on its edge, each extruded face being unconnected to its adjacent extruded faces. If you pick multiple faces and use this extrude faces action, you will notice that unlike the extrude edges action, any transformations will be performed relative to each face – try the two faces opposite each other on a cube. Draw a polygon in the top view, select the face and set the local transform options for Polygons|Extrude Face to -1 for translate Z and 20 for rotate Z. Press apply and close the options box. The new face will still be selected, so pressing "g" will extrude the face with these new settings until a twisted column is produced. The Polygons|Extrude Face action will create a new face with a similar transform manipulator and when moved will create a polygon face between the new edge and the old one.

Very quickly the rough shape of a model can be built up, but so far only from using the faces supplied by the polygon primitive. A problem now arises when you need to extrude two faces from one – for example, when you need to create two new extruded faces from the bottom of a cube to form legs. Use the Split Polygons tool in the Edit Polygons menu to create a new edge in between two other edges. LMB click the first position on an existing edge that the new edge will start from and complete the operation by LMB clicking onto another edge to define its end point. Press Return to finish the operation, although more than one edge can be defined before pressing Return. This method not only grants new faces to extrude but is

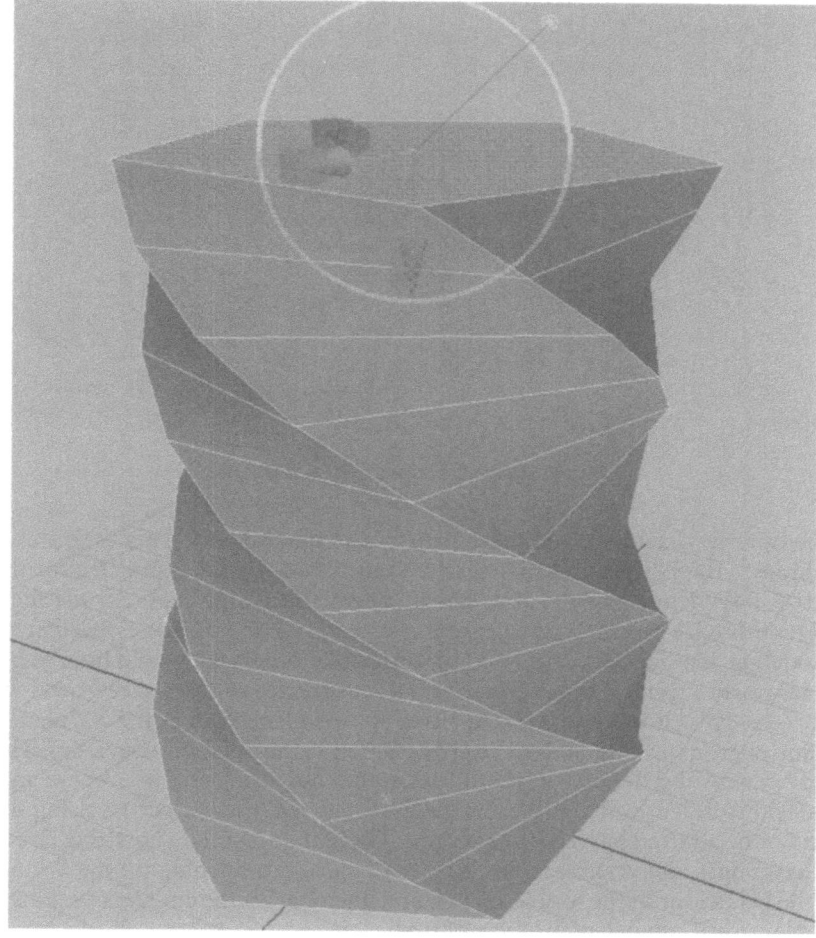

Figure 4.17 A Twisted Column Created from a Polygon Face Extrusion. Note the Special Manipulator at the Top.

also a good way to remove twisted faces. Twisted faces occur when the vertices of a face no longer lie on the same plane (they are said to be non-planar). This can only happen with faces that are created from more than three vertices, as three vertices will always be planar. Non-planarity can give unexpected results when deforming polygonal geometry or when rendering it, as polygon faces may not be consistently interpolated between their control points. Select a single vertex of a polygon cube and translate it so that the face it is part becomes non-planar; if you rotate the perspective view around it, you can see the problem as Maya tries to represent this face. The problem can be reduced by splitting the face between two of the opposite pairs of vertices, depending on the final result required.

Using `Edit Polygons|Poke Faces` will give similar results to the Split Polygon tool when used on polygon faces, but the face will be divided into four triangles and a translate manipulator will automatically be placed at the new vertex, allowing speedy editing of the polygon

Figure 4.18 A Selection of Poked, Wedged and Cut Faces.

surface (the options determine the placement of the new vertex). This action operates in a similar fashion to the Extrude Faces tool when returned to in the inputs list for the polygon surface. Edit Polygons|Wedge Faces lets us select a face and then extrude them about a selected edge (this edge must form part of the selected face). This action is extremely useful for roughly modeling shoulders and other connections that otherwise would have to be extruded a multiple number of times. The Cut Faces tool lets us create arbitrary slices through a selected polygon surface. This slice can be created along an axis plane such as the XZ plane, a custom defined plane or from an interactive slice (this action is the default behaviour). These different types of cut can be defined in the options box, but using the interactive method best demonstrates this tool at work. When the LMB is released, the cut occurs using the line and can be seen on the affected parts of the polygon. This cut does not do anything else apart from introduce new edges and vertices to the polygon object, but opening up the options box lets us change the behaviour of the tool so that it can either extract the cut faces a set distance from the slicing plane or it can delete the faces entirely.

Other methods to provide more faces on a polygon surface are to select a face or faces on a polygon surface and use the Edit Polygons|Subdivide action to divide each face into a new set of polygons or to use Polygons|Smooth which will act on selected faces or a selected object to subdivide and alter the polygon surface to provide a smoother definition. The effect of the Smooth action can be altered in the options box, which covers whether the action will be exponential or linear (linear can give better control over the final poly face count). Additionally, we can use Polygons|Smooth Proxy which will let us smooth our polygon surface using the same options, but will display this new shape inside the mesh of the original polygon object. This allows us to continue to work on a lightweight polygon object whilst observing the upstream effects of the smooth action on our model.

If we want to reduce the number of faces on a polygon surface, we can use Edit Polygons|Delete Edge to delete this type of component and have the rest of the model resolve itself around the remaindered components. The same will work for vertex deletion: create a new polygon cube, try to delete a corner vertex and the error message will say that the vertex has "too many complex connections" but using Edit Polygons|Delete Vertex will solve this. However, deleting a selected face using the backspace key will create a hole in the

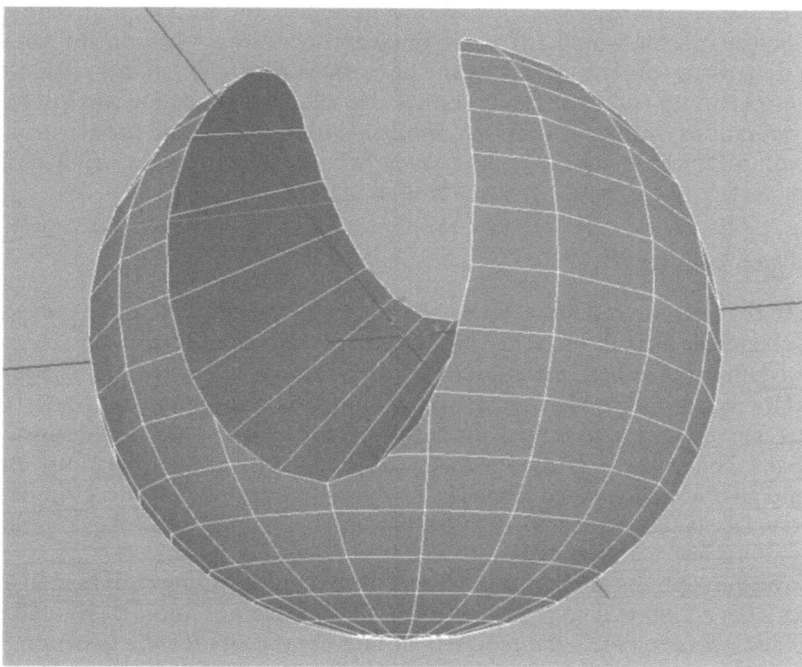

Figure 4.19 A New Polygon Object Created from a Boolean Operation.

polygon which will have to be filled by using the extrude edges and merge edges method, as will deleting vertices and edges using backspace. `Polygons|Reduce` will also cut the number of faces on a polygon surface, but may not always result in a pleasing geometry or one that animates well – try it on a reasonably dense polygon sphere.

Boolean Objects

This is a branch of modeling known as Constructive Solid Geometry (CSG) which deals with the manipulation of geometry at an object level, not concerning itself with the component level of modeling. Boolean algebra was developed to provide a means of manipulating sets, and each polygon object can be seen as a set of vertices. Manipulations of these sets/surfaces in different ways (union, intersection and difference) can be used to edit sections of polygon surfaces in a method similar to machining surfaces. The Boolean operation requires two polygonal surfaces that are reduced to transform positions and then return a new polygonal surface. Create a polygon sphere and a polygon cone, move the cone into the sphere and duplicate these objects two more times so that they are all adjacent to each other. Select the first set of objects and use `Polygons|Booleans|Union` to create a new surface. One thing to notice here is that the original surfaces are now just transforms that feed into the placement of the vertices of the new Boolean surface. Select one of the transforms and move it. The Boolean surface will update until the construction history is deleted, which will delete the two existing transform surfaces. Another difference between the Boolean "Add" and a polygon Combine operation is that the vertices that lie within the objects do not exist. If you were to take two polygon objects and perform a `Polygons|Combine` action, the vertices that were in the interior of the object volume would still exist. Boolean operations work on the volume of the objects and discard any other surfaces that lie beneath. Perform the other two Boolean operations on the remaining surfaces, but note that the selection order for the Intersection and Difference operations will yield different results. With the original surfaces still available, interesting volumetric animations can be created from transforming the original objects over time, such as surfaces being eaten into or volumes being slowly created.

Refining Polygon Surfaces

In addition to the polygon modeling operations that we have covered so far, polygon surfaces can also be created as a result of NURBS surface modeling. The output surfaces can be converted to polygons via the particular surfacing operation or at a later time by converting the NURBS surface into a polygon surface. If you open up the options for `Surfaces|Loft`, there is a checkbox that allows you to output the final surface as a polygonal mesh, a process known as "tessellation". This is the only change to the action, history, partial curve use etc. that will still work, and all that has changed is the final surface description. Various options cover how the NURBS surface is subdivided into a polygon mesh based on either a fixed number of faces or based on interpolating the underlying NURBS surface description.

These conversion options can be explored more thoroughly by using `Modify|Convert|NURBS to Polygon`. This action will convert a selected NURBS surface into a polygonal mesh. The options will allow you to create the required surface complexity for the situation. For example, if you are limited to a total scene or model size in terms of the number of polygons then using the `Count` option to limit the number of polygons created will be helpful. You could create many polygon versions of the same object and use the count option to constrain their level of detail depending on the object's distance to the camera. If you do have a scene or model limit, this can be aided by using the "heads up display" which will show the total number of polygon faces, vertices, edges and UVs in the scene and on a selected surface. This can be activated from `Display|Heads Up Display|Poly Count`. Whether you choose to convert to triangular faces or quads is generally up to the situation, but for the number of faces used, a curved surface can be approximated with triangular faces better than with quadrangular faces.

Create a NURBS sphere and delete its history. Select it and open up the options for `Modify|Convert|NURBS to Polygon`. Set the `Tessellation` method to Count (set that to 150), the `Type` to quads, click Apply and move the resultant mesh away from the original NURBS sphere. Select the sphere again (the polygon copy will turn purple, as there is still a connection from the NURBS surface to the polygon surface via the Convert function), change the `Tessellation` method to Control Points and click Apply. This method creates the same number of vertices on the polygon copy, as there are CVs on the NURBS model. The other options are related to how closely the curvature of the NURBS surface is replicated in a polygon form. For example, using a `Standard` fit method of tessellation will allow you to control how many faces are used to represent large changes in curvature. Select the NURBS sphere and tessellate it using the standard fit method. In order to see the faces of a polygonal object more clearly during shaded mode, turn on `Wireframe on shaded` under `Shading|Shade Options` to define the edges clearly. If you transform a couple of CVs from the NURBS sphere, changing its shape, you can see how the number of faces will adaptively resolve themselves near areas where the curvature changes. The `General tessellation` method will just try to approximate curvature over the entire NURBS surface. Polygon meshes can also be triangulated or quadrangulated using either `Polygon|Triangulate` or `Polygon|Quadrangulate` with the latter requiring an angle that specifies whether adjacent triangles will be merged (0 degrees will only combine triangles that are co-planar). Too many polygons can be dealt with by using `Polygon|Reduce`.

To save time it is often easier to model a surface along an axis of symmetry, duplicate it, scale it and then attach it to create a complete model – double the surface in half the time. Create a NURBS sphere with an end sweep of 180 degrees, edit its shape but do not change the profile at the edges, convert it to polygons and delete the NURBS sphere. Open the options for `Polygon|Mirror Geometry`. This function will reflect the selected polygon object around a specified axis and create one piece of geometry from the two pieces. Turn on the `Merge` option if you wish the two halves to be connected physically by faces and edges, otherwise any gaps at the edges of the surface will not be filled. Without using the `Merge` option, the effect will be the same as if you had scaled the surface by a negative amount and then used `Polygon|Combine`, which just takes the list of vertices from one object and adds them to the list of vertices of the other object (try it on two polygon objects that aren't touching). To break a polygonal surface into separate objects you will need to select the faces where you wish the cut to occur and either delete them and then use `Edit Polygons|Separate` or use `Edit Polygons|Extract`.

A Polygon Teapot

We're going to model another teapot, but this time in polygons so that we can see how the method of working will differ as you use explicit surfaces. One way the polygon teapot could be made is to select each NURBS surface, convert to polygons and then use a Boolean union operation to connect each surface together. But that won't exactly demonstrate any of the tools or methods that we have looked at. We are going to begin with a basic primitive surface, which will give a three-dimensional starting point.

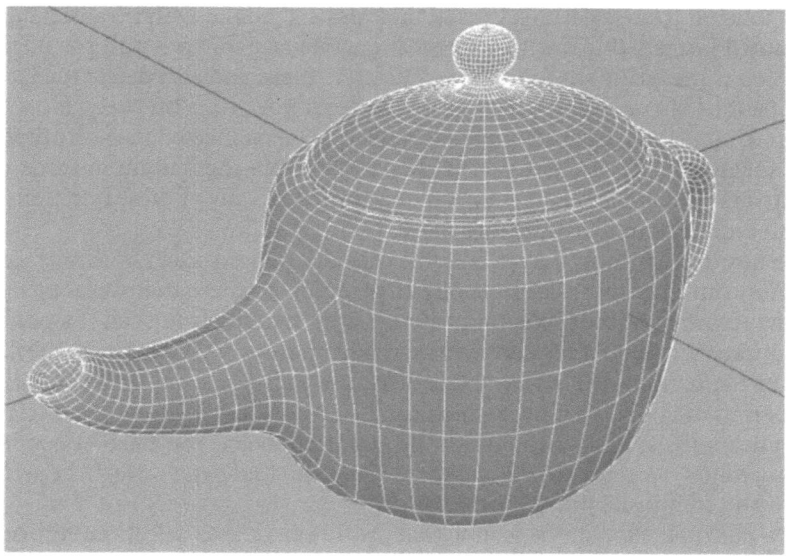

Figure 4.20 The Polygon Teapot.

Create a polygon cylinder with ten subdivisions in Axis, three in Height and two in Caps, then delete the history.

Scale and move the vertices of the cylinder into the rough shape of a teapot body. We're going to create the spout as a face extrusion, so on the front face of the teapot body you need to make a new face for this operation. This face can be made from either a newly drawn polygon using the Split Polygon tool or by extruding the existing face. Select the face using the RMB marking menu to bring up the choice of components and use the Extrude Face action. Scale the face down to a square size, pop the side view to the foreground and then pull the new face out a little from the body of the teapot. You can use the side view to extrude the face four or five times just using the manipulator to get the rough shape of the spout. For now, you only need to get the rough shapes of the surfaces at this time, as polygon modeling allows you to come back to areas and refine the amount of detail locally. While in the side view, change to vertex component mask mode and get the shape of the spout correct. However, because the extrusions had been done in the side view, the spout hasn't been scaled in the top view that gives a very blocky look. You can use the construction history to step back through the extrusions instead of changing the shape at a vertex level. Pop the perspective view forward, select the teapot as an object and select the second extrusion node name from the bottom of the inputs list. Using the Show Manipulator tool, you can access the original manipulator for the extrusion function. Scale the spout using this method (notice that each change made to an extrusion node has a knock-on effect) and edit any vertices if needed, to get the spout looking correct.

Connecting the teapot body to a new polygon handle will create the rest of the main surface. Two faces will need to be made that can be connected to the handles' ends. Select the rear face of the teapot body and extrude it once. Without moving it, scale this new face down in Y until the rear is now split into three faces. Select the top and bottom faces and extrude those as well. These faces should be scaled in X so that there are now three faces along the top row and three along the bottom. Select the middle face of each row and extrude them. Scale the faces in a little bit and pull them out from the teapot body. These will form the connection points for the handle. In the side view, use the Create Polygon tool to draw the outline of a handle as a polygon face, select this central face and extrude it. Don't translate this new face but scale it down instead, this way we can get a separate face for each polygon edge that forms the outline. Select the face(s) in the centre and delete them and also delete the face at the end so that a horseshoe shape is left. Select all of the faces now, turn on "keep faces together" in Polygons|Tool Options, because these faces need to be connected to each other (try it with "keep faces together" off) and extrude these out to create the handle in three dimensions. Delete the history of this handle, as you won't need to access any of these functions again. Now move the three-dimensional handle into place.

There are now two surfaces that need to be made as one, so select both surfaces and combine them. You can only select a single object made up of these two surfaces, meaning that these are now regarded as one polygon made up from two shells (a shell is a polygon surface that has a boundary, a polygon object may be made up from multiple shells). Delete the faces at the ends of the handle shell and the faces that are opposite on the teapot shell. There are now four holes in the polygon object which can be bridged using the Append to Polygon tool creating a continuous surface throughout the polygon object. You have to combine the two surfaces beforehand, because the Append to Polygon tool won't work between different objects, only one composite polygon surface.

To create a hole in the top of the teapot, that the lid can fit into, select the vertices at the centre of the top and use Edit Polygons|Delete Vertex to combine the edges that the vertices form into one large face. Select this face and scale it outward until there is a smallish gap between the edges of this face and the edges of the teapot body, as this face will define the edge of the hole. Now extrude the face a couple of times to form the rim of the hole. With this central face still selected use `Edit Polygons|Extract` which will extract and detach the selected face from the polygon object. Extrude this face enough times (use the side and front views to ensure that the edges of the lid match the edges of the rim) until the outline of the lid and handle has been created.

Select the teapot and the lid and use `Polygon|Smooth` to create a smoothed version of the polygon. Usually, changing the Divisions between 1 or 2 for the exponential method will yield a smooth enough surface. If you want to edit the shape without waiting for a slowed update, set divisions to 0 – this will effectively disable the operation for now – or use `Polygons|Smooth Proxy` prior to this to see how the teapot model will turn out. It is possible to apply smoothing to individual faces, but it can become difficult to ensure a good surface continuity between smoothing boundaries. If you find that you need to work on further parts of the model, add extra edges etc., then delete the smoothing node in the Hypergraph or select the node in the Attribute Editor and then delete it.

Subdivision Surface Modeling

A Subdivision surface is an interpolated surface that uses a polygonlike shell to control its basic shape. What is different about a subdivision surface is that it can be composed from a hierarchy of components that allow local subdivision and detail whilst still having a curved surface. So we can now model individual parts of a subdivision surface with as much detail as

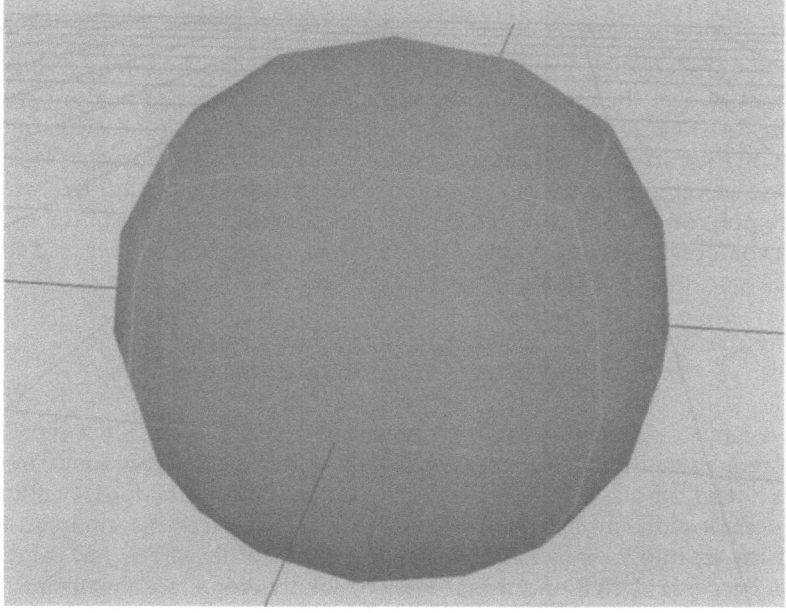

Figure 4.21 A Subdivision Surface.

possible without increasing the overall complexity of the surface. Create a subdiv sphere from `Create|Subdiv Primitives|Sphere` and set the smoothing to "3". The surface looks like it is composed of curved four sided patches similar to a NURBS surface but it is a closed surface (there are also no options for any of the primitives under `Create|Subdiv Primitives`). Using the RMB marking menu over the sphere we can see that it is composed of polygon components and there is also a new set of menu items: `coarser`, `finer` and `polygon`. If we select `edges` from the RMB marking menu, the edges that are displayed are in the shape of a polygon cube, as are the vertices and the faces. This is the base shape and is at level 0 of the subdiv surface hierarchy; all edits will build upon this base. Because this base shape is created from a polygon cage, we can use most of the polygon modeling techniques to give us the basic shape that we want. But first we need to switch into modeling mode, so select `polygon` from the RMB marking menu (this menu item will now toggle to `standard` to let us switch back to subdiv modeling mode). When we jump from polygon to standard mode, any changes made to the polygon cage will have their history deleted so that it does not interfere with the editing of the subdiv surface.

- Select `faces` from the RMB marking menu and select the top face of the polygon cube.
- Extrude this face and move it upwards by a small amount.

The new extension to the polygon cage has now extended the subdivision surface that it shapes. The surface still tends towards curvature but to retain this, there is now a new subdivision level on the surface.

- Move into subdiv mode by selecting `standard` from the RMB marking menu.
- Select `vertex` and then select `finer` from the RMB marking menu.
- Move the center vertex upwards to form a point on top.
- Select `coarser` from the RMB marking menu and move a level 0 vertex.

We use the `finer` and `coarser` menu items to traverse the surface hierarchy giving us different degrees of control over the sections of the surface and this can also be done from the subsection of the RMB marking menu: `Display Level`. The vertices (and faces, but not edges) are labeled with the current level to make things a little more straightforward. Unless we are in polygon mode we cannot use polygon tools, so if we wanted to extrude a face we would have to go back to polygon mode and select the face. We can refine any part of the subdiv surface by picking a component (at any point of the hierarchy) and using `Subdiv Surfaces|Refine Selected Components` or selecting `refine` from the RMB marking menu.

- Select two faces at level 1 of the hierarchy on the subdiv sphere.
- Use `Subdiv Surfaces|Refine Selected` and translate the new faces.

Each time we refine a selection, we create a new subdivision level on the surface by adding a new level of refinement. Each refinement will not only add a subdivision level to the selected components but will also affect the surrounding components so that the transition of surface curvature does not suddenly change. As we translate the new faces, the subdiv surface accommodates this by creating new faces/vertices/edges at the border of the new subdivision level components. Because subdivision surfaces work by subdividing a face equally into parts, make sure that all faces of the level 0 polygon proxy object have four edges per face otherwise the subdiv surface will create odd vertices.

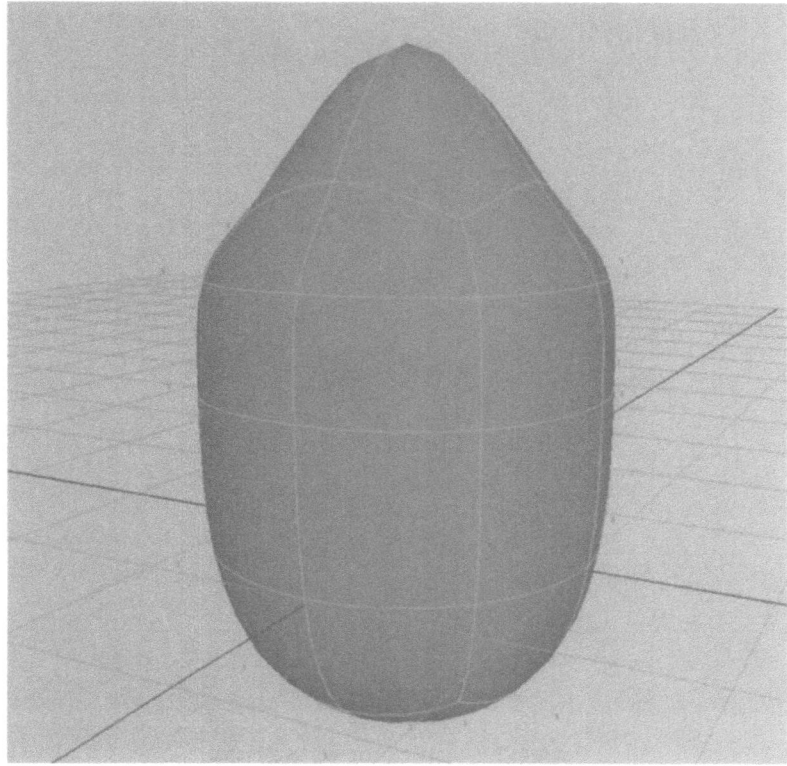

Figure 4.22 The Subdiv Sphere with Level 1 Vertices.

Converting to Subdivs and Back Again

Subdivision surfaces can be created in three ways: as subdiv primitives, as output surfaces from modeling operations such as revolve or as the end result of a convert operation. NURBS and polygons can be converted into subdiv surfaces from the Modify|Convert menu heading. The options cover the maximum number of faces and vertices that the base mesh may have, whether we keep the original object and whether the converted surface will become the subdiv base 0 polygon cage or not (which is why Keep Originals is turned off when this option is selected).

Of more interest is the facility to convert subdiv surfaces into polygonal surfaces and NURBS surfaces. Conversion options for subdivs to polygons govern the method used to create polygon faces, sharing of texture sets and what happens to the original object. The subdivs to NURBS options govern the resultant surface type (NURBS or Beziers) and what happens to the original object. If the subdiv surface cannot be represented by a single NURBS patch, multiple patches will be created and grouped together ready for attaching or stitching.

Creases, Mirroring and Attaching

If we want our subdiv surface to suddenly change in curvature or have a hard edge in places, we can create a crease at a selected component.

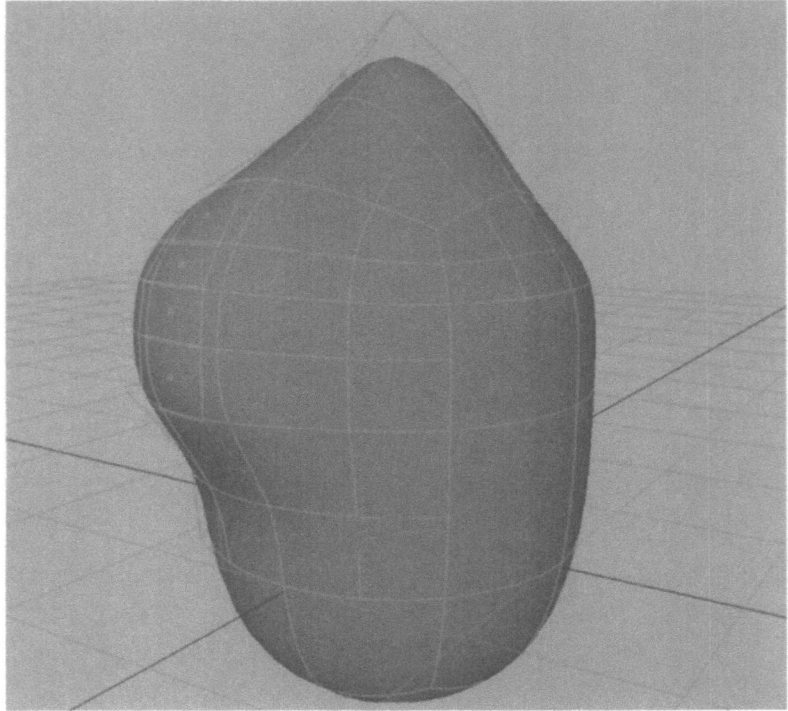

Figure 4.23 The Subdiv Sphere with Level 2 Faces.

- Select an edge on the subdiv sphere at display level 1.
- Use Subdiv Surfaces|Full Crease Edge/Vertex.
- Translate the creased edge outwards from the surface.

Because we have changed the surface again, our subdiv surface has added the appropriate new components at a subdivision hierarchy level higher than the currently selected level in order to smoothly transition across the surface. The edge is now displayed as a thicker broken line to designate that it has a crease attached to it; we can also crease vertices to create sharp points but these do not have their display changed or necessarily create a new subdivision level. If we are unhappy with the effect then we can use Subdiv Surfaces|Uncrease Edge/Vertex but this will not remove the newly created subdivision level. If the crease is too sharp then using Subdiv Surfaces|Partial Crease Edge/Vertex will create a smoother version at the component. As with modeling any object, we can mirror and attach subdiv surfaces in much the same way that we can polygon surfaces, however the options for Subdiv Surfaces|Mirror do not specify any attachment criteria like the polygon version does, just which axis we wish to mirror across; so we have to use Subdiv Surfaces|Attach which lets us specify whether we merge both UV sets (surface texturing coordinates) and whether there is any maximum threshold over which edges etc. will not be attached or closed.

Combining new polygon objects to a subdiv polygon shape (the level 0 base shape) will not automatically create a subdivision surface within the new polygon. To do this we have to

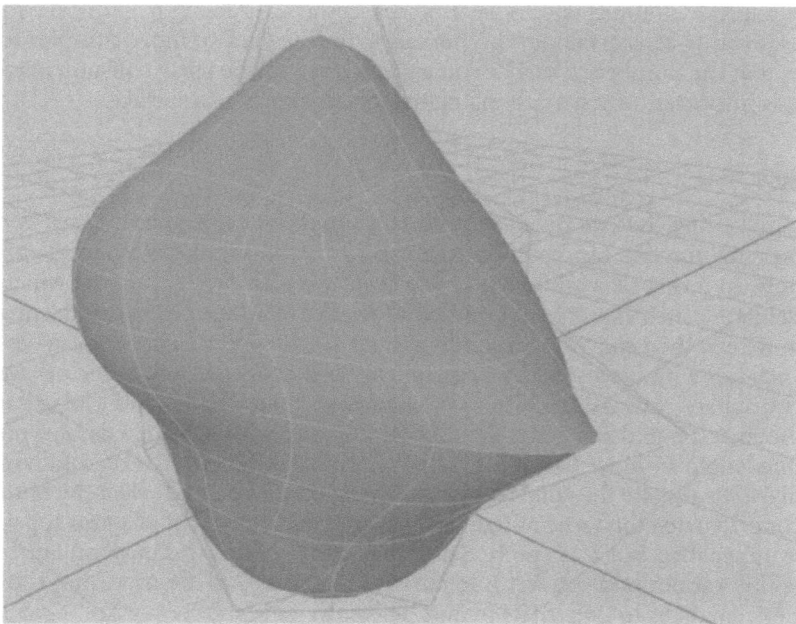

Figure 4.24 The Subdiv Sphere with a Crease.

combine our polygon object with the base polygon using `Polygons|Combine`. This will create a new polygon object which we can then model and then convert to a subdivision surface using `Modify|Convert|Polygons to Subdiv` with `Keep Original` turned off. As soon as we have done this we can see that any subdiv modeling that had been done on the previous subdiv polygon that we combined with will be carried over to the new subdiv surface that we have just converted to. This lets us build our surfaces in a modular manner, so that we don't have to have the entire model in front of us.

Optimizing Subdiv Surfaces

The first thing we can do to start optimizing the subdiv modeling process is to remove unwanted information. Generally, subdiv surface information can be split into components we have edited or components we have not touched. If we refine a surface in places but only edit a portion of this surface, then there may well be a large amount of refined surface that we never actually use (apart from the additional borders that the operations such as creasing create) which can end up extremely heavy in a large model. Using `Subdiv Surfaces|Clean Topology` will remove any components that have been created as part of a refine operation but never edited/transformed. Using `Display Filter` from the RMB marking menu lets us either see all components or only those which have been edited. When we have finished the subdiv model and are ready to texture (and/or animate) or have got to a point where there is a lot of subdivision levels on our model we can lower the hierarchy count by collapsing levels into each other. `Subdiv Surfaces|Collapse Levels` will move edits from higher levels into lower levels, so that the surface remains constant. The options box for this gives a slider from 1 to 2 so that if we select 2, all levels will move 2 places upwards unless it is necessary for a subdiv surface to retain edits at a certain level. This can make the surface more complex looking but it also means that the number of vertices on a given level will be fairly constant across the surface and this is important when applying deformers or skinning a surface.

A Subdiv Squid

Because the first thing that we need to build is a simple polygon mesh to act as our level 0 base the modeling practice can be fairly freeform, as we should have a decent grasp of poly modeling tools. In terms of workflow it is worth keeping an original model which has all of the modeling history such as extrusions and point tweaks and duplicating this to create a "clean" model which we can then convert to a subdiv model. If the subdiv surface doesn't look right or there are difficulties with the surface, we can quickly and easily go back to the original polygon surface and work back through the history to change or delete actions and tool use such as face extrusions. Because a squid is a generally tubular creature with a main axis of symmetry that runs down the length of it, we can begin with a polygon cone with 6 Axis subdivisions and 3 Height subdivisions. Rotate the cone so that it is lying on its side and select the bottom face or base of the cone. Extrude this face enough times so that the main shaft of squid appears to come out from the upper shell, but at no point delete the history. Name this polygon Squid_Base.

Duplicate this surface and convert it to subdivs to check that the modeling is on the right track, make any changes to Squid_Base and delete the new subdiv surface. Now we need to place eyes onto the mid body and fins onto the upper shell. Select the flat side edges of the upper shell and extrude and shape these until they resemble fins, then pull the edges of the smaller upper fins out a little. The eyes will be placed on the body shaft as it comes out of the upper shell, so we need to select the two large faces at the side and make them a little more square. Then extrude these faces until we get a square "eye" coming out of a square eye socket.

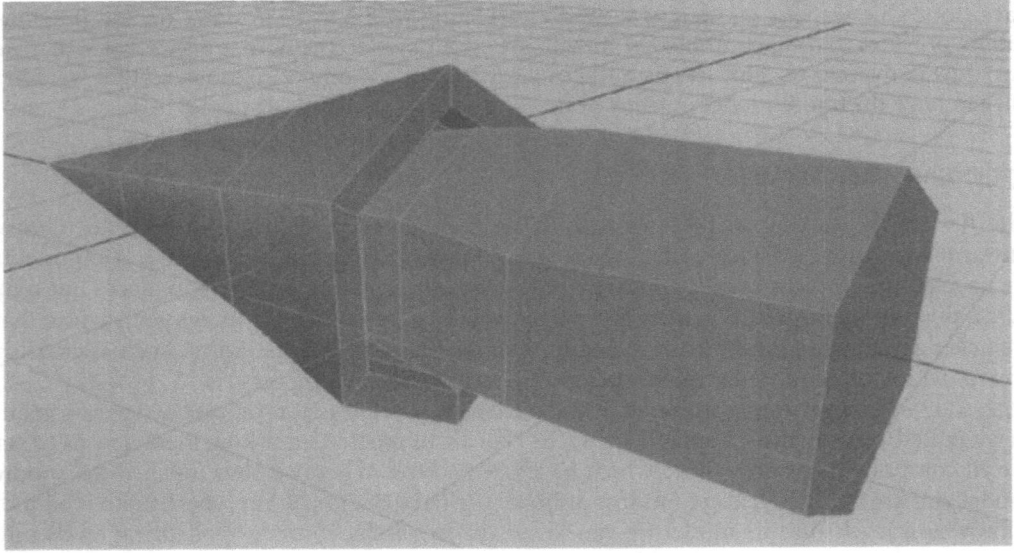

Figure 4.25 The Start of the Polygon Cage for the Squid Subdiv.

Select the face at the end of the Squid_Base model and use Edit Polygons|Extract Face to create a copy of the base face. This operation creates a group under which is placed the two remaining polygon surfaces and a transform. Delete the history of the new surfaces, call the new face tBase, scale it so that it will just fit inside the face it came from and lock its scale. Rename the original surface nBaseSquid, delete the transform and call this new group SquidGrp. We are going to work on tBase to create the tentacles and then re-attach it to the main squid body but in order to re-attach it, we need to use the extract action as this will provide us with the necessary border edges to append between. Now that we are at the end of our polygon level 0 modeling we can duplicate the surface and then convert to a subdivision surface, naming it subdivSquid. Although there is a hole in the polygon surface we can still use a subdiv surface but we can also select the polygon level 0 surface and use Edit Polygons|Fill Hole and then delete the face when it comes time to re-attach the two polygon surfaces.

Start work on the level 1 edges and vertices, adding creases to the edges of the shell and adding wrinkles around the eyes. The second half of the squid, namely the tentacles can now be created, independently of the main body and added on afterwards. Working like this means that we can split the workload and also not have roughly modeled sections obscuring the modeling views. Hide subdivSquid and select the face of tBase. Duplicate this face twice so that we have a small lip around the edge and then six large faces round this. Use the split polygon tool to split the top and bottom two faces in half and then extrude and scale down all ten faces so that they can form the base of the tentacles. Extrude all of the tentacles and shape them converting duplicates to subdiv surfaces to check progress. We will be connecting them together but we need to prepare the end of tBase as it has to have border edges. Select the six large outer edges on the starting hexagon shape and transform them away from the model. This should pull out a large face which has been hidden. Delete this face so that there is a hole where the end used to be. To connect the two sections back together, select the polygon base 0 surface from subdivSquid and the polygon tentacles and use Polygons|Combine to attach

Figure 4.26 The Basic Subdiv Squid.

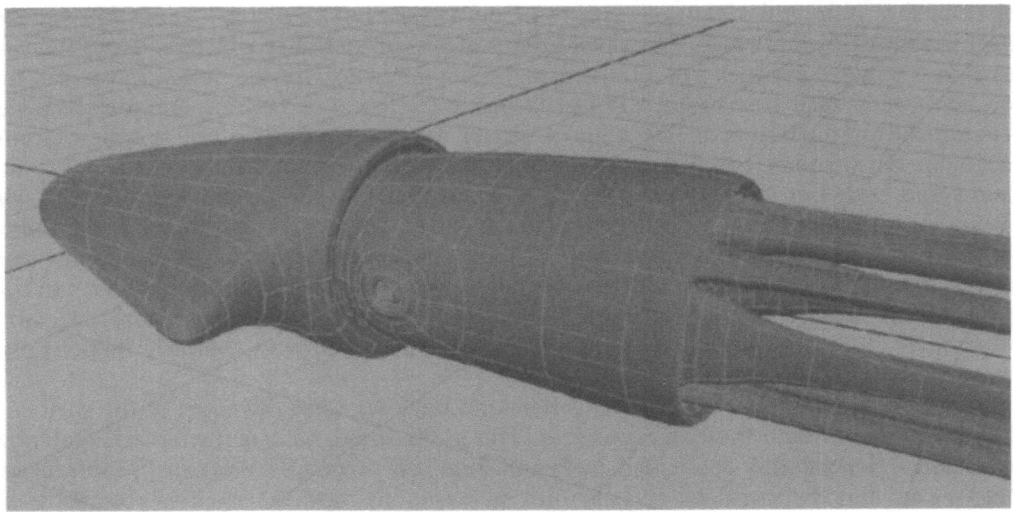

Figure 4.27 The Final Subdiv Squid.

them, which will duplicate them out as a single polygon surface yet still retain the subdiv surface history of modeling changes that were made to subdivSquid. Delete the face at the end of the main body, select both polygon surfaces and use Polygons|Combine to create a new polygon surface which should have its history deleted.

Remove the necessary groups, clean up the polygon surface (make sure that the option to triangulate quads is turned off) and convert this surface to a subdiv surface. This should now have carried over the original subdiv edits that were made on the original subdivSquid surface whilst now incorporating the new tentacles.

Sculpting with Artisan

For a more intuitive method of modeling and refining models, Maya has a surface-sculpting tool that uses the Artisan interface. This interface is a brush-based method of working where you can specify four operations upon your designated surface, NURBS or polygons, there is no sculpt tool for subdiv surfaces. For NURBS this tool is found under Edit NURBS|Sculpt Surfaces Tool and for Polygons, is found under Edit Polygons|Sculpt Polygons Tool. Because you will need to change how the tool functions, while you use it, it is imperative that the options box for the tool is opened. Create a NURBS or polygon sphere (make sure that they have a fairly heavy surface in terms of isoparms or vertices), delete the history and while the sphere is still selected, open up the relevant sculpt surfaces tool option box. First, you should see the brush "footprint" moving over the NURBS surface – this is the area of effect. This footprint size can be changed using the Radius U slider (the Radius L slider will only come into play if a pressure-sensitive stylus is used with Maya) and this will update on the surface automatically. The operation that the tool will perform speaks for itself – push, pull, smooth or erase. For the first two operations, the amount of displacement is set by the Max Displacement slider but the effects can be tempered by the Opacity setting – multiply the displacement by opacity – this also affects the smooth or erase operation too. The direction of an operation is determined by the settings found under `Sculpt Variables` and you can set the tool to only update the changes made – useful if you have very heavy geometry or a struggling graphics card. Other options for the Sculpt Surfaces tool govern the functioning of the brush over the surface or surfaces and can be found under the other named tabs.

If you start sculpting a surface using this tool, you can see that the changes made by the tool really only occur at isoparms or vertices and not in between these points. So to sculpt well, you need to make sure your surface has the detail you need either by adding more isoparms or subdividing the polygon mesh. This tool can also be useful to refine a surface after more "traditional" modeling methods. For example, if you have been working on a head using methods such as lofts or revolves, you can smooth the entire surface out and remove any strange kinks by using the "Flood" button while set to "Smooth". This will apply the current operation and opacity to the entire surface, universally smoothing the relationship between the isoparms or edges. Because this is such a flexible tool and more akin to modeling with a lump of clay, very complex surfaces can be quickly built intuitively.

Summary

Choose the surface type that will be correct for the job that you are doing or that you feel happiest working with. Remember that the modeling process is usually the first step in making a piece of digital work, so any decisions made at this point will have an influence on how you will be using them at a later date. What are you modeling for? If you are modeling props or scenery, then you need to make sure that the surface can be textured easily – this can be aided by having an even distribution of components across the surface, this is where rebuilding surfaces and curves becomes very useful. If the surfaces are being created for animation then as well as providing a good surface for texturing, look at how the surface will be moved and deformed, that is, the amount of component control and complexity that the surface has at the important deformation points. Flow lines (edges or isoparms) that show the connections between components need to be observed, as they will affect how the critical areas will deform and/or crumple.

Animation 5

Introduction

Animation in the context of using Maya means changing attributes or values over time. All nodes contain unique attributes and as these attributes change we can create different effects, from lifelike movements to cartoon action to complex mathematical forms. What this chapter will concentrate on is the different ways that these attribute changes can be effected. At the simplest end of the spectrum, animation of a channel can come from a varying value over time provided by a waveform. At the more complex end, the values driving an attribute can be derived from a weighted blend of multiple inputs from multiple nodes. In this chapter, animation will come in two different forms – rigid body animation and shape animation – and will have two different variants – keyed and procedural. Keyed animation involves setting keys that are specific values at a point in time for specific channels; procedural animation involves creating values for a channel over time as a result of input from equations or from the relationship with another channel's value.

The Animation Environment

At the bottom of the Maya GUI is the Time Slider. The Time Slider controls the display of the current point in time, the amount of time (in frames) that will be played back and the display of keys for currently selected channels. The current place in time can be moved by either LMB dragging the indicator or LMB clicking to a point on the timeline. Either of these actions will cause any time-based functions to update. If you don't want to move the mouse button away from a point of interest, then holding down "k" and LMB dragging will also change the current time. The current time is also displayed in a text field at the right-hand side of the Time Slider (new times can also be entered into here).

At the side of the Time Slider are the transport controls. These look and act exactly like the controls on a DVD player apart from two specialized buttons which step forward and backward one key. Below the Time Slider and the Transport Controls is the Playback Range. The Playback Range will allow you to define the start and end of playback in the scene; more importantly, the Playback Range can allow you to concentrate on portions of the total time range. This is useful because you can set a start and end time for your scene using the outer fields, then define what part of this you wish to concentrate on using the inner fields or the slider in the middle. To modify the slider, LMB drag on the box icon at either end to shorten the amount of time the slider focuses on. This slider can also be LMB held in the middle and slid back and forth changing the focus range over the entire scene time. This can be useful when playing back ten frame sections of animation; just set the slider to cover frames 1 to 10 and then slide it forwards when you wish to examine the next ten frame sections. Additionally, these Playback Range values can be entered manually.

Prior to starting to animate within Maya, the correct preferences need to be set up. Open up the Animation Preferences from either Window|Settings/Preferences|Preferences or LMB click on the Animation preferences icon at the right-hand side of the Transport Controls and open the Preferences section. This allows you to set the time value (you will generally be setting this to PAL, NTSC or Film) so that the keys you create will be played back correctly. Now open the Timeline section. Set the Key ticks to Active and the Playback Speed to Real-Time so that when you press play using the transport controls, you get a real time playback of your animation. Other settings should be set as desired, such as whether the playback will loop and, more importantly, whether all of the views will update when you press play or just the active view (this can drastically affect the playback speed as Maya tries to play in real-time). Open the Keys section and check the boxes for Weighted Tangents and Auto Key, the reasons for these will become apparent later on.

Keyed Animation

In this section, we will look at the steps needed to create an animated bouncing ball. There are three areas that will be explored during this, one is to set the ball up for animating, the next is to animate the ball using the animation tools in Maya and the final stage will be to edit and refine the work. This bouncing ball exercise will introduce you to the basics of keyed animation in Maya – how to set and edit keys, how to play back animation, how to connect attributes together and how to set up a character. Setting up a character for animation is as important as animating the character itself; it means that when you come to work with the character, the controls and utilities that you have created are laid out in an easy to use manner. Importantly, you may be working on a project that requires the character to be set up and then be animated by somebody else. This means that you will have to provide somebody with an interface that can be used quickly and without explanation, instead of the animator having to work around any personal idiosyncrasies.

Setup

To explore the process of animating within Maya, we are going to look at one of the oldest animation exercises: the bouncing ball. In order to make the actual process of animating as easy and as straightforward as possible, the character (the ball) should be set up so that you are presented with a clearly labeled set of controls (you should only ever see the channels that you are going to be concerned with). Before starting to set the character up, you should consider what it will be doing during the course of the animation. The ball will be moving up, down, forwards and squashing; so these are the controls that should be presented to the animators and these are also the channels that should be engineered into the character. It is going to be easier to use only the correct "levers" to move this ball than be faced with a potentially confusing and redundant set of controls with no clear organization. For this part, you will need the Outliner visible.

- Create a NURBS or polygon plane, scale it by 10 units in X and Z, freeze the transformations, delete the history and name it `Ground`.
- Create a NURBS sphere and place it so that the bottom is resting on `Ground`, delete its history, freeze the transformations and name it `Ball`.

It isn't strictly necessary to freeze the transformations for `Ball`, but it means that one animated position is at zero making it much cleaner to animate from. You are now going to break up your workload; instead of animating `Ball`'s channels, you are going to divide the labour up so that the object in front of you will only do one job: be a surface. Its job will be to reflect light and be concerned with all things visible. Translations will be handled by using groups. Now select `Ball`, group it once and rename this group `Ball_Scale`. This group will be concerned only with squashing the ball when it hits the ground. Because we are going to be animating the position of `Ball` first, we don't want to find that its underside moves away from the ground when we scale it, so the scale pivot needs to be at the bottom of the sphere not the centre. The `Ball_Scale` group will have its pivot set by default to `0,0,0`, which should lie conveniently at the bottom of the sphere.

We are only going to be using the scale Y channel at the moment to squash `Ball`, but looking at the Channels Box, there is an awful lot of extraneous information that isn't relevant to the job or character. If we regard this as an interface, then all this extra information just clutters up the working area. With the group selected (remember you can display the selection handle for the group) open up the Channel Control Editor found under `Windows|General Editor|Channel Control`. This allows you to change attributes into channels so that they can be keyed (and vice versa) and to lock attributes/channels so that they cannot be changed by accident (very important). Using this editor, you can control the information that is available to anybody wanting to animate this character. Select all channels apart from `scale Y` and use the `move >>` key to make these selected channels unkeyable (this also removes them from display in the Channels Box, clearing up the interface). However, this won't stop the attributes being changed by manipulators – select the Transform tool and the manipulator will be displayed, meaning that this attribute can be changed even if it cannot be keyed; so all of the common transform attributes should be locked. Open the `Locked` tab and select all of the transform attributes (except `scale Y`) and move these over to the left-hand side to lock them. Now selecting the Translate manipulator will bring up a greyed out manipulator. The `Ball_Scale` group is now set up for clear and easy animating – all the relevant information is presented and any other transformation attributes cannot be accidentally affected.

The next stage is to set up a node for the remaining channels – `translate Y` and `translate X` – to give up/down and forward/backward. This node will be at the top of the hierarchy and pass all translations down to the other group and to the surface. Select `Ball_Scale` and group it once more, naming this new group `Ball_Trans` and move the pivot to the bottom of the sphere. In the Channel Control Editor, set all channels apart from the `translate Y` and `translate X` channels to `Non keyable` and `Locked`. To be extra sure about attributes and channels, select the sphere (`Ball`) itself and turn off all channels apart from visibility, so that the only job that this node can handle will be to display orientated tasks. Looking at the hierarchic set up now, you can quickly see what each group is responsible for. If this was passed to another animator who wasn't familiar with this scene, they could very quickly see what is responsible for what and wouldn't be able to change any other attributes. At this stage, it's probably worth saving the scene.

Keys

Setting keys in Maya is a fairly simple affair, but there are many different ways to accomplish it. The easiest way to set keys will be through the various options found in the "Set Key" action and by using the Channels Box. The workflow for keyframing the bouncing ball will be methodical, which keeps operations simple as the focus is on the methods used. You should define your time range and playback range, so enter a value of 1 in the Start Time field and a value of 100 in the End Time field, keep the Playback Ranges the same too. Set the Current Time value to 1 so that you can start at the start.

The first keys that you will set will be for the Y translation of the sphere; once these have been created the other values for scaling and movement can be keyed. Because of this, the Ball_Trans group should be selected as that is the object responsible for translations. The first keys will be for the lowest Y value of the ball, where it touches the ground, so open up the options box for Animate|Set Key. This has a few varieties that can be important when using the Set Key action or its hotkey "s"; normally it is set so that all manipulator handles will have a key set at the current time for the current values. Click the Set Key button and you will see that all of the channels for the currently selected object will now be coloured orange. When you see a channel that is coloured this way, it means that it is being driven over time by some input and as such cannot be driven by any other input. So, all of the channels for Ball_Trans are now controlled by keys. This option for the Set Key action creates a lot of wasted keys, as any values that are keyed will be evaluated by Maya even if they do not change and in a large scene this can really slow things down.

To explore the other options for Set Key, you should break the connections that are driving these channels, so highlight the channel names and bring up the marking menu for the Channels Box with the RMB, go to Break Connections and release. This marking menu will act only on the highlighted channels. Set the options in the Set Key dialogue to "Current Manipulator Handle", keep the time option as "Current Time" and keep the dialogue box open. Activate the Translate tool and select the translate Y handle (so that it turns yellow) and now click the Set Key button. A key should be placed for the current manipulator, the channel will turn orange and the key will be represented as a red tick in the timeline.

Now select the translate Y channel in the Channels Box. We are going to set the same key values at intervals throughout the playback range using a function of the Set Key options. Select the translate Y manipulator (this can accomplished quickly by highlighting the translate Y channel), set the time option to "Prompt" and click the Set Key button again. A prompt box will now pop up allowing you to set keys for the current channel at the current value at set intervals. Type in 20, 40, 60, 80, 100 making sure that the values are separated by commas and then click OK. Keys will now be set at these positions for the current time, speeding things up considerably. Set the value for translate Y to 5 and then use the prompt option to set keys for this value at frames 10, 30, 50, 70 and 90. Playing back the scene will now give the basic animation of a bouncing ball, enough for you to start working with.

Now you need to set the keys for the scaling of the ball; squashed on contact with the ground and stretched a little when at the apex of its bounce. Set the current time to 1, select Ball_Scale and set the scale Y channel to 0.6. Highlight the channel name in the Channels Box and select Key Selected from the RMB marking menu to set a key at the current time. Move to frame 20 when the ball is on the ground again and use this marking menu to set

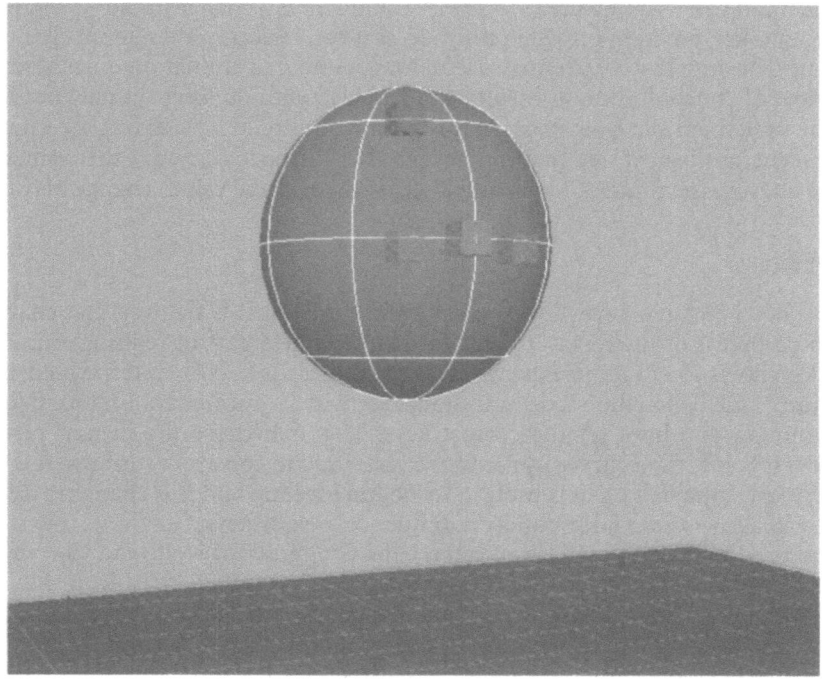

Figure 5.1 The Ball Stretching at the Apex of Its Bounce.

another key for the scale Y channel, now repeat this for the other frames where the ball is in contact with the ground. The ball is just rising and falling at the same scale, however, so set the current time to 10 and set a scale Y key with a value of 1.1 here. Playing back between frames 1 and 20 the animation is now looking correct, but you will have to keep changing the scale Y value in the Channels Box for each new key that you want to set. Instead, you can change the current frame without Maya updating by using the MMB to place or drag the current point in time to the desired position and then set the keys using the RMB marking menu in the Channels Box. Set in scale Y values of 1.1 for the frames where the ball is at the top of its bounce using this method. This method becomes extremely useful if you are working on a scene that is slow to update and you know the values that you are going to enter and key.

Playback now should yield a rough animation of a bouncing, squashing ball. There is one final channel that needs to be set (translate Z) and there is another method of creating keys that becomes invaluable to working swiftly in Maya: the auto key function. Now that the ball is bouncing up and down, it can easily be moved along in the Z axis to give the impression that it is bouncing somewhere. Set a key for the translate Z channel at frame 1. Turn on the auto key function by clicking on the key icon below the transport controls; when this function is activated, any detected changes made to values will be keyed no matter where in time you are. Note that the auto key requires that the channel to be affected already has a key set somewhere (this effectively lets the function add keys to an existing connection).

Set the frame to 20 and move the ball three units or so down the Z axis using the Translate tool. A key will be set for this channel by the auto key because of the change to the value in the channel. Repeat this for the other keys and move the ball 3 units down the Z axis every time using any method you wish (all the auto key is looking for is a change in the value). Remember to turn the auto key function off when finished as it can seriously alter keyed channels if forgotten about. The auto key is extremely useful for roughing in animation quickly so you don't lose your flow of concentration or inspiration and although the keys set may not be perfect, you can fine tune them at a later stage. At this point you should have a roughly animated ball, so save the scene, as the next step that you have to take will be to fine-tune this animation. This will involve altering the timing of keys and altering the way the values change between keys.

The Graph Editor

So far we've been creating keys. Keys are values in time but it is the way that changes occur between them that is of interest to us and forms the largest part of refining animation. The Graph Editor allows you to change the way that the values for keys are interpolated; if you look at the motion of the ball in the Y axis, you should see that the movement isn't particularly realistic even though you have set the correct keys. This is because the default interpolation between keys is a spline, a curve similar to the ones used to construct surfaces. It is this interpolation that gives the ball's Y axis motion its floating feeling and it is changing this interpolation that will allow you to add subtlety and nuance to your keys.

First, you need to make sure that you can see the Graph Editor while you view the playback of the character you wish to affect. Click the Graph Editor/perspective view icon at the left-hand side of the Maya GUI below the tool box, but change the perspective view to the side view in order to correctly observe the up and down movement of the ball. The Graph Editor is so called because the interpolation of the keys for a currently selected channel is represented as a curve plotted between values in the Y axis and time in the X axis. Whichever node you select, all of the channels that are animated will be shown here. This is why it's worthwhile breaking up the work that each node has to do. A complex character could have over 60 different animated channels, it would be unwieldy to select a node that has maybe 30 of these channels and see them all laid out in the Graph Editor. This is one reason why you should split up the work done by nodes and thus thin out the display of curves in the Graph Editor when editing and refining.

Navigating within the Graph Editor window is the same as navigating within any orthographic view: use Alt key combinations to zoom in and pan around the viewport, the "f" and "a" hotkeys will also work on selected items in this window as well. Select the Ball_Trans group channels in the left of the Graph Editor to see a list of the nodes and their animated attributes; select the translate Y heading. In the main area of the Graph Editor you can now see how the keys for Y axis translation are interpolated. Play back the scene and notice how the curves pass through each key as the timeline advances, it is this classic spline shape that gives the motion its floating feeling. Instead of this floating feeling, we want the ball to bounce sharply from the impact with the ground and to hang just a little at the apex of its upward movement. All keys possess tangents which control the slope of the curve as it enters and leaves itself (in tangent and out tangent respectively) and it is these tangents (and the resultant curve tangency) which will control how the animation is evaluated. You can also set the time and value of each key or selected keys in the two numeric fields at the top left of the Graph Editor, while keys can be translated and scaled using the same tools from the toolbox (or hotkeys).

The first alteration you should make is to change the slope of the curves for the bounce. Select all of the keys at the bottom of the curves so that they are highlighted (you can see the tangents displayed for each key here) and in the menu set local to the Graph Editor, use Tangents|Linear to change the slopes of the curves. Play back now to see the effect this has

Figure 5.2 The Shape of the Translate Y Graph before Editing.

had on the ball's motion. There is a more pronounced feeling of impact and rebound now, all from just changing the interpolated curve, but this can still be worked on further.

- Deselect the curve and click "f" to frame the whole curve in the Graph Editor for a better view and select the first key so that the tangents are showing.
- Select the out-tangent for this key (the tangent on the right is always the out-tangent because time advances from left to right) and with the move tool MMB drag it so it is vertical.
- Select the next key's out-tangent and move it, but unfortunately the in-tangent now moves with it. The default nature of in- and out-tangents is for them to be unified so changes to them affect both sides of the animation curve's tangency.
- With one of the tangents selected use Keys|Break Tangents to break this relationship and move both tangents so that they are vertical.
- Repeat this for each of the keys and tangents that control this bounce position for the ball.

Playing back now should show that the ball has a more realistic movement in relationship to its impact with the ground. The next state is to introduce a slight hanging at the apex of its bounce. This will be achieved by flattening out the curvature of the translate Y curve as it passes through the keys at the top. You can only move the tangents in relation to a vertical and horizontal attitude, which won't change the shape of the curve in the manner that you require. What you need is to unlock the tangent weight for each key so that the curve's tangency can be further controlled.

- Select the second key, select one of the tangents and use Keys|Free Tangent Weight (the tangent now looks different – there is an empty box at the end of it).

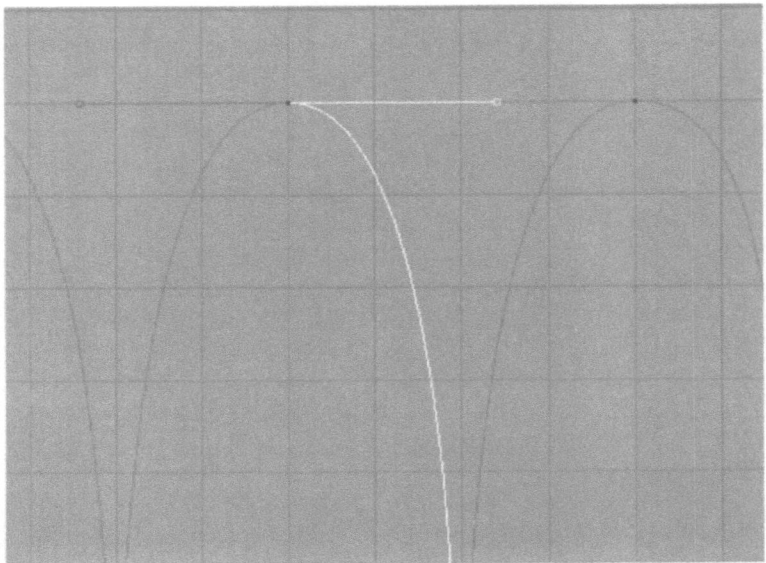

Figure 5.3 Changing the Weight of a Key Tangent.

- Move the tangent outwards so that the curve flattens.
- Flatten the curve for all of the other apex keys, but Shift-select all of the tangents so that you don't have to keep repeating the same action over and over again.

This is why the weighted tangents option was turned on in the animation preferences, otherwise this wouldn't be possible. Changing this preference is not retroactive so you would have to re-key everything prior to activating this preference.

Icons represent all of these operations across the top of the Graph Editor window as well. Changing the shapes of the graph and the values and positions of the keys are important operations and are the key to mastering animation within Maya. However, this can be a long process and Maya can provide help to give us the correct feedback when implementing any changes.

- Select the translate Z attribute to display the graph in the editor.
- Turn on Show Results, which is under the View menu.
- Move one of the keys and you should see that Maya is now showing the original position of the key and the original curve until the key is released.
- Reselect the translate Y curve and click on the curve itself so that it turns white.
- Use Curves|Buffer Curve Snapshot and turn on the display of this buffer curve using View|Show Buffer Curve.
- Move one of the keys to reveal the snapshot of the curve that you took.

These two methods allow you to compare and contrast changes that you make to the original curve via tangents and key positions and the latter operation becomes a very useful analytical tool. If you change the curve for the worse you can always use Curves|Swap Buffer Curve (and then take another snapshot to begin the process again) to undo all changes.

Figure 5.4 Changing the Shape of the Graph and the Underlying Buffer Curve.

To change the tangency of the curve as it passes through a key, or just the tangency of the curve as it passes into or out from the key, you can use the Tangents Menu to automate this process somewhat, instead of changing tangents by hand. The default for curve interpolation is spline. Useful settings are Clamped, Stepped and Fixed as they alter the relationship that one key has to another instead of how the curve interpolates between keys. Clamped will keep the value of the curve constant between keys if the keys are close together, which is useful for animating pauses in motion. Fixed allows you to change the value of a key without altering the angle of the key's tangency. Stepped will keep the current key's value constant until the next key occurs, which is useful for creating camera cuts when the camera must suddenly move from one position to another over the space of one frame. Changing tangency settings will affect the shape of the curve as it passes through a key position, but a further degree of control can be attained by using the In Tangent and Out Tangent menu headings under the Tangents menu heading. This can allow you to change the shape of the curve on the left or right-hand side of the key, an effect similar to breaking the tangents of a curve, giving independent control at either side.

If you wanted to have the ball's up and down animation looping indefinitely, select the respective curve (translate Y) and select Curves|Post Infinity|Cycle. This will now cycle the entire curve forever (and the same effect will happen before the first key under the Curves|Pre Infinity) after the last key. The other settings under this menu heading will change how the curve is extrapolated. Cycle with Offset will add the last key's value to the first key's value so that the animation is incremented each cycle (the time between the

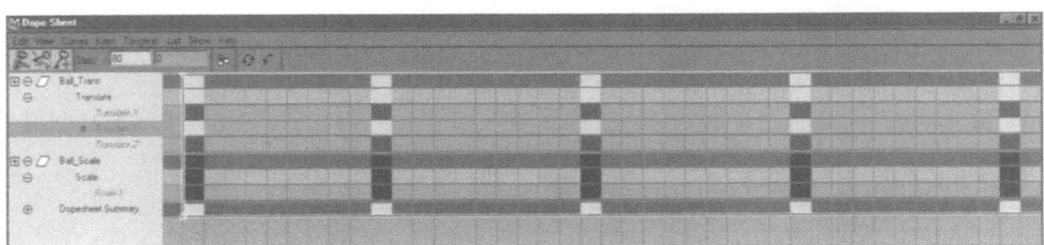

Figure 5.5 The Dopesheet with the Channels Folded out at the Left-Hand Side.

first and last keys). Oscillate will bounce the animation by adding an inverted curve to the end of the normal curve and then cycling them. Linear will extrapolate the value of the last key to infinity and Constant will set the value of the channel to that of the last key set (the default setting).

In addition to the tools and techniques that we have just looked at, it may well be necessary to move or scale keys in time to finesse the timing. Using the move or scale tool in the Graph Editor can create the problem of moving keys to non-integer time positions which can become untidy, so use the Snap to Time or Snap to Value aids to keep any changes made to keys as integers. Sometimes these operations can spoil the time spent adjusting the tangency of the animation curve as it passes through a key: move the key and the curve will change, so turning a key into a "breakdown" can avoid this situation. A breakdown will keep its position and tangency in proportion to its neighbouring keys, so that any changes to the adjacent keys will mean that the breakdown will keep the same relationship in time, value and tangency that was already there. Try this quickly on one of the keys in the scale Y curve: change it into a breakdown using Keys|Convert to Breakdown and then move an adjacent key (this can be reversed using Keys|Convert to Key).

The Dopesheet

The Dopesheet is an editor that displays the position and value of keys. We can use this editor to change all aspects of a key apart from displaying the manner of interpolation. Change the Graph Editor window to the Dopesheet by using Panels|Panels|Dopesheet in the menu heading local to that panel (navigating around this panel is the same as navigating within the Graph Editor). For each node selected, the Dopesheet displays all of the channels that have animation in them, grouped under the relevant heading, so translate Y will be grouped under Translate. Each key is represented by a coloured tick (grey if the value of the key is zero) which will turn yellow when selected. Keys can be selected individually by clicking on them, drawing a box over them or selecting all keys in one channel by selecting the channel name. Selection is hierarchic, so selecting the Translate heading will also select all channels under this heading. When a key is selected, it can be moved or scaled using the normal move and scale tools allowing rapid changes and fine-tuning of events to occur, while additional manipulations can be performed using the cut, copy and paste utilities.

The ball is bouncing up and down fairly well right now but the scaling in Y leaves a lot to be desired in terms of timing and interpolation. It would certainly look a lot more natural if the ball only scaled at the points surrounding the keys (the large changes in velocity) so that the ball has a scale Y value of 1 at any other times. New keys can be created quickly in the

Dopesheet using either the Add Keys function or the Insert Keys function represented by the two icons at the left of the dope sheet. Adding keys will create a new key at the point specified by MMB clicking in the Dopesheet but the key will have the tangency of the adjacent keys, whereas inserting keys will keep the tangency of the curve and not disrupt its interpolation. Here we want to have the ball scale back to normal size in Y two frames after it leaves the ground and one frame before it hits the ground.

- Create a new key using the Add Key tool two frames after the first scale Y key in the Dopesheet. This key will have an averaged value, which can be seen in the right numeric field to the left of the Add Key tool.
- Add another key one frame before the next key (the scaling at the top of the bounce) and another key two frames afterwards.
- Keep doing this until new keys surround all of the original keys.
- Shift-select all of these new keys and enter 1 in the value field, which will affect all keys selected.

Now the ball should retain its shape until a change in velocity and direction occurs.

You can double this animation by copying the keys that you have already created and pasting them onto the end using the Dopesheet. At this point, the Dopesheet is only displaying the keys for the currently selected node, so Shift-select the Ball_Trans group as well so that all the keys that you want to manipulate are available in the left-hand side layout. Unfold the hierarchies so that the relevant channels can be displayed and then select all of the keys by either dragging a selection box over all of the keys or by Ctrl-selecting the channel names. Use Edit Keys|Copy to place these keys on the clipboard, move the time slider to the position that you wish the copied keys to begin from and use Edit Keys|Paste to place them at the current time. Options within this menu item cover how the keys are placed in relation to the existing keys and also where in time the keys will be positioned. Keys can be deleted using the Delete key, Backspace key or Edit Keys|Cut.

Playing back the Animation

You can play your animation back in movie format by using the Playblast utility. A Playblast will advance each frame and perform a screen grab of the currently selected window, then using either the default movie player or the Fcheck utility, you can play back the animation in real time. In the timeline use the RMB to bring up the marking menu and then open the options box for Playblast. The important option here is the Viewer option where you choose what software will play the movie back. Other options govern the size of the frames that are grabbed (window size as it appears, global render sizes or a custom resolution) and whether the temporary files that Maya has created will be deleted or not once you are finished watching the Playblast. The length of the Playblast is the length of the timeline, but you can cut the generation of the Playblast short by pressing the Esc key.

- Select the window that you wish to view the animation from.
- Scale the timeline so that it encompasses the range of the animation.
- Use the RMB to open the Playblast options.
- Set the Viewer to Movieplayer, the Display Size to Custom and enter 400 and 300.
- Turn on "Remove Temporary Files" and click Playblast.

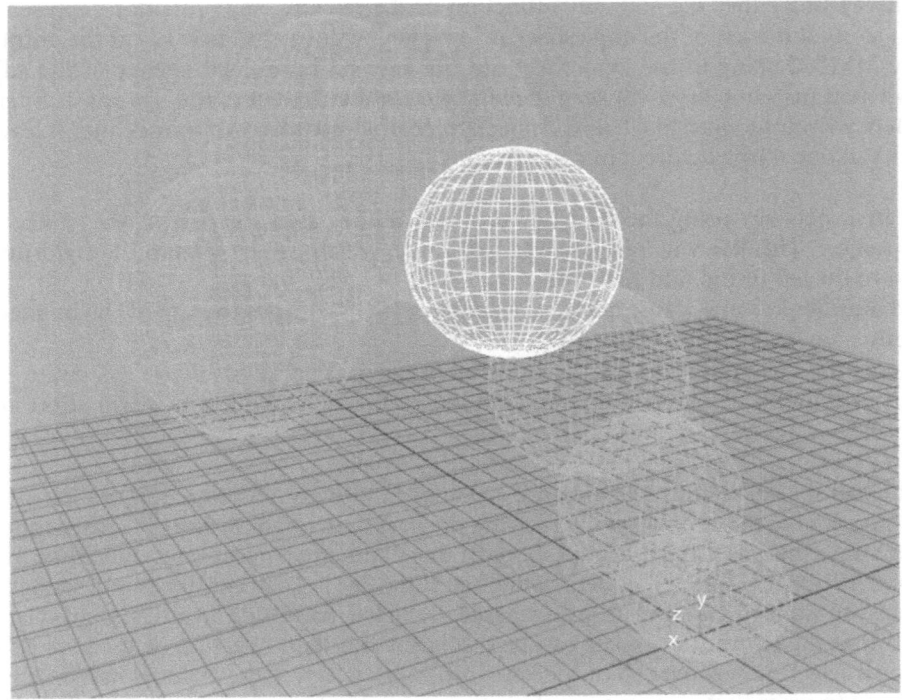

Figure 5.6 The Ghosted Ball.

Once the frames have been stepped through, the Playblast will appear in the movieplayer, from which you can also save the animation out to a permanent file. Because the Playblast is a screen grab, the Maya window must remain at the foreground of current windows; if the Playblast will take time, disable any screensavers or they will be captured instead. Playblasts are a quick and efficient way of watching and archiving rough animated work without having to render out a final scene, which means that lunchtimes and short breaks are the perfect time to Playblast work.

The Timeline and Motion Analysis

Some of the functionality of the Dopesheet is also mirrored in the timeline, as you can cut, copy, paste, move and scale the keys which are represented as red ticks. You can select a key or a sequence of keys by holding Shift and LMB dragging across the keys that you want to manipulate. Then the desired operation can be executed from the RMB marking menu associated with the timeline. The selected keys can be moved or scaled by LMB dragging the arrows at either end to scale or LMB dragging the selection using the central arrows to move the keys. In conjunction with auto-key this can allow you to place keys very quickly without having to open up the Graph Editor or the Dopesheet.

You can analyze the motion of any animated object by using motion paths and ghosting. Select the Ball_Trans group and activate Display|Object Display|Ghosting. This will now show you a faint display of the object's position before and after the current frame in order to give a better idea of how an object will move through space. Turn off ghosting with

`Display|Object Display|No` Ghosting and instead select the object and use `Animate|Create Motion Trail` to display the position of the object each frame. The motion trail will update interactively from any changes to key values or positions that you make in the Graph Editor or Dopesheet.

Now that the ball's position and scaling has been animated, there is one more piece of work to do. The scaling of the ball is in one axis only and as such does not change volume, meaning that instead of squashing, it just shrinks. This could be quickly remedied by keyframing the scale X and scale Y channels at the relevant time, but if you need to change any of the times that the ball does squash, then you will have to change three sets of keys. The next section in this chapter will concentrate on making this squashing an automatic function of the `scale Y` keys that have already been set.

Procedural Animation

Procedural animation allows you to control the channels of an item without using keys. It allows you to create automatic animation that will look after itself while the timeline advances. We use this style of animating to create actions that would be too difficult or tedious to key, such as the flickering of a broken neon light or actions that are best created by mathematical descriptions such as the movement of a flock of birds or swarm of insects. Within Maya there are two ways of creating this type of animation: *expressions* and *driven keys*. An expression is a mathematical description which is evaluated once or at each frame to give a result. Driven keys are connections that are made between attributes and channels that can simplify the animation process. Once either of these methods is chosen, you cannot use another way of controlling the channels – you cannot key a channel if you are controlling it with an expression.

Expressions

As mentioned, an expression is a mathematical description that controls a channel. At the heart of an expression is the evaluation or the "=" sign. An expression can be one line long or many hundreds of lines long depending on the requirements, but it will boil down to "left side = right side" or "value of channel = value of expression". The first things you need to know about expressions are how these channels are accessed and where these expressions can be written. Expressions are time dependent and are evaluated every time the current frame changes.

Create a polygon cone and rename it pCone then open up the Expression Editor from `Windows|Animation Editors|Expression Editor`. The Expression Editor is divided into two halves, the upper half controls the way the expression is created and utilized, the lower half is where the expression itself is written. In the top half the selected node and its attributes are listed allowing you to write an expression per attribute (and name it as well). Click on the selected object (pCone) and the attribute you wish to control (`translateY`) and you should see that this is represented as `pCone.translateY` in the `Selected Object` and `Attribute` text field. This syntax will be the same for all objects and their attributes – `object.attribute` – and will be the same whenever you need to edit or enquire about an object and its attributes. Highlight the text and MMB drag the text into the expression area. To drive this channel you will need to create the right-hand side of the expression. Type `=pCone.translateX;` to complete the right-hand side (expressions have to be terminated with a semicolon).

Once the expression has been completed click the Create button. If the expression syntax is correct, then the Create button will change to Edit so that you can update this expression at any time, also the translateY channel will be coloured showing that it is now controlled. If you translate the cone in the X axis then it will also move correspondingly in the Y axis; if you select the Y axis with the move tool you won't be able to affect it this way. You can also delete the expression and its control over a channel using the Delete button or by using Break connections from the RMB menu accessed in the Channels Box. Close the window using the Close button. If you open the Expression Editor again, the expression that you wrote will not be displayed. You need to change the filter type to show expressions in this window not the attributes that the currently selected object has. Use the Select Filter menu in the Expression Editor and change the filter type to By Expression Name which will now give a list of all the expressions in the scene, so naming any expressions created will be most useful. Other filters can be set that may allow you to hone in on the type of expression that you want to edit through the Object Filter and Attribute Filter menus. There is a discrepancy though, between the name of an attribute in the Channels Box and the name in the Expressions Editor. This is because the Channels Box displays the names of channels as "nice" which is purely for presentation purposes. You can display the "proper" names of channels using the Channels menu in the Channels Box. Under this menu go to the Channel Names heading and set the names to Long or Short. Either of these names are correct syntax for expressions so either pCone.translateY or pCone.ty is acceptable.

We are going to explain how to use an expression to finish the animation of the bouncing ball. Although the translate attributes were set, the squashing was only half finished. The ball was only scaling in one axis, which isn't squashing, as squashing involves a change in shape but not volume. Because the expression will use the value of the scale Y channel to drive the scale X and scale Z channel, you would only have to change the value of the scale Y channel to effect a change to rest of the squashing action.

Open up the saved scene of the animated ball, select the Ball_Scale group and open up the Expression Editor with the select filter set to Selected Object/Attribute Name. Click on the

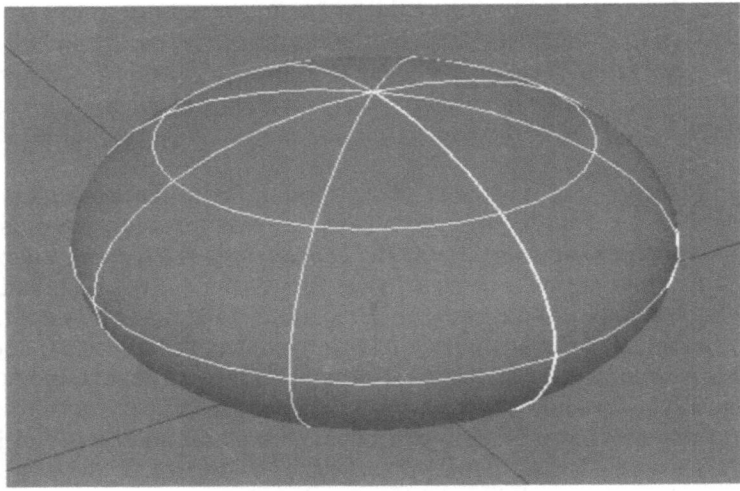

Figure 5.7 A New Squashing Effect for the Ball.

scale X attribute and MMB drag it to the expression area in the bottom half. The expression will now change the value of this channel in relation to the value of the scale Y channel

- Type Ball_Scale.scaleX=1/Ball_Scale.scaleY;
- On the next line, type 1/Ball_Scale.scaleZ=Ball_Scale.scaleY;
- Click Create and play the animation back.

The ball should now scale automatically in the X and Z axes without you having to set any keys whatsoever – quite convenient once the correct expression has been determined. Looking in the Hypergraph may give a better idea of how these expressions work. Select the Ball_Scale node in the Hypergraph and use Graph|Input and Output Connections to display the node connections. The node representing the expression receives information regarding the current time in the scene and also the value of the scale Y channel from the Ball_Scale node along with message information. In return, the expression nodes also output the values of the scale X and scale Z channels which are returned to the Ball_Scale node. Save this scene again and either delete everything or create a new scene from File|New Scene. If you had deleted everything, Maya will automatically do the house keeping and delete any expressions that were linked to the deleted nodes.

Because you were linking the attributes of the Ball_Scale node, the values of the scale X and scale Z channels were not time dependent, in that their values would change in relation to the values of another channel. If you create a sphere (name it ball) and type ball.translateY +=1; you would expect the value of the translate Y channel to increase by one every time the value of the current frame changes (this includes operations such as jumping to a new frame, playing backwards or rewinding). But if you didn't want the expression being evaluated whenever the current frame changed (which would be useful if you wanted to place an object in a random position using an expression), you can turn off the Always Evaluate feature. Now changing the current frame value will not affect this expression.

Other ways to change the values of channels and attributes is to create expressions that use functions. Functions cover a wide range of uses from cyclical functions like cosines to random functions like noise. Other functions can also be used to modify values such as the abs function. To animate some butterfly wings, you could key the values for the rotate channels and then cycle the curves in the Graph Editor post-infinity. It would become harder to do this for a high number; if a scene required perhaps 10 or 15 butterflies then it might be easier to create an expression that works for one butterfly and then cut and paste it to the other butterflies:

- Create a sphere, scale it in X and Y so that it is roughly cigar shaped, delete its history, freeze its transformations and name it BflyBody.
- Create a locator, name it RwngLoc, move it to the right side of BflyBody and then freeze its transformations.
- Create a grid, call it RWing, move that to the right side of the BflyBody and parent it to the RwngLoc.

We are going to have an expression affect the RwngLoc rotation channels and not the RWing object, so that if we want to alter any of the transformation channels of the RWing we will be free to do so:

- Parent the RwngLoc to the BflyBody and edit the shape of the RWing so that it is more winglike.
- Select the RwngLoc, duplicate it, scale the resulting wing and locator by −1 in X.

- Now move it to the other side of the BflyBody, freeze its transformations and change their names accordingly (RWing to LWing and so forth).

Select RwngLoc, open the Expression Editor and select and MMB drag RwngLoc.rotateZ to the lower half. We are going to use a cosine function to drive this rotation; the cosine function returns a value between −1 and 1 in a cyclical fashion depending on the input value. You can use this to drive the wing rotations by using the current frame or time to act as the input value for the cos function (time is defined as frame/frame rate). Type =cos(time);, press Enter and then play back the scene. Two things should be evident: the wing cycles ever so slowly and the amount of rotation is tiny (the frequency is too long and the amplitude is too small). To change the frequency you need to increase the value of time as it is seen by the cos function, so change the cos (time) line to cos(time*10) instead. Additionally, there is only one wing moving so in the next line type LwngLoc.rotateZ=RwngLoc.rotateZ*-1; so that any changes that are made only have to be made to one locator's expression.

Now that the frequency is correct, the amplitude or value needs to be boosted somewhat as the cos function only returns a value between −1 and 1. This can be achieved by multiplying the output value from the cos function, so change the expression to RwngLoc.rotateZ= cos((time*10)*55); so the wings have a much larger rotation value. The wings now flap equally, but their start and end position may need to be changed because butterfly wings tend to meet at the end of the upstroke and rarely go too far below the centreline on the down stroke, so we need to shift the values. This can be done by adding the amount that you wish to shift the rotation by at the end of the line, outside of the brackets.

The final expression should read RwngLoc.rotateZ=cos((time*10)*55)+35; and playing this back should reveal the wings now flapping in a correct manner. If this isn't correct, then the changes can be implemented easily by changing any of the numbers. The butterfly can now be moved around the scene by any means and the wings will carry on flapping tirelessly.

Functions can be inserted easily by using the RMB menu and choosing one from a large selection under Insert Functions. For instance, the flickering of a light can be controlled by a random function such as noise, sphrand, dnoise and gauss. The inputs to these functions can also be driven by external sources so instead of just typing a number, it could be created as a variable (a variable in an expression is represented by a dollar sign and the variable's name). At the top of the expression type $amp=55; and replace the 55 in the body of the main expression with $amp. This will allow you to quickly edit the values for the expression, so unless you wish to alter the actual framework of the expression, you don't need to start selecting values that lie in the expression itself.

Another way to control these values would be to create some new attributes for the character and then use these attributes as the variables. Now, if you wanted to change the value for the amplitude you wouldn't even have to open the Expression Editor, just change the value of the channel in the Channels Box.

- Select BflyBody and go to Modify|Add Attribute... to open the editor for this operation.
- Name the attribute amp, set the data type to integer and then click the OK button.
- Open up the Expression Editor, select the expression and where the variable declaration and assignation is, delete 55 and type BflyBody.amp.

Now you can control the amplitude of the wings without going near the expression that you wrote and could do the same with all of the other values that you are using to control the values of the right-hand side of the expression.

Figure 5.8 The Butterfly Flapping.

Driven Keys

Driven keys work by connecting the output of one attribute or channel to the input of another channel or attribute. So instead of manually keyframing a hand to open and close, finger by finger, it will be faster to create a custom attribute called clench and use the output of this channel to drive the rotation channels of the fingers so that you only need to key one value. This way of working also allows you to keep all of the important controls for a character in one area of the interface, so for varied objects and actions, the channels are all grouped under one item. Although the driven key sounds like an expression where one value is connected to another by using an equals sign, one difference here is that because they are key based, you can alter the interpolation in the Graph Editor.

- Create a sphere and a cube, name them Ball and Block respectively and translate the sphere to -5 units in the Z axis.
- Open the Driven Keys Editor from the options box under Animate|Set Driven Key|Set.

This window is divided into two halves each with object and attribute sections. We are going to be affecting the cube's translate Y channel with the sphere's translate Z channel, so the cube is the driven, the sphere the driver.

- Select Ball and click the Load Driver button.
- Select Block and click the Load Driven button.

There is a list of the attributes each object has, so to create the driven key you have to highlight the channels you wish to connect and when they are set to the correct values in the Channels Box, click Key.

- Highlight `translate Y` for `Block` and highlight `translate Z` for `Ball` and click Key.

This has now defined the start conditions. The end conditions now need to be defined:

- Translate `Ball` to 2 units in the Z axis and translate `Block` 4 units up in the Y axis and click Key again.
- Now move `Ball` back and forth down the Z axis.

This driven key is irrespective of time because it is just looking at the relationship between two values and nothing else. The time factor will only come in if you key the driver channel. Unlike an expression, the driven key has no effect outside of the values that have been keyed, so moving `Ball` to −20 in the Z axis doesn't affect `Block`'s translation in the Y axis. However, `Block`'s movement is fairly linear and you can change this by selecting the driven object/item/node and opening up the Graph Editor. You can now see the curve is plotted with driver in the X and driven in the Y and you can make any changes to this curve as you did when animating the bouncing ball, including adding new keys if necessary or changing the values of the keys. Change the shape of the graph so that `Block` flies out of the path of `Ball` at the last moment. If you want to undo this kind of connection, then either select the curve in the Graph Editor and delete it or select the driven channel and use the RMB menu to choose `Break Connections`.

Driven keys can be utilized to make not only the task of animating complex functions easier but to present the interface for these functions in a simpler manner while keeping the underlying transformations transparent to the user. The following example shows how to make a robot arm complete with pincers and use a small set of custom attributes to drive the animation of the arm (feel free to embellish the robot arm with any additional modeling).

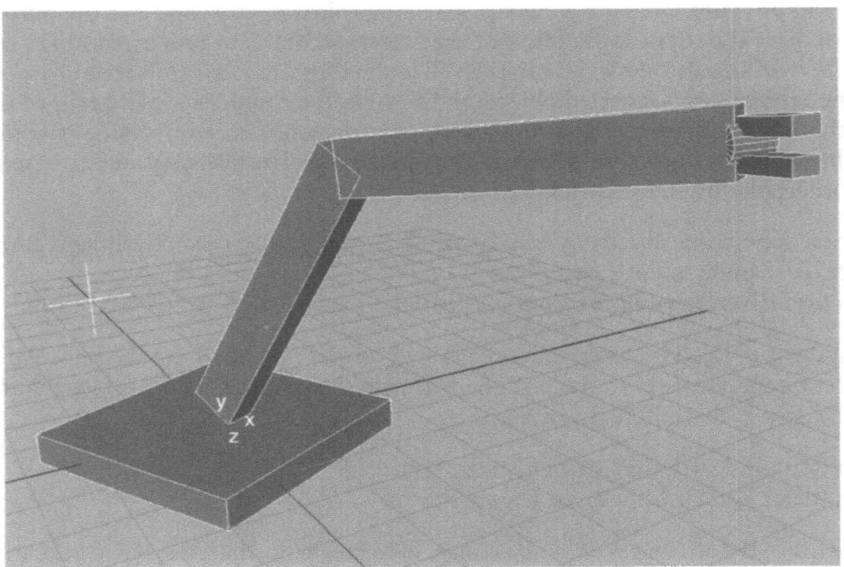

Figure 5.9 The Robotic Arm.

First, you will create the basic objects and set up the hierarchies:

- Create a polygon cube, scale it 4.0, 0.5, 4.0, delete the history, freeze the transformations and rename it Base.
- Create another polygon cube, scale it 5.0, 0.8, 0.5, delete the history, freeze the transformations and rename it "LArm".
- Move the pivot for this arm to the end of the cube.
- Duplicate LArm and rename this new object Uarm.
- Duplicate Uarm, scale it 0.2, 0.3, 0.6, freeze the transformations and rename it Tpincer.
- Duplicate TPincer and rename this object Bpincer.
- Create a polygon cylinder, rotate it 90 degrees in X, scale it 0.25, 0.25, 0.25, delete the history, freeze the transformations and rename it Ppivot.
- In the Outliner, MMB drag and drop BPincer and TPincer onto PPivot, drop PPivot onto Uarm, drop Uarm onto Larm and drop Larm onto Base.
- Now move the various objects into position until they look like a robotic arm.

The robotic arm should function correctly and you should be able to rotate the various parts of the hierarchy to produce an animated arm. However, even if you were to pare down the number of channels for each section using the Channels Control Editor, it would still be an arduous task to keep selecting and reselecting each component to animate it. Now you can create a locator, give it some custom attributes and use these to drive the animation of the robotic arm, without ever having to select the hierarchy.

- Create a locator and name it RoboBoss, move it out of the way of the robotic arm and freeze its transformations.
- Open up the Channel Controls Editor from Window|General Editors|Channel Control and set all of the channels for RoboBoss to Non Keyable.
- While RoboBoss is still selected, use Modify|Add Attribute... to create a new attribute called Swivel.
- Make this attribute a float data type, set the maximum to 10, the minimum to -10 the default to 0.
- Click Add to create the attribute with its associated settings, but keep the window open. You should be able to see the new attribute appear in the Channels Box.
- Create a new attribute called ArmUpDown with the same data settings and click Add.

We've made a mistake here as the attribute name isn't particularly useful (there are two arms in this hierarchy), so highlight the ArmUpDown attribute in the Channels Box and use Modify|Edit Attribute... to rename the attribute LArmUpDown and click Close. Note that you can change any aspect of the attribute's function here.

- Create a series of attributes called UArmUpDown, HeadLR and HeadUD with the same data settings as LarmUpDown.
- Create an attribute called OpenClose with a float data type a maximum of 5, a minimum of 0 and a default of 5.

All of these data types were created as a float because a floating-point number allows a smoother transition when changing. This is important because we are going to be driving rotation values between 180 and −180 degrees to a range of −10 to 10, so having the precision of three decimal places (in the Attribute Editor) will allow a smoother mapping.

- Open the `Set Driven Key` option box and load in `Base` as the driven and `RoboBoss` as the driver.
- Highlight the `Swivel` and `rotateY` attributes, make sure they are both set to 0 and click Key.

To check that the required attributes are at the correct settings, you can change the current selection of an item by clicking on its name in the Set Driven Keys box. This allows a quick way to select and verify attribute values before setting the driven keys.

- Set `Swivel` to 10, `rotateY` to 90, click Key, set `Swivel` to -10, `rotateY` to -90 and click Key again.
- Change the values of `Swivel` to verify that the driven keys have been set.

Now we will continue with the driven keys for the rest of the hierarchy:

- With the `Driven Keys` window still open, select `Larm` and load it in as the driven object.
- Highlight `LArmUpDown` and `rotateZ`.
- Set `LArmUpDown` to −10, click Key, rotate `Larm` 140 degrees in Z, set `Swivel` to 10 and click Key again.
- Set `LArmUpDown` to 0 and load in `Uarm` as driven.
- Highlight `UArmUpDown` and `rotateZ`, set `UArmUpDown` to −10, rotate `Uarm` −160 degrees in Z and click Key.
- Rotate `Larm` to 0 degrees in Z, set `Swivel` to 10 and click Key once more.
- Load in `PPivot` as the driven object, highlight `rotateY` and `HeadLR` and click Key.
- Set `rotateY` to −45, `HeadLR` to −10, click Key, set `rotateY` to 45, `HeadLR` to 10 and click Key.

If you have set driven keys incorrectly, the reason is usually forgetting to load in the correct driver or driven, forgetting to click the Key button when updating a value or forgetting to update a value when clicking Key. Either select the attribute in question and break the connections using the RMB menu and then key it again, or change the values of the keys on the Graph Editor. For the rest of the attributes that `RoboBoss` has (`HeadUD` and `OpenClose`) set up the relevant driven keys for the other attributes so that all of the controls are now working. Now, to control and key the movement of the robot arm, it should just be necessary to select `RoboBoss` and animate the six channels presented. Open up the Attribute Editor and fold out the `Extra Attributes` section. The custom attributes are here and are represented by sliders with accuracy to three decimal places. You can now change and key these attributes by holding down the RMB over the numeric field and selecting `Set key`.

Connections can still be made between one area of animation and another. Consider creating a factory floor populated by these robots. The animation of most of the background robots could be created and controlled by an expression that feeds into any of these driven keys. For instance, all of the keys could be controlled by sin and cosine waves to give a whole feel of automation, just offset some of the expressions or insert a randomization function into the result for each robot arm to give that small bit of differentiation between them all. If the expressions are driving driven keys that are driving the channels of an object, then changing the shape of the curves for the driven keys will add another layer of complexity to the animation.

Non-Linear Animation

Non-linear animation techniques allow us to store portions of animation as clips or positions of characters as poses giving us the ability to mix and match these pieces together without the

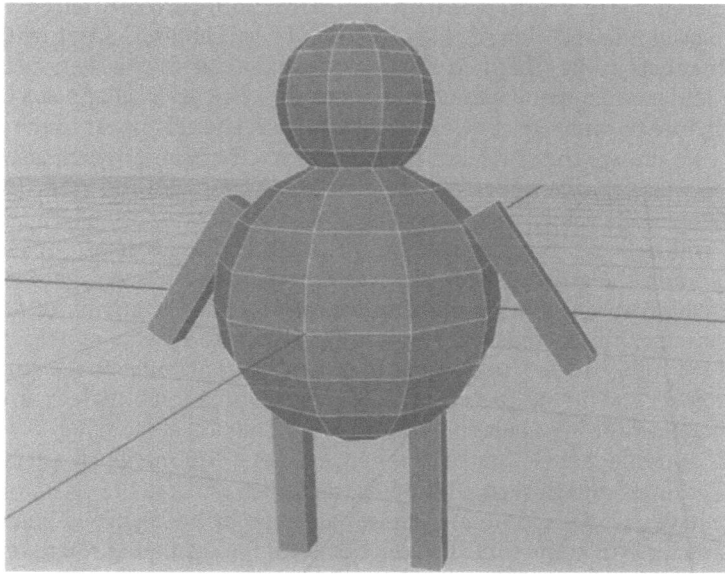

Figure 5.10 The Simple Character Ready for Non-Linear Animation.

constrain of absolute timing or positioning in a scene in a similar fashion to editing. Moreover it allows us to save these clips or poses out as separate files which can be opened up in different scenes to allow the non-linear animation process to continue in a scene independent manner.

In order to use the non-linear animation functions that Maya provides we need to create a Character node which is a collection of all the channels for a character that we would normally animate with over the course of a normal animation scene. This needs to be used because Maya has to know which channels to export values from and store in clip form. This means that we don't need to collect absolutely every channel that is used in a character, just those which will be transforming objects and those channels that affect driven keys for deformers and expressions for example.

- Create two spheres and transform them so that they represent the torso and head (of an extremely simple character) and name them accordingly.
- Create, scale and place four cubes for the arms and legs (and reposition their pivots), naming them Larm, Rarm, Lleg and Rleg.
- Place all the objects into a hierarchy that starts under Torso.
- Group the torso once and name this group Trans.

To create a character node all we have to do is to start with our main transform node and place this into a character node first. Maya will let us add or subtract channels from any character node at any time and also has the facility for creating subcharacters that sit under our main character node. This hierarchy of subnodes lets us create a very straightforward and organized structure with which to animate with. Select Trans and open up the options box for Character|Create Character Set. First we should name our top level character set, so we'll call it Senor. Then we need to pick which attributes from our currently selected node (Trans) we want to be placed into this character set. Turn on From Channel Box, highlight the translate and scale channels in the Channels Box and press Create Character Set. Immediately a few things should have happened: the name of our new character set appears in the playback range line just before the auto-key button and the new set should appear in the Outliner. If we fold out Senor, we can see the attributes that are collected under it, which also appear in the Channels Box if we select the node. We could now animate with this node by selecting the channel and changing its value.

Because we will also use Trans to give us the general movement of our character in the scene, we should add the attributes for torso to our character sets, so that we can have fine control over any body movement. In this case we can just add the attributes for Torso to the main Senor character set so that we don't end up with too many subcharacter sets. Use Character|Add to Character set to add these selected attributes to the currently selected (Senor) character set and do the same for the head, both arms and both legs. If we have attributes we wish to remove from a currently selected set, Character|Remove from Character set will do this and Character|Merge Character sets will merge all attributes from sets selected in the Outliner into the last selected character set.

Now that we have a working character set we can begin by saving poses. Poses are just positions that a character is in at the time, but can be useful for animating rough layouts or creating key poses to animate from. Although the character set is available for us to use, we don't get any of the transform manipulators which can make animating quite tedious and although it looks like the channels are being driven when we select an object, they are in fact just members of the character set, so we are free to animate with them as we wish using the transform manipulators. Select Senor and open the options box for Animate|Create Pose. Change the name of the pose to Rest and press Create Pose. This first pose lets us now access the resting position for all of the objects. Position the character into a mid walking pose with the left leg forwards and create a pose called L_Walk, change the pose so that the character is walking with the right leg forward and call this pose R_Walk. All poses that are created are accessible from

Figure 5.11 The Three Poses.

Visor which is an interface where we can access Maya internal files as well as stored project files. Open the tab titled Character Poses and we should see the stored poses. RMB over any of the poses and select Apply Pose which should position our character in the correct pose. This is why it is always worth storing a default pose first so that all poses and animations can be reset if needed. We can actually animate from any of these poses or even use these poses as key positions and let Maya do the inbetweening.

So far we have only been creating poses using the main character set, so make sHead the currently selected set and create a pose called Head_rest, then rotate the head so that it is looking to the left, save a pose called Head_L and save another pose looking off to the right called Head_R as well. We can now use these subset poses to affect our main poses. In Visor, apply L_Walk and then apply Head_L so that we can see the effect of a sub set's pose on the main set's pose. The main set pose will always overwrite the sub set pose, so if we apply L_Walk again, the head is returned to the position that it was in when this main character set pose was created.

The Trax Editor

The actual business of non-linear animation is conducted in the Trax Editor which can be opened using Windows|Animation Editors|Trax Editor and which looks like the dope sheet with the available character sets in the left hand side, the clips of animation and their respective tracks on the right and a timeline at the bottom of the window.

The Trax Editor is where we will be mixing and editing our animation clips which are represented as bars in the track for the character sets. So the first thing we need to do is to create some animation and save it as a clip. At frame 1, select the Senor character set, apply the Rest pose and key all the channels in the Channels Box. At frame 10 apply the L_Walk pose, key again and at frame 20 apply the R_Walk pose and key this. Playing back we should see that the character moves from a rest to a short walk. We can now begin building clips of animation.

- Open the options box for Animate|Create Clip.
- Change the name of the clip to walk_from_rest.

Figure 5.12 The Trax Editor.

- Turn off `Leave Keys in Timeline` and turn on `Put Clip in Trax Editor and Visor`.
- Specify the Start and End of the clip as 1 to 20.
- Turn off all other options and press `Create Clip`.

In the Trax Editor we can now see our clip represented as a bar from frames 1 to 20 in the track for the Senor character. This clip can now be moved back and forth in the Trax timeline by using the cursor (no transform tools work here) so that we can arrange the clips at any point in time. Because we turned off the option to leave the keys in the timeline, all the animation is now stored in this clip, letting us carry on and animate our character. If we want to just keep animating different actions without this stored clip affecting the scene, we can disable it by bringing up the RMB marking menu over the clip and turning off `Enable Clip`. Conversely, the clip can be re-enabled by turning this option back on. Because the Trax Editor will display all animation tracks and clips for all of the character sets, we can neaten things up a little by folding up the display for each character. Now the total length of the animation clips is displayed as a single bar letting us view the overall animation length for a character set quite easily.

Now that we have a clip inside our editor, we are free to manipulate it as we wish. If we want to change the length of the clip, just move the cursor to the edge of the clip until it turns into an arrow and bar icon and just stretch the clip to desired size. If we want to cycle the clip instead, move the cursor to the bottom corner of the clip edge until the cursor turns into a circular arrow with a bar and then drag the clip; inside the clip itself are small lines representing where the cycles begin. The clip can be cut, copied and pasted using the RMB marking menu and also instanced. If we instance the clip, any changes to the master clip will ripple down to all instances. For now, just select the clip, copy it and then paste it which should place it in a track below the original clip. Move the start of the new clip to the end time of the first clip, select both clips by dragging a selection box over them and enable them. Playing back the scene should now show that the character now cycles, apart from the point that the second clip begins and the position snaps back to the rest pose.

Drag the timeslider to the point in the second clip that the rest pose stops and the L_Walk pose begins and select Split Clip from the RMB marking menu, which should break the clip up into two sections, placing the split at the current time (the options for `Edit|Split Clip` in the Trax menu allow the specification of a split time manually). We can also merge clips, but only from the Trax menu. Select the useless clip section and delete it with the backspace key. We now have two clips in a track each, but at the end of the first clip the character is in the opposite position to that of the start of the new clip. Maya allows us to blend between clips to provide another measure of editing power.

- Move the second clip so that it starts ten frames after the end of the first clip.
- Select the clips so that they are both highlighted.
- Open the options box for `Create|Blend`.
- Set the Initial Weight Curve to `Ease In Out` and press `Create Blend`.

There should now be a curve between the end of one clip and the start of the other and if we play the scene back, the blend should fill in the gaps.

Editing Clips

Now that we have the basics of non-linear animation editing, we can change the source information for a clip to give us a further degree of flexibility on top of using the Trax Editor. Select

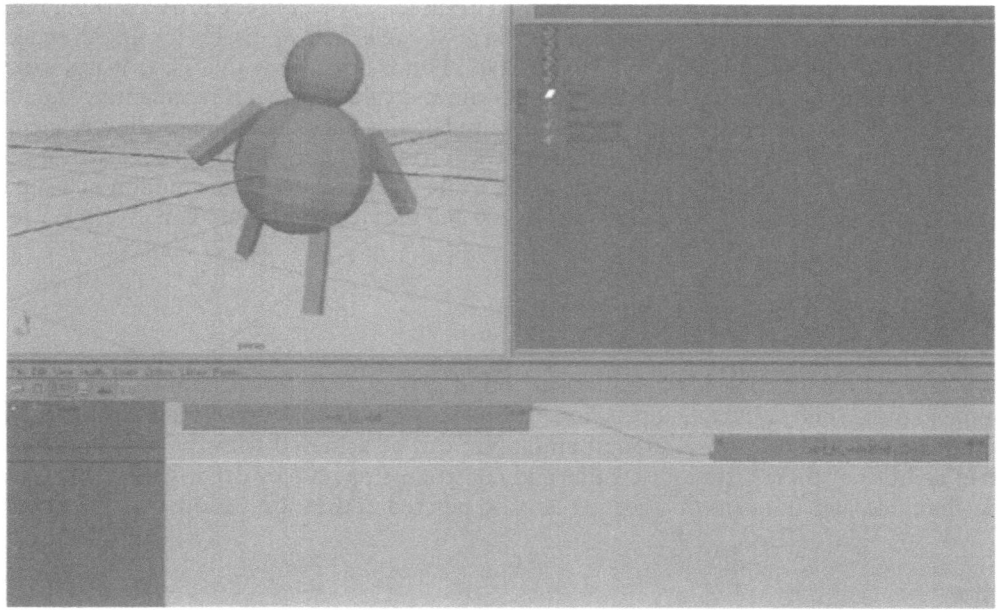

Figure 5.13 The Blended Clips.

a clip and bring up the Attribute Editor, using either CTRL+a or from the RMB marking menu. In the Attribute Editor we can change the weight of the clip which will alter how much influence it has over our character set, whether the clip has an absolute or relative offset for the channels it drives in terms of 3D space, the start and end time of the clip in the Trax Editor, whether the clip cycles and whether the clip is enabled or not. If we decide that the source clip isn't working well or could do with some tweaking, we can change the keyed values for the channels. Select the first clip so that it is highlighted and use Modify|Activate/Deactivate Keys so that the clip turns green. The keyframes that we originally set for the clip are in the timeline and if we select the Senor character set from the Outliner, we can see the keyed channels. Go to the second keyframe in the timeline, alter the position of the head and key this change, then use Modify|Activate/Deactivate Keys again to turn off the key selection. We could also add new keys into an activated clip wherever we wish on the timeline, so secondary motion for the head can be added with no real difficulty. Now when we play the clips back, this change should appear in the first clip (but not the second as it is a copy not an instance). Additional keys can be set onto a character by selecting the character, setting a key for all the channels at the beginning of the timerange and setting keys at the end of the timerange. This now lets us add new keyframes onto our character in the traditional sense, with the beginning and ending keys marking the start and end of the hand animated section. We can also change the interpolation between keyframes in a clip in the Graph Editor, using View|Graph AnimCurves (which will also work if we selected a blend).

Further to changing the animation curves and keyframe characteristics, we can go to a higher level of editing and use Time Warps which affect the total change over time in the clip. Time Warps can be created when a clip is created or can be added later on using Create|Time

Warp (the options let us create the warp enabled or disabled) or from the RMB marking menu over the clip in question. If we create a Time Warp, we can enable or disable it using the checkbox in the Attribute Editor. Opening up the Graph Editor on a clip with a Time Warp, we can see there is a curve stretching from 0 to 100 in time and value, each axis representing the total percentage of value against timing. We can manipulate this curve in all the usual ways including adding more keys to it or even deleting it if we don't need it, but it provides an extra level of control over the evaluation of a clip. We can use Time Warps to reverse the motion of a clip by setting the value of the first Time Warp key to 100 and the value of the last Time Warp key to 0.

Paths and Constraints

Paths and constraints provide another method of driving transform channels and are very simple to utilize and animate in operation. Complexity can be built up very swiftly using these methods and some otherwise difficult animation can be achieved with the judicious use of either or both of these techniques. Paths and constraints operate by driving the transformation channels, which means that groups can also be used in these operations.

Paths

Path animation is a method of controlling the position and rotation of an object by driving its channels from a derived position on a curve. Effectively we are going to be attaching an object to a curve (which when used in this manner becomes a "path") and specifying how long it takes the object to move down the curve, somewhat like a carriage on a roller coaster.

Create a NURBS cone and draw and shape a curve so that it changes shape in all three axes. Select the cone then Shift-select the curve and open the options up for Animate|Motion Paths|Attach to Motion Path. These options control the way that the selected object's translation and rotation channels will be driven. Most of these can be set in the Attribute Editor after this operation, so the main options to set right now will be the start and end frames that the object will be moved along the path (use the time slider option for now) and click Attach. Clicking Play will show the object move along the path between the specified times, at all other times it will sit at the start or the end of the path because its translate channels are now being driven by a position along the path. The object is positioned and animated on the path by moving its translate pivot along the curve, so we can alter how the object sits on the path by repositioning its pivot using the insert key method. Two markers at either end of the path give the time that each position will be reached, so select either of these and MMB drag them so that the path animation can now be altered within the length of the curve.

You can affect how the cone's position is evaluated by changing the way that the position on the path is evaluated. Select the cone, open the Attribute Editor and select the tab named motionPath1. Turn on the Parametric Length attribute and play the animation back. The motion of the cone will speed up and slow down as it moves along the path, whereas if you turn this attribute off, the cone will move along the path in a linear motion. Parametric Length means that the time to move along the path is divided equally between the CVs of the path. Moving along a section that has two CVs close together will mean that the 3D movement of the cone will be slower than moving between two CVs that are widely spaced apart. However, having only two known quantities (start and end frame) about this path animation is not enough as you don't have any control over where the object is between these two points

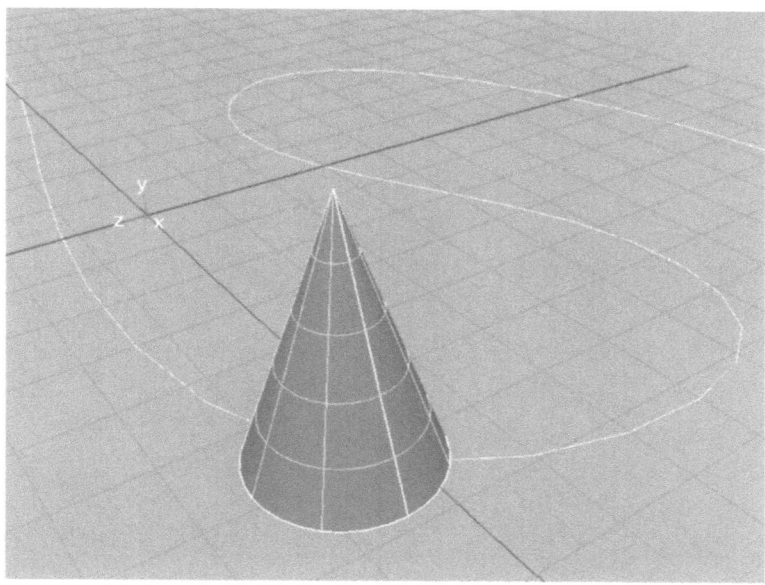

Figure 5.14 A Cone on a Path.

in time. Select the cone and open up the input node named motionPath1. The channel that we are interested in is the U Value channel that controls the position along the curve with respect to time. Play back and then pause the animation so that the cone is about midway along the path, highlight the U Value channel and use the RMB marking menu to set a key, creating another path marker with the appropriate time value. The inverse of this is to play the animation until the cone is at a desired point along the path, MMB drag the current time marker to the desired time and then set a key. The position of the cone along the path is now being controlled by another influence (the U value along the path) but this is a keyed influence and as such, the interpolation of these keys can be changed in the Graph Editor, so select the cone and open the Graph Editor. The curve for the U value can be seen here and adjusted in the same manner as all aspects of keyed channels for the bouncing ball were adjusted.

Now that the cone is moving sufficiently well along the path, you can start using some other attributes to give the animation a different feel. For instance, what we have right now is good for objects moving along conveyor belts but the cone has no orientation. You can use further attributes of the path to now drive the rotation channels of the cone so that it appears to be looking ahead or at least to have directionality (this why these examples use a cone and not a sphere). Select the cone, opening the Attribute Editor at the motionPath1 section and turn on the Follow attribute. This will now align the cone on the curve using the attributes Front Axis and Up Axis. Front Axis will determine which local translation axis will point down the curve and Up Axis will determine which local translation axis will be used to keep the cone in the correct orientation as it moves through the scene. The Up Axis of the object is kept pointing up by setting a World Up Type that the object's Up Vector will align itself with constantly. Now that the cone is following the path as it moves through space, it can be made to bank, or lean like a motorcycle, as it moves through curves in the path. However, the cone has

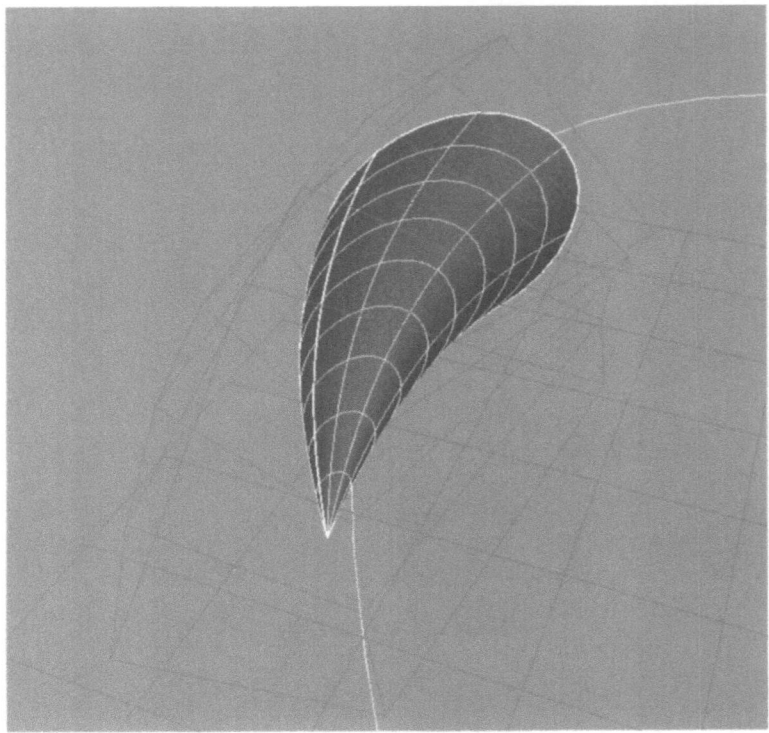

Figure 5.15 A Banking Flowing Cone.

a circular cross-section and having it bank won't produce appreciable results, so scale it in Z so that it is taller than it is wide and turn on Bank in the Attribute Editor. The two attributes underneath Bank are Bank Scale, which controls how the reaction of the object to curvature (set this to a negative number to get the object to lean away from the curve), and Bank Limit, which sets an upper limit on the amount of banking done.

So far, all of these methods will work very well for rigid objects moving along a path. One further attribute can be given to the object in cases where the animation should suggest a flexible object moving down the path. This is an attribute called a Flow Path Object and is applied to either the object or the path. Essentially this creates a deformer (more on these later) called a lattice about the chosen item, which allows the deformation of the object to occur relative to the shape of the path. This is a lot easier to see in action than to visualize, but do increase the complexity of the cone's surface by changing the number of spans to 3 or 4 in the inputs section of its construction history (if you deleted its history, then just insert a couple of isoparms).

Select the cone and open up the options box for Animate|Motion Paths|Flow Path Object. The only thing you should be concerned with is that the lattice is created around the object; the rest of the options can be left alone. However, if you were to create the lattice around the path, then you will need to change the number of T divisions to something higher than the default. Click Flow and the lattice should be created around the cone and now control the shape of the object as it and the lattice move down the path – a useful technique for fish, dolphins, snakes and cartoon vehicles.

There may be a time when you wish to create a path animation but are either unsure of exactly where you will be creating the path or wish to roughly make the path and fine-tune it later.

- Create a new object or delete the path and lattice that are involved with the cone.
- Select the object, set the current time to 1 and use `Animate|Motion Path|Set Motion Path Key` to create the first CV of a motion path.
- Change the current time, move the object to another position and use `Animate|Motion Path|Set Motion Path Key` again to create the next CV until you have a completed path.

This function can also be used to add additional path positions to the start or the end of a current path and extend it.

Constraints

Constraints allow you to drive the transformation channels of an object by constraining these channels to various attributes or properties of another object. The most basic type of constraint is the point constraint. This will constrain the position of an object to a target or targets (there are no limits to the number of point constraints that can be placed on an object). All constraints have an offset value which is keyable, letting us further alter the nature of the constraint if we so wish. Create a locator (a locator is a position in space that carries a transform node), create a sphere and move the locator away from the sphere. When creating constraints select the target and then the object which will be constrained; so select the locator, Shift-select the sphere and open the options under `Constraint|Point`. The options allow you to add or remove a constraint and also to assign the weight of the particular point constraint. If there is more than one constraint affecting an object, the weight of each constraint will determine which constraint has the greatest influence over the object. In the options, set the `Constraint Operation` to `Add Targets` and click Add/Remove to create the constraint. The sphere should now snap to the position of the locator, a constraint node should be added to the sphere's node hierarchy and a weight should be apparent as a channel in this node.

Create another locator and move this to another point in space, Shift-select the sphere again and use `Constraint|Point` to add another constraint to the sphere. The sphere should now be centred between the two locators and moving the locators will now affect the position of the sphere as a weighted average of their positions. Changing the weights will affect the final position of the sphere. This can be very useful if animating a character who is picking up a ball: the ball can be constrained between two locators, one at ground level and one in the character's hand. Animating the constraint weights will transfer the ball from the ground position to the hand position smoothly. The offset values can also be used to add further movement to the sphere as it travels between locators.

The scale channels of an object can be controlled by using a scale constraint, which operates in exactly the same manner as the point constraint: a target is specified with a weighting and the scaling of the object is controlled as a weighted average of the scale channels of the target object(s). The orient constraint works in the same manner, as the rotation channels of your object are controlled by the rotation channels of the target(s). These three types of constraints work in a relatively simple manner but when layered together, sophisticated animation can be created. If you wish to remove the effect of a target from the object and its channels, select the target and the object, set the `Constraint Operation` to `Remove Targets`

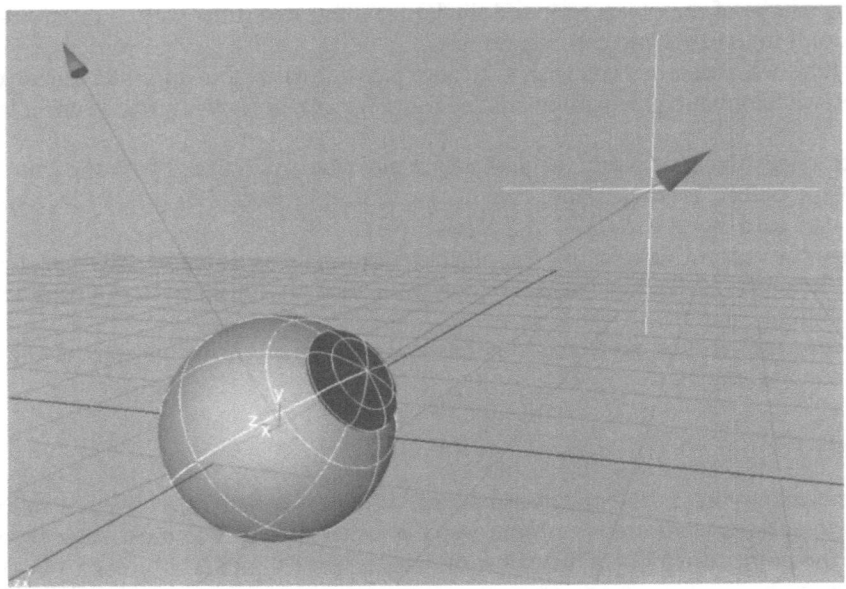

Figure 5.16 An Eyeball with Aim Constraint.

and click Add/Remove. Another way would be to display the input and output connections in the Hypergraph and to delete the connections. The constraint node should never be connected unless you wish to remove all constraint operations of that type.

The next type of constraint that can be used is the aim constraint. This constrains an object's axis to point at a specified target thus controlling its rotation channels. Create a sphere and a cone and move the sphere away from the cone. Again, select the sphere first and then the cone (target then object) and open the options up for Constrain|Aim. These options are similar to the options for an object following a path and you need to specify which axis is used to aim and which axis will be used for the up vector. In the cone's case, the aim vector will be the Y axis so that the pointy bit points and the up vector can be the X axis (change the World Up Type to Scene Up and click Add/Remove). Move the cone or the sphere around and the cone will now track the position of the sphere. A very useful application of this kind of constraint is to constrain the aim vectors of a character's eyeball to a locator so that the character will look at the locator making it an easier task to animate these rotations, as only the locator needs to be moved.

The tangent constraint is used to affect an object's orientation using the curvature and direction (tangency) of a NURBS curve. This is similar to using a path for the animation of an object except that the object is not being moved down the path. Draw a NURBS curve and create a cone. Select the curve and then the cone and open the options for Constrain|Tangent. Because you are going to be controlling the orientation of an object by a target, the same options such as aim vector and up vector need to be set. Set the aim vector to 1 in the Y axis and the world up vector to 1 in the X axis and click Add/Remove. Translate the cone around to see that its orientation is now controlled by the tangency of the target curve.

Another method of controlling an object's translation and rotation channels is to constrain it to the surface attributes of a target. These kinds of constraints can be weighted between different targets but the effect does not lend itself easily to animating as the change of position between targets occurs only when one weight is zero and the other is one. You will be using two types of constraints for this effect: a geometry constraint which will set the object's position to that of the target's surface and a normal constraint which will set the orientation of the object's axis to remain normal (perpendicular) to the target's surface. Create a NURBS plane, give it 6 patches in U and V and scale it by 10 units in X and Z. Push and pull the CVs so that the plane now has a lumpy aspect to it (or use the Sculpt Surfaces tool). Create a NURBS sphere, set its end sweep attribute to 180 and delete its history. This hemisphere will be our impromptu boat, but because we are going to be using constraints, we need to make sure that its pivot is in the correct place, so use the insert key to move the pivot to the outer edge of its surface in the Z axis.

Select the plane and then Shift-select the sphere, open up the options for `Constrain|`
`Geometry`, use the default settings and click Add/Remove. The "boat" should now be stuck to the surface of the plane and if moved around, should follow its contours. The surface is followed but the orientation of the boat doesn't change relative to the surface, so selecting the plane and then the boat again, open up the options for `Constrain|Normal`. These options echo the options found under the Aim constraint settings. The aim vector for the boat will be −1 in the Z axis as you want this axis to point perpendicularly at the surface it is constrained to, and you want the up vector to be 1 in the Z axis. Keep the `World Up Type` to `Scene Up` and click the Add/Remove button. Moving the boat about now should show how this combination of constraints can be used – it is no coincidence that the operations to create these constraints mean that you don't even have to change your selections. Modeling and moving thorns onto the surface of a cactus can be made far easier using these two constraint processes – if it's just for positioning then the constraints can be deleted later.

Deformers

So far in this book we have seen how to move objects and nodes in three dimensions by changing the values of the attributes in their transform nodes. So far, we haven't been able to change the the shape of geometry except for the results of scaling and moving the components manually. This section will look at how to change the shape of an object using deformation effects, which are applied at the component level (this is why scaling is not a deformer). Maya provides a set of tools known as deformers and splits these into two categories: *non-linear deformers* and *linear deformers*. Deformers can be applied to an object or to a selection of points, thus a deformable shape is one composed of points. You can use deformers to improve the animation of a character by changing its surface over time, such as giving the illusion of skin being changed by the underlying muscles. However, deformers are extremely useful modeling tools, allowing you to achieve shapes that would otherwise be hard to create using normal modeling methods (sometimes, fantastic shapes can arrive purely through serendipity); at any point, select the deformed surface and duplicate it. This will duplicate the current node without any input nodes, resulting in a "fresh" surface.

Both types of deformer operate on the component level by applying their effects to a set of points. In Maya, a set is a non-homogenous collection of items: anything (component or object) can be in a set and a set defines a collection, nothing more. You can create sets either by intent or by the use of a tool or an action. Maya uses sets to keep track of items or components that need to be considered by various nodes in the scene and for this reason, you are going to be using and manipulating sets as you use deformers. When you create a deformer, Maya will create a deformation set that holds all of the points to be considered by the

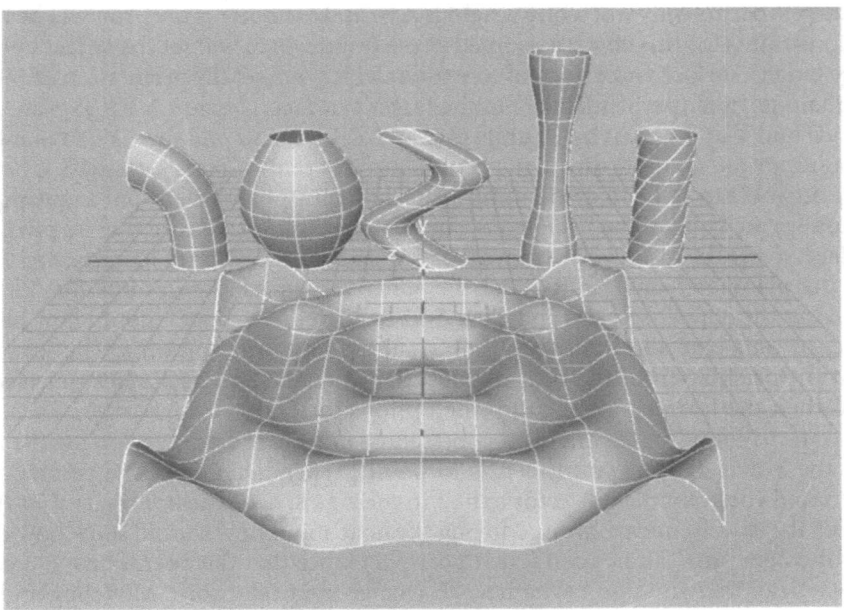

Figure 5.17 The Non-Linear Deformers.

deformer. You can use various operations on them to change the number of points in a set and therefore edit the effect of a deformer on the shape of an object.

Non-Linear Deformers

Non-linear deformers work by applying a specialized type of deformation (such as bending or rippling) to a set of points. These specialized deformations will not reposition points in a linear manner, hence the name. The attributes for each of the non-linear deformers are straightforward in effect and are tied in with the action of the deformer itself. The simplest way to explore their function is to create five NURBS cylinders (eight sections, six spans) and one NURBS plane (10 patches in U and V).

- Move the cylinders and the plane so that they are apart from each other.
- Select the first cylinder and use `Deform|Create Nonlinear Deformer|Bend` to put a bend deformer into the cylinder.
- Create a Flare, Sine, Squash and Twist deformer in the other cylinders.
- Create a Wave deformer in the NURBS plane.

All of the non-linear deformers are represented visually by a deformer handle which allows you to manipulate the effect of each deformer without having to change or access any attributes in the channels box. This type of deformer is comprised of a transform node and an input node and it is the input node that contains the attributes relevant to the deformer. Changing these attributes can be done using either the Channels Box or the Show Manipulator tool. The Show Manipulator tool will only display the handles to change a deformer's attributes if the title of the input node is LMB clicked to display the attributes. Additional effects can also be gained from transforming the non-linear deformer (NLD) in 3D. Because the handle is treated as an object with a transform node, scaling, rotating and translating will change the area of effect that each NLD will have. Ripples and bends can not only be animated in terms of their deformation effect but also in terms of the area of effect that they have. For example, if the upper and lower bound of the flare deformer is changed so that the flaring looks like a bulge, then translating the deformer handle will give the appearance of an object moving through the cylinder in a cartoon fashion. The squash deformer could be parented to the animated bouncing ball and a driven key or expression could drive the squashing attributes.

Clusters

Moving on from NLDs, we come to the simplest (in mechanism) deformer in Maya. Many of the functions and properties that a cluster has are similar in function for all of the other deformers and this will let you explore how deformers work, while keeping the details of each operation simple. So although this section may appear lengthy in comparison to the sections on other deformers, it is not in proportion to the complexity of a cluster, it just allows you to examine the framework of deformers in one fell swoop.

A cluster allows you to transform a set of points in 3D and each point in the set can be given a different weight that will change how much of the cluster's original transformation will be passed on to it (similar to weighted constraints). In effect, a cluster could be seen as a smart group of points. It is possible to transform and key points in space without using clusters (or other deformers), but it is a procedure that is relatively difficult to control. Create a NURBS sphere and select several of its CVs. You can see the selected CVs in the Channels Box by folding out the list under CVs (click to show). Each CV that you select will have its position represented in the Channels Box as purely an X, Y, Z position with no transform node attached to it (this is because a CV can only have positional data, rotations will be interpreted purely as a change in position and scaling makes no changes to a point). So you can key their position in space using the normal RMB menu method, but it is a method that is unnecessarily difficult, especially when you have to keep changing the selection mask mode every time you wish to change their position.

Select a series of CVs on a NURBS sphere and use Deform|Create Cluster. A small green "c" should appear in the view and this will have a transform node and an input node. Select the cluster and transform it in space. The points that you have selected will now be moved; if you rotate or scale the cluster, this will change the position of the CVs relative to the pivot point of the cluster – in effect you could see a cluster as a smart group for points. Why a smart group? One thing groups cannot do is assign a weighting to the items that it contains. With clusters and other deformers, you can change the effect that the deformer has by assigning a weight to the points it affects, so the transformation that each point receives from a deformer will be multiplied by its individual weighting.

In the cluster options box, there are two tabs labeled Basic and Advanced. The advanced options deal with the order in an object's inputs that the deformer is going to be placed in and whether the deformer will be the only thing that can affect these points. These advanced options are the same for every deformer and we will look at the effect that these will have later on. The basic options are the options relevant to the currently selected deformer type, for example the only options we have for a cluster is whether it acts in a relative or absolute manner. When a cluster is transformed, these transformations are passed on to the points that it affects. If a cluster is in "relative" mode, then only transformations applied to the cluster itself will have an effect on the points.

- Create two NURBS spheres.
- Pick some CVs on one sphere, create a cluster with "relative" turned on and group both of them (name the group Rel).
- Repeat for the other sphere but turn "relative" off and group both of them (name the group Abs).
- Move both clusters so that the surface of each sphere is deforming.
- Select Rel and translate it.
- Select Abs and translate it.

Because both clusters are in a hierarchy, they are being transformed by its parent's transformations being passed down to them. The cluster with the relative attribute turned off is interpreting these hierarchic transformations and applying these to the points it deforms, even though the cluster itself doesn't actually move. This attribute can have a profound effect on how the surfaces will deform, so fortunately you can change its value in the Attribute Editor. However, keying a cluster is extremely easy and any of its animated channels can be dealt with in the same fashion as any other transformed object in terms of connectivity and curve interpolation.

Editing Deformation Sets

We talked about the collection of points that the cluster deforms and that the cluster passes a weighted sum of its transformations to the points. This mechanism is accessible to us using two different methods, which yield the same result.

- Create a NURBS plane with 10 patches in U and V and scale it by ten units in X and Z.
- Select the object and create a cluster (at this point all of the points are equally weighted and considered by the cluster, so moving the cluster will appear to transform the whole surface).

Now, the only way to create any form of local deformation is to change which CVs are affected by the cluster and what their particular weighting is when transformed. As soon as the cluster was created, all of the surface's CVs were put into a set (in this case a deformer set). When the cluster moves, all CVs in this particular deformer set are moved as well, so if you remove CVs from this set, you remove them from the transformation effects (and vice versa).

All of the sets within Maya can be referenced and manipulated in the Relationship Editor. The Relationship Editor is a multi-function editor, that allows you to manipulate and view all of the different kinds of sets that exist in Maya, so open it up from Window|Relationship Editors|Sets... and change the fold-out to Deformer Set Editing (as you can see, the Relationship Editor covers a large variety of functions). On the left-hand side is a set called clusternSet and you can see all of the points in this set by clicking on the fold-out icon to the side of the title. You can now use the menus in the editor to add and remove CVs from your deformer set.

- Select all of the CVs at the edge of the NURBS plane.
- Select the set in the Relationship Editor.

- Use `Edit|Remove Selected Items` to move the CVs from the currently selected deformer set.
- Display the list of CVs in the deformer set, highlight a few and use `Edit|Remove Highlighted from Deformer Set`.

Using the `Add` version in the menu can reverse all of the above operations. Additionally, all of the items/points in a set can be selected by highlighting the set and using `Edit|Select Set Members`. Now that some CVs have been removed from the deformer set you can start to weight the remaining CVs so a more interesting deformation can occur. You can change these weights using the Component Editor, which brings up a spreadsheet for anything that could affect our currently selected components.

- Select a row of CVs on the NURBS surface that are affected by the cluster.
- Open the Component Editor from `Windows|General Editors|Component Editor`.
- Open the `Weighted Deformers` tab to display a list of the selected CVs and the deformers that are affecting them.
- Change all of the weights to 0.2 and close the window.

Now these CVs will only be transformed a fifth of the amount of the other CVs. The Component Editor is a useful window when you wish to "get under the hood" of Maya and change values on a component by component level. However, these two methods will quickly become time consuming if you ever wish to make large changes to deformers, CV sets and the effects they have on one complex surface, let alone a series of characters. Maya provides faster methods of changing all of these values while also providing useful visual feedback. You can change whether a point is considered by a cluster or not by using the Edit Membership tool, which allows you to quickly move points in or out of its deformer set.

- Move the cluster so that the surface of the NURBS plane is deformed sufficiently.
- Activate the tool from the `Deform|Edit Membership Tool` menu.
- Select the deformer whose sets we wish to edit.
- All points within its set will now be highlighted yellow.
- Points can now be added to the deformer set using `Shift+LMB` and can be removed using `Ctrl+LMB`.

Painting Set Membership

Any points that have been removed will now assume their original untransformed positions and any points added will be transformed with a default weighting of one. Now that deformer sets can be easily edited without opening another window or editor, it will be equally useful to edit the weights of the CVs without opening any editors. You can change the weights using a variation of the artisan tool that was used to sculpt surfaces, allowing you to paint values over a deformed surface.

- Select the deformed surface.
- Open the options box for `Deform|Paint Cluster Weights` because you will need to change the values of the artisan tool.
- Paint corresponding values for the deformed points.

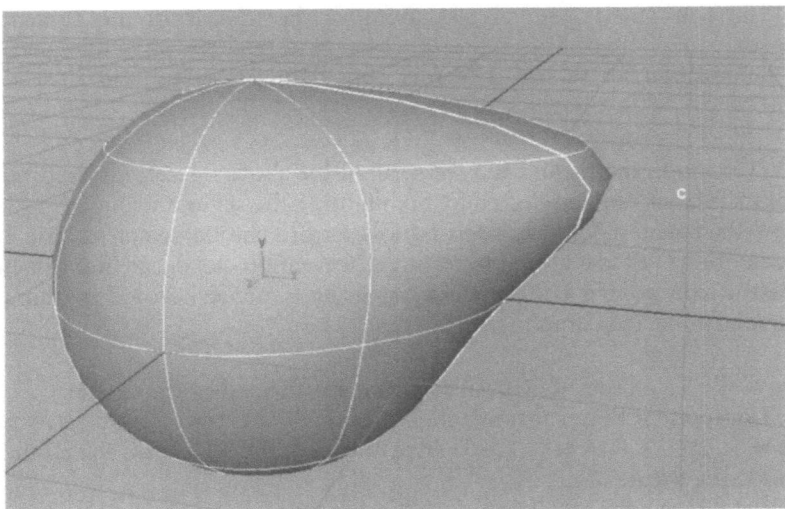

Figure 5.18 Deforming the Sphere Surface with a Cluster.

You will only be able to paint values for the points that are in the deformer set, which may limit the overall deformation effect.

- Delete the cluster.
- Select the object.
- Create another cluster (so that the deformer now affects all of the CVs).
- Open the Paint Cluster Weights tool, set the value to zero, the operation to Replace and click the Flood button.
- Now start painting the required values.

You can also remove all of the points with a weight of zero from the deformer set by selecting the surface and using Deform|Prune Membership|Cluster, which will remove all points with a weight of zero or points that are currently undeformed. If there is more than one cluster affecting a surface, you can also use the Paint Set Membership tool (found under Deform) to add, remove or transfer points between the relevant deformer sets.

    If you wish to keep the points that each cluster affects separate from the other cluster (and this technique is the same for all deformers), you can place both deformer sets into a partition. A partition is a collection of sets, but placing sets within the same partition means that the sets cannot share members. You cannot add sets to partitions if they already share members with a set that is in the partition, so you have to make sure that the items are not shared at all. One way is to edit the set membership using the techniques that we have already seen. Another is to use the advanced options in the options box when creating the deformer. These options allow you to either create a new partition when creating the deformer or to add the new deformer to existing partitions (if the new deformer has any points that are already members of another deformer set, then Maya will move them to the new deformer's set).

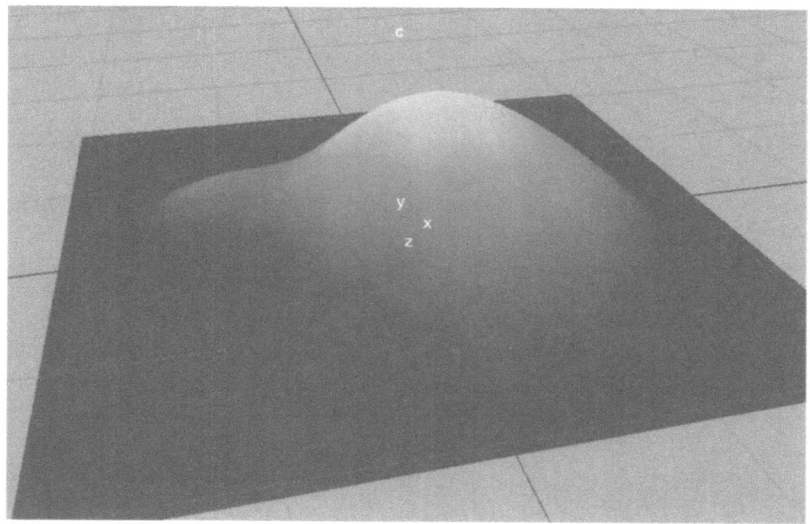

Figure 5.19 Painted Weights for the Cluster Deformation.

- Create a new NURBS plane with ten patches in u and v.
- Select two-thirds of the CVs and open the options box for Create Cluster.
- In the advanced section, turn on Exclusive, set partition to use to Create New Partition (calling this partition C1Part) and create the cluster.

Opening up the Deformer Set Editor, you should be able to see the deformer set. Change the editor to Partition Editing and you will see that the C1Part partition is visible and that it contains the newly created deformer set. With C1Part highlighted, you can select all of the members of the sets by using Edit|Select Partition Members. Select the other remaining CVs by using Shift-select as a toggle over the entire surface, plus add a few rows of CVs that are already members of the other cluster's set and open up the advanced tab in the Create Cluster options box. Keep the exclusive option checked, set the Partition to Use to C1Part and create the cluster. The new set created for the cluster will appear inside C1Part, but will not share members with any other set inside the partition.

    Turning back to deformer set editing in the Relationship Editor, you can add and remove CVs from each set as you wish.

- Select a row of CVs that the first cluster affects.
- Select its deformer set and use Edit|Remove Selected Items.
- Highlight the second deformer set and use Edit|Add Selected Items.

Alternatively, you can add or remove items from a selected set by using the plus or minus icons at the top of the Relationship Editor.

Sculpt Deformers

A sculpt deformer creates a spherical deformer (a sculpt sphere) at the centre of a selected surface or points which exerts an influence over the points, (the effect of this influence depends

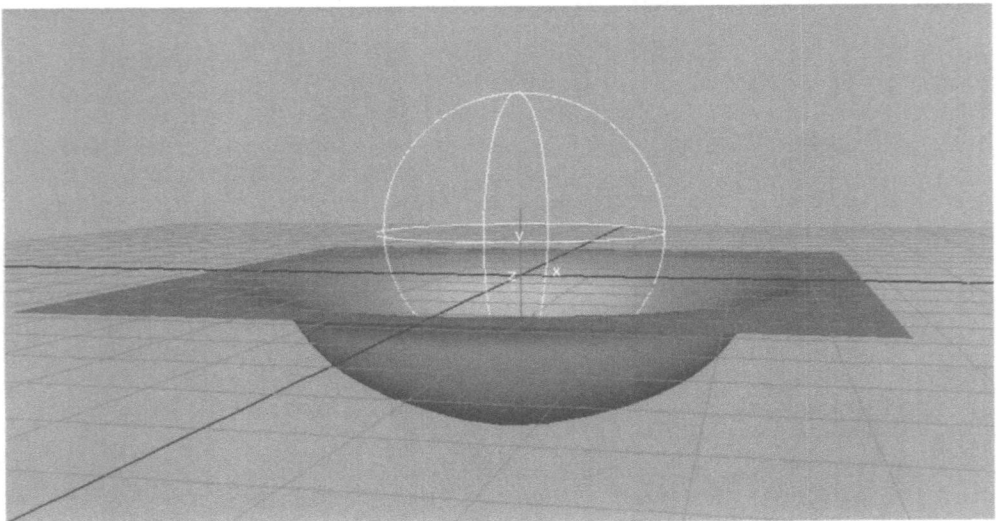

Figure 5.20 Deforming a NURBS Plane with a Sculpt Sphere.

upon the mode of the sculpt deformer). Movement and positioning of the sculpt sphere will also affect the deformed points relative to the attributes of the deformer. The sculpt deformer's modes are flip, stretch and project and are affected by additional attributes (whether set at creation time or afterwards in the Attribute Editor).

- Create a NURBS plane with ten patches in u and v and scale it ten units in all axes.
- With the plane selected, open the options box for Deform|Create Sculpt, set the Mode to Stretch and the Inside Mode to Even and click Create.

The sculpt deformer is represented as a spherical object plus there is now also a new locator. This locator is created when the sculpt deformer is in stretch mode and is known as the "base" as it allows the deformer to ascertain how far the sculpt sphere has moved and therefore how much deformation is to be applied to the set of points. Moving the sculpt sphere will deform the surface and scaling the sculpt sphere will increase the deformation across the surface as its local influence grows. With the sculpt deformer still selected, open the Attribute Editor. If you change the Inside Mode to Ring you can change the way the points are deformed inside the volume of the sculpt sphere (Even will spread the points throughout the sphere whereas Ring will tend to deform only the points near the edge of the sphere). Change the mode to Project and not much will happen; you need to change some of the other attributes:

- Move the sculpt sphere so that it is in the centre of the NURBS plane, there should be a small amount of dimpling near the sculpt sphere.
- Increase the Max Displacement attribute until a noticeable deformation begins.
- Change the Dropoff Type to Linear and the effect of the deformation will now be smoothed at the edges.
- Move the sculpt sphere up and down to see the "flip" effect.

In this respect, the Max Displacement attribute and the Dropoff Distance and Type can adjust the effect of the deformer; experiment with these while changing other attributes such as the scaling of the sculpt sphere and also the scaling of the surface itself. Setting the mode to Project will try to project the surface or the set of points onto the surface of the sculpt sphere. Changing Dropoff Distance and Max Displacement will have a pronounced effect upon the nature of this deformation type. One option which cannot be changed after creation is the option to centre the sculpt deformer within the selected surface. If this is turned off, then the sculpt deformer may be moved about until it is in the correct position to create a more localized effect. It would be difficult to create a cartoon bump rising from a character's head without moving the sculpt deformer to the top of the skull. However, it would be possible to achieve this by grouping both the sculpt deformer and the locator and then transforming the group across the surface instead.

Jiggle Deformers

This deformer is used in conjunction with other animation to create secondary animation to a surface by adding wobble or "jiggle" to it. This is useful for creating the effect of a moving volume underneath a character's skin, for example the muscle shudder that travels up a leg when a mammoth places its foot down while walking. The jiggle deformer has various attributes describing the motion of the surface in relation to any movement that has been keyed (this movement can be in the form of the standard 3D transformations or in the form of shape deformation created from the use of other deformers). The jiggle deformer can also have its weighting across a surface edited by painting in the same way that a cluster's deformation weights could be painted.

- Create a NURBS sphere and key its movement in the X axis so that it travels 10 units in 25 frames.
- Select the sphere and open the options for Deform|Create Jiggle Deformer.
- Set the Stiffness to 0.1, the Damping to 0.5 and leave the other options as they are.
- Play back the animation over 100 frames.

The entire sphere appears to jiggle when it stops, but to create a more believable jiggle it may be worth adjusting some of the deformer attributes. Select the sphere and open the Attribute Editor; the attributes for this deformer are under the Jiggle n heading. The attribute that will have the most impact on the scene is the Enable attribute which enables you to define whether the jiggle will occur at all times, when the deformer comes to a halt or not at all. Change the settings between Enable and Enable Only After Object Stops and view the difference in deformation when playing back. The stiffness and damping attributes will control how much deformation will occur by retarding the jiggling if set high and will create a more elastic and reactive effect when both set low. The direction of the jiggling can also be influenced by the Force along Normal and the Force along Tangent attributes. Once these values have been adjusted to give the correct deformation the Jiggle Weight attribute can then scale the effect over the whole surface.

   Instead of the jiggle affecting the whole surface, the artisan interface can be used to paint the deformation weight over the affected surface creating areas that will jiggle more than others.

- Select the sphere and open the painting interface by selecting the options box for Deform|Paint Jiggle Weights Tool.

- Set the Value to zero, the Paint Operation to Replace and click the Flood button so that the weights for all points are set to zero (playback will confirm that there is no jiggling happening).
- Set the value to one and paint the sphere on the side that is facing the direction of travel.
- Close the paint weights tool and play back the scene.

Now the sphere has a localized wobbling. This can be accentuated by increasing the Motion Multiplier attribute, which multiplies any effects created while the Enable attribute is set to Enable Only After Object Stops.

Two problems can arise when using this deformer in a scene, however. One is the accuracy while playing back the animation and the other is the effect on accuracy as surface complexity rises. If you scrub the time slider back and forth you will notice that Maya will not update the effect (especially if scrubbing backwards), which can make life difficult when attempting to fine-tune any jiggle effects. This is because Maya creates the deformation on an incremental basis, not as an overall deformation. If you want to see an accurate picture of the deformation on a frame-to-frame basis then you have to create a disk cache. A disk cache stores the deformation of each point for each jiggle deformer and will play these values back for the frame range that you have saved. This saves Maya trying to calculate these values and is indispensable when using multiple deformers on a character. You can also edit the accuracy of the caching by changing between Over Sample and Under Sample and using the Rate attribute to edit the frame-to-frame sampling of the deformer.

- Open the options box for Deform|Create Jiggle Disk Cache.
- Set the Cache Time Range to Time Slider and click Create.

Maya will play through each frame and save the effects to disk. Once finished you can scrub the time slider back forth and the jiggle will be played back for each frame. If you make any changes to the deformer's attributes or the object's attributes or animation then you will have to recreate the disk cache again, otherwise Maya will play back from the cache. You can also delete the cache by opening up Deform|Jiggle Disk Cache Attributes... and selecting Delete All Caches.

Lattices

A lattice is a cuboid array of points that surrounds a selected surface or points. Each of the lattice's points has a local effect over the nearby points of the object, so deformation is created when the lattice's points are moved. These points can be moved in the same manner as any other points can and can be keyed as such, the effect working on the points of a surface using deformer sets in exactly the same way that a cluster works. A lattice comes in two parts – an *influence lattice* and a *base lattice* – and it is the difference between these two shapes that determines the amount of deformation that is applied to the surface or points. A lattice allows you to create freeform deformations (FFDs) upon a surface, which is why a lattice and its base will be prefixed with "ffd".

- Create a NURBS or polygon sphere.
- With the sphere selected, create a lattice with Deform|Create Lattice without using the options.

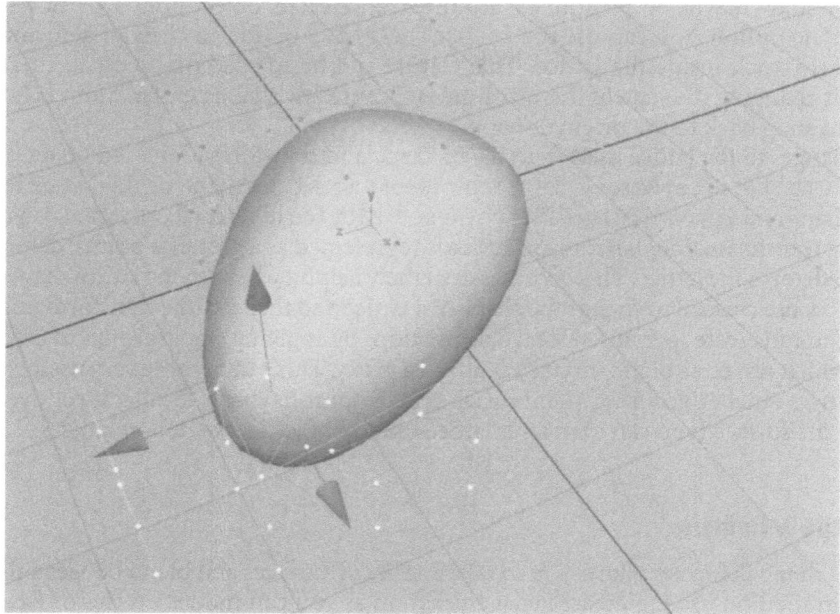

Figure 5.21 Using a Lattice to Deform a NURBS Sphere.

Surrounding the sphere will be a lattice, represented by a connected network of points in a cuboid shape. Use the RMB marking menu over this to select the lattice points and transform the lattice points in space to create local deformations on the object. If you move the lattice, the entire surface will move because the lattice is controlling all of the points. If you move the base, however, the surface will undergo a deformation as the 3D relationship between the relative shapes of the lattice and its base change. If you select the object and translate it, the surface will deform in relation to its position within the base lattice's volume. This effect can create interesting deformations based purely on the position of the object in reference to the lattice (for example, a tomato squishing as it hits the floor).

Further refinement can be made on the way that a lattice operates upon its set of points by way of the creation options. Delete the lattice and its base so that the sphere returns to its original shape, select the object and open the options box for Create Lattice. The first settings that will be immediately important are the divisions. Divisions are defined in terms of s, t, and u (the local space of the lattice) and they determine the number of lattice points that are available (this can also be changed in the Channels Box after the lattice has been created). Local mode means that each lattice point will only have an effect over the part of the surface close to it. This can be further influenced by the Local Divisions option, which sets the maximum distance (in s, t, u divisions) that a lattice point can have an effect over part of the surface. This local effect can be seen quite easily by deforming the shape of the lattice, opening up the Attribute Editor at the ffdn tab and turning local mode on and off. The options for Grouping and Parenting mean that the lattice and base can be created in a neater manner, as it will often be useful to have the lattice and base grouped together and more often than not, useful to have them parented to the surface to be deformed. When the lattice is created, you can choose whether it will be positioned around the selected object/points or not using the Positioning option. You can use the Freeze Geometry option to keep all deformed points permanently stuck inside the lattice. This feature can be toggled on or off in the Attribute Editor, but changing the state of this attribute will cause any shape deformations created while "frozen" to snap back to the original shape.

Any changes to the lattice itself in terms of shape and transformations can be reset by using Deform|Edit Lattice|Remove Lattice Tweaks to set the shape of the lattice back to its original shape and Deform|Edit Lattice|Reset Lattice to reset all operations on the lattice (including transformations). Because a lattice is represented as a group of points, deformers can be used to deform the lattice. This becomes extremely helpful when keying lattice shapes because you can now use clusters to change the shape of a lattice and then key the transform nodes of the clusters. You can create specialized local deformations by applying whole groups of deformers to a lattice, which can control the surface's shape as a proxy. This can become very useful as you are now editing a smaller group of points, each lattice point having a local control over a set of points on the surface (you can even layer lattices on top of lattices on top of lattices . . .).

Blend Shape Deformers

The blend shape deformer allows you to take a series of surfaces and blend between them. This is the main method used to create facial animation as you can model a series of facial shapes such as smiling and frowning and then use this deformer to blend between them. To use the blend shape deformer, you will need a series of target shapes and a base shape. The deformer will then deform the base shape by creating a weighted blend between the shapes of the target shapes. This deformer also creates a GUI for you to use so that the process of animating the blends is streamlined and easy to work with. The only caveats for using this deformer are that the base shapes and target shapes must be the same surface type.

- Create five NURBS spheres, name them T_Up, T_Left, T_Down, T_Right and Base, delete their histories and move them apart from each other.
- Select the CVs at the top of T_Up and move them upwards.
- Select the CVs at the left of T_Left and move them to the left.
- Select the CVs at the top of T_Down and move them downwards.
- Select the CVs at the top of T_Right and move them to the right.
- Select the target shapes and then the base shape (the base shape is always selected last).
- Open the options box for Deform|Create Blend Shape.

Two types of blend shape deformation with two types of effect can be created. It will be worth naming the blend shape node Balls as this will avoid any difficulty finding the node later on if the deformer needs to edited or deleted. The two types of blend shape deformation are determined by the Target Shape Options: if this attribute is unchecked, then there will be a slider controlling the amount of blending for each target shape. If this attribute is checked on, then there will be a single slider that will interpolate between all of the target shapes. If the blend shape style is to be In-Between then the order in which the target shapes are chosen is important, but for now, keep this option checked off. The two types of effect for the blend shape deformer are Local or World. If set to World then the blend shape deformer will take into account any changes in the target shape's transforms, if set to Local then the deformer will only include changes in the target shape's components.

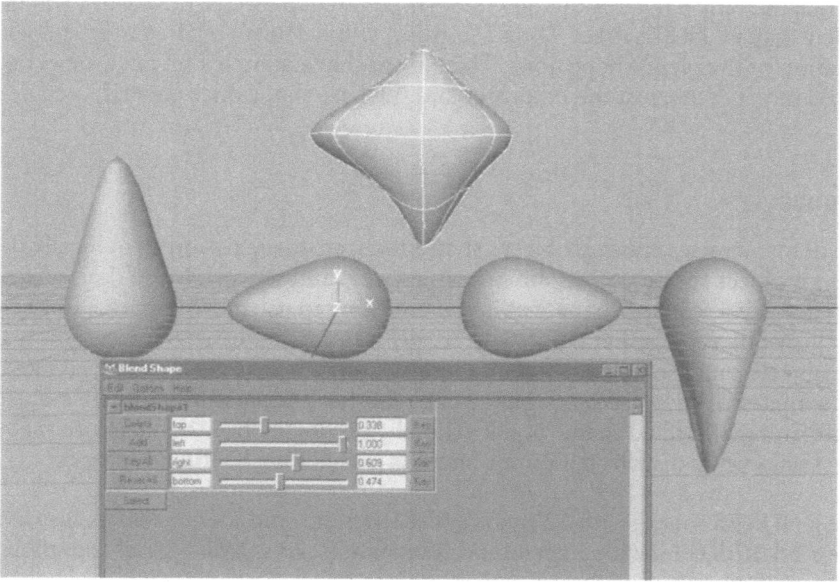

Figure 5.22 The Four Target Shapes and the Resulting Blended Base Shape.

- Set the `Origin` attribute to `Local`, turn off `In-Between` and click Create.
- Bring up the Blend Shape GUI from `Window|Animation Editors|Blend Shape...`

There is a slider for each target shape that allows you to blend and key the amount of influence each node has on the base shape. If you want a slightly more compact version of this interface, then you can change the interface style with the `Options|Orientation...` menu item. You can remove target shapes from the currently selected deformer by selecting the target shape, then the base shape and using `Deform|Edit Blend Shape|Remove`. You can add new target shapes by using `Deform|Edit Blend Shape|Add` and you can swap the order of target shapes by selecting the relevant targets and using `Deform|Edit Blend Shape|Swap`. These alternatives allow you to create a blend shape deformer and edit the target shapes that it considers as you work. So if you need to have a new shape in your deformer (if your face animation needs a sneer, for example) you can add it as required without having to create a new deformer (which would mean destroying any keys that you had set). The options for these menu items let you choose the node you are affecting and the target shape you want to add, remove or swap. As with any deformer, you can create any number of blend shape deformers for each base shape, because each blend shape deformer is a node that blends the different positions of components together. If you do need to destroy a blend shape deformer, then click the Select button for the node in the `Blend Shape` panel and press the Backspace key.

The remaining two options for the `Create Blend Shape` action are `Check Topology` and `Delete Targets`. `Check Topology` forces Maya to check that the components for the base shape and the components for the target shapes are the same. If they differ and this option is checked on, then Maya will reject the action and a blend shape node will not be created. If this option is checked off then Maya will accept any surface, irrespective of differences in their components; the only danger is that it will be impossible to foresee how Maya will interpolate the blended shapes. The `Delete Targets` option will delete all of the target shapes involved in the creation of the blend shape node. This means that a complex set of surfaces do not have to be stored in the scene, just the deformer and the base shape once created.

Wrap Deformer

The wrap deformer uses another object's shape and transform attributes to locally deform the surface of an object (these objects are known as wrap influences). More than one object can be used to deform a selected shape, but if you are going to use more than one object you must group all those objects together before you create the wrap deformer. However, note that wrap influence objects can also be added after a wrap deformer has been created; so like the Blend Shape deformer, workflow does not have to be rehashed. Because the influence object's shape will be deforming a selected shape, it will generally be worthwhile to make sure that the influence object has evenly distributed points and less points than its intended target.

- Create a NURBS sphere with 12 spans and 12 sections and then delete its history.
- Create a NURBS cone with 3 spans and 5 sections, scale it by 0.3 in all axes then delete its history and freeze its transformations.
- Move the cone so that the tip is just protruding from the top of the sphere.
- Select the sphere, then the cone and open the options box for `Deform|Create Wrap Deformer`.
- Turn on `Use Max Distance`, set the `Max Distance` to `0.1` and click Create.

If you select the cone, the sphere will turn purple to indicate that the cone is influencing the node structure of the sphere at some point. Moving the cone will pull an area of the sphere with it. This deformed area is defined by the local position of the cone's CVs relative to the CVs of the sphere and also by the `Max Distance` setting, which limits the distance at which an influence object's point can have an effect. Instead of moving the cone and influencing the sphere's shape with the cone's transform node, change into component mask mode and transform some of the cone's CVs to deform the sphere. Open the Attribute Editor and open the tab named `Wrapn`. Weight threshold will effectively alter the smoothness of the deformation effect by increasing the influence that a point has over a surface. Changing the `Max Distance` attribute will alter the area of the local effect that the influence object has over the surface (in Maya units); setting this to zero means that each CV has an infinite influence distance. To add another influence object, simply follow the same workflow as before; select the object to be deformed, Shift-select the new influence object and use `Deform|Edit Wrap|Add Influence`. Alternatively, influence objects can be removed from the deformation effects by selecting the deformed object, Shift-selecting the influence object in question and using `Deform|Edit Wrap|Remove Influence`.

Wire Deformer

The wire deformer uses a NURBS curve to locally deform surfaces. When created, the wire deformer will only deform the surface points near and along its length, whose area can be

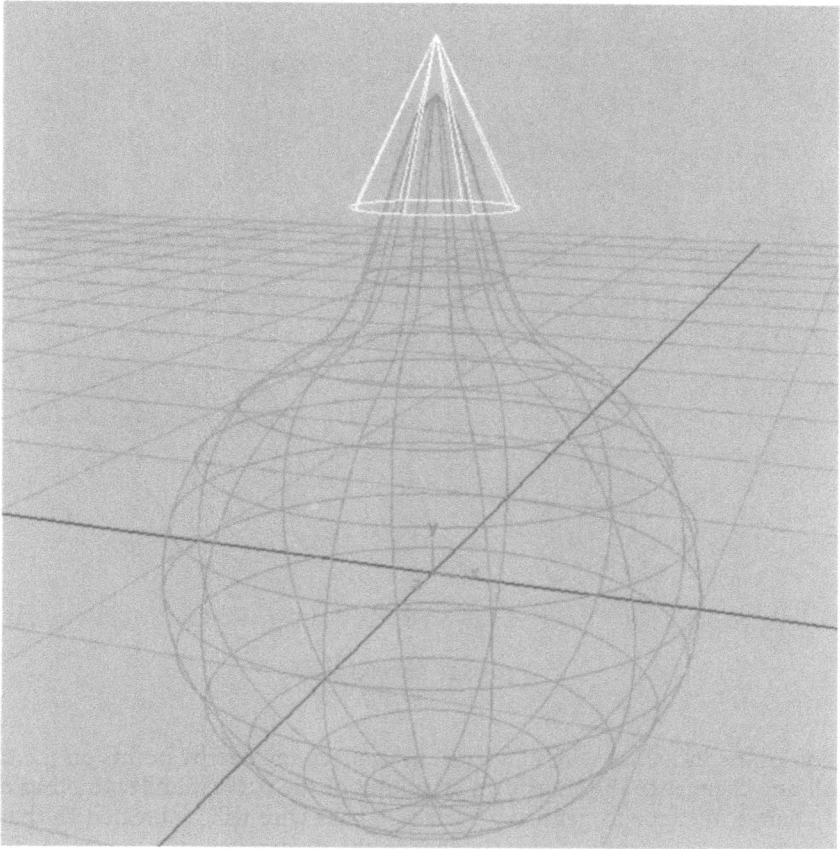

Figure 5.23 Using a Cone as a Wrap Deformer on a Sphere.

limited using several attributes or a series of curves called "holders" which define the edges of the deformation area. Wires can be easily implemented into a model and its surface using any of the curve modeling techniques, meaning that their inclusion into a character is straightforward.

- Create a NURBS cylinder with 6 spans and 12 sections, scale it three units in Y and delete its history.
- Make the surface live and use the EP curve tool to draw a curve on the surface.
- Turn off the Live action, select the curve and use Edit Curves|Duplicate Surface Curves (the wire deformer needs the curve to be defined in three dimensions not in the two U and V dimensions in which a curve on surface is defined).
- Hide the curve on surface and delete the newly duplicated curve's history.
- Activate the Wire Tool using Deform|Wire Tool and follow the instructions, picking the shape and then the curve.
- Select some of the CVs of the curve and transform them to deform the surface.

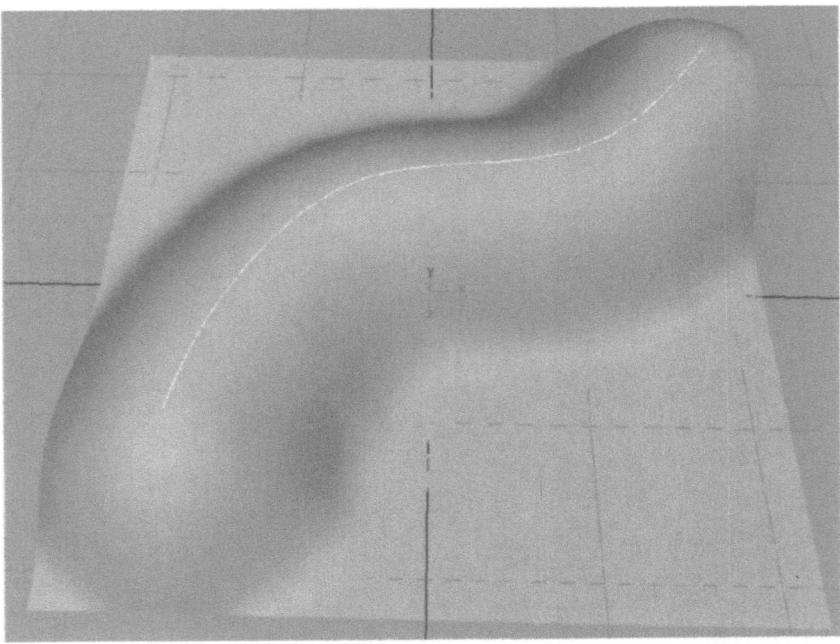

Figure 5.24 A Wire Deformer.

The position of the influence wire's CVs will now affect any nearby points on the target surface, as will any changes to the transform attributes of the curve. Similar to other deformers that use a change in shape to deform a surface, a base wire will be created so that the wire deformer node can keep track of any changes in the deforming influence wire. Turning on group checkbox in the options will group all relevant wires together (deformer, base wire and any holders). We can also turn on the display of the basewire using Deform|Edit Wire|Show Base Wire and Deform|Edit Wire|Parent Base Wire will parent both the wire deformer and the base together.

Select the surface and open the wiren tab in the inputs for the surface. The two channels that will alter the deformation right now are Scale [n] and Dropoff Distance [n]. These channels are represented with a subscript so that different influence wires can have different values for these channels. This means that the wire tool can have more than one curve when created, or new wires can be added. Select an existing influence wire, select the new curve you wish to add and use Deform|Edit Wire|Add (the inverse can be achieved using Deform|Edit Wire|Remove). Alongside these menu items, any deformations can be reset by selecting the relevant influence wire and using Deform|Edit Wire|Reset. Any of the effects for the deformer node can be changed for the entire surface using the Rotation, Local Influence and Tension attributes. When two or more wires come near each other on the deformed surface and especially if they cross each other, the effects for each adjacent wire can be controlled using the Crossing Effect attributes so that each wire has a cumulative effect or a smoothed effect.

The effects of the influence wire can be further edited by creating dropoff locators along its length. A dropoff locator defines a position along the influence curve and allows further attributes to be brought to bear on the local effect of the deformer.

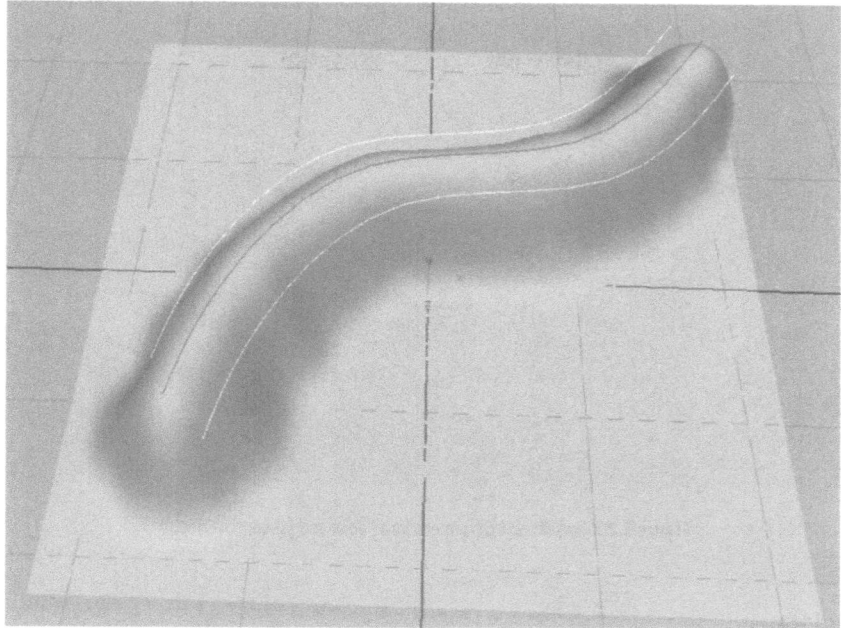

Figure 5.25 A Wire Deformer with Two Holder Wires to Limit the Deformation.

- Select the influence wire you wish to edit with locators.
- Use the RMB marking menu to change to Curve Point.
- Select a point along the curve and use Deform|Wire Dropoff Locator.

Nothing will happen when you create the locator, because it affects the wire's deformation local to its position. While the locator is selected, open the Attribute Editor and the Wiren tab and fold out the Locators heading. The attributes for each locator control the position of the locator along the curve (Param), the tangency of the surface at the locator point (Twist) and the amount of effect (Percent and Envelope).

The deformation of each influence wire can be further limited by the use of holder wires. Holder wires allow an area to be marked out on the deformed surface, so any deformation does not cross these boundaries. Holder wires can either be created when the wire deformer is created or they can be added at a later stage.

- Create a NURBS plane with ten patches in u and v and in the top view draw three roughly parallel curves.
- Open the options box for the Wire tool, turn on Holders and click the Close button.
- Follow the instructions for the tool that appear in the bottom left of the Maya GUI (to add another holder wire to the existing influence wire, you will need to select it a second time during the wire tool process).

When you now move the influence curve, the position of the holder curves will limit the deformation across the surface giving a more readily available way of affecting the deformer than changing dropoff attributes.

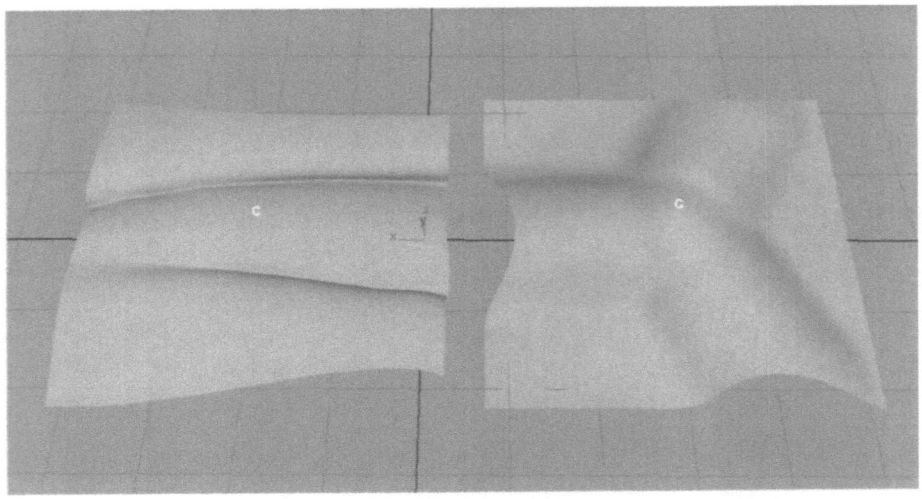

Figure 5.26 Two Wrinkle Deformers with Radial and Tangential Effects.

Wrinkle Deformer

The wrinkle deformer is a fusion of a cluster deformer that controls several wire deformers. Now that we have covered the mechanics for these two deformers, the operation and effect of wrinkle deformers will come as no surprise. They are used to provide a localized wrinkle and pinching to surfaces. Any attributes that the wrinkle deformer node contains will be from the cluster and wire deformers. The wrinkle deformer comes in three flavours: tangential, radial and custom. These flavours describe how the wrinkle will be applied across the surface. Additionally, the first two types of deformer can only affect one NURBS surface, the last can affect multiple surfaces of any description.

- Create two NURBS planes with ten patches in u and v, scale them both by ten units in all axes and move one of the planes to the left of the other.
- Deselect the patches, open the options box for the wrinkle tool from Deform|Wrinkle Tool, set the Type to Tangential and click on one of the patches.
- Red lines indicating the extents of the wrinkle deformer should enclose the patch, but for now we'll leave these alone to show the effect over the whole surface.
- Press Enter to finalize this stage of the process.
- Select the cluster handle and move it upwards to demonstrate the effect of the tangential wrinkle deformer.
- Repeat these stages but with the wrinkle tool set to Radial.

As can be seen from the radial and tangential deformers, each has a very different effect on the area chosen, which is set out by the various options for creation. The main effects of the wrinkle deformer are controlled by the transform node of the cluster handle, so not only transforming the handle, but scaling and rotating it will also affect this particular deformer. If you look in the Outliner, you can see that the wrinkle node has created a cluster handle with several influence wires grouped under it plus the accompanying base wires. We can fine tune the wrinkling effect by selecting the deformed surface and changing the attributes for the individual wire, and cluster deformers will further affect the final shape of the wrinkle deformation. Note that there is no "Wrinkle Node" per se, only a node for clusters and a node for wires in the Hypergraph and Attribute Editor.

Deformation Order

The order in which you apply deformers to surfaces will have a large impact on the final shape that is created. This becomes extremely important if you consider that characters may well have more than one deformer acting on a local surface area, such as a blend shape for the lips, wrinkle deformers near the corners of the mouth and sculpt spheres near the cheeks. The order in which you apply these deformations to a surface becomes of paramount importance.

- Create a NURBS cylinder with eight spans, scale it four units in the Y axis and duplicate it.
- Add a Bend NLD followed by a Flare NLD to the first cylinder.
- Add a Flare NLD followed by a Bend NLD to the other cylinder.
- Set the curvature attribute of each Bend handle to one and the curve attribute for each Flare handle to one.

The overall effects are very different as each cylinder has its points moved by the handles. The order in which the deformers were applied will define how the points are deformed; so for the first cylinder, the surface is bent and then has a sine wave passed through it and vice versa for the second cylinder. The main problem with this is when you decide to create and add deformers to objects and you want to change the order around. Instead of writing down a list of the deformers that you would like to have, deleting the current deformers and then recreating them in the correct order, you can simply switch the deformers' orders as they feed into the shape node of the surface. Bring up the RMB marking menu for one of the cylinders, move down to Inputs and select All Inputs ... (opening the options box for any of the current inputs will bring up the Attribute Editor). The list of all inputs for the currently selected node is here and you can change the order by simply MMB dragging and dropping one node onto another. Additionally, you can also turn off each node so that it doesn't affect the upstream node(s) that it feeds into, by changing the Node State from "normal" to "has no effect". This can also be achieved in the Attribute Editor under the Node Behaviour fold-out. Using this facility can speed up the playback or interaction of the scene if you have surfaces or a scene with many deformers.

Skeletons, Bones and Joints

In Chapter 3 we described how to create a stickman using a hierarchical structure that allowed you to change the rotations of each object to create a compound set of rotations. This structure allowed you to set up and animate your character. However, there were several limitations:

1. You could only use one method of animating.
2. You could only animate a character composed of rigid surfaces.
3. You had to build the objects and then put them into a hierarchy.
4. You could only animate the transforms of the rigid surfaces.

All of the above aren't large stumbling blocks if you wanted to animate a stick figure or robot. If you want to animate a dolphin, a hobgoblin or any character that will have the appearance of a surface being deformed by the movement of its limbs (real or not), then you will need to utilize a different set of tools.

Maya provides a set of tools that govern the creation and animation of items called *skeletons*. The analogy goes further, as these skeletons are created from connected hierarchies of *joints* and *bones* (bones being the straight connecting bits, joints being the point of rotation for the bones). Creating a skeleton is fairly straightforward and will allow you to bind a polygonal or NURBS surface to it and deform it as a result of changing the position of the skeleton's bones. One additional thing that skeletons do automatically is create a hierarchy, so when the first joint is created, the second joint will automatically be a child of this joint and will be connected with a bone. This should begin to address some of the limitations identified above.

Bones, Joints and Forward Kinematics: Setting up the Skeleton

Pop the side view to the foreground and create a new shelf called Skel to hold the new tools you are going to be using. To draw a skeleton, use the Joint tool underneath the Skeleton menu heading. Open up the options box for the Joint tool, because analogous to a real skeleton, a skeleton in Maya is the underpinning for animating a character and choices that are made at this point can have important ramifications further down the line.

In the Joint tool options box, there are three types of option that are of concern at this point: degrees of freedom, orientation and scaling. The "degrees of freedom" options will control which axes the joints can rotate in, the "orientation" options will also affect the local axis of each joint and the "scale compensation" option determines whether a child will inherit its parent's scaling. Only the first of these options can be changed in the Attribute Editor after creation, so deciding which manner of creation options you wish to use will have an impact on how much work you need to do on the skeleton in order to have it functioning correctly. We shall explain how to create a small three-bone hierarchy using different options to see how these affect the function of each skeleton. For now, leave the options as they are. The first click in the window will place the first joint, which will be the root of the skeleton hierarchy; the next LMB click will place the second joint, which will automatically be connected by a bone to the joint preceding it. You can drag the position of a joint around (until you release the LMB) in the same fashion that you could when placing CVs while drawing curves. If you place a joint and decide that it was the wrong one, then pressing Backspace will delete the current joint but you'll still be able to place a fresh joint down as the Joint tool will still be active. To finish drawing a skeleton, just press Return and this will finish the process and pick the select tool as the current tool.

Joint Orientation

Notice how the cross in the centre of each joint orients itself to the next joint when you draw it. This is the local axis of each joint and corresponds to the orientation of the rotation handles when using the rotate tool. Joint orientation, as set in the options, will affect how each joint's local rotation axis is aimed. If set to x,y,z then the X axis of each joint will aim towards the next joint (thus the X rotation handle will be perpendicular to this axis), the Y axis will point at right angles to the X axis and the Z at right angles to these, all according to the right-hand rule of axis orientation. What this means is that the local rotation axes can be

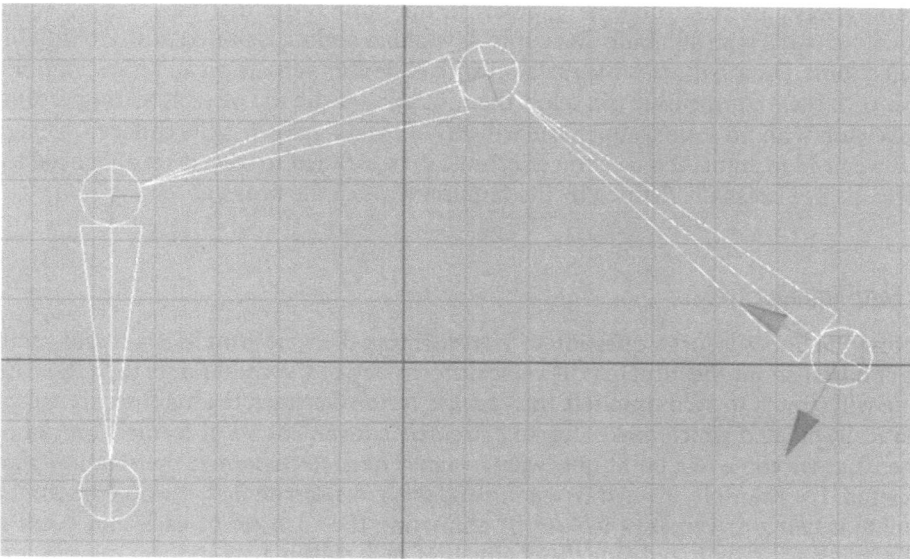

Figure 5.27 A Three-Bone Hierarchy.

pre-set before you create the skeleton by changing this setting, so create a series of three-bone skeletons with different settings to explore how these affect your skeleton. If you set the Auto Joint Orient to None the local axis for each joint will be aligned with the global axis. This may not be much use, but it could mean that if you draw your skeleton in the side view, then all the joints will all rotate about the Y axis in the same manner which brings us to an extremely important point about animating using the rotate tool – there are three incarnations of the rotate tool: global, local and gimbal. Select a joint and double-click on the rotate tool icon to bring up the options for this tool (double-clicking on all icons in the toolbox will bring up an options box if it has one) and set the Rotate Mode to Global. The rotate handles will be aligned to the scene global axis and if you rotate the joint using the X axis handle, you will see that the rotation for the joint in the Channels Box is not in the X axis. Change the rotate mode to Local and the rotation handles will now orient them with the local axis of the joint, ensuring that the handles and the axis are correct – rotate in Z and the rotateZ channel will be affected. The last mode is Gimbal and ensures that only one axis can be rotated about at any one time (local may still transform an item in more than one axis) – so there is no perpendicular yellow ring about the rotate manipulator. Gimbal mode is important because when rotation channels are animated, the order of the rotation animation will affect the final orientation of the item and this is dependent on the rotate order.

Select a joint and open the Attribute Editor. There is a fold-out menu labeled Rotate Order and this will hold every combination of X, Y and Z. This will control the order in which each channel is evaluated (first, second or third) by Maya when rotating the object over time. So if the rotate order is x,y,z and you animate the object rotating X then Z then Y, the object will have the channels animated differently to the way you intended. If you apply X, Y, Z rotations in a different order then you will have a different composite rotation and this will greatly impact how any animation works. So when rotating any object for animation, use Gimbal mode and always animate rotation channels in the same order that they will be evaluated. Scale compensate is an attribute that controls whether scaling is passed down to the children of a scaled joint. Draw a three-bone skeleton with scale compensate on and draw a three-bone skeleton with scale compensate off, select the root joint at the top of each hierarchy and scale it, the skeleton with no scale compensate will pass all scaling down to its children. This can be useful if we need to adjust the skeleton size, but can be difficult to reset if we only need to scale one bone. Its use is usually defined by the requirements of the project.

Editing Local Rotation Axes

Animating the bones is just a question of transforming the root joint in space and rotating it and its children about the local axis. If we transform any of the child joints then the connecting bone will stretch to accommodate this change. In the Outliner, the hierarchy has also been automatically created which makes for an extremely convenient set of features for animation purposes. But we come to a point now when we may need to customize the rotation planes of our skeleton. For example, if we draw a hand and wish to animate that, it would be convenient to animate it using driven keys instead of animating the rotation of each and every finger bone. Driven keys ask you to define the channels of each driven item and you can select multiple objects at once. It is obviously going to be more straightforward if you drive only one rotation channel for every finger bone, being that they are all hinge joints and will only use a single axis for animation. But the Auto Joint Orient function can often place the axes of each joint incorrectly as Maya tries a best guess policy, so you are going to need a method of re-orientating the local axes of joints to allow you to animate correctly. In this example, you are going to draw a simple hand and look at some of the issues that arise, not only while creating but also when starting to set up the skeleton for animating.

- Pop the top view to the foreground and with the joint tool set to x,y,z, all of the degrees of freedom ticked and with scale orient on.
- Place the first bone in the view and then draw the first finger (this is where using the "snap to grid" aid can become very useful).
- Without pressing Enter to end creation, move back up the current hierarchy using the up arrow key until you are at the root joint again.
- Draw the next finger and use the arrow key to traverse the hierarchy and then draw the last finger.
- Press Enter to finalize the skeleton.

To check if one of the fingers will rotate correctly about a single axis, select the joint at the top of the finger and use Edit|Select Hierarchy. This will select all joints in the skeleton hierarchy (check the outliner for confirmation) and allow the same rotation value to be passed to each selected joint's channel. Using the rotate manipulator, rotate in the Y axis to clench the finger and repeat for each finger. If all of the fingers rotate and "clench" correctly then you've been lucky and Maya has orientated the rotation axes as you wished. Draw the hand again and you may find that the axes aren't working in the way you want, meaning that the behaviour of the joint tool is unpredictable and should be watched. So if you have a finger that is rotating incorrectly, it means that the local axis of some or all of the joints needs to be re-aligned to suit your purposes. In this case it means that you want them to rotate around the Y axis uniformly so that a driven key can easily be created.

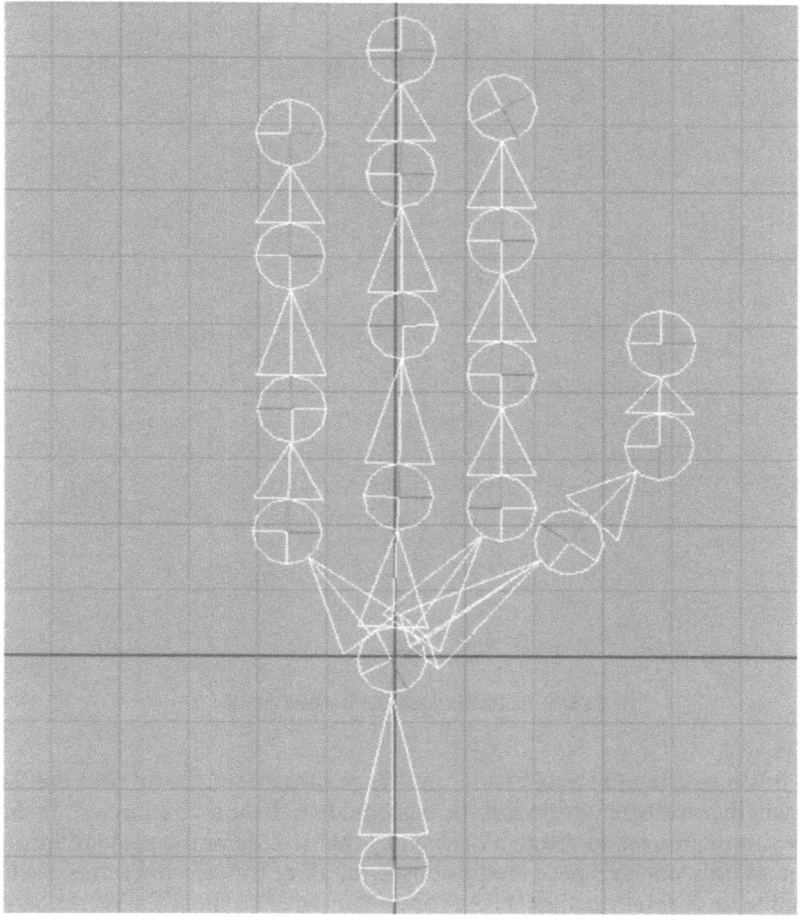

Figure 5.28 The Finished Hand.

Set all rotation values back to 0, select all the bones of one finger and use Display| Component Display|Local Rotation Axes. Now you can see the orientation of each local axis for each joint and see that some of them aren't orientated correctly. If you don't wish to display these axes, the command acts as a toggle. You can now rotate them so that they are all aligned in the same direction and because your finger joints are all hinge joints, you only need the Y axis of each joint to point in the same direction.

- Look for an axis that is orientated incorrectly and change to component mask mode.
- Turn all component masks off and then LMB click on the question mark mask icon (RMB clicking will display the underlying choices) to activate a mask of type Local Rotation Axes.
- Select the local rotation axis in question and use the rotate tool to change its direction so that it matches the other axes in the hierarchy (use the rotate tool in Local mode for this as Gimbal will not work).
- Go back to object mask mode and now rotate all of the bones in the finger hierarchy.

Figure 5.29 The Local Rotation Axes Aligned in the Hand.

This can also be done using the Skeleton|Orient Joint action (the options are for the orientation and whether the orientation is to be passed down the joint hierarchy). It should now be a relatively simple process to create a driven key that will drive the same rotation channel for each finger, as only one axis needs to be chosen for all of the selected joints. Save a button for displaying the local rotation axes (LRAs) onto your shelf so that this operation is quicker when toggling the display for each selected joint. When creating a more complex skeleton, there are tools to aid the process, as different hierarchic sections will have to be added or subtracted until the correct shape is achieved. This editing process is as quick and expedient as possible, meaning that you will be able to spend more time on creating the correct structure, without having to delete everything and start all over because you forgot to include something. It also means that you can create a rough understructure for a character and only add more complex pieces when you need to or when you have created them. For example, you could draw the character's skeleton and attach the hands with full driven key functionality at a later time, allowing you to use this rough skeleton straightaway.

Drawing a Skeleton

We're going to extend our range of tools now, by creating a skeleton for a humanoid character. First, the spine and the hips will be created and the limbs will be added as necessary. Draw the first joint (the root of the entire hierarchy) in the front view and place the next joint fractionally above this first joint. This allows you to isolate the root of the hierarchy, which will be important later on when you start animating.

- With the tool still active, pop the side view to the foreground and draw a curved spine.
- Use the arrow keys to traverse the hierarchy back down to the root joint and pop the front view to the foreground.
- Draw the hip joint to the side of the root joint.
- Draw the thigh and the shin bones and press Enter to complete the process.

Before adding more limbs to the skeleton, it is worth doing a little bit of editing. Select the knee joint and open the Attribute Editor. This knee joint is a hinge joint and you can edit its behaviour so that it won't be accidentally rotated in the wrong axis. Open the fold-out menu labeled Joint and turn off the axes which won't apply under Degrees of Freedom, so that when you use the rotate tool in Gimbal mode, all the irrelevant axes are greyed out as well as in the Channels Box. While the Attribute Editor is open, you can also control how far this joint will rotate as well, so that it won't be rotated by accident past a certain point. Open the fold-out section labeled Limit Information and fold out the sub-section labeled Rotate. Only the axes that have freedom of movement will be available for editing and you can define a maximum and minimum rotation value for each selected joint using this section. Rotate the knee joint so that it is just forward of the thighbone and if it is a positive number, click the arrow button that points to "max" (and vice versa). Rotate the knee joint so that it is fully bent in accordance with the natural bending of the knee and click the arrow key pointing to "min" or vice versa. Now you will not be able to rotate the knee joint past these set limits.

Editing the behaviour of the bones is useful, because it allows you to start defining characteristics of how the skeleton moves which will have an effect on how the skeleton is animated. If you set all of the bones to have a very small rotation range, then you could make the action of the skeleton mimic a very old character by restricting the options that an animator would have. When setting up joints in this manner, always have an idea of what you or the animator will require from a situation, especially if the animator will be wanting to use extremes of rotation such as breaking of limbs to exaggerate speed. This type of set up should be done with the animation requirements of each character and project in mind.

In the spine, you may need to edit the actual position of the joints and also whether you need to include or remove any joints (you can leave the rotation freedom of each joint alone, as the spine should be as flexible as possible). In the side view, zoom in on the spine so it is clearly visible. There should be a larger proportion of smaller bones on the lower half of the spine than in the upper half, as it is this area that will have the most flexibility (again, depending on the character) and you should move each joint until the correct shape is achieved. Normally, if you move a joint, it will move all of its children, which can be inconvenient if it is the position of this joint that is incorrect. You can move the selected joint by moving it as you would move a pivot point. In fact, you are just moving a pivot point, because apart from being in a hierarchy, that is all a joint essentially is.

- Select a joint in the spine that could do with being repositioned.
- Press the Insert key and now move the joint.
- When the joint has been repositioned, press Insert again.

If you wish to delete a joint or insert a joint into the existing skeleton, you can use specialized tools and actions in Maya. To remove a joint, simply select the joint in question and use Skeleton|Remove Joint which will then connect the parent of the removed joint to the next joint. To add another joint into the hierarchy use the Insert Joint tool found under the Skeleton heading. This will ask you to pick the joint that you wish to insert the new joint after, so just drag the new joint to the correct position. Place these tools onto your shelf, as you will be using them time and time again as you edit the skeleton's shape.

Now that the skeleton has a leg, a spine and a hip, you need to add an arm to the spine. You should think about what kind of joint set-up to use, because one thing that a skeleton can be used for is to deform geometry so that it acts as a skin to the character. As such, the skeleton should allow some minor articulation in the shoulder area instead of the skeleton just moving the arm from the shoulder mimicking the movement of the clavicle and shoulder blade (look at how the shoulder moves when you raise your arm above your head). Afterwards you will need to connect your arm hierarchy to the main skeleton.

- Pop the front view to the foreground and draw the clavicle and then the arm.
- Select the end of the arm hierarchy, Shift-select the spine joint that you wish to connect to and then open up the options for Skeleton|Connect Joint.
- Set the mode to Parent Joint and click Connect.

The two hierarchies should now be merged into one with a connecting bone.

Two other ways to perform this operation would have been to use Edit|Parent or to MMB drag and drop the arm root joint onto the selected spine joint in the Outliner. All these different operations do is to create a new hierarchical connection, which the joints and bones interpret in a correct manner. Conversely, you can detach joints by selecting them and using Edit|Unparent, use the MMB to drag and drop the joint out of the hierarchy and into a separate place in the Outliner or use Skeleton|Disconnect Joint. Make sure you set up the attributes for the elbow joint, in the same way as you did for the knee joint. Using the same method, draw three bones for the head in the side view and connect it to the top of the spine.

Mirroring Joints

Now that half of the skeleton is created, you can mirror the leg and arm in the same way that you mirrored the leg and arm of the stickman created earlier. One of the useful things about mirroring joints is that any joint attributes that have been set up (such as degrees of freedom), will be copied onto the mirrored joints. If you set up attributes for each joint section as you go along, you will really only have to do half the work in comparison to the number of joints. Also, the mirrored joints will be automatically connected to the main hierarchy. The options for mirroring are whether you choose to mirror the behaviour or the orientation of the selected joints, which plane you wish to mirror across and whether a search/replace for text needs to be done on the new joints so their names conform to the other names in the hierarchy. Mirroring orientation means that the new LRAs will be aligned with the original LRAs so that rotations will be applied in the same direction.

- Select the top of the leg and open the options box for Skeleton|Mirror Joint.
- Set the Mirroring Plane to yz, the Function to Orientation and click Mirror.
- Select both knee joints and rotate them so that both legs are bent.

Select both the thigh joints and rotate them in the X axis. With the orientation mirrored, both legs should rotate in the same direction. Delete the new leg and repeat the above process, but with the function set to Behaviour, and now when you rotate both hip joints, the rotations should be mirrored. How you have this set up will be dependent upon what the character will

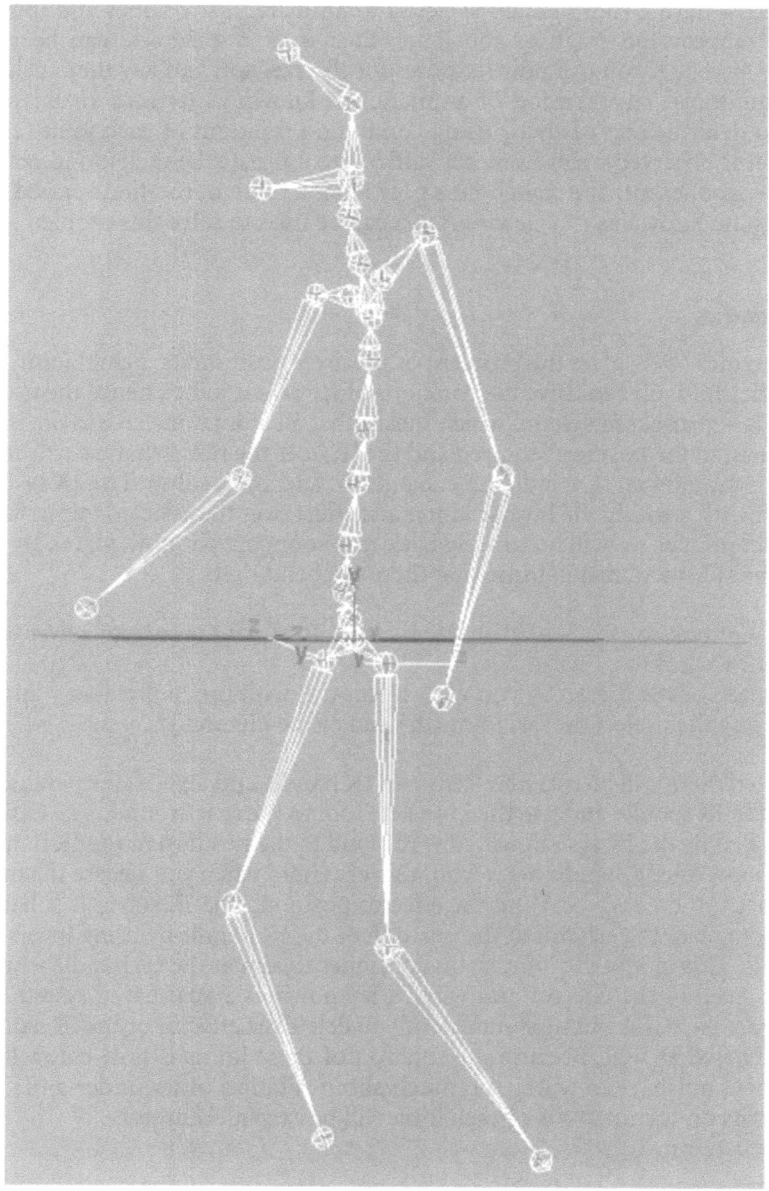

Figure 5.30 The Finished Skeleton.

be doing and how you want to animate it. Select the arm and mirror it with the function still set to Behaviour and you will probably find it more convenient to animate using this set-up as one arm's movement will tend to mirror the other when moving away from the torso. If you find that the rotations are incorrect then you can just delete the sections and re-mirror them, or just rotate the relevant LRAs for each joint until they satisfy requirements.

You should now have a rudimentary skeleton to animate. If the bones and joints that have been created appear too small or too large, then their display size can be altered using Display|Joint Size. You can now set poses for the skeleton and key them using the translate and rotate tools. This method of animation is known as *forward kinematics* (FK) and allows you to describe arcs easily by using compound rotations of each joint (as long as the rotation order is observed). However, it is difficult to animate the skeleton to reach for a precise point in space because the child bone's position is a result of rotations passed to it from its parents. A system known as *inverse kinematics* can be used to solve this problem.

Inverse Kinematics

Inverse kinematics (IK) solves the problem of precisely positioning a child joint, by using the position of the child joint to drive the rotations of its parent joints, hence the use of the term "inverse". IK is a goal-based system, which means that all animators have to do, is to move the end of the chain to the position required and the IK does the rest. What we will create is an IK system, which contains an IK handle, an end effector and an IK solver. This IK system will then concern itself with creating the inverse kinematic effect over the selected joints. Save the scene with the skeleton in as we will be coming back to it soon, but for now, just draw a three joint skeleton in the side view, making sure that there is a bend in it.

- Open the options box for Skeleton|IK Handle Tool, set the current solver to SC Solver and close the window.
- Select the top of the hierarchy you wish to control with the tool cursor – in this case the shoulder and then select the last joint (the end of the hierarchy).

In the Outliner, there will be two new items: an IK handle and an effector parented to the last joint. Select the IK handle and use the Translate tool to move it around. The entire hierarchy that is controlled by the IK system will now respond to the position of the IK handle by rotating. You can move the IK handle away from the joints and when you release the mouse button it will snap back to the last joint and the effector position. The IK solver is solving the problem of trying to place the effector at the position of the IK handle by using inverse kinematics to achieve this. This is why the joint chain continues to aim at the IK handle when you move it out of the reach of the effector and why IK is known as a goal-based system. All of these components are part of the same system, so if you delete the effector or the IK handle, then the rest will be deleted as well. Because the rotation of these joints is now controlled by an IK system, you will not have to worry too much about rotation order under an IK system, but setting up limits on the rotations of each joint will be extremely useful.

Single Chain IK Solvers

Open up the scene with the skeleton that you have created, so that you can now implement IK systems into the arms and legs. First, delete any keys that you may have created and set the rotation of any of the limbs back to zero so that they are completely straight. With the solver type set to SC solver create an IK system for each leg, select one of the IK handles and open up the Attribute Editor. However, if you try and move the IK handle, it will be impossible. This is because you created the joints for the leg straight and the IK solver does not know which way to bend the legs.

- Delete both IK handles.
- Select a knee joint and rotate it back a little.
- Move the cursor over the joint and use the RMB to bring up a marking menu.
- Select Set Preferred Angle, release the RMB and set the rotation of the knee joint back to zero.
- Create a new IK handle for the leg.

If you move the new IK handle, the leg will rotate in the direction of the preferred angle, so do the same for the other leg. Now select an IK handle, open the Attribute Editor and fold out the section labeled IK Handle Attributes and set Stickiness to Sticky. You should see a red dot appear at the position of the IK handle, repeat this for the other IK handle on the other leg. If you now select the root of the hierarchy and move the whole skeleton up and down, the IK handle will stay in one place forcing the legs to bend. This Stickiness attribute mimics the function of an IK handle when keyed, allowing you to test and edit the behaviour of our animation controls before we start animating. Once an IK handle has been placed into a joint system, it will be copied across to the new set of joints if the Mirror Skeleton function is used, again letting you only work on one half of the skeleton.

Rotate Plane IK Solvers

The type of solver that we are currently using is called an "SC solver" in the tool options, which stands for "single chain solver". This type of IK solver will attempt to position the effector where the IK handle is and match its position and orientation. But it will not be able to change the orientation of the whole leg in terms of twisting, such as turning the feet inward or outward. To accomplish this, you will have to use the other solver – the RP solver, which stands for "rotate plane". The RP solver will only try and match the position of the effector to the position of the IK handle, orientation is controlled by a different method, but this does allow us far more control over the joints and their rotation. Delete the IK handles for the legs, set the solver type in the IK Handle Tool options to RP solver and then create an IK system for each leg.

   The first difference that this new type of IK solver contains is that at the top of the IK system is a rotate plane. This plane is perpendicular to the handle vector (the line that runs between the top of the IK system and the effector) and shows how rotation will affect the leg. There is another disc at the bottom of the IK system called the twist disc and this will control the twisting of the joints controlled by the IK handle.

- Select the IK handle and activate the Show Manipulator tool.
- Select the Twist Disc at the bottom of the IK system and MMB drag to twist the joints changing the value of the Twist channel in the Channels Box.

As you twist the joints a white triangle in the rotate plane moves with the joints. This indicates the orientation of the joint system showing which direction it will bend in and it also describes the plane that this joint chain lies in, called the "joint chain plane". Additionally, there is also a Translate manipulator with a green line attached to the start joint of the system. This is the pole vector and creates another plane known as the "reference plane". It is the difference in position as measured about the rotate plane's axis (the handle vector) that tells Maya which way the joint chain is facing and which way it will bend.

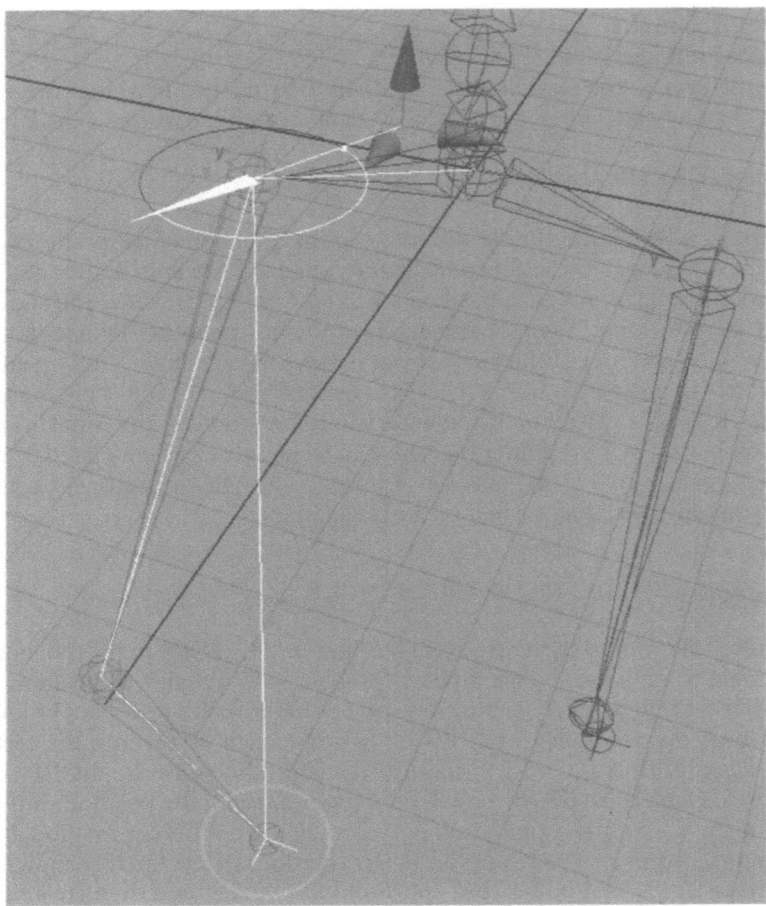

Figure 5.31 An IK Handle with the Rotate Plane and the Pole Vector.

If you move the pole vector around using its translate handles, the joint chain will twist again. However, you do not have two ways of controlling the orientation of the joint chain. Due to the mathematics of inverse kinematics, if the reference plane and the joint chain plane ever cross each other, the entire joint chain will flip over by 180 degrees. So the pole vector is used to stop this happening and the twist plane is used to control the orientation of the joints. All you need to make sure is that the white Joint Plane Indicator is kept away from the pole vector indicator while animating.

Pole Vectors and Joint Flipping

Making sure that the pole vector is in a certain position as indicated and using the Show Manipulator tool to keep it away, can become tiresome when animating, especially as we keep

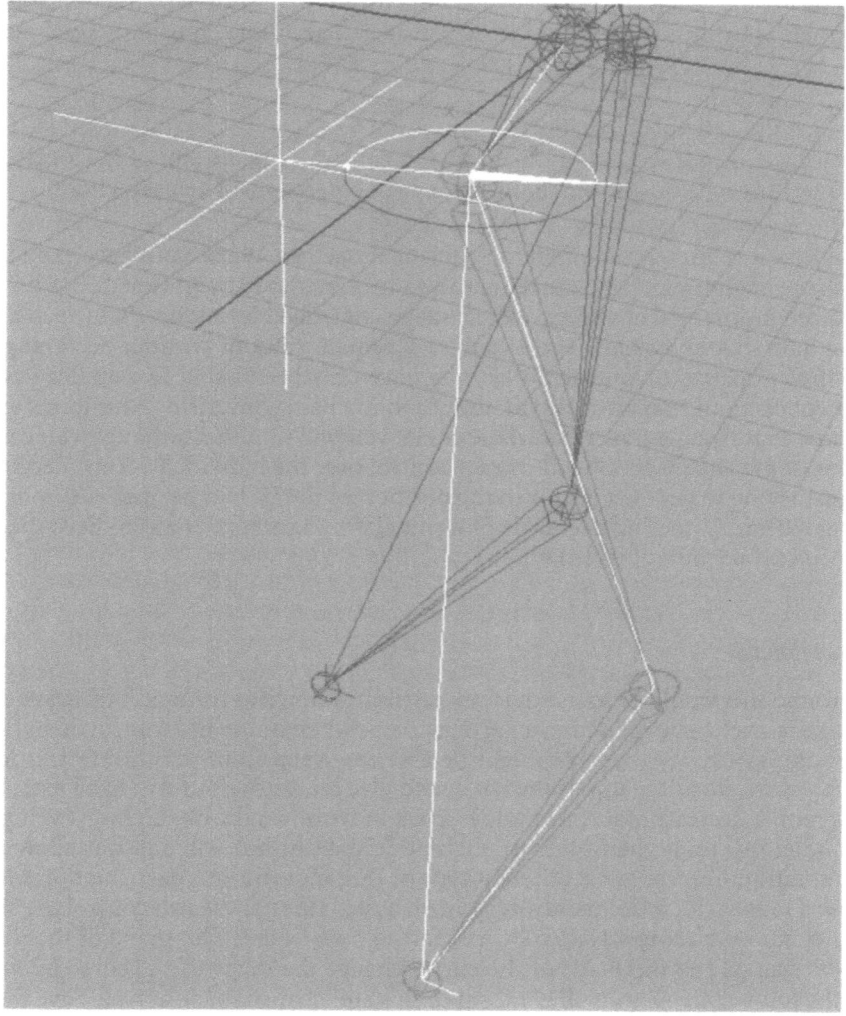

Figure 5.32 The Pole Vector Constraint Linked to a Locator.

changing context as far as tools go. So Maya has a specialized constraint called a "pole vector constraint" that allows you to control the position of the pole vector using a locator.

- Create a locator, position it behind one of the leg joints and name it PVL01.
- Select the PVL01, Shift-select the IK handle for that joint chain and use Constraint|Pole Vector.
- Now change the Twist channel to 180 so the legs can be bent in the correct orientation.

Now as long as the joint chain plane does not cross the reference plane while you animate, the leg should not flip. If it does, all you have to do is to animate the position of the pole vector by translating the locator instead.

Set up IK handles and pole vector constraints for the arms of the character. The only area left to animate is the head and the spine. The head can be animated using several methods:

1. Forward kinematics.
2. Driven keys to control orientation.
3. By creating a locator in front of the head and constraining the aim of the local axis to the position of the locator (setting up the neck LRA correctly will be useful here).

The spine, however, presents a different problem altogether. We need to have explicit control over the shape of the spine while making the control method straightforward. This problem extends to other objects that will have their shape controlled by a joint chain such as a tentacle, an elephant's trunk or hair. The shape must remain sinuous without becoming a nightmare for the animator to control. So far, you have only been using IK handles to control a chain of two joints and no more. If you draw a joint chain comprising four joints and create an IK handle that stretches over the whole chain, you will find that although you can control the skeleton somewhat, it is difficult to gain control over the individual joints. Because the IK solver is just trying to get the effector to the position of the IK handle, the local control is lost and is no good for animating a tentacle or a spine, where you may want to have specific flexing in a localized portion of its length.

The IK Spline Handle

One way round this would be to use the joint attribute known as stiffness. Stiffness determines the joint's resistance to be rotated in a particular axis when under the control of an IK handle. This attribute is one way that you might be able to give a simple control to this long joint chain. Select the joint at the top of the chain and give it a stiffness of five in all axes, then give each child joint a decreasing stiffness value as you move down the hierarchy. Now if you move the IK handle, this joint chain will act slightly differently, but will still not allow any local change in rotation. You can use a different type of IK handle for this particular problem when controlling a long series of joints: an IK spline handle. This handle will control the shape of a long joint chain by placing a NURBS curve through its length. The shape of the joint chain will then be snapped to the shape of the curve; change the shape of the curve by moving its CVs and the joint chain shape will conform to this and change shape as well. Save the current scene and draw a long joint chain in the side view. Select the IK Spline Handle tool from the Skeleton menu heading and create the handle from the start of the joint chain to the end of the joint chain. In the Outliner and in the current view you should see that a curve has been created along with an IK handle and an effector. Select the curve, change into component mask mode, move the CVs about and this will now change the shape of the joint chain (using the stiffness attribute of each joint along this chain can still affect the animation especially if on a spinal column).

To animate this shape change over time, the position of the CVs need to be keyed. What can often make this task easier is to cluster each of the CVs responsible for the curve's shape so that you don't have to switch between object and component mask mode in order to animate your character's skeleton. You can also display the selection handles for clusters so that each cluster is in easy reach. Remember that clusters can hold CVs with different weights and overlap between different clusters, which can allow you to create a more subtle control method over the IK spline. The only thing that cannot be changed using the curve shape is twisting of the

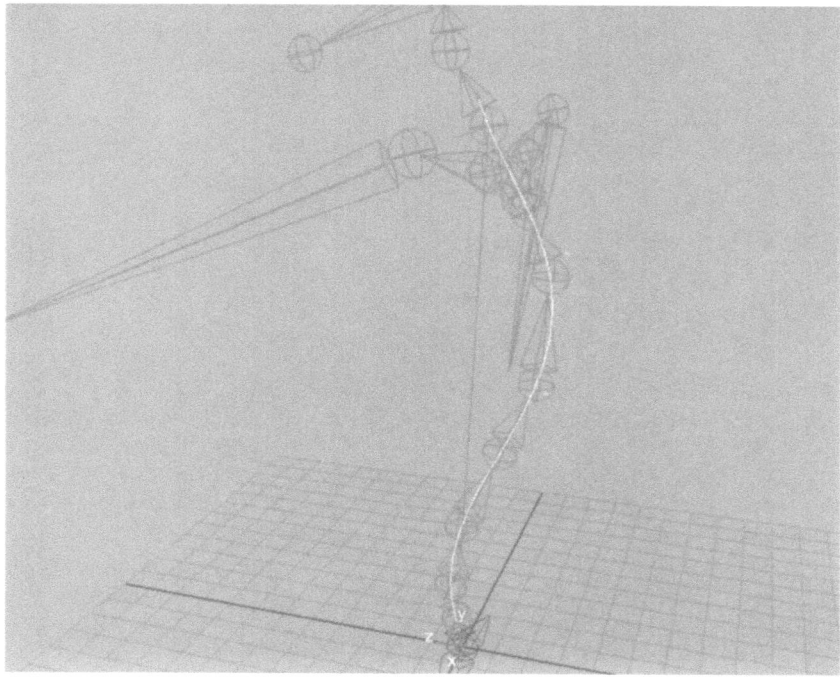

Figure 5.33 The IK Spline Handle Controlling the Bones in the Spine.

joint chain, so select the IK handle and select the Show Manipulator tool. Two rotate planes will appear at the top and bottom of the IK spline, which drive the Roll and Twist channels of the IK spline handle respectively. These can be manipulated using the MMB, LMB or in the Channels Box to change the rotation of the joints along the length of the affected chain and give a useful twisting effect (such as the roll of a character's shoulders and waist when walking). By default, the Twist attribute will have a linear effect across the whole joint chain, but this can be changed in the Attribute Editor. Select the IK spline handle, open the Attribute Editor and fold out the menu labeled IK Solver Attributes. The Twist Type attribute can now be changed from Linear to various other choices. These other options will determine the strength of the twisting along the joint chain, so Ease Out will twist the joint chain more at the start than at the end.

The default creation options for the IK Spline Handle may not create a NURBS curve with enough CVs, so delete the IK handle and open the options box for the IK Spline Handle tool. Set the number of spans to 4 and create the IK spline handle now; there should be a large amount of CVs giving greater control over the shape of the curve. If you should need even more CVs then turn off the Auto Simplify Curve option and one CV will be created for every joint. The simplest way to animate and control the shape of an IK spline is to use a cluster for each CV, so be efficient with the number of CVs that you create on the curve. Otherwise it can become a little unwieldy to animate. Remember that you will be editing the shape of the curves between the keys in the Graph Editor, so the more clusters keyed, the more curves and tangents, so try to find an optimum number of CVs for the IK spline handle. It is possible to

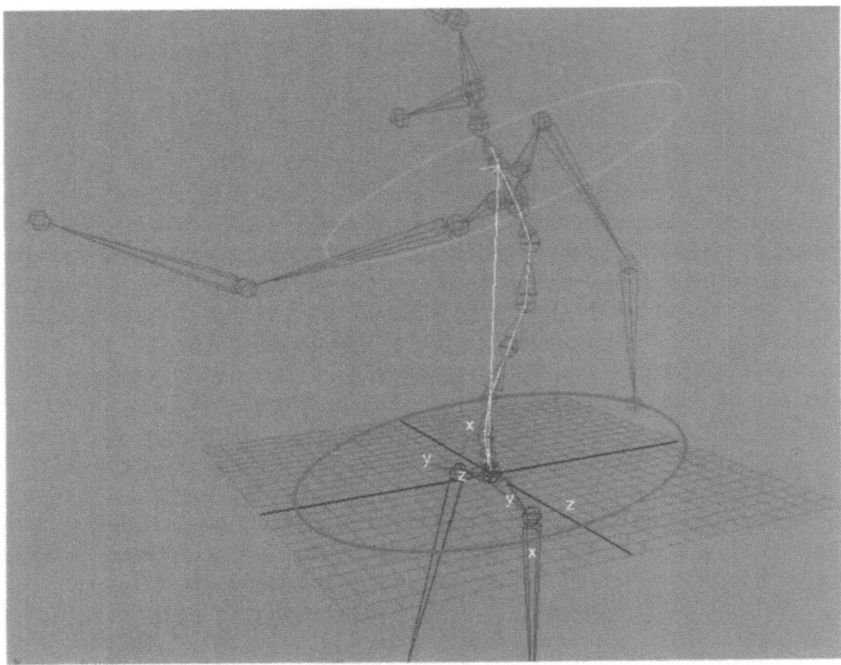

Figure 5.34 The Rotate Disks in the IK Spline Handle Twisting the Upper and Lower Halves of the Skeleton.

supply your own curve – by turning off the `Auto Create Curve` option, the IK Spline Handle tool will then ask for the curve to be picked after you have defined the start and end of the joint chain. If the `Snap Curve to Root` option is on, the curve will be placed at the start of the joint chain, otherwise the joint chain will be moved to the curve's position.

Using the IK spline handle, you can animate the motion of a snake across the floor by using a combination of options:

- Draw a seven joint chain in the Top view and draw a long curve across the view that will represent the path of the snake.
- In the IK Spline Handle tool, turn off the `Auto Create Curve` option and the `Snap Curve to Root` and select the start and the end of the joint chain and then select the path.
- Use the `Offset` attribute in the Channels Box to move the joint chain along the curve.

Even more interesting effects can be created if you turn off the `Root on Curve` option, as this will allow you to move the entire joint chain off the curve by translating the root joint.

Switching between IK and FK

Now that the skeleton is set up, you can begin to animate it using the IK handles. An IK handle is not very good at precise arcs; try moving just the forearm of the skeleton or any child limb in an IK-controlled chain. Because the IK solver is only trying to solve the problem of putting the effector where the IK handle is in space, the relative rotation of the joints is of no concern. It is possible to switch between using IK and FK while animating, but it is important to decide how you are going to be working. The best way to work is if you know that you are going to be using combinations of IK and FK, and this will come from knowing what the character will be doing in the scene. Set keys for the IK handle's position by using `Animate|IK/FK Switching Keys|Set IK/FK Key` and at the point that you wish to change over to FK, turn off the IK solver using `Animate|IK/FK Switching Keys|Enable IK Solver`. Once the Solver has been turned off, select the joint you wish to animate and on the frame in which you turned off the IK Solver, use y to set an FK key. When you want to switch back to IK, turn on the IK Solver, select the IK handle and set an IK/FK switching key and carry on keyframing with this method. This will then allow you to add precise FK animation at any time.

If you wish to insert FK animation into an IK-controlled skeleton that has already been keyed using translation keys, you will have to key the `Solver Enable` attribute of the IK handle to "on" at the start of the scene's animation. You will have to define a range in time that the IK animation will be overwritten, so at the end of the section that you will be animating with FK set an IK/FK switching key, and then at the start of the section set an IK/FK switching key. This now defines the boundaries for Maya to switch between IK and FK and you just need to turn off the IK solver with `Animate|IK/FK Switching Keys|Enable IK Solver`. Between these boundaries you can set keys for the rotation of the joints using `Animate|IK/FK Switching Keys|Set IK/FK Key`. Then select the IK handle, turn on the IK solver and set a key for the `Solver Enable` attribute (on) at the first frame again.

Binding a Surface to a Skeleton

Now that you've got a poseable skeleton that will respond to a series of custom animation controls, it will be worth clothing it; one reason to do this is that the joints themselves will not render. You can very quickly place geometry onto the skeleton by creating cubes and transforming them so that they are the same sizes as the joints you wish to cover and then just swiftly parenting the cubes to the joints. But if you have been modeling a character that you wish to animate, you need to be able to move the model using the position of the joints and the skeleton. In this sense you want the geometry to deform as the joints move, giving the semblance of a skin with muscles driving the shapes underneath. This deformation is known as "binding" or "skinning" and is an operation that can only be performed with skeletons and surfaces.

Maya will take all of the points of a surface, be they CVs or vertices, and deform them according to the movement of the closest bone or bones. This deformation effect is worked out at the time that you bind the surface to the skeleton by utilizing the deformation pipeline seen in the last section. Because binding a surface or set of points to a skeleton is a form of deformer, you can also create additional deformers that can help either to fine tune the skeletal deformation, or to add new types of deformation to the surface. For example, a blend shape controlling facial animation as the body and head is deformed by skeletal animation. Maya will create a series of deformer sets that will be affected by the position of each joint and bone. The workflow for this process is to create a surface in either polygons or NURBS and build a skeleton inside it. This way you only have to edit the shape and proportion of the skeleton and not the model (it is a lot easier to edit the construction of a skeleton as well). Once the joints have been created and the appropriate controls set up, you can bind your chosen surface to the skeleton. This process is as repeatable as the process for construction of a skeleton, meaning that you can bind a surface, see if it works, unbind it if necessary and edit the skeleton and/or the surface. This allows both the modeler and the animator to have a freer development process until an optimum has been achieved.

Because the starting position of the joints will determine the amount of deformation that is applied to a surface when they are rotated, it will be important to have the limbs straight at the elbows and knees. Additionally, it will also be important to have a start position for the entire skeleton, so that the geometry is not deformed at this position whatsoever. This is known as a "bind pose" and there are several ways to achieve this position. Once this binding has been achieved, the second level of editing starts as you change the way the deformation is applied to the geometry by the underlying skeleton. After this, you can begin to add specialized deforming objects to add the appearance of a working musculature and wrinkling skin.

Rigid Binding

There are two methods of binding a surface to a skeleton within Maya, one is called "rigid binding" the other is "smooth binding" but apart from the few differences in operation and editing, the workflow is essentially the same. You will need geometry to deform and to use as a reference for building a skeleton in, so the following process explains how to build a simple NURBS leg and use it as a bound surface.

- Create a NURBS cylinder with eight sections and eight spans. Scale it seven units in the Y axis, freeze its transformations and delete its history.
- You need to have more surface definition around the areas that are going to be deforming the most, so select the middle three rows of CVs and scale them in the Y axis to bring them closer to the centre line, where the knee will be bending.
- Select the next outer rows of CVs and scale their position in Y so that they now lie in the middle of each upper and lower section.
- Scale and position the rest of the rows of CVs so that they are in the centre of their respective halves.
- Remodel the NURBS surface until it looks like a leg and rename it Leg.

The leg should appear to be in a relaxed state; that is to say, that the underlying muscles should have shape but not be overly defined. This is because the binding and editing process that will follow will create the illusion of muscles contracting and relaxing. It will be worth creating three layers called Skin, Skeleton and Deformers to contain and manipulate the display of the various items that will be in the scene, so place Leg into the Skin layer and template it. Now that you have a surface to deform, you can begin building your skeleton and controls into it.

- Draw a three bone skeleton that fits into the templated geometry and make sure the joints are straight.
- Rename the upper bone Thigh and the lower bone Shin.
- Rotate Shin so that the joint chain is bent in the correct direction, set the preferred angle for the joint and set its rotation back to zero.
- In the Attribute Editor, turn the Shin joint into a hinge joint by allowing it freedom in only one axis.
- Limit the rotation of the joint so that it cannot rotate more than 120 degrees.

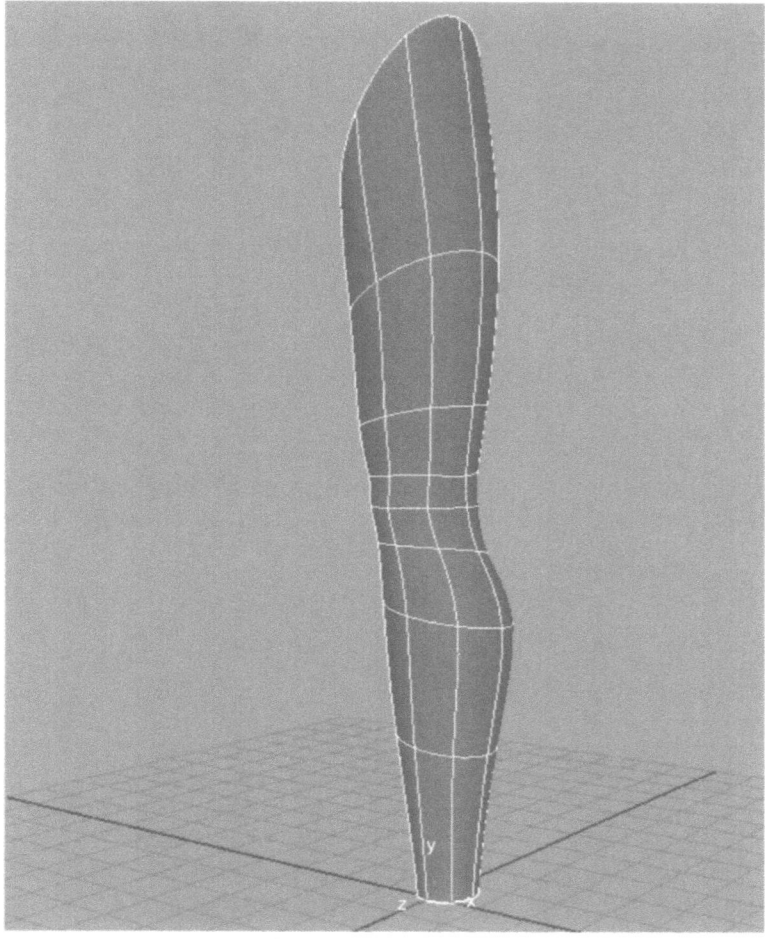

Figure 5.35 The NURBS Leg Surface.

- Create an IK rotate plane handle, a locator and constrain the pole vector of the IK handle to the locator.
- Place the joint chain, the locator and the IK handle into the Skeleton layer and untemplate the Skin layer.

To bind the geometry to the joint chain, select the Surface, then the root of the joint chain and open the options box for Skin|Bind Skin|Rigid Bind. The most important option within this options box is the Bind to option. If you set this option to Complete skeleton then you don't have to select the root of the skeletal hierarchy, as Maya will apply the skinning operation to the whole set of joints. The option to apply the skinning process to only selected joints will allow you to tightly define which objects are bound to which joints, this can be useful if you wish to test how a piece of geometry will act but only when bound to a series of local joints. For example, you may want to see how a glove will deform, but you only want the joints

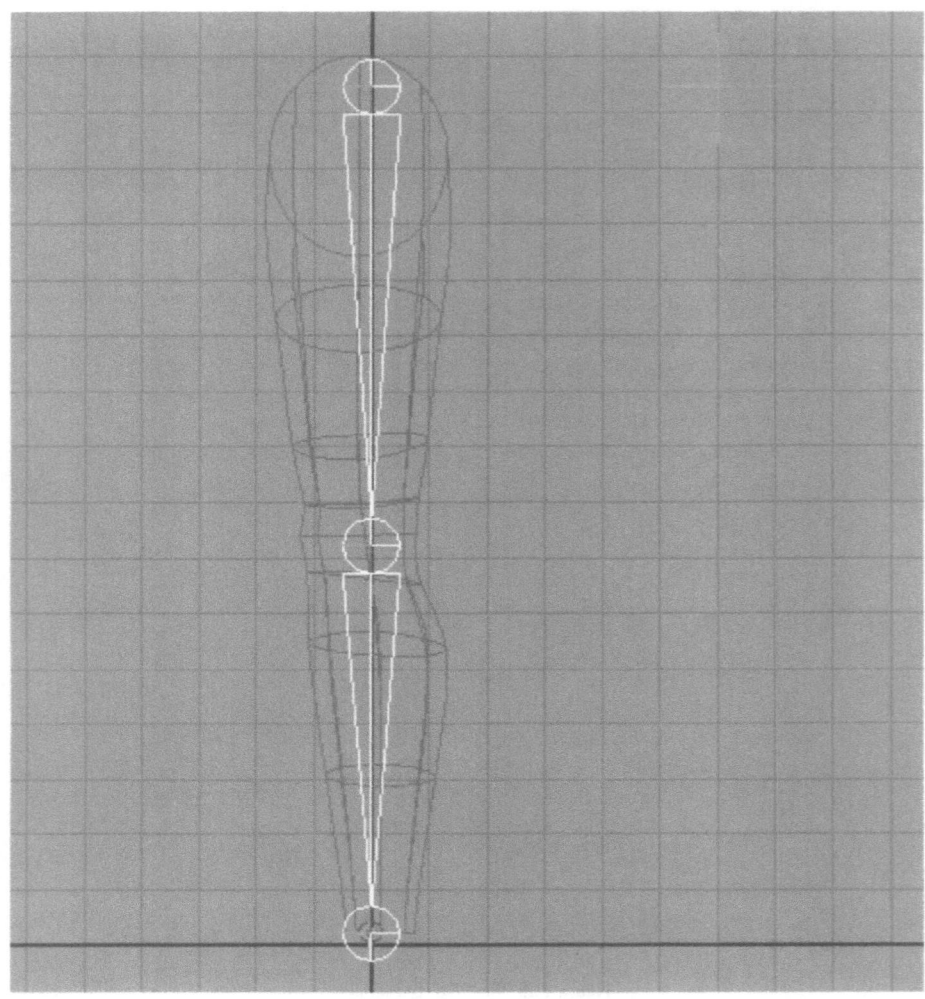

Figure 5.36 A Skeleton and IK Handle in the Templated Leg Surface.

in the hand to affect it, not the entire skeleton. If this latter option is used, all of the bones must be Shift-selected, not just the top of the hierarchy.

Turn on `Colour joints`, set `Bind Method` to `Closest point` (whether Maya will let the closest joint to a point deform it, or the closest joint to a prepared set of points) and then click Bind Skin. Maya should do a little thinking and then bind the skin. The geometry will appear purple to show that the currently selected item (the skeleton) has an effect on it. Select the IK handle and move it, which will deform the geometry relative to the position of the joints. If you look closely at the geometry surrounding the joint, you will see why this method of binding is named "rigid bind". There is no smooth deformation of the surface; rather, it is bending like a thick layer of cardboard. This type of deformation occurs because the CVs on the surface have been divided up into sets, one set for each bone, and it is these sets

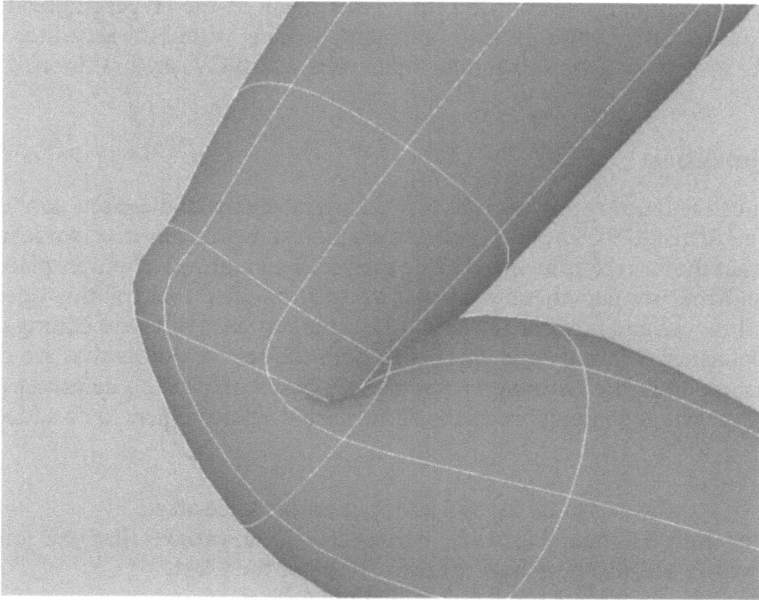

Figure 5.37 The Deformation Created with a Rigid Bind.

that are used by Maya to decide how to deform the geometry (not surprisingly these are called "deformer sets"). So each CVs position can only be changed by one bone's influence, and so as default behaviour the rigid bind will not smoothly stretch the geometry around a rotating joint.

The Bind Pose

If you decide to, you can unbind the surface from the skeleton so that you can edit either item, but you need to return to the bind pose so that the skeleton can be in the ready position for eventual binding again. This bind pose is also useful, because it is the pose where zero deformation is occurring and as such, is important when determining any before and after effects from editing the deformation. Select the root of the skeleton and use Skin|Go to Bind Pose. Unfortunately, this will not happen because the rotational values of the joints are controlled by an IK system. The IK solver node needs to be temporarily disabled, so use Modify|Evaluate Nodes and turn off IK Solvers (or you could quickly use Disable All as well). Now you will be able to return to the bind pose, from which you can select the skin and then use Skin|Detach Skin (leave the options as they are) to remove the relationship between the geometry and the joints. You can see how these sets function by opening an editor from Windows|Relationship Editors|Deformer Sets. On the left-hand side are the available deformer sets in Maya (a set is a collection of items) and on the right-hand side is everything else that exists in the scene. Highlight the set named ThighSet1 and the objects that this set affects or has connections with will be highlighted in the other side. Click the little "x" icon beside the set and you can see a list of CVs that this set contains. This is how Maya knows which CVs to transform, because each deformer set is linked to a bone via a skin cluster, which is a node that provides the deformation effect (you can examine this relationship in greater detail in the Hypergraph). Highlight the deformer set named `ShinSet1` and (from the menu heading within the set editor window) use `Edit|Select Set Members` to show in the main view which CVs are in this set.

Editing Joint Membership

The next part of the binding process is to edit the membership of these sets so that the correct bones affect the correct CVs. The CVs around the knee quite probably need some minor editing to make sure that the correct influence is being exerted. This editing will purely place a point into a different deformer set and thereby change its position. The tool for this operation is the Edit Membership tool and it works in exactly the same way as if you were editing the membership of any deformer (Maya creates clusters to hold the sets of points that are bound to the skeleton). Because all of the skinning procedures are based on existing deformer mechanisms, this integrates the whole binding process to allow additional deformers to be added to a bound surface.

- Select the IK handle, bend the leg and zoom in on the knee area.
- Activate the Edit Membership tool and select a joint (notice that the joints are now coloured which will also be echoed by the colours of the CVs).
- The CVs that the joint affects will be highlighted yellow.
- You can add or remove CVs from the deformer set that the selected joint influences by using either `Shift+LMB` to add to the current set or `Ctrl+LMB` to remove CVs from the current set.
- Change some of the CVs of the knee so that when the leg bends, the knee retains some kind of shape.

This is the first part of the editing process and is probably the smallest part. In order to get around the rigid deformation effect, you can add a certain type of deformer called a "flexor". As we have seen, deformers can be layered on top of each other to achieve subtly layered effects and it is this mechanism that enables the use of flexors: as another layer on top of binding. The available flexors are lattice, sculpt and cluster and the reason that these are used is that by definition, these deformers operate on a shared set of points. It allows you to smooth the deformation around each joint. These flexors should be placed when the skeleton is in its bind pose.

Flexors

Move the IK handle down to the bottom so that the leg is relatively straight and select the knee joint. Bring up the flexor creation dialogue from `Skin|Edit Rigid Skin|Create Flexor...` and select `Lattice` from the fold-out menu. Have only `Selected joints` turned on because you want to create a flexor at the currently selected joint only. However, you cannot change the number of s, t and u divisions so if it doesn't behave as you want, just delete the flexor and try again. Click Create and the lattice flexor will be centred about the joint (if you want to position it manually then turn on `Position the Flexor` in the options box). Now when you bend the leg, the lattice flexor will smooth out the deformation of the surface. As well as this smoothed deformation, there are also various attributes that are unique to this deformer type. With the leg still bent, change the attributes in the Channels Box that affect how this deformer

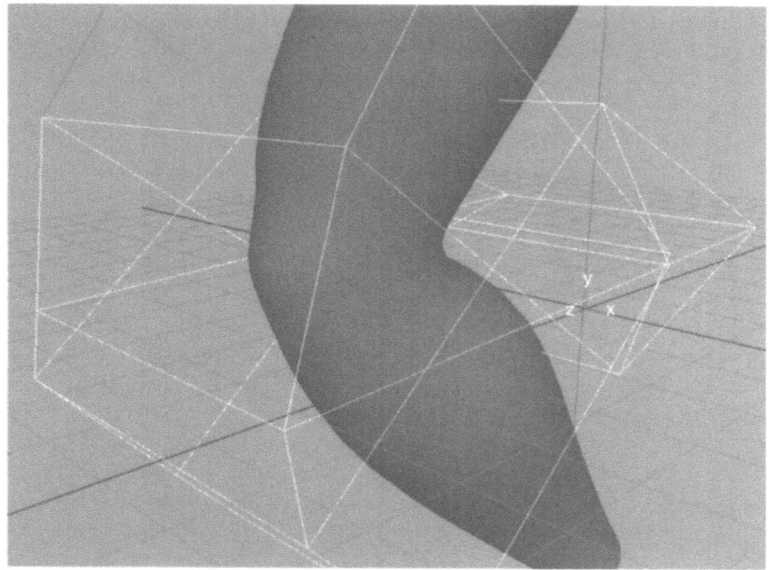

Figure 5.38 A Lattice Flexor on the Knee Joint Smoothing the Rigid Bind Deformation.

works, such as creasing or rounding. Select the flexor, place it into the Deformers layer and hide the layer. This will make it easier to observe the effects of the flexor. If you create a lattice flexor on a selected bone, you can edit its channels so that the lattice bulges, relative to the child joint's rotation.

The sculpt flexor can be utilized to create the effect of muscle contracting (on top of any lattice flexors) when placed at a selected bone. However, the sculpt flexor does not have the same automatic animation controls linked to the rotation of the joints that the lattice flexor has, so when setting this type of flexor up, a driven key will need to be set up. Select the thigh and create a sculpt flexor on this selected bone. Changing the settings on how the sculpt flexor operates (dropoff, mode etc.) plus moving the flexor itself into the correct position will yield the correct muscle bulge. The driven key will then usually connect the rotation of the child joint to the Envelope attribute of the flexor. This Envelope attribute can also be driven to go above one, thereby increasing the deformation of the sculpt deformer at the maximum or minimum of the joint's rotation. What can make this type of flexor more versatile than the lattice bone flexor for muscle contraction is that the use of driven keys will allow you to edit the curves in the Graph Editor. Thus, you can create a more natural movement for the effect of the muscle contraction instead of the linear automatic action of the lattice flexor. Again, hide this flexor by placing it in the Deformer layer.

The third type of flexor that can be created is the jointCluster. This flexor can only be created at a joint, because it is used to further smooth the deformation about the joint as it rotates. Set the leg back to its bind pose, select the knee joint and create a jointCluster flexor. There are no options for this type of flexor except whether it is created at the selected joint or at all joints. Evaluate all IK solvers and bend the leg. Select the jointCluster and select the Show Manipulator tool to display two rings that are placed at the top and bottom of the joint at

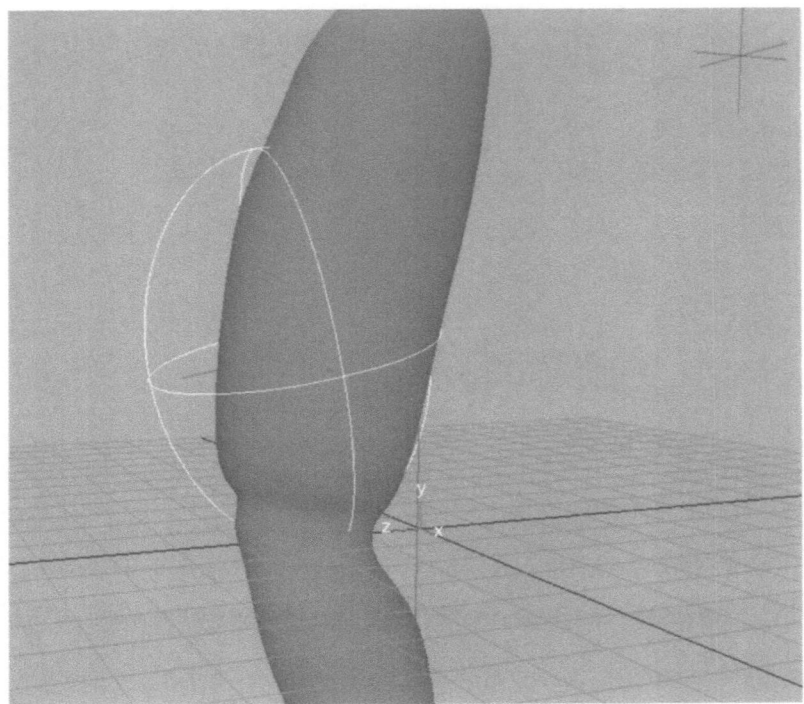

Figure 5.39 A Sculpt Flexor on the Thigh Joint.

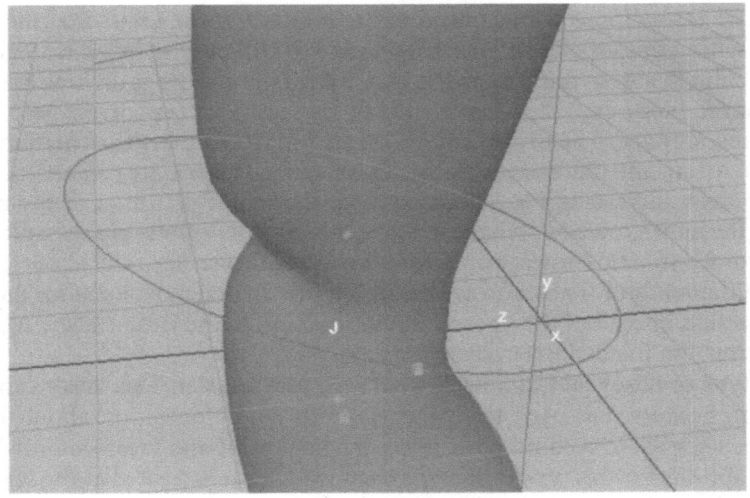

Figure 5.40 A jointCluster in Action around the Knee Joint.

which the cluster was created. The blue diamond at the centre of each ring will allow you to move the ring along the bone, whereas the blue diamond at the edge of the ring will control the amount of smoothing that this flexor exerts over the area defined by the rings.

Flexors can be copied from one joint to another by selecting the required flexor and then Shift-selecting the destination bone or joint and using Skin|Edit Rigid Skin|Copy Flexor, although this should be done (as with all operations of this kind) while the skeleton is in the bind pose. This now means that you can set up half of the bound surface and once ready, copy all of the flexors across to the skeleton's opposite limbs. Not only will this save time, but it means that the behaviour of the bound surface will also be the same across the body. Moreover, this means that you can copy flexors between different characters once the default behaviour has been set up.

Smooth Binding

The other method of binding a surface or set of points to a skeleton is known as smooth binding and allows a point to be influenced by more than one joint or bone. This creates a much smoother deformation as a default action and, as such, the editing process is concerned more with adding to the existing smooth deformation instead of creating deformers to create a smooth deformation. Save the current scene, delete all of the flexors that you created and detach the surface from the skeleton so that you don't have to model anything new for this next type of binding.

With the leg and skeleton displayed, select the geometry, then the root of the skeleton and open the options for Skin|Bind Skin|Smooth Bind. Because you now have to determine the amount of proportional influence each bone will have over each CV (or vertex), the number of options for the smooth bind action have increased compared to the options for the rigid bind action. You still have the choice of whether you wish to bind to the entire hierarchy or just the currently selected bones. The next option for smooth binding is the choice of how the bones are going to affect the selected geometry, either using Closest joint or Closest distance (keep this set to Closest joint). The other method will use the distance between a joint and any available points to bind, which can have problematic effects if used when the choice of joints and surfaces is unclear – for example, if a character's legs are side by side. Max Influences sets the upper limit on how many joints can influence a single point and Dropoff Rate controls how fast each joint's influence on a point tails off with distance. Keep all of the options as they were and click Bind Skin. If you now move the IK handle (remember to re-evaluate all IK solvers if you returned to the bind pose), you will be able to see straightaway the effects that smooth binding has. The geometry now deforms smoothly and evenly as each joint has an effect across the surface.

Editing Smooth Skin Deformation

The first task now is to edit the deformation around the knee, as the default behaviour of smooth binding still requires a little work. If you tried using the Edit Set Membership tool to add and remove CVs from deformer sets, you would find that each bone affects all of the CVs on the surface. The smooth deformation effect is created by a weighted deformation (there will only be one skin set in the Deformer Set Editor) in the same way that a cluster works. Because of this similarity, you can use an incarnation of the Artisan Tool to help to change the

Figure 5.41 Painting Different Weights on the NURBS Leg.

weights of the bound geometry; this tool operates in the same manner as the Paint Cluster Weights tool.

- Bend the leg so that the binding action can be clearly observed.
- Pop the perspective view to the foreground.
- Select the skin, change into shaded mode and set the smoothing to the highest setting.
- Open the tool from Skin|Edit Smooth Skin|Paint Skin Weights Tool.
- In the Influence window select Thigh. The areas that the Thigh will influence and deform will be coloured the appropriate colour from one (white) to zero (black).
- Painting differing values using this tool will create different effects when the joints are bent.

In the Skin|Edit Smooth Skin menu, there are a number of useful actions that can be of help when painting skin weights. If you need to go back to the original settings of the skin weights, you can use Skin|Edit Smooth Skin|Reset Weights to Default and you can use Skin| Edit Smooth Skin|Prune Small Weights to remove any weights under a certain value as set in the options. In keeping with the workflow for skeleton and flexor creation, you can mirror skin weights across the skeleton and surfaces. This means that you can halve the time spent adjusting weights and also keep the same values for each limb (as long as the number of joints and points are similar) using Skin|Edit Smooth Skin|Mirror Skin Weights. Skin weights can also be transferred between characters with a similar skeleton and geometry using Skin| Edit Smooth Skin|Copy Skin Weights. Although the characters do not necessarily have to have the same number of joints and surface points, it will certainly help the operation and save time when re-editing.

If required, we can also copy or mirror skin weights between sets of CVs as well, so that we can use propagate minor edits to areas across characters, for example the area behind the knee can be copied from one knee to another and even used as the reference for other skin weights. For both of these operations, the source CVs are selected, then the destination CVs are shift-selected and then either the Mirror Skin Weights or Copy Skin Weights action is used. For these kinds of operations, it is often easier to create sets of CVs using the set editor so that we can easily refer to the CVs in question. If these sets are placed into a user-defined partition there will be no danger of accidentally sharing the same CVs amongst the sets.

Editing Weight Behaviour

This, like the process for refining the rigid bind, is only the first part of editing the behaviour of the smooth bind. You can also change the skin weights on a point-by-point basis if you wish, to gain the greatest control over the deformation. Select some of the CVs in the crease of the knee and open the Component Editor from the Windows|General Editors menu. The Component Editor allows you to change any kind of value or data that the currently selected component(s) might have associated with it, so in this case you are going to change the values for the Skin Clusters. Select this tab and you can see the CVs listed at the left-hand side, the joints at the top and the values in the middle. All of these values will add up to one, because the weights for the skin are normalized allowing you to view the skin weights as relative to each other. If required, you can disable these upper and lower bounds of zero and one by using Skin|Edit Smooth Skin|Disable Weight Normalization, which will allow you to assign absolute values to your point weighting. Skin|Edit Smooth Skin|Enable Weight Normalization will reverse this process, but only when you start painting weights again. Because the skin weights can be represented as a black and white colour across the surface of the bound geometry, you can also save these weights out as Skin Weight Maps.

- Select the Leg surface.
- Select Skin|Edit Smooth Skin|Export Skin Weight Maps (the options deal with the size of map and the type of map).
- Name the map LegMap and click Write.
- With the Leg geometry still selected, use Skin|Edit Smooth Skin|Reset Weights to Default to reset the deformation of the leg.
- Select the Leg geometry and use Skin|Edit Smooth Skin|Import Skin Weight Maps to open the import options box.
- Select LegMap.weightmap and click Import.

Influence Objects

The final part of the editing process for a smooth skin deformation is to use influence objects. Influence objects affect the shape of the underlying smooth skin by using changes in their transform nodes or changes in their shape to modify nearby surface points. These influence objects can be used to not only add to the smooth skin deformation, but can also be used to stop any undesirable effects of smooth skinned deformation. An influence object can be any shaped surface, NURBS or polygon, which means that you can create your influence object to be any shape you require (such as a shoulder blade) instead of being limited to the shape of a particular deformer. For now, the following will explain how to use influence objects to create the illusion of thigh muscles bulging.

- Set the leg back to its bind pose and create a NURBS sphere (deleting its history).
- Shape and position the sphere so it roughly resembles a quadriceps muscle, rename it `ThighMuss`.
- Select the `Leg` geometry, select `ThighMuss` and open the options for `Skin|Edit Smooth Skin|Add Influence`.
- Keep the options as they are and click Add (the options here control the dropoff of influence over distance, the accuracy of samples relative to each surface type and whether the influence object affects the painted weights of the smooth skin or not).

Maya should calculate for a little while, the influence object will remain selected while the geometry that the influence object is affecting will run purple indicating a connection.

There is an additional object in the Outliner, known as the "base" object, which determines how much deformation to apply to the bound geometry by checking the difference in transformation between the influence object and itself. If you now transform the influence object, it will deform the bound geometry, so it is just a matter of setting up the driven keys for the leg surface deformation. This could be done several ways:

1. The joint rotation could drive the translation, rotation and scaling of the influence object.
2. The influence object could be transformed so that it is already deforming the surface and the joint rotation could drive the `Envelope` attribute of the `skinCluster` for the influence object.
3. The influence object could be deformed by some other deformer and the joint rotation could drive this secondary deformation.

We are going to use the third method, as the first two are similar to the way the sculpt flexor was driven for the rigid skin. The process will create a blend shape, which will be driven by the joint rotation, so you will need to create two duplicate objects and change them at a component level, because blend shape deformers do not change objects at a transform level. First, you need to detach the influence object from the smooth skin.

- Set the leg back to the bind pose.
- Select the `Leg` geometry and the influence object then use `Skin|Edit Smooth Skin|Remove Influence`.
- Leave `ThighMuss` where it is and duplicate it.
- Call the duplicate `ThighMussBig`.
- Change the shape of `ThighMussBig` using the CVs.
- Select `ThighMussBig`, then `ThighMuss` and open up the options box for `Deform|Create Blend Shape`.
- Name the node `Tmuss`, set the target shape options to `In Between` and click Create.
- Test the blend shape is working in the Blend Shape Editor and delete or hide `ThighMussBig`.

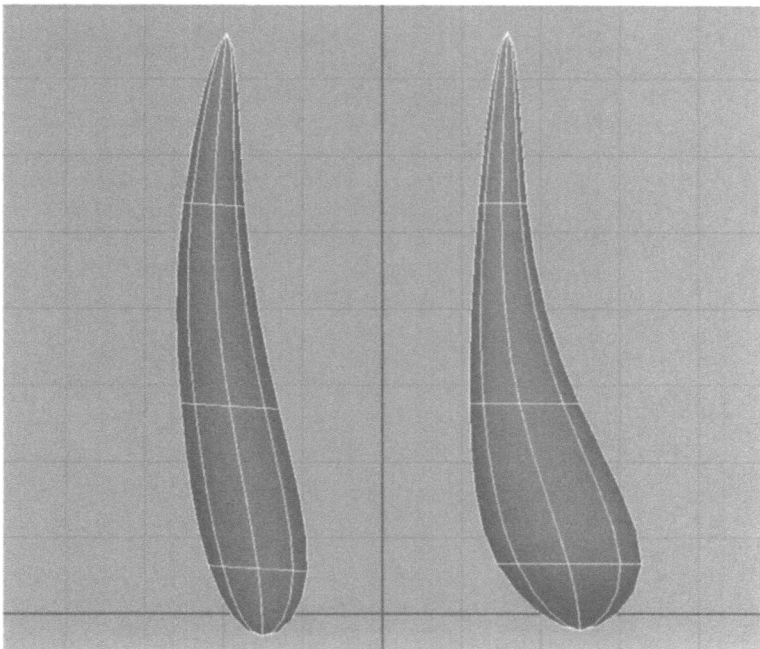

Figure 5.42 The Small and Large Versions of ThighMuss.

Now add the ThighMuss influence object back to the Leg geometry. If you try using the slider in the Blend Shape Editor, however, you'll notice that no deformation occurs. Open the Attribute Editor on the skinCluster tab and turn on Use components. This now lets the influence object change the shape of the smooth skin using changes at a component level. Now the final operations for this muscle bulging effect can continue, but first re-evaluate all IK solvers.

- Parent the influence object and its two base objects to the thigh bone.
- Select the knee joint, open the Driven Keys Editor and load this joint in as the driver.
- Click Select in the Blend Shape Editor and click Load Driven to load the blend shape node and its attributes.
- Select rotate Y for the knee joint and Muss for the Blend Shape node.
- With the leg straight, move the slider in the Blend Shape Editor to one so the leg's surface is deformed and click Key in the Driven Key Editor.
- Move the IK handle so the leg is bent, set the slider in the Blend Shape Editor to zero and click Key in the Driven Key Editor.
- Hide the influence objects.

These methods of binding geometry to a series of joints represents the mechanism that Maya uses when deforming any piece of geometry; the only real difference is that due to the nature of joints and bones, a specialized set of tools and functions can be utilized. The workflow for creating a deforming, hierarchical character is open to editing at any stage as long as the

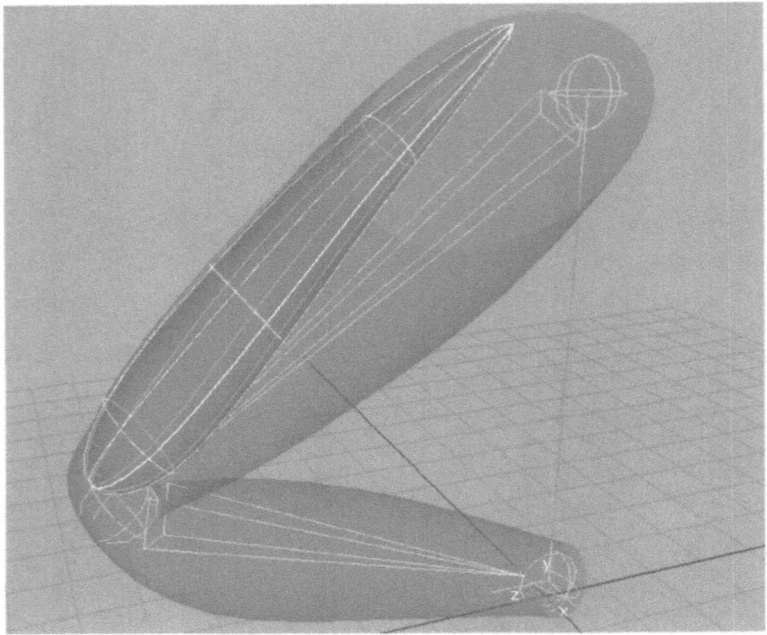

Figure 5.43 The ThighMuss Working under the Surface of the NURBS Leg.

various caveats are observed. It is worth noting that when you skin something, you are deforming a set of points like any deformer, so you can also bind objects such as a lattice or a wrap deforming object because they consist of sets of points too. This means that you can use the lattice or wrap as a proxy object so that the point-by-point editing process is made a little easier as each point on a lattice has a local effect over a series of points on the geometry.

Summary

Although several different methods for changing the values of an object's transform and shape nodes have been explored and used, what should be clear is that all of these methods can be combined. We saw the result of combining different channels to create a single value when we used driven keys. Here we are using a relationship to control another channel, affecting it indirectly. If a node has attributes that can be converted into channels, then the node can be animated, for example modeling processes such as lofting, extrusions and polygon Booleans can be animated to create shape and surface animations such as growing plants and automotive cut-aways. Deformers can be added to the input for a surface at any time, skeletons can be created to control the overall shape of a hierarchically animated surface and paths can serve to animate the position of objects, lights and cameras. As many techniques as there are available can be used to create animation of great complexity. With the increase in complexity comes the need for control, repeatability and flexibility. It is no good having a character that uses all of the techniques we have covered but also has 300 controls just for walking, which once set up cannot be changed easily without wrecking the setup of character. Remember that the script for the project will determine how the character will need to be built and controlled, so assess these requirements and place them in order of importance and implementation. Then decide what method will give the animator the greatest control and keep these controls transparent, so that the interface for a particular node is uncluttered and straightforward. If a problem does occur with the character, it will be easier to troubleshoot a clearly created collection of nodes than an ad hoc set up. All of the above skining and deforming methods work with polygons and subdiv surfaces, the only requirement is that the surfaces are clean, have no history nodes and in the case of subdiv surfaces, have a straightforward hierarchy of detail levels.

Rendering 6

Introduction

Now that we have created all the components for an entire scene, the only missing elements are lights to light the scene, materials and shading networks to colour the surfaces and a camera and renderer to create the final part of the creative process: rendered frames. From what we've discovered when modeling and animating, Maya is based upon the relationship between different nodes, a functionality that is demonstrated ably by the Hypergraph. When we start creating surface colour and detail we will now be using a similar window to explicitly connect nodes together, enabling us to have intuitive control over your surface appearances. Lighting scenes within Maya is a straightforward process and any knowledge of studio lighting can be adapted to CG scenes easily combined with fast feedback via an interactive renderer.

Lights

In order to see objects in Maya, we need to cast light upon them. All of the lights within Maya are represented as primitives and can be found under the Create menu heading. This means that lights are treated as physical objects within Maya and contain a shape node and a transform node: moving and orienting them in space is done through the use of the normal transform tools. The Show Manipulator tool can also be used to change attributes particular to lights, such as the size of a spotlight's cone.

The Five Types of Light in Maya

Maya has six different lights which all perform one task: casting light upon objects. The manner in which they cast light will determine which light is best suited to a particular task or application.

- *Point light.* A point light casts light uniformly in all directions from the position of the light source, similar to a light bulb.
- *Ambient light.* An ambient light source casts light across the scene in two ways. It can apply an equal amount of light to all surfaces irrespective of whether the light can "see" the surface and it can shine like a point light, with light coming from the ambient light's position in space.

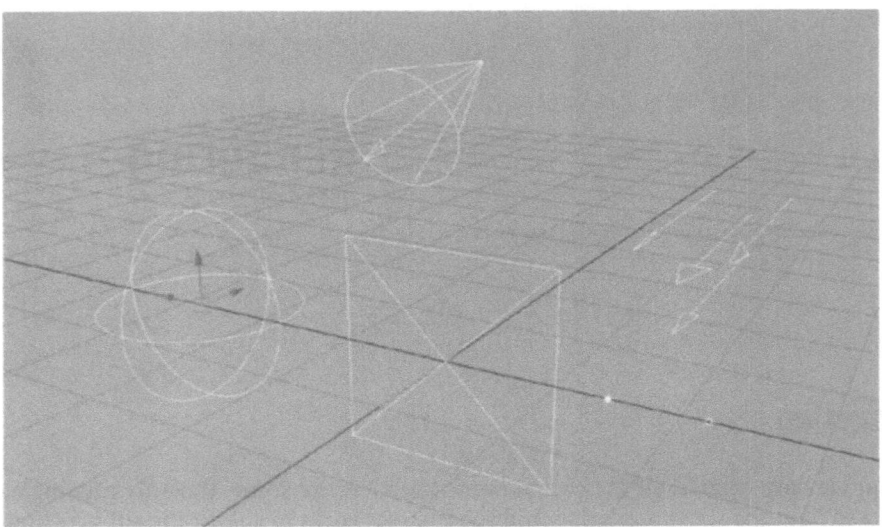

Figure 6.1 The Different Lights and Their Icons.

- *Directional light.* A directional light casts light in one direction creating parallel rays. The light does not come from a source but has a direction only as if it were emitted by the sun.
- *Spotlight.* A spotlight casts light within a cone from the location of the light.
- *Area light.* This simulates the light that is cast from a surface, such as a striplight or a photographer's reflector by creating a rectangular light source surface.
- *Volume light.* This light operates like a point light but has a controllable falloff and many other features that allow the shaping of the light.

We are going to explain how to create a few simple objects and light them with a single light, which will enable you to quickly determine how changes made to the lights' attributes will affect the scene. Since you are going to be working purely on the visual aspect of the scene, turn off all the superfluous user interfaces (timeline, help line etc.), giving a much larger viewport.

- Create a grid, a sphere, a torus and a cone.
- Scale the grid so that it fills the field of view and position the other primitives in a ring around the origin.
- Delete the history for all of the objects.
- Create a new perspective view, renaming it "MyCam", swap one of the orthographic views for this new view and position it for a pleasing composition.

We will be using MyCam to render any snapshots of the scene, so all other viewing operations will be conducted from the standard perspective view. This means that you will be getting the same render every time from MyCam, which will be useful for the purposes of comparison. Because MyCam should stay in the same position, you should set up a bookmark for the current position (a bookmark is a placeholder for the current camera position and settings that can be recalled at any time) using the View menu heading in the camera viewport.

- Open the Bookmarks Editor from View|Bookmarks|Edit Bookmarks...
- Click the New Bookmark button and change the name of it to "MyView_01".
- You can now recall this position from the View|Bookmarks menu item which will display all of the available bookmarks.

The bookmarks are relevant to each camera view as are any other camera-specific commands from these menus. As well as using bookmarks, you can also keep track of the positions of the camera using the camera journal and the Previous view and Next view commands. The camera journal allows you to undo any changes made to the camera position and the Previous view/Next view commands allow you to step through the positions in which you have put the camera. The journal can be turned on from View|Camera Settings|Journal, and the Previous and Next view commands can be accessed from the View menu heading, but the "[" and "]" hotkeys will make this process faster. As we are going to be creating lights and rendering the results, you should change into the Rendering menu set.

A Brief Note on Rendering

We will get to grips with some of the aspects of rendering now, but any questions that remain will be answered later in this chapter. To render the currently active view, use Render|Render Current Frame or click the clapperboard icon. Maya will render the current view into a new window called the render view, but this window can be assigned to any of the other panels or even to the MyCam viewport. If there are no lights in the scene, then Maya will create a default light when rendering the scene so that the frame does not render black. All of the objects are shaded with the default surface lambert1, whose attributes can be changed in the Attribute Editor. This shader is assigned to every new surface so that they can be seen when you render.

Within the render view window there are several menu headings, with some of the more commonly used items represented as icons. You can re-render your current view at any time by using Render|Redo Previous Render or by clicking the clapperboard icon. If you wish to render a section of your scene instead of the whole view again (for example, if you only want to see the changes made to a single object) then you can use the LMB to draw a rectangle in the view and use Render|Render Region or the clapperboard with red rectangle icon. If you go to the Options menu heading and turn on Auto Render Region then you won't have to draw a rectangle and then select the menu item. If you wish to render a different camera, then you can select any available camera from the Render|Render menu. All of the menu options for the render view can be accessed from the floating menu brought up by holding down the RMB in the window. You can change the size of the image rendered by using the Options|Test Resolution menu item to change between three proportions of a pre-set resolution or to render the image as the size of the current window in pixels. The standard orthographic view controls can be used to pan and zoom the picture (normal size can be returned to by LMB clicking the "1:1" button).

Exploring Light Attributes

We will start by exploring the most basic light in Maya and moving upward in terms of complexity. Complexity for a light is represented in terms of its transform node and its shape node, which will carry attributes relevant to the actual operation of the light, all lights carrying the default shape node attributes of light colour and intensity. The simplest light is the

Figure 6.2 The Render View Window.

ambient light which seeks to address the problem of bounced light in a scene by applying an equal amount of illumination to every point on a surface no matter its orientation and to also shine light from its position.

- Create an ambient light from the Create|Lights menu.

Move the new light to a position above the objects and render the scene.

As we can see, the whole scene is evenly lit with some slight diffuse colour showing that some light comes from the position of the ambient light. Open the Attribute Editor to examine the shape node attributes for this type of light. The first attribute common to all lights is the colour. This can be changed using the slider to adjust the value of the colour from light to dark. LMB clicking on the colour swatch will bring up the colour chooser, which will allow you to change the colour of the light over the entire range of the spectrum. The next attribute common to all lights is the intensity of the light. Intensity is used to modulate the amount of light received by a surface which in turn affects the amount of colour that a surface receives, so for the ambient light you can use this as a dimmer switch. The attribute that is unique to the ambient light type is ambient shade and describes the amount of light that is cast directionally and the amount of light that is cast uniformly. Set the ambient shade to zero and the entire scene will be coloured uniformly with no shading characteristics, set the ambient shade to one and the light will behave as a simple point light.

In the Attribute Editor, turn off the `Illuminates by Default` attribute for the ambient light so that it doesn't contribute any light to the scene. Create a point light, move it into the centre of the objects so that it is a few units above the ground plane and render the scene. The light source emits light in the manner of a light bulb and if you look at the Attribute Editor you can see that there are a few new attributes for this light's shape node. You now have the `Decay` attribute to work with, which has three settings other than `No Decay` and describes the relationship that the light intensity has with distance from the light source, i.e. the change in light as a function of distance. Real world light intensity changes as an inverse square of the distance from the light source, which is represented in Maya as the `Quadratic` decay setting.

- Render the scene with Decay set to `No Decay`.
- Use `File|Keep Image in Render View` which will store the current image in the render view memory (or use the icon with the arrow pointing into the bucket).
- Set `Decay` to `Linear`, render the scene and use `File|Keep Image in Render View` to store this next image.
- Change the settings to `Quadratic` and then `Cubic` while rendering the scene and storing the image.
- Now use the slider at the bottom of the render view to move between stored images to compare the changes in the light decay.

When you want to remove any stored images from the render view, use `File|Remove Image from Render View` or the corresponding icon to remove these from memory. The images have to be removed from the back of the queue so that the last image left is the most recent render. If you wish to keep any images permanently, you can save them to the hard disk from the render view by using `File|Save Image` which will then allow you to save the current image in any format. You can also use the render view to display previously saved images from the hard disk using `File|Show Image`. Now that you have a main light source for your scene you can examine the effect of the previously created ambient light source. You can quickly select the ambient light source by using the `Focus` menu item in the Attribute Editor, which will allow you to change the focus of the Attribute Editor to any node that has previously been edited.

- Under `Focus`, select the ambient light source and turn on the `Illuminates by Default` attribute.
- Change the ambient shade attribute to zero and the intensity to 0.4.
- Select the point light source and change its decay rate to `None`.
- Render the scene.

The ambient light source when set to full ambient effect now adds some light to every surface, lightening the scene a little. The only danger with using ambient light sources in this manner is that all surfaces are affected, no matter their orientation, but if the scene needs to have the overall light values increased, then this light type will be perfect. For now, delete the ambient light source in the scene, which can be done through the Attribute Editor by having the focus on the ambient light, clicking the Select button and then pressing the Backspace or Delete key.

A very useful change that can be made to a light source in the Attribute Editor, is to change the actual light type. This allows you to very easily change the light source until you arrive at the desired solution for your lighting requirements. Use the `Type` setting to change the point light to a directional light source – the Attribute Editor will update to reflect the new attributes that the light source has (or has missing) and so will the scene. As can be seen from the icon in the perspective view, the directional light has a series of arrows indicating the direction in which the parallel rays of light will be cast. This does not indicate the direction from which the light rays will be cast, however, but the transform node allows you to move this icon in order to keep it near the relevant points in the scene. The directional light has no decay rate, simply a colour and intensity. The directional light will be created pointing parallel to the XZ plane, and moving it in the scene using the transform manipulator will not change the orientation of the light source, so the direction that the light is cast from will not change.

- Render the scene.
- Translate the light in the scene.
- Render the scene again.

The light source here casts light in a very different manner to any of the other lights, as it simulates the parallel light rays cast from the sun, so the light will be directional no matter where an object is. If the directional light is parallel to the ground plane then the light rays cast will not touch it, but if the light is rotated, the entire plane will be lit no matter where it is on space. So you won't be able to edit how light propagates through your scene from this light, as you could using the decay factor for the point light. If you want to change the orientation of the light, you can use the rotate tool to do this, but a more intuitive way to change the orientation of the light is to use the Show Manipulator tool. This tool will bring up specialized manipulators for each light, depending on what can be changed. For the directional light, the tool will display two translate handles allowing you to change the orientation and aim of the light easily. Beside the light icon is the `Index Manipulator` which allows you to cycle through the various manipulator handles for each light. Clicking on this will bring up the next available manipulator handle for the directional light, which allows you to change the pivot position about which the light rotates.

- Display the pivot handle and LMB drag it halfway down the vector that is drawn between the light icon and its aim point.
- LMB click on the pivot so that the centre is filled (enabling it) and now move the light source icon.

This manipulator will allow you to rotate your light about the new pivot position, but only when using the Show Manipulator tool, because any changes made by the standard transform tools will override any other transform changes. LMB clicking the pivot so that its centre is not filled will disable its effect and the Show Manipulator tool will function as normal.

Position the directional light so that it is at a 45 degree angle to the ground plane, render the scene and keep the image, then change the light source into a spotlight and render the scene again. The spotlight only casts light within a specific cone that extends from its origin to its aim point, which is why we can now see the edges of the spotlight's cone on the ground plane. Changing between the saved images in the render view also shows that the light itself has a very different effect upon the objects in the scene, because the rays that now emanate from the spotlight are not parallel any more, but spread out from the origin. The spotlight now has three new attributes that concern the cone of light it casts plus it has the decay attribute, like the point light. The attributes that shape the cone of light are the cone angle, the penumbra angle and the dropoff; there are also decay regions to make use of, which help to precisely shape the light that is cast. All of these attributes can be changed in the Attribute Editor or by using the Show Manipulator tool in the viewport. The spotlight has the largest amount of attributes among all of the lights in Maya, but allows you to direct exactly how much light will fall on a surface and exactly how much light will propagate through 3D space.

- Remove any saved images from the render view and render the current scene.
- Select the spotlight and keep the Attribute Editor open to examine any changes made.
- Select the Show Manipulator tool and click on the `Index Manipulator`.
- The first index after the standard origin and aim point manipulators is for the pivot.
- The next index is for the cone angle. LMB drag the blue indicator to expand or contract the size of the spotlight cone; if the indicator is still active (yellow) then the MMB can be used to change the value.
- Set the cone angle to 30 degrees.
- The next index is for changing the penumbra angle and specifies where light starts to fall-off: from cone centre out to the penumbra edge.
- Set the penumbra to 20 degrees.
- Render the view.

A penumbra has been added to the outer radius of the cone angle so the total angle that the spotlight spreads its light over is now 50 degrees, which determines light fading from the inner edge to the outer edge. If the dropoff is set to 30, then the light begins to dropoff from the

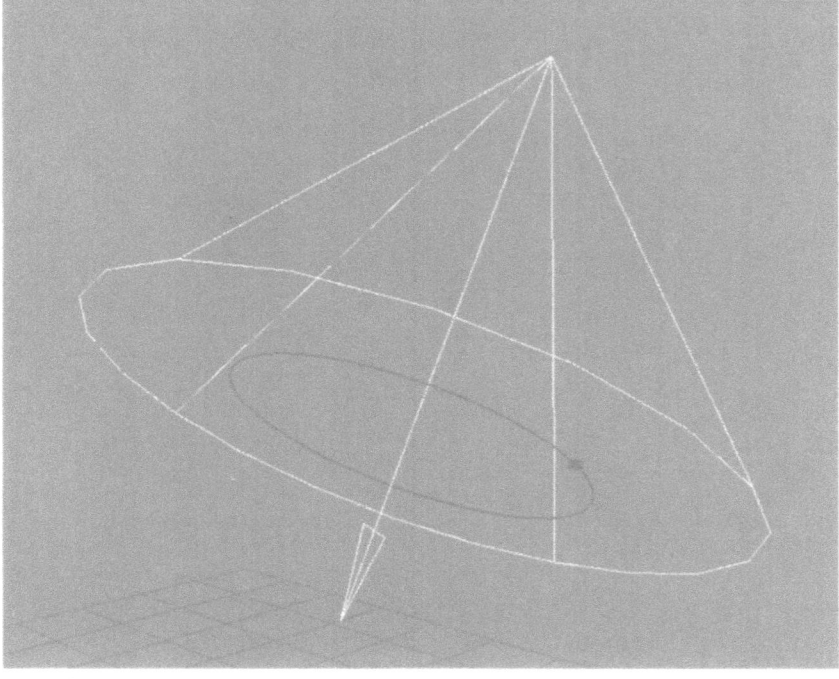

Figure 6.3 The Spotlight Icon with Penumbra Edge.

centre of the cone to the outer edge of the cone. So changing the values for penumbra and for dropoff can now alter the amount of light that hits any surface within the cone shape. The intensity of the spotlight can be modulated using the decay settings, but the spotlight also carries with it a set of decay regions that can further modulate where the spotlight will be casting light. The decay regions of a spotlight can be displayed by LMB clicking the Index Indicator five times. These regions are conic sections that allow you to define where light will be cast and can be moved along the cone's aim vector by LMB dragging their edges back and forth.

- Hide the current objects and create a new NURBS plane.
- Scale and rotate the plane so that it almost bisects the spotlight, so we will be able to see the spotlight's cone of light cast down the plane.
- Move the view of MyCam so that you can see the NURBS plane side on and render this view.
- In the Attribute Editor, open the fold-out menu titled Light Effects and the fold-out menu under it titled Decay Regions and turn on Use Decay Regions.
- Set the penumbra to zero, the dropoff to zero and the intensity to four.
- Change the position of the decay regions.
- Render again.

These decay regions now enable you to direct the light exactly, so that you are able to define how the light will be cast in the scene. One further attribute that spotlights have, which is

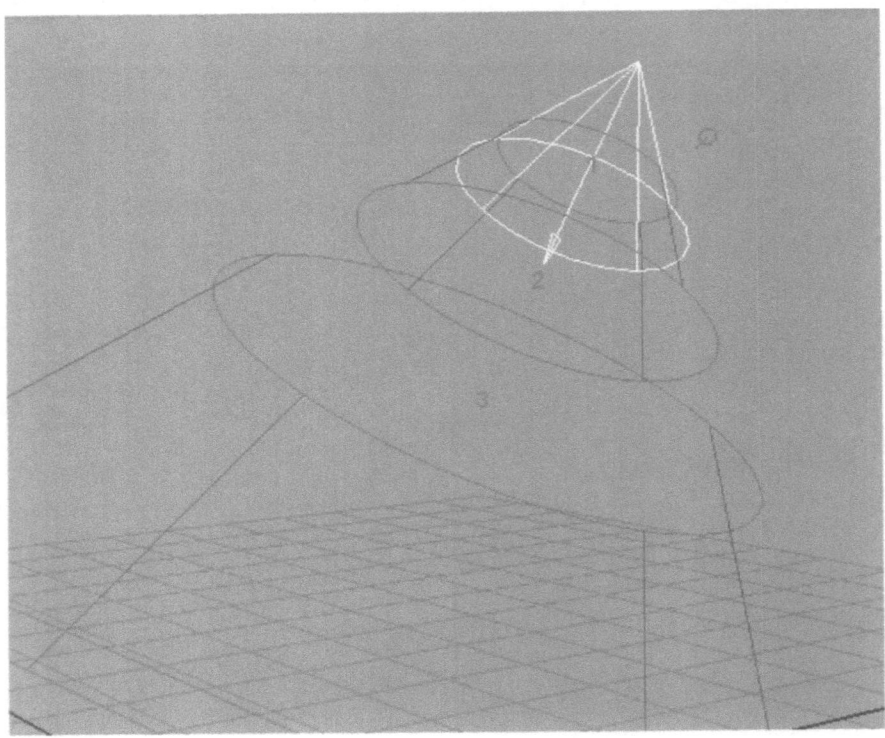

Figure 6.4 The Decay Regions for a Spotlight.

found under the Light Effects fold-out menu is the use of barn doors. These allow you to shape the cone of light by moving imaginary shutters in front of the light, simulating the physical characteristics of the lights upon which Maya spotlights are based. The barn door attributes specify the angle that they sit at on the front of the spotlight, so if the cone angle is set to 40 degrees then the default angle (20 degrees) for the barn doors means that they will sit at the edge of light cone. These can be a lot easier to visualize than to set up and render, so there is a useful function of Maya that lets you look through the currently selected item.

- Delete the plane, display your original objects, in the Attribute Editor for the spotlight turn off Decay Regions, turn on Barn Doors and set the intensity to one.
- In the perspective view use Panels|Look Through Selected.
- You can now move the light about using the normal camera controls (Alt+LMB etc.) while seeing the "footprint" of the cone of light in the viewport.
- Activate the Show Manipulator tool to display the barn doors.
- You can now change the position of the edges of the barn doors either in the Attribute Editor or by LMB dragging the edges in the current view.
- Render to see the effects.

The next light that is available in Maya is the area light, which simulates light cast by a surface. Because it is based upon physical simulation, all of the attributes for the light are modulated through the light's position and size. Area lights create rectangular-shaped highlights on surfaces, creating a shaped specular highlight, such as that from a windowpane. All of the

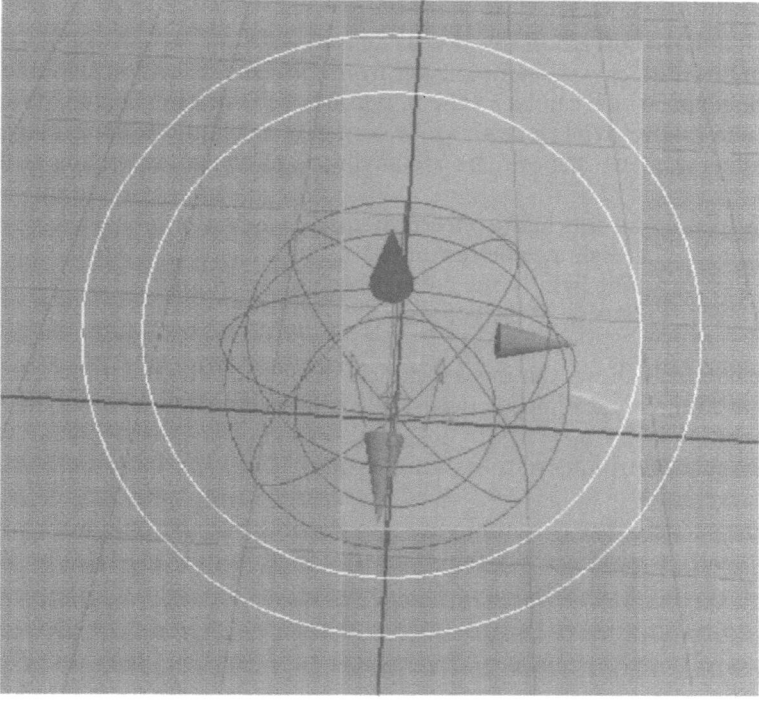

Figure 6.5 Looking through the Spotlight with Barn Doors on.

other lights (apart from the directional light) cast light from a single point so all light sources will create round highlights. The area light will cast light rays from across its surface and as such will create a soft diffuse light across the scene.

- Delete the spotlight and create an area light from the `Create` menu.
- Move the light so that it is pointing at the objects in the scene.
- Scale the area light up by four units in all axes and set the intensity to 0.75.
- Render the scene.

To increase the amount of light emitted from the area light a combination of the intensity and the size of the area light has to be used. If the size of the area light is increased using the scale tool, the amount of emitted light is increased proportionally. The area light won't cast light rays beyond its edges, so if a small footprint is required, then the intensity needs to be increased due to the relatively small size of the area light. Area lights can also be useful for simulating the light that diffuses from surfaces to create a bleeding effect from nearby coloured surfaces or to create subtler light effects like those produced from a bounce card.

The next light that is available in Maya is the `volume light`, which lets us change the falloff of the light instead of just using the decay rate and also lets us change the shape of the light and effect it has.

- Delete the area light and create a volume light from the `Create` menu.
- Move and scale the light so that its surface/volume is covering all the objects in the scene.
- Render the scene.

The volume light has a soft falloff towards its defined edge and we can also change the shape of the light and how quickly the light falls off from the centre. The first attribute that defines the light is the shape, which can be a sphere, cylinder, cone or box. This shape can be scaled, transformed and rotated in all three axis so we can have an elliptical shape if required; for the sphere, cylinder, and cone shapes there are attributes to control the shape of the primitive (`Arc` and `Cone End Radius`).

Our next attributes for this light concern themselves with the colour and direction of the light as it is emitted. The light can be cast outwards, inwards or downwards and we can use a colour ramp to control the light in the cross section of the volume (from right to left in the ramp is from center to outside in the volume).

- Set up the volume light so that it is a spherical shape and IPR render the result.
- Change the colours and interpolation style for the colour ramp to see the effect on the emitted light.
- Change the shape attributes of the volume light.

Changes to the shape of the penumbra are also possible but will only work when the light shape is a cylinder or a cone. Again, the shape is formed from left to right on the ramp and defines how the falloff is controlled.

Shadows

Now we understand the ways that the various lights in Maya work, a real world attribute that is missing from these lights is the creation of shadows. In all of the renders that you have been

Figure 6.6 Shadow Casting.

creating, the shadows have been missing and as such any perceived realism has been lost due to their absence. With most of the lights, shadows can be created through two different methods: *depth mapped* and *raytraced*. Both of these methods have their own caveats on use and how they are generated, so what you wish to use them for will decide which method will be best suited to your work.

Because you are going to be creating a lot of lights for the rest of the examples in this chapter, it will be useful to be able to access any of the light creation menu items. The easiest way to set this up is to use Ctrl+Alt+Shift and the relevant Create|Lights menu item. This will create an icon for each light type in the currently selected shelf. Useful as this is, as you create more and more shelf items, you will have to move the cursor up to the shelves and their items making this no faster than having to select menu items. Instead, then, you can use Maya's marking menu system to provide instant access to any functions that you have saved to the shelf. You have already seen several marking menus in operation in and around the Hotbox, and holding down a hotkey (like "h") can also access a marking menu. Marking menus mean that you don't have to move the cursor from its current position when you hold down an associated key, so you can create a new menu and set up a new hotkey to be associated with it.

- Create an icon on the current shelf for each of the four main types of light in Maya (point, directional, area and spotlight).
- Open the Marking Menu Editor from Window|Settings/Preferences|Marking Menus ...
- Click Create Marking Menu – this will bring up the template for the menu item positions.
- MMB drag and drop a light icon from the shelf onto a space in the template (you can test the functionality by using the demo area in the bottom left of the window).
- Give the menu a name (call it light_types) and click Save.

- Select light_types from the Marking Menu Editor and use the fold out to set the marking menu's use to "Hotkey Editor".
- Click Apply Settings and close the window.

You have now created a marking menu, but still need to set up a hotkey for it.

- Open the Hotkey Editor from Window|Settings/Preferences|Hotkeys.
- Scroll down the Categories section until the User Marking Menus category is found.
- Highlight this category and the action for light_types_press.
- Assign the "l" key to this item (Maya will ask if you want the same hotkey attached to the release action).
- Click Save and close this window.
- Test it out.

Depth Mapped Shadows

Depth mapped shadows are created from a light by rendering a depth map from the light's point of view; a depth map is a rendered file image that represents distance in terms of the greyscale colour of the pixel. To determine whether a surface point is in shadow or illuminated, Maya calculates the distance of the light to the surface point in question and compares it to the corresponding distance for that pixel stored in the shadow map. If the surface point is further away from the light than the pixel for the depth map, then it is in shadow.

- Delete any lights in the scene and create a spotlight that illuminates the scene.
- Render the current scene so you can be sure of the correct framing.
- In the Attribute Editor for the spotlight, open the fold-out titled Shadows and the sub-fold-out titled Depth Map Shadow Attributes and turn on Use Depth Map Shadows.
- Render the scene.

The depth map is stored as a square map whose XY size is determined by the Dmap Resolution attribute. Try and keep this as low as possible, as the larger the depth maps, the longer it will take to generate. For all depth map shadows, an attribute called Use Mid Dist Dmap is available, which averages the distances used to determine whether a surface point is in shadow or not. If this is turned off, streaking and spottiness may occur in the scene so it is set to on by default. When determining the resolution for a depth map shadow, a good rule of thumb is to start the Dmap Resolution at the same size as the currently rendered picture (found under the Options|Test Resolution menu in the render view) and increasing or decreasing the map to suit. Increasing the size of the depth map can reduce any blockiness at the edge of the depth map as this increases the accuracy of the map to distance comparison. Keep rendering the scene until the shadows are acceptable. If soft edged shadows are required then you can use the Dmap Filter to blur the shadow – this lets you keep the shadow map to a small size, as the blockiness will be blurred out:

- Set the Dmap Resolution to 320 and set Dmap Filter Size to 5 and render.
- For softer shadows, set the Dmap Filter Size to 15.

In addition to blurring the shadows, the shadow colour can also be changed to give different lighting effects (soft shadows can be made to look almost transparent by setting the shadow colour to a light grey).

Figure 6.7 Blocky Shadows due to a Low Depth Map Resolution.

Figure 6.8 Depth Map Resolution Set to a Higher Value.

Figure 6.9 Blocky but Filtered Shadows.

The type of light used will also determine how the shadows will look. A directional light is the only light that will give parallel edged shadows, but some problems can occur if lighting a scene with one. If you are using a directional light to simulate the sun's rays then you may find that you have to increase the size of the shadow depth map in order to correctly cast shadows for everything in the scene. Because a directional light is the size of an infinite plane perpendicular to the direction of the light rays, Maya uses an attribute called Use Dmap Auto Focus to create a shadow map just large enough to cover all shadow casting objects. Turning this attribute off does allow you to tune the width of a shadow map by using the Dmap Width Focus value to scale the depth map within the area of the light's illumination.

- Move the objects in the scene into a line.
- Delete any lights in the scene and create a directional light that shines on the objects at roughly 45 degrees (turn on depth map shadows too).
- Render to make sure that the shadows are falling evenly from the objects.
- Turn off Use Dmap Auto Focus and render with a Dmap Width Focus value of 100.
- Render with a value of 10 and then 1000.

With a setting of 1000, the shadow is so scaled that it hardly resembles a shadow at all, but with a setting of 10, the shadow is sharper and only covers the middle object. So, setting the Dmap Width value allows you to optimize shadow casting and the size of the depth map used. One further attribute that can be used to fine tune the creation of a shadow map is the Bias setting. Bias allows you to change the position of the edge of the shadow that is cast from a surface, in effect allowing you to move the start of the shadow away from or towards the shadow casting light. This attribute allows you to solve any calculation errors that may cause the shadow to become detached from the surface.

Plate 1 The NURBS teapot reflection mapped using an environment cube and scanline rendering.

Plate 2 The NURBS teapot raytraced in the same environment.

Plate 3 The iridescence shader.

Plate 4 An advanced iridescence shader on butterfly wings.

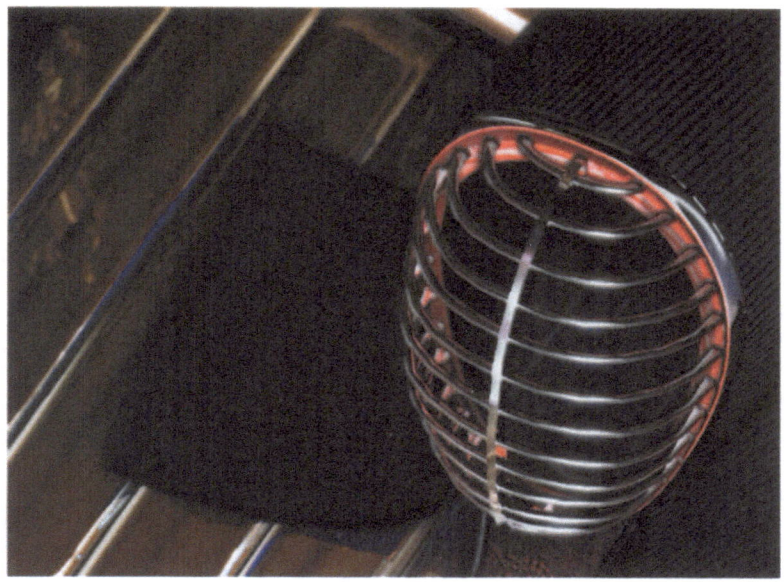

Plate 5 Image rendered using combinations of multiple layers of raytraced and scanline rendered passes.

Plate 6 Image courtesy of Seth Dubieniec.

Plate 7 Image courtesy of Seth Dubieniec.

Plate 8 Image courtesy of Jessica Groom, Claire Pakeman and Alison Muffet.

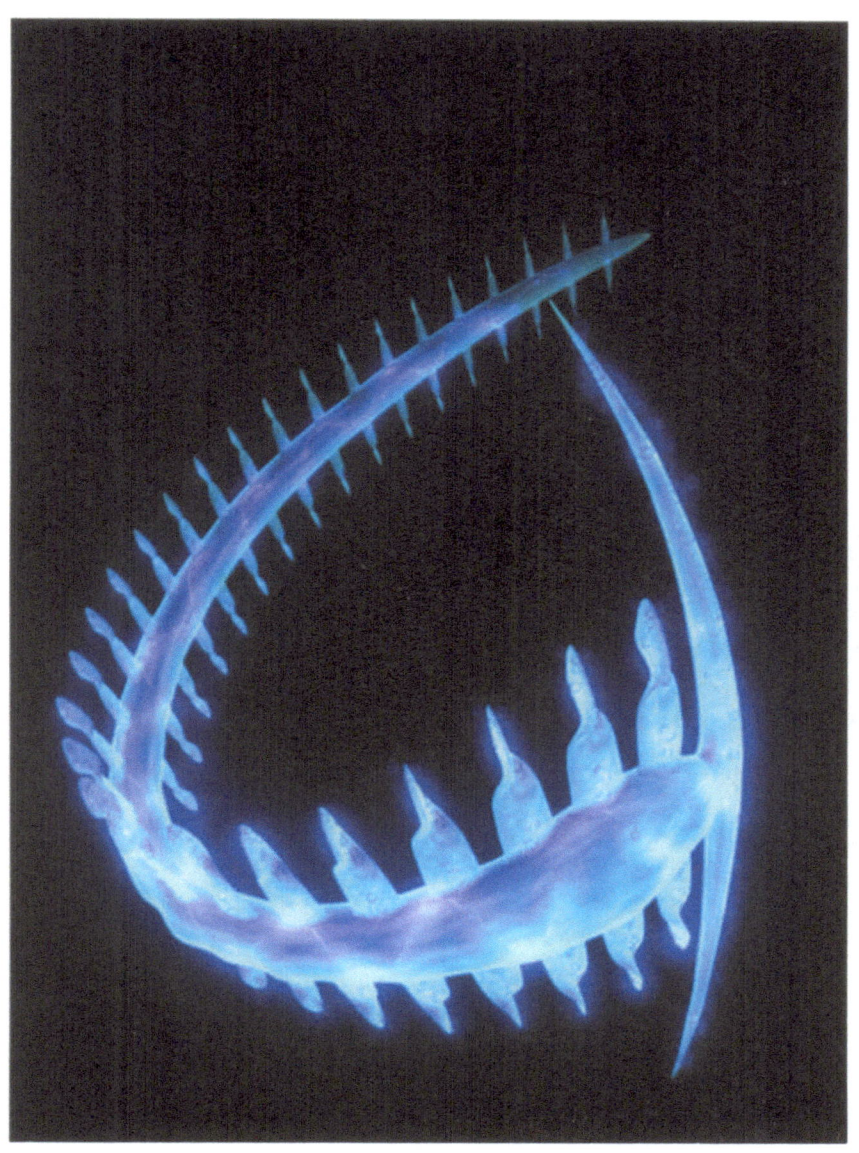

Plate 9 Image courtesy of Mark Hatchard.

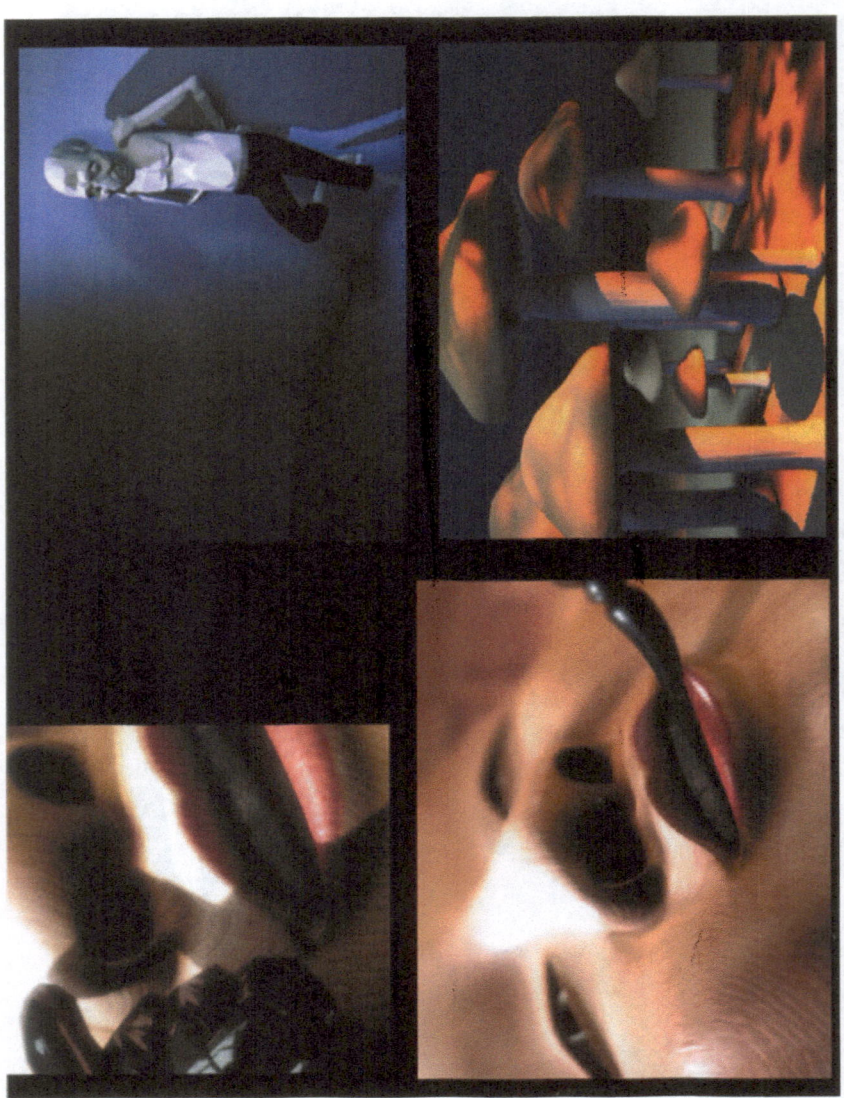

Plate 10 Image courtesy of Ben Toogood.

Plate 11 Image courtesy of Gawain Liddiard, Unnstein Gudjonsson, Jordan Kirk, Stefan D'Hont and Mohamed Sohby.

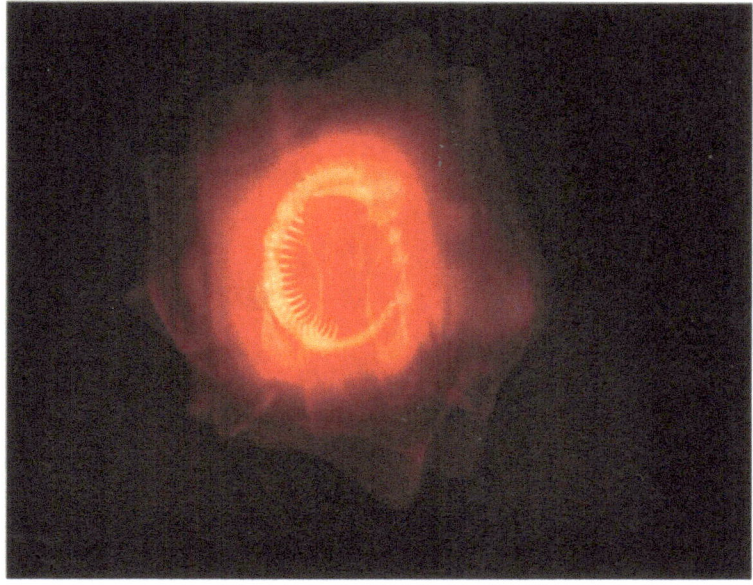

Plate 12 Image courtesy of Duncan Price.

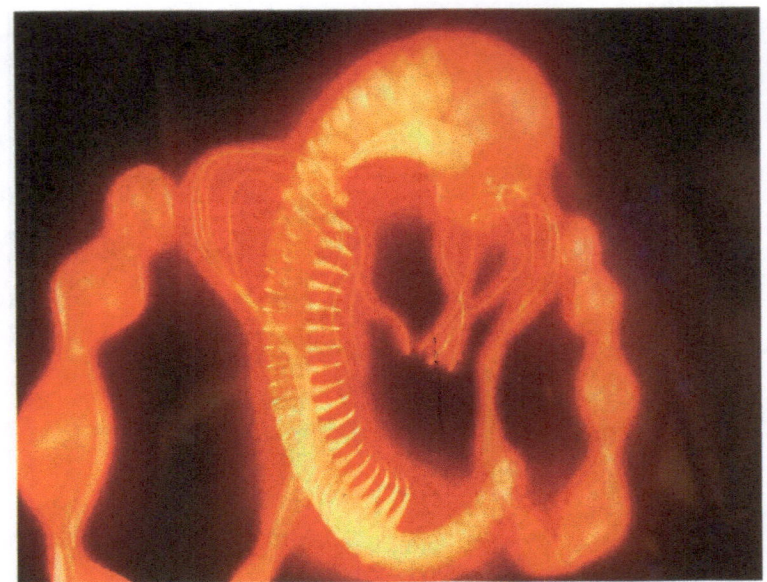

Plate 13 Image courtesy of Duncan Price.

Plate 14 Image courtesy of Tom Greybe.

Raytraced Shadows

So far, when rendering shadows and scenes we have been using a technique known as scanline rendering. This splits up the screen into lines and renders each line according to the light falling upon each visible surface point in the line. Another method for rendering that Maya can utilize is called raytracing, which casts a ray of "light" from the screen, which is then traced through the scene collecting colour values each time it encounters a point. This can provide very accurate details about the surfaces used and accurate shadow shapes as well, but because of the nature of this technique, render times may slow down. Because the shadows are generated as the scene is rendered, optimizations such as saving shadows to disk can't be created either. Maya can use both rendering techniques at the same time – this will be expanded on later in this chapter.

Select the shadow casting light and in the Attribute Editor, turn off Use Depth Map Shadows. Open the fold-out titled Raytraced Shadow Attributes, turn on Use Raytraced Shadows and re-render the scene. No shadows appear. You need to enable the use of raytracing within the renderer, as it is not turned on by default. The reason for this is that raytracing can incur a very large time overhead when rendering and as such, a conscious decision should be made to enable this rendering method. Options that pertain to the renderer can be found under Window|Rendering Editors|Render Globals in the main window, or from the Options menu within the render view. The Render Globals allows you to change various rendering attributes such as the quality of the final image (anti-aliasing), the size of the rendered image (resolution) and the enabling of raytracing. Open the fold-out titled Raytracing Quality and turn on Raytracing. Leave the other attributes as they are, close the Render Globals and re-render the scene.

Because the shadows are created during the raycasting process, there are only a few available attributes that control the resultant shadows. The most important attribute is the Shadow Rays attribute, which defines how grainy the resulting shadow will be. This is important, because one of the major differences in shadow quality when using raytraced shadows is that you can correctly calculate soft shadows. Before, with depth map shadows, you could simulate softened shadows by using the depth map filter, but this was only uniformly blurring the result of the shadow process. Raytraced soft shadows can correctly produce diffused, soft shadows but the number of shadow rays used to create the effect determines their quality. Too few rays and the result will be grainy due to the lack of shadow sampling.

Area lights will produce raytraced soft shadows by default because the light casts light rays from a surface not a point. Looking at the shadows cast from a naked bulb and the shadows cast from a diffused light source will demonstrate this and all of the lights in Maya, bar the area light, will cast shadows like a naked bulb, unless otherwise told to.

- Delete all the lights in the scene and create a directional light pointing straight up.
- Set the intensity of the directional light to a very low setting, as this will provide some bounce light for the objects.
- Create an area light and position, scale and adjust the intensity so that it is illuminating all of the objects.
- Turn on Use Raytraced Shadows and render the scene.

As you can see, the area light is creating soft shadows, but the shadows are only being sampled once. Change the number of shadow rays to ten and re-render. The shadows should now be created with a much higher quality, but at the cost of an increase in time to render. It is important to get the mix between shadow rays, quality and render times right – this can only be done by adjusting the number of shadow rays cast until an acceptable trade off is found.

Figure 6.10 Raytraced Soft Shadows from a Polygon Sphere.

The size of the area light will also affect the softness of the shadows cast: the larger the light, the softer the shadow, like a photographer's diffuser. But the larger the light the larger the number of shadow rays required to stop the soft shadow from becoming grainy. If you want soft raytraced shadows from any of the other lights, then the Attribute Editor provides the necessary attributes relative for each light.

- Change the area light into a spotlight and reposition it so that all of the objects are evenly illuminated (you may need to adjust the intensity accordingly).
- Render the scene.

Although the number of shadow rays is set to ten, no soft shadows appear. This is because the spotlight casts sharp edged shadows by default, not soft ones; so the Attribute Editor has created a new attribute called Light Radius which allows you to pretend that the light covers an area in 3D space. Analogous to the area light, a larger setting will create softer shadows. This attribute exists for point lights as well, but for a directional light, the attribute is called Light Angle instead. In general, point lights will produce softer shadows than directional lights, which in turn will produce softer shadows than spotlights. Experiment with different settings between the three lights, but keep the number of shadow rays the same. You can stop a light contributing to a render by hiding it, so you can create three lights and quickly compare effects between them using the hide and display actions.

Light Linking

Now that we have covered the methods for creating and editing light attributes in Maya, we can start using some more functions to fine tune the effects of lights on the scene. Many of the functions let you change options for the lights to either optimize rendering time or to create a more pleasing aesthetic. Another available option is to change various ways that lights act which don't correspond to any real physical properties. Because the lights and renderer don't obey the actual physical phenomena of light within the scenes, there is also a lot to play with in terms of tricks within the environment. The most useful property that can be changed about lights is whether they cast light on objects, known as light linking. This technique is important for three reasons:

1. Unless the light has a fall off, it will shine on any objects in the scene irrespective of distance; this is especially true for directional lights which have no decay settings.
2. If the light is casting shadows then you may want it to cast shadows from certain objects only, especially if you want different objects to cast different coloured shadows from the same source.
3. When rendering, Maya doesn't have to calculate whether all of the objects are being lit if there is a list defining which objects will be lit by which light.

The Relationship Editor can be used to review and define which lights affect which objects. By default all lights are linked to all objects, placing these lights into a set called the defaultLightSet which can be seen in the Outliner.

• Create three objects, three directional lights and a ground plane.
• Move the lights so that they are illuminating all of the objects and change the colour of the lights so that one is red, one green and one blue.
• Render the scene (it should come evenly lit in grey shades as the three light colours additively mix to create white).

To access the light linking window use Window|Relationship Editors|Light Linking| Light Centric. Because you are using light-centric linking, the list of available lights appears on the left and objects on the right, meaning that you select a light and then edit the list of objects it affects; object centric is the opposite of this.

• Select the green light and all objects it affects will be highlighted.
• Toggle off all objects apart from the ground plane and one object.
• Do the same for the other two lights so that they each shine on the ground plane and a separate object.
• Re-render the scene.

Now that this relationship has been set up, you can further individualize the effects of the lights without affecting the other objects in the scene; for instance, you can now turn on shadows and have some soft and some sharp plus change the colour of them if you want. You can also make and break light links by selecting the relevant items and lights and using Lighting/Shading|Make Light Links or Lighting/Shading|Break Light Links. In order to keep abreast of which lights are affecting which surface without the Relationship Editor, the Lighting/Shading|Select Objects Illuminated by Light and Lighting/Shading| Select Lights Illuminating Object allow you to quickly display these connections in the Outliner and viewports.

Negative Light Sources

If you find that you need to darken some areas of the scene, you can remove light from the scene by using a negative intensity. This will obey all of the other light attributes such as decay, fall off and linking but can serve to create areas of darkness that would otherwise be difficult and time consuming (for you and the renderer) to achieve using shadows. This can be extremely useful when darkening a character's mouth using a negative point light with a sharp decay rate.

Lens Effects

Although the lights illuminate the scene and in the case of an area light have a surface, they do not actually appear within the final render. For example, if you wanted to show a spotlight as it shone into the camera or a sun rising over a planet, then you would have to create an object which represented the light and/or create some form of lighting effect. Maya provides a node called `Optical FX` that can be attached to a light to generate 2D light effects.

- Create a point light and open the `Light Effects` fold-out.
- LMB click the map button (chequer-patterned) beside the "Light Glow" text field to create an Optical FX node which is attached to the light (the map button indicates that a rendering node can be attached to this attribute).
- Render the scene with the light source in view.

The Optical FX node provides many attributes that control how light glow and lens flare are rendered. When rendering a spotlight or area light with an Optical FX effect connected, make

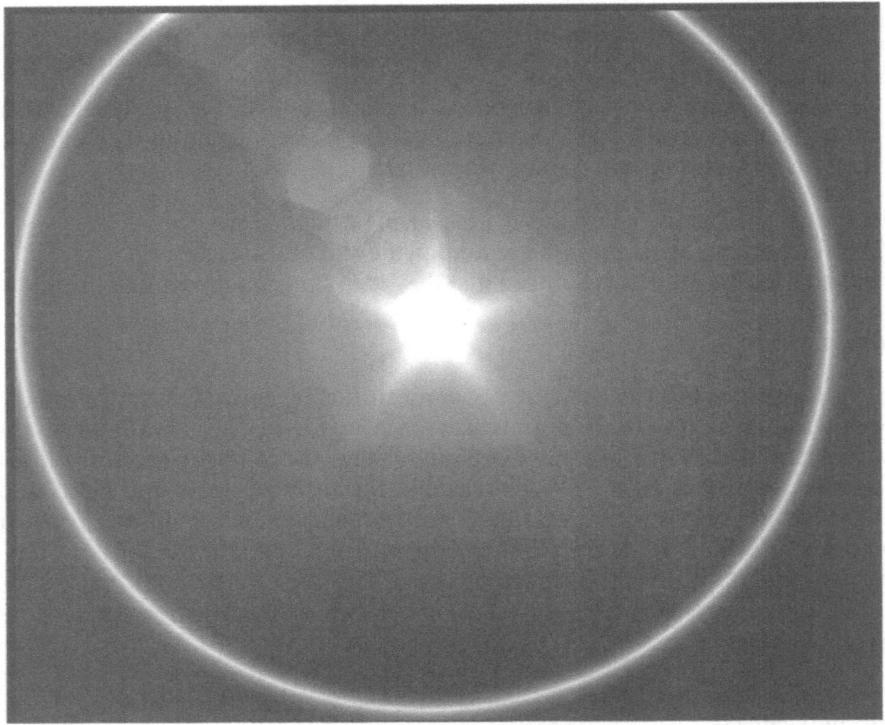

Figure 6.11 Lens Flare when Looking Directly at a Light.

sure that the light is facing the camera. Whenever an Optical FX node is attached to a light, Maya will create either a sphere for point lights, a disc for directional lights or a rectangle for area lights. These are used to determine whether foreground objects are hiding the light glow. Each of these glow objects has a scale attribute that allows you to change their size, which may be needed when trying to occlude the light glow with an object.

Light Fog

You can simulate the interaction of light cast from a spotlight or a point light with particulate matter in the environment, to create a light volume.

- Create a sphere and a spotlight directly above it.
- In the Attribute Editor open the Light Effects fold-out and LMB click the map button to create a light fog node.
- Render the scene.

This node gives an evenly distributed light fog within a cone that is created and attached to the spotlight. Changing the scaling of the cone will change the volume of the light fog. If you wish to have objects casting shadows within the light fog, then you need to have the light in question casting depth mapped shadows not raytraced. Turn this attribute on and re-render the scene to give the effect of a volumetric shadow within the fog. In the light attributes, Fog Spread will control how the fog is distributed from the centre of the fog cone and Fog Intensity will scale the overall colour of the fog. In the fog node itself, colour and density can be changed which will also tend to scale the overall colour and effect of the light fog, density controlling how easy it is to see objects obscured by the fog. The fast Dropoff attribute works with the density attribute and distance to the rendering camera to control the amount that an object in or behind the fog is obscured. A further attribute that can control the visibility of objects is Colour Based Transparency, which will combine density with colour to control the visibility of objects. So set the colour of the fog first, and turn on the required attributes and use density to then change the overall visibility of objects.

The IPR Renderer

As you are going to be changing surface attributes in addition to lighting attributes, it will make sense to use the IPR renderer. IPR stands for Interactive Photorealistic Renderer, with the emphasis being on interactive. Unlike the normal render view window, the IPR renderer takes a snapshot of the scene in terms of colour but also in terms of shading calculations (an IPR file). An IPR file contains the shading calculations that define the image such as material shininess, shadow colour and light position, and means that changes to these attributes will update in real time, thus re-rendering the scene will not be necessary. Although the results do not echo the final frame in terms of total quality, they provide very fast feedback when setting up and tuning shading networks.

- Create a sphere and a few lights.
- Invoke the IPR renderer by clicking on the IPR icon in the main GUI window or from the render view.

- Select a portion of the rendered view that you wish to tune.
- Select a light, open the Attribute Editor and begin changing attributes.

Limitations to the IPR renderer will be geometry changes, shadow map changes (apart from colour), raytraced attributes and transformations (apart from lighting transforms). You can keep the current IPR file for as long as you wish to tune from the current viewpoint and different sections can be marquee selected to tune. Once the IPR file is finished with, flush it from memory by LMB clicking the red IPR icon at the top right of the window. Whenever selecting a portion of an IPR file, make sure that the file can be kept in memory, the size of which is shown in the top right corner. IPR files can also be saved to disk if required, but will obviously represent the scene at that time and not update if the scene changes. Because this renderer allows you to quickly view changes made to render nodes, this chapter will use the IPR renderer. If we want to make several changes but don't want the IPR renderer to activate we can press the pause button in the Render View, make the changes and then unpause the IPR renderer which will then update.

Materials and Shading Groups

Now that objects can be illuminated in the scene, we need to start defining how surfaces reflect the light. In Maya, materials are used to define these reflections and to determine an object's colour, shininess, opacity, and surface detail. All surfaces, when initially created, will have a default material attached to them so that you can see them when you render a scene, in the same way that Maya creates a default light. Most of the following work will be done in the Hypershade – a window that allows you to create all of the shading nodes you need and will display connected networks in much the same way that the Hypergraph does.

With a fresh scene, open the Hypergraph from `Window|Rendering Editors|Hypergraph`. The Hypershade is divided into three sections:

1. The far left-hand side (the Create Bar) displays the type of nodes that can be created.
2. The top section displays shading nodes of a type controlled by the tabs (`Materials, Textures, Utilities, Lights, Cameras and Projects`).
3. The bottom section provides an area where you can examine shading networks and connect nodes or load in shaders.

As with the Hypergraph, you can navigate about the Hypershade with the orthographic camera controls. Nodes can be deleted by selecting them and pressing Backspace and can be connected by MMB dragging one onto another. The Hypershade display can be modified to present the clearest picture at any time by using the display buttons to show or hide the Create Bar and the icons at the top right to show or hide the upper and lower sections of the Hypershade. In the Create Bar you can limit the display of available nodes that can be created by using the various options from the triangle icon (a fold-out menu). As with the Hypergraph, all of the menu items are represented in a RMB marking menu.

A material defines several attributes of a surface when it renders: how shiny it is, how reflective it is, how bumpy it appears and how transparent it is, to name but a few. All surfaces reflect light using surface normals, which are vectors that lie perpendicular to a surface. If the normals are facing roughly towards a light source, then the surface will reflect light. Normals can be displayed for each surface type using `Display|Nurbs Components|Normals (Shaded mode)` and `Display|Polygon Components|Normals`. All surfaces are created double-sided in

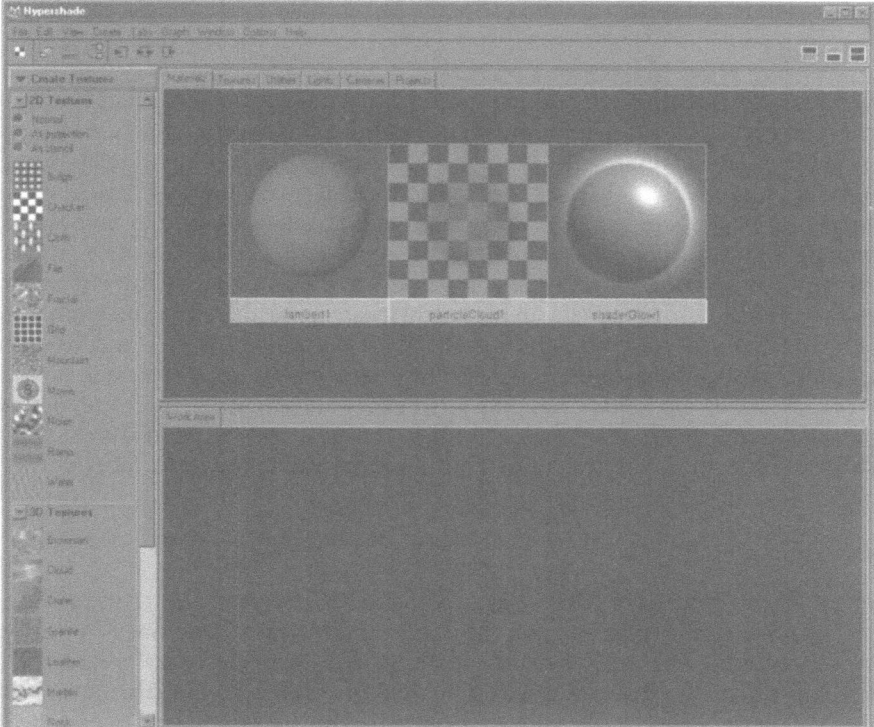

Figure 6.12 The Hypershade.

Maya, which is why you can see the interior of objects after you delete faces or trim surfaces, but you will only see one set of normals as Maya will just double up the normals. Create four spheres and a ground plane, light them and move the camera so that you can see them all. Create an IPR render for the view. Open the Hypershade and pop the view to the foreground and draw a marquee selection over the objects so that you can begin investigating the five basic surface materials.

Surface materials all share some basic attributes and as materials change, new attributes will be added. The most basic material is the Lambert. In the Hypershade, set the Create Bar to `Create Materials` and LMB click the Lambert Material icon. Although there already is a Lambert material in the scene, you should leave this alone as it is applied to all new objects created. Select the ground plane in the Outliner (or in any view), in the Hypershade move the cursor over the picture or swatch of the new Lambert material and use the RMB marking menu to select `Assign Material to Selection`. You can also assign materials/shaders to an object by MMB dragging and dropping it onto the surface when it is in an IPR render or a view, by selecting the object in any of the windows and using `Lighting/Shading|Assign Existing Material...` or by using the RMB marking menu over any object – this will allow you to assign an existing material or to create a new one. The IPR renderer will update as a change to the ground planes shading network has been detected, but nothing else will really change as the new Lambert material is the same as the default grey one. Double-click on the swatch and you can see what a Lambert material represents in terms of shading attributes.

Types of Materials and Shaders

Lambert Material

The Lambert material is a perfectly diffuse material that has no specular shading attributes, so it will reflect no highlights from light sources. All of the other five materials are built on top of Lambert, so they share attributes like Colour (LMB click on the colour swatch to bring up the Colour Chooser and the slider in the Attribute Editor will then lighten or darken this colour), Transparency and Ambient Colour. These attributes are all controlled by colour values and so can only have inputs from other nodes that are represented as colours, float triples or vectors. Generally, you will be connecting shading nodes to these attributes, but it is important to note that if you were to use an expression to control these values, then the expression would have to feed into all three red, green and blue values. Diffuse, Translucence and Translucence Focus are all controlled by single floating point values whereas a shading node can only control the Bump Mapping attribute. Changing any of the values that are represented here (apart from Bump Mapping which will be dealt with in the next section on textures) will quickly demonstrate the effect that the attribute has on received and reflected surface light.

Phong Material

The Phong material simulates a glossy plastic surface In the Hypershade, create a Phong material, apply it to one of the spheres using the RMB marking menu and open up the Attribute Editor for the material. The IPR view will update again showing that the Phong material has a specular component added to its shading attributes, echoed in the Attribute Editor in a Specular Shading section. In addition to the controls for the colour and size of the specular highlight, the Phong material also has a reflectivity value and colour. These attributes can be used to either simulate a reflected environment or to accurately reflect the environment when used in conjunction with raytracing. Reflection, refraction and raytracing issues will be looked at later on in this chapter.

Phong E Material

The Phong E material simulates a shiny plastic surface, whose highlights are softer edged. Create a Phong E material and attach it to another sphere. The highlights on the surface of the object have a much softer edge to them, represented by the controls in the Attribute Editor. You can compare different attributes between nodes by LMB clicking the Copy Tab button at the bottom of the Attribute Editor and then changing the focus of the original editor back to the Phong material. Because the Attribute Editor will remember every node that it has displayed so far, the Focus button lets you quickly change between regularly viewed nodes without having to move between windows. The Phong E material can control the smoothing of the edge of the highlight and the colour of the highlight but cannot create sharp edged glossy highlights like the Phong material.

Blinn Material

The Blinn material simulates the properties of a metallic surface by changing how light is reflected from a surface. Create a Blinn material and apply it to the penultimate sphere. Open the Attribute Editor and examine the `Specular Shading` attributes for this material. The specular attributes control not only how large the highlight appears, but also how the highlight looks when the angle of view changes. If you look at an object with a Blinn material from a low grazing angle, the spread of the highlight will be different than if you viewed it from overhead. The `Specular Roll Off` attribute defines how much this changes. Experiment with this by rendering and compare different views of a flat surface with a Blinn material. To finish the look of a metallic material, the highlight colour should be similar to the diffuse colour.

Anisotropic Material

The Anisotropic material simulates a material with tiny scratches or grooves in it, creating highlights that are dependent on the viewer's position (isotropic means that reflection is identical in all directions). Real world objects that exhibit these properties are CDs, satin and brushed aluminium. The tiny grooves serve to break the light up creating a reflection that moves around when the spatial relationship between viewer and surface changes. Create an Anisotropic material and attach it to the final sphere. Within the `Specular Shading` attributes are values controlling the way that the specular highlight occurs across the surface and the colour of the highlight.

Layered Shader

A layered shader allows you to combine several different materials together to attach to a single surface. This is useful when you want to represent a material whose light reflecting attributes change, such as the bottom of a ship which is covered in barnacles and other gunk but the rest of the hull exhibits shiny metallic reflections. A Lambert material can be used for the lower portion, while a Blinn material can be used for the upper portion of the surface with the layered shader combining both of them – this is then attached to a surface. A texture is generally used to modulate between the different materials but this means that the layered shader will render substantially slower than other shaders.

Ramp Shader

The ramp shader lets us control every aspect of surface shading using ramps, either colour ramps for attributes such as incandescence and specular colour or position ramps for attributes such as specular rolloff and reflectivity. Because ramps are used for attributes we can map textures to any colour entry position giving us unlimited control for special shading characteristics.

Shading Map and Surface Shader

Both of these materials allow you to create non-realistic shading effects. The shading map allows you to use a material like a Phong and use the brightness calculations from the surface to define a colour at that point. For example, you could use the brightness of a surface to define boundary colours similar to the colours in a 2D cel cartoon. The surface shader allows you to ignore shading calculations like diffuse and specular contributions and change only the colour, transparency, glow and matte attributes. These can be controlled by any input that provide the correct data – for example, an object's translation channels could provide the input for the shader's colour attribute.

Use Background

This material lets you use the colour values of any background colours or images that you are using to define the colour of your surface without any other shading calculations. This is useful when you want to composite CG objects into live action backgrounds and need an image or environment to use as a reference for transparency, reflections or refractions, or to composite scenes directly within Maya itself.

Diffuse and Specular Components

It can be seen that most materials are made up of either just a diffuse component, in the case of a Lambert material, or a combination of diffuse and specular components. You can easily see what amounts are included in the shading of the final surfaces by either setting the Diffuse attribute to zero or the Specular Colour to zero. You can also change the contribution to the diffuse or specular shading of a surface from lights by toggling the Diffuse or Specular checkboxes for each light. This function, combined with light linking allows you to closely define how a light will interact with a surface. If you want to generate a subtle bounce light from the ground plane in the scene, all you need to do is to create a directional light pointing straight upwards. Set the intensity of the light to a low value and change its colour to that of the material attached to the ground plane and turn off Emit Specular in the Attribute Editor.

Translucency and Glow

Having explained how these materials work in terms of specular and diffuse shading, there are two remaining attributes common to most of the materials: *translucency* and *glow*. Whereas transparency controls how much light passes through an object, translucency simulates the diffused transport of light through an object, for example, how light tends to "leak" through lampshades or leaves; glass is transparent, white Perspex is translucent. So for a lampshade, we wouldn't want to see the bulb behind it, but would like to see the effect on the surface from the light that hits it instead.

RGBAL Channels and Mattes

In the render view you have the option of viewing different channels for each rendered image. Each image is composed of a red, green and blue channel and optionally of an alpha (or matte) channel. These channels can be displayed in the render view along with a luminance channel by either using the Display menu item to select various channels or the two beach ball icons below it (one for "all channels" and one for "alpha channel"). The Matte Opacity attribute common to most materials controls what components of the image are used to create the alpha channel and what effect this channel has on the surrounding alpha channels of other items. The default setting is Opacity Gain and allows the material to gather alpha values from transparency, shadows and raytraced reflections. Changing the Matte Opacity

Mode to `Solid Matte` and changing the value of the `Matte Opacity` with the slider can set a constant value for the alpha channel across the entire material. You can also use the object to remove the colour and alpha values from an image by changing the `Matte Opacity Mode` to `Black Hole`.

- Move one of the spheres partially in front of one of the other spheres.
- IPR render the area and display the alpha channel.
- Set the foreground sphere's `Matte Opacity Mode` to `Solid Matte`, change the `Matte Opacity` to zero and then display the colour channels.
- Set the foreground sphere's `Matte Opacity Mode` to `Black Hole` and look at the alpha and colour channels.

Textures and Texture Mapping

Texturing is a method of controlling some or all of the various attributes that are seen within the surface shaders, for instance colour or transparency. Instead of assigning a constant colour or value across the entire material, a texture can be used instead. This allows you to vary the values of a shader's attribute across the surface of an object and begin to build up more complex shading networks. A texture can either be a file or movie texture or a procedurally generated texture, and once this has been defined, the next process is to map it to the surface which has the shader assigned to it. Because the mapping of a texture involves the use of a surface description at some point, textures are mapped to NURBS surfaces and polygon surfaces in different ways, as each surface type is defined in a different manner. A procedurally generated texture can be defined in terms of two dimensions or in terms of three dimensions, whereas a file/movie texture is imported from the hard disk. All of the 2D and 3D procedural textures that ship with Maya are presented in a straightforward manner within the Hypershade window as swatches, but the best way to examine their effects is to create a simple test on a simple object with some simple lighting. This way you can see how the texture changes shader attributes without having to wait a long time to render a complex object.

NURBS Texturing

As we know from modeling, NURBS surfaces are defined in two dimensions – U and V – which can make things very easy if you want to apply 2D textures to them. Both the surface and the texture have only two dimensions, so the mapping of a point on the texture (whether a bitmap or a procedurally generated texture) to a position on the surface can be very simple to do. This one-for-one mapping is known as UV mapping as it uses the inherent parametric positions on the NURBS surface to look up the colour value of the chosen texture. Beyond UV mapping you can also use projection mapping which allows you to project your texture from a geometric shape, thus enabling you to define a more specialized texture placement. Use `Display|NURBS Components|Surface Origins` to show where the U and V parameters start from on each patch.

UV Texture Mapping

Start a new scene and create a NURBS sphere. Set up the perspective camera so that you can see the sphere clearly and create a few lights to evenly illuminate the object. In the Hypershade,

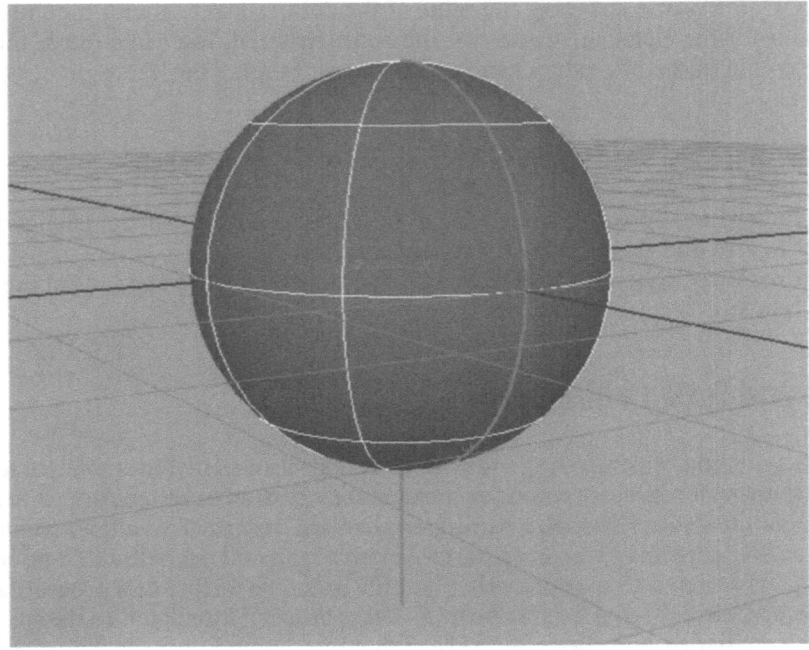

Figure 6.13 U and V Surface Origins.

create a new Phong material, apply this to the selected surface and IPR render the sphere. Normally you would control the colour of the sphere by changing the colour of the Phong shader, but instead we are going to use a texture to control this attribute. The quickest way to add a texture control to an attribute is to open the Attribute Editor (double-click on the Phong shader swatch in the Hypershade) and to LMB click on the Map button at the right of the attribute. Clicking on the Map button will bring up the Create Render Node window, which is opened at Texture and mirrors the Create... menu bar at the side of the Hypershade. It can be seen that there are four varieties of textures (2D, 3D, Environment and Layered) with three methods of applying them (Normal, Projection and Stencil). Because we are going to be using the NURBS surface's inherent UV mapping to position the 2D texture, it needs to be Normal so that it can access the surface information of the sphere. Click on the chequer pattern and the IPR render should update, as should the Attribute Editor, giving access to the relevant attributes for the chequer texture. The texture doesn't change any of the other characteristics of the shader such as shininess or diffuse amount as you are only controlling the colour value across the surface. Note that a texture can also be applied to an attribute by using the RMB menu when the cursor is over the attribute name (the cursor will also change display indicating that a menu can be brought up).

In the Hypershade, select the Phong material (the swatch has now changed to reflect the new attributes) and show the Input and output connections for the shader. You can see in the lower portion of the Hypershade, that the Phong shader has two nodes downstream and it also feeds into a node upstream. The node upstream is a Shading Group that collects the series of different nodes which can be used to affect a surface under one roof. Double-clicking on this node, you can see that it collects together a Surface material, a Volume material and a Displacement material and so forms the logical end of a shading network. The Attribute Editor for the chequer pattern allows you to affect attributes concerned with colour but not with placement or with the number of chequers that appear in each row. For these attributes, you need to examine the 2D placement node. This node controls all of the information about where the colour pattern is placed in relation to the NURBS surface description. This can be seen in the Hypershade by moving the cursor over any of the connecting lines, which will display the upstream and downstream attributes that are connected. From the 2D placement node to the chequer node, you can see there are two attributes connected. One is `OutUV` to `uvCoord`, which places and generates the pattern over the surface, and the other is `outUvFilterSize` to `UvFilterSize`, which is concerned with making sure that the texture doesn't flicker when rendered.

Double-clicking on the 2D placement node will allow you to see its attributes, which are common to all 2D placement nodes. The chequer pattern is generated from a repeated set of colours, which you can see, by setting the repeat UV attributes to one. To increase the amount of squares in U and V change the repeat UV values, or to create stripes in either direction set one of the values to 0.5. The other attributes that are available control how the co-ordinates for the texture are mapped to the co-ordinates of the NURBS surface. Changing attributes such as `Coverage` or either of the rotate attributes will have an immediate effect on how the texture is mapped to the surface, as will adding some noise to the UV co-ordinates. If you want to change these attributes in the camera view, click the Interactive Placement button. This will invoke the Texture Placement manipulator and display the extents of the UV texture on the surface as a series of red lines representing the boundaries. You can now use the MMB to drag these edges or other icons in order to affect the placement, which will update in the Attribute Editor. You can quickly navigate through all of the related nodes in the shader network using the `node input` and `node output` buttons.

Textures can be used to control every aspect of the shader's appearance, but you need to make sure that the output from the node matches the required input. In the Hypershade, make sure that the full shader network for the Phong material is visible and create a 2D noise texture (keeping `Normal` selected). We are going to use this texture to change one of the Phong shader's attributes; this can be done in one of three ways, if you create a node using the `Create` menu bar in the Hypershade.

1. MMB drag and drop the texture node onto the required attribute in the Attribute Editor (Maya will display a "no entry" sign if this connection is not possible).
2. MMB drag and drop the node onto the shader node in the Hypershade, which will bring up a sub menu asking what connection you would like to make.
3. Use the arrow connectors – these allow you to connect the output of the node to the input arrow of another node.

MMB drag and drop the noise texture onto the transparency attribute for the Phong shader and adjust the values for the 2D noise node so that only spots of the surface are transparent (use the `Density` attribute). The effect of the transparency attribute will work better if the sphere is re-rendered against a background, because the IPR renderer didn't take into account the backfaces of the sphere when creating the first IPR file. Maya has automatically connected the out colour from the noise node to the transparency of the Phong shader, because transparency is defined as a colour so that we can get realistic effects like white light passing through coloured glass. Disconnect the noise texture from the Phong shader by using

Break Connections from the RMB menu in the Attribute Editor or by LMB clicking on the connecting line between the two nodes in the Hypergraph and pressing Backspace to delete it.

You can have more control over connecting attributes by MMB dragging and dropping the 2D noise node onto the Phong shader node. Because the default attribute is being controlled by the chequer texture, a menu of the various attributes you might want to connect is presented. Because the default output of the noise node is a colour value, Maya will present us with colour-related inputs for the Phong shader. If you wanted to connect to some other attribute, such as the diffuse value which requires a single floating point number, then you would have to choose Other, which would bring up the Connection Editor. The Connection Editor allows you to connect left side attributes (outputs) to right side attributes (inputs), as long as the data from one side to the other is of the correct form. For example, if you click on Out Colour (which has a fold-out indicating that it is composed of multiple values), you will be unable to select any illegal connection choices. So, if you wanted to have the noise texture affect the diffuse input, you would need to select the Out Alpha and connect it to the Diffuse attribute, because Out Alpha is a single floating point value.

The same control over attribute connection can be exerted using the arrow connectors, which function in much the same manner as dragging and dropping one node onto another. Create another chequer texture, LMB click and hold on the arrow icon on the right-hand side of the texture swatch and select Out Colour. Move the cursor and it can be seen that an attribute connection line is being created, so LMB click on the arrow icon on the left-hand side of the Phong shader swatch and select Transparency. The connection will be made and IPR view should update. Again, you can open the Connection Editor using this method as well. In the Attribute Editor for the chequer texture, change the values of the Repeat UV to 5.0, 0.5 and set the Rotate Frame attribute to 30.0. The work area in the Hypergraph can also be tidied up using Graph|Rearrange Graph.

UV Bump and Displacement Mapping

One section of the Phong shader's attributes that is not automatically obvious is the Bump Mapping attribute. The only way that this attribute can be made to work and altered is by connecting a texture to it. Bump mapping perturbs the way that light is reflected from the surface of an object to give the illusion of bumpiness without actually changing the surface description.

- Delete all of the textures apart from the chequer texture that feeds into the colour attribute of the Phong shader.
- Create a 2D cloth texture and connect it to the Bump Map attribute of the shader.

The IPR renderer will update this change because the bump map purely changes the way the surface is shaded. The edge of the sphere hasn't changed from its original form and is still smooth and curved, despite the effect of the bump map on the area that can be seen. As such, this makes bump maps ideal for small changes to a surface that won't be seen edge on or that define the edges of shadows (e.g. the fine wrinkles in the palm of a hand). If you want to change the depth of the bump map, open the Attribute Editor for the newly created bump2D node and adjust the Bump Depth attribute. If you want to use a texture to actually change the surface description of the NURBS sphere to provide a change in silhouette and shadow casting, you need to use a displacement map. This takes the black and white values from a texture and changes the surface at render time, which means that although rendering of the sphere might significantly slow down by using a displacement map, the sphere itself is still the same lightweight NURBS object in the workspace. Displacement maps are attached to a surface using the Shading Group.

- Delete the cloth texture from the Hypergraph and create a noise texture.
- MMB drag and drop the noise texture into the Displacement Mat section of the Phong Shading Group.
- Render using the normal renderer.

It can be seen that the surface of the sphere has been exploded by the Displacement material that has been applied, but in the Maya workspace it is unaffected. However, you cannot change the amount of displacement for the bump3D node, as it is controlled by the out alpha value of the noise texture. In the noise texture node, change the alpha gain attribute to 0.25 to ramp down the value of the displacement. The change in speed for rendering is quite large, so use displacement mapping judiciously. You can still use textures to create bump maps on top of displacement maps for further detail on a surface, so map a bulge texture to the displacement material instead and use the noise texture as a bump map. If we want to quickly see the effect of texture values as they affect displacement height, we can use a height field utility. The height field is a square surface which will only show in the interactive window and attempt to show the size of the texture displacement.

- Create a height field from the utilities section in the Hypergraph and open it in the Attribute editor.
- MMB drag and drop the noise texture onto the Displacement attribute.

Projection Mapping

Projection mapping can be used to apply textures to surfaces if the UV mapping method isn't correct for the situation. Instead of directly mapping the UV co-ordinates of a 2D texture to the UV co-ordinates of a NURBS surface via a place2Dtexture node, a 2D texture with two new nodes that help project the texture through space from 3D world co-ordinates is created instead, analogous to using a slide projector. The types of projections available are Planar, Spherical, Cylindrical, Ball, Cubic, Triplanar and Concentric; which all describe the way that the texture is projected.

- Delete all nodes feeding into the current NURBS sphere and IPR render the grey Phong shaded object.
- Change the type to Projection in the Create bar and create a 2D chequer texture.
- Connect the chequer texture to the colour attribute of the Phong material.

The chequer texture is now projected over the surface of the NURBS sphere but does not follow the UV description of the NURBS surface, because two new nodes now control the look. In the perspective window you can see the texture placement icon (set out as a planar projection) and you can change the shape and placement of this projection by activating the Show Manipulator tool or transforming it using the standard transform tools. If you scale and translate the texture placement icon, you can always return it to its normal position by clicking the Fit to Group Bounding Box button in the projection node. If you move the texture placement node so that it is only projecting across half of the sphere, the IPR render still

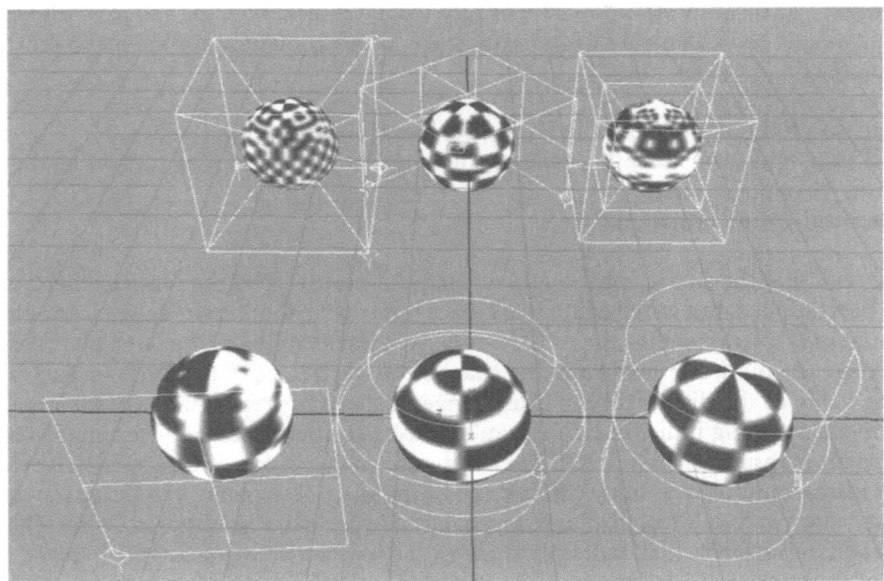

Figure 6.14 The Different Texture Projection Types.

shows all of the texture is projected across the whole of the NURBS surface. Open the Attribute Editor for the place2Dtexture node and turn off Wrap U and Wrap V, which will keep the texture to within the 3D bounds of the projection icon. If the Attribute Editor's focus is turned to the project node, you can change the type of projection interactively and explore how the different projections affect the colours on the surface of the sphere. When using projected textures, you should always parent them to the transform node of the surface you are texturing otherwise the colours across the surface will alter drastically when you move the object. Projections can be extremely useful when you wish to place a texture onto your shader without following the UV lines. Using a spherical projection, you can move the texture placement icon to get a chequer colour that doesn't shrink at the poles of the sphere.

3D Textures

A 3D texture is a procedural pattern that is defined in 3D space, so that the final appearance is as if the object had been carved from a block of this texture. This involves no real mapping apart from the procedural 3D texture co-ordinates to the object space of the surface (which is why there is only a cubic placement manipulator). 3D textures do not smear themselves when placed on surfaces, but surfaces will appear to move through the texture if the placement icon isn't parented to the surface that is moving. In the attributes for all 3D textures are three checkboxes, which can control how the texture is propagated through 3D space and across surfaces. If local is checked off and the material containing the 3D texture is applied to several objects, then the objects will appear to have been carved out of a large chunk of the same material. If local is checked on, then the objects will have the 3D texture centred at the local space co-ordinates of each object. If wrap is turned off, then this is the same as turning off

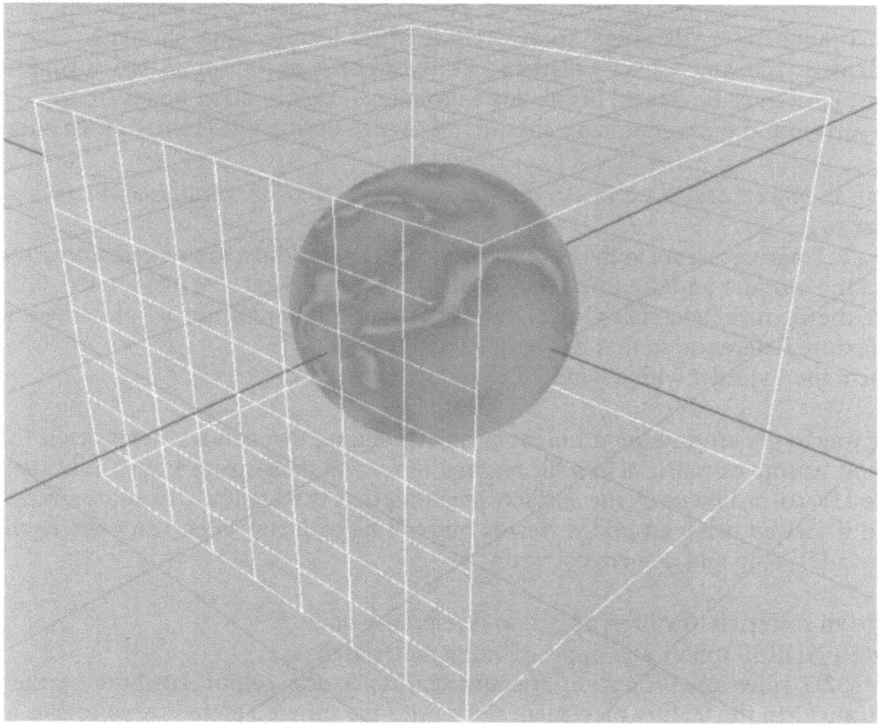

Figure 6.15 The Projection Node for a 3D Crater Texture.

Wrap U and Wrap V in the 2D texture placement nodes, the surface will only have texture on it if it is within the cubic volume of the 3D texture.

Deforming Surfaces

We have seen the three ways that a texture can be mapped to a NURBS surface. Of these methods, UV mapping is the most stable, because no matter where the surface is or what shape it is changed to, the mapping retains a continuous relationship. If we were to UV map a NURBS sphere and deform the sphere in a lattice, the texture would move and stretch with the surface. However, this does not apply to projected and 3D textures, because the UV co-ordinates of the 2D texture are projected into 3D space and the 3D textures are defined at the intersection of the 3D texture procedure and the 3D position of the surface. So for standard transforms, we can just parent the texture placement node under the transform node and any transformations will be applied to the texture placement node as well.

If you want to deform your surface and have the texture stretch with the surface you have to do one of two things:

1. Use a texture reference object.
2. Convert your textures to file textures and then re-apply as a UV texture.

A texture reference object is a duplicate of the original undeformed object with the texture locked to it, allowing the deformed surface to find where texture values should be on its surface as it deforms, in the same way that a lattice uses a base object to determine its deformation. This reference object must be created before any animation or deformation nodes are applied to the original surface and the components should not change through the course of the animation.

- Delete all objects and materials in the scene, create a NURBS cylinder and attach a Phong shader to it.
- Map a 3D marble texture to the Phong's colour attribute, adjust to suit and render the scene.
- Select the cylinder and use `Lighting/Shading|Create Texture Reference Object`.
- Move the Texture Reference Object out of the way and parent the 3D placement node to the Texture Reference, so that it is templated as well.
- Deform the Cylinder with a Bend NLD and render again.

Another way to get around the problem of objects sliding through texture space is to export the current texture or material as a file texture. Maya will then create a bitmap of the texture from the UV co-ordinates of the surface, meaning that the texture will appear warped and stretched if viewed using an image viewer, but will fit perfectly when reapplied to the same surface as a UV map and deform correctly.

- Delete all materials, textures, objects and reference objects.
- Create a NURBS sphere and apply a Phong material to it.
- Map a 2D spherical projection chequer texture to the colour attribute of the Phong and transform the texture placement node until the sphere's texture is no longer uniform (otherwise you might as well have used a UV mapping).
- Select the material and shift-select the object it is attached to and in the Hypergraph, open the options box for `Edit|Convert to File Texture`.
- In the options box, turn on `Anti-alias`, click `Convert` and close.

Maya will then save a file texture to disk, create a new material with this file texture and attach it to the selected object as a UV map. If odd coloured edges are creeping into the file texture, set the `Background Mode` to `Extend Colour Edge` to clear up any pixels along the edges that weren't included in the conversion process.

Layered Textures and Layered Shaders

Layered shaders and textures allow you to combine textures and shaders together to create a composite surface description. A layered texture lets you combine multiple textures together that feed into a material shader attribute, whereas a layered shader allows you to combine different shaders together to obtain varied material effects over a surface, such as specularity and bump mapping. Common to both nodes is the method of layering, in that it is usual to use a texture to create a transparency between two levels. You can use multiple textures in the layered texture and then save it out as a UV map if required so that calculation time is reduced on the final object render.

- Create a Phong material, a layered texture and attach to a NURBS sphere.
- IPR render the scene.

- Create a leather texture, a ramp texture, a chequer texture and open the layered texture in the Attribute Editor.

The layered texture collects the texture swatches and applies them to the selected surface from left to right, with the texture swatch at the left appearing at the top. MMB drag and drop the leather texture into the layered texture and delete the empty green swatch by clicking on the "x" icon at the bottom of it. MMB drag and drop the chequer and then the ramp texture onto the layered shader. You could change the transparency value for each texture by clicking on it in the layered texture and then adjusting the Alpha value, but this changes the value across the whole surface. Using the Blend Mode fold-out, which provides a variety of different modes, you can change the blending for each layer.

- Select the leather texture swatch in the layered texture and MMB drag and drop the leather texture onto the Alpha value.
- Select the chequer texture swatch in the layered texture and MMB drag and drop the chequer texture onto the Alpha value.

In this way you can use the original texture's colour position to affect its own blending with the layers below it. A layered shader functions in exactly the same fashion except that you are now layering materials together, which can cause a noticeable slowdown when rendering as different shading networks are combined, especially if they are composed of layered textures. These materials can each have a bump map assigned to them, but because the layered shader feeds into a single shading group, only one displacement map can be used.

Texturing Polygons

As we know from modeling, polygons are defined in terms of vertices, faces and edges and unlike NURBS surfaces, aren't always products of a regular mathematical formula. Because of this we need to provide polygonal surfaces with texture co-ordinates so that we can map a two-dimensional texture to a three-dimensional surface. In addition to the normal set of components on a polygon surface, there are also UVs, which can be selected using the RMB marking menu if activated over a polygon object. These UVs cannot be transformed because they are locked to the polygon surface, but they do allow you to map texture co-ordinates to them. All polygon primitives can have UVs attached to them in the create options and all polygon surfaces must have UVs in order to render with textures. As you create more complex polygon objects or convert NURBS surfaces into polygon surfaces, you will need to create UVs for these objects.

- Create a polygon cube, light it and IPR render it.
- In the Hypershade, create a Phong material and assign it to the cube.
- Connect a Chequer texture to the Phong shaders colour attribute (make the texture normal).

The chequer has been evenly applied to each of the cube's faces because each face carries its own UV co-ordinates. These UV co-ordinates allow the cube to have the two-dimensional chequer textures applied to it and each face has a UV span of zero to one per side. Changing the number of repeats in U and V and other related mapping attributes in the place2dtexture node will have an effect on each face. To change how the texture fits onto each face and how the UVs are used by the polygon surface, we need to use the UV Texture Editor. The Texture Editor will present a flat image of the mapped texture and the cube folded out onto the two-dimensional plane of the texture. Close the IPR renderer and turn on hardware texturing under the Shading menu in the perspective view (or use the hotkey "6") so that you can see any changes in the polygon's texture mapping. Select the cube and open the UV Texture Editor from the Window menu item. The chequer texture is laid out as a repeating colour across the U and V domain (V being vertical) and the edges of the selected cube are in white. This shows how the texture is applied to the faces and you can zoom out to see the extents of the entire chequer texture using the normal orthographic camera tools. When using hardware texturing, we can define what material property is displayed using the Hardware Texturing foldout in the Attribute Editor for the relevant material. This foldout lets us choose the channel we wish to display (it will display as a colour) and also the resolution that we wish to display at, quickly letting us see the placement of transparencies or other channels that we would otherwise have to render.

What you can do in the UV Texture Editor is move the UVs of the polygons around until you arrive at the desired effect. You can select any component in this window using the RMB marking menu, so select UVs and drag a selection box over a corner. This selection will also be represented in all of the views and you can also select UVs in the views, which will select them in the UV Texture Editor. If you move the selected UV in the UV Texture Editor you should see that the chequer texture will appear to slide across the surface of the cube. This is because the mapping co-ordinates (UV positions) have changed in relation to the texture. What this does mean is that you can apply textures to faces and surfaces with precision as you can select the faces that need editing and change their mapping in the UV Texture Editor. The display for the image can be turned on or off using Image|Display Image and you can govern how

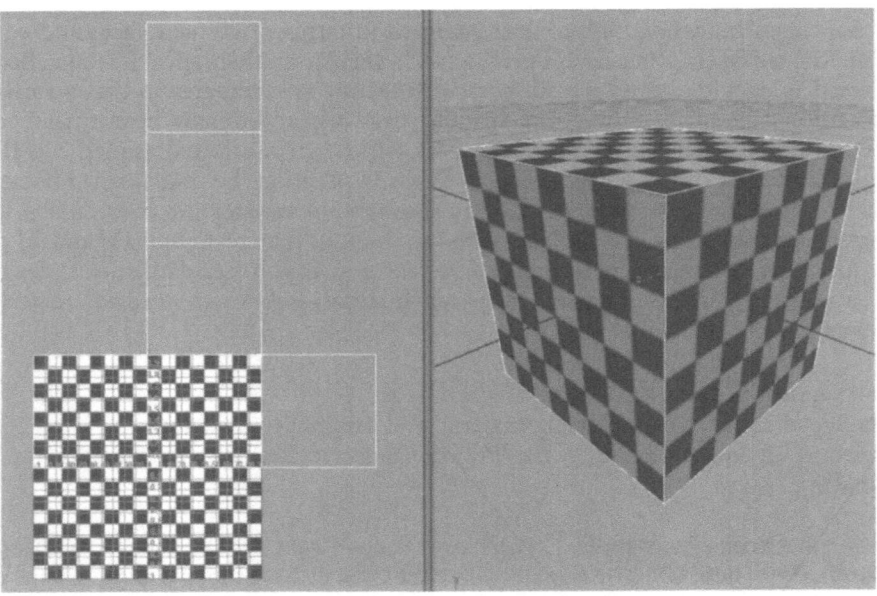

Figure 6.16 A Textured Polygon and the Unwrapped UVs in the Texture View Window.

much of the image is displayed (important for endlessly repeating procedural textures) by set-ting the options in Image|Image Range. You can also limit the amount of information shown by using View|View Contained Faces to only show faces when the number of selected com-ponents complete a face and using View|View Connected Faces to show faces that are con-nected together by the currently selected component.

It can be advantageous to separate the surface into smaller parts to provide more flexibility in the Texture View window. Select one of the edges of the cube on the UV Texture Editor and use Polygons|Cut UVs to separate UVs. Change the selection mask to UVs, click on one of the corners and move the UV away. You can now cut the cube up into component faces, even down to individual faces if you want. If you need to sew these UVs back together, select the edges and use Polygons|Sew UVs. If, however, you wanted to connect a new set of edges you should use Polygons|Move and Sew UVs to move the selected faces to a more useful relative position. These techniques become useful when you start working with more complex mod-els. Complex models will need their own set of UVs defined and more often than not will need these UVs moving so that a more regular and easy to edit structure will be displayed. It is use-ful to keep the painted textures as efficient as possible in terms of size and memory. You can paint all of the parts of your character in strips and areas, cut up your polygon object into components and move these components to their respective texture areas. So you only need to paint one arm and move the UVs for both arm surface to this position in the texture.

Mapping a More Complex Object

When you create a new polygon surface that has either been created as a result of operations upon a polygon primitive, as a result of surface creation or from converting NURBS to poly-gons you will need to create UVs for it. Using projection mapping techniques, UVs can be cre-ated on the polygon surface which fixes the UVs in 3D space relative to each vertex. The technique is extremely simple but you need to determine which method will yield the clearest result in the UV Texture Editor. You have a choice of Planar, Spherical, Cylindrical, Camera View or Automatic mappings and you should use the mapping shape that most closely resembles the shape or symmetry of your object.

- Delete the current cube and create a new polygon cube.
- Model the cube into a rough humanoid shape.
- Select the character and open the options window for Edit Polygons|Texture|Planar Mapping.
- Turn on Smart Fit and set it to Fit to Bounding Box.
- Set the projection plane to the plane that is perpendicular to the character's front.
- Turn on Insert Before Deformers.
- Click Project.

The character should now appear in the UV Texture Editor, but because you applied a planar projection, you can only see what the plane sees. If you wanted to give your character the same textures front and rear, then this would be ideal, although there would be significant smearing along the sides of the character, like any planar projection. But this is a good starting point for your character, because the main parts of the surface are presented in a clear and undistorted manner. You can now unwrap the UVs for the surface so that they are all visible by selecting the surface and using Edit Polygons|Texture|Layout UVs, but open the options dialogue. Set the Separate to Folds, turn on Flip Reversed and Rotate for Best Fit, set Layout

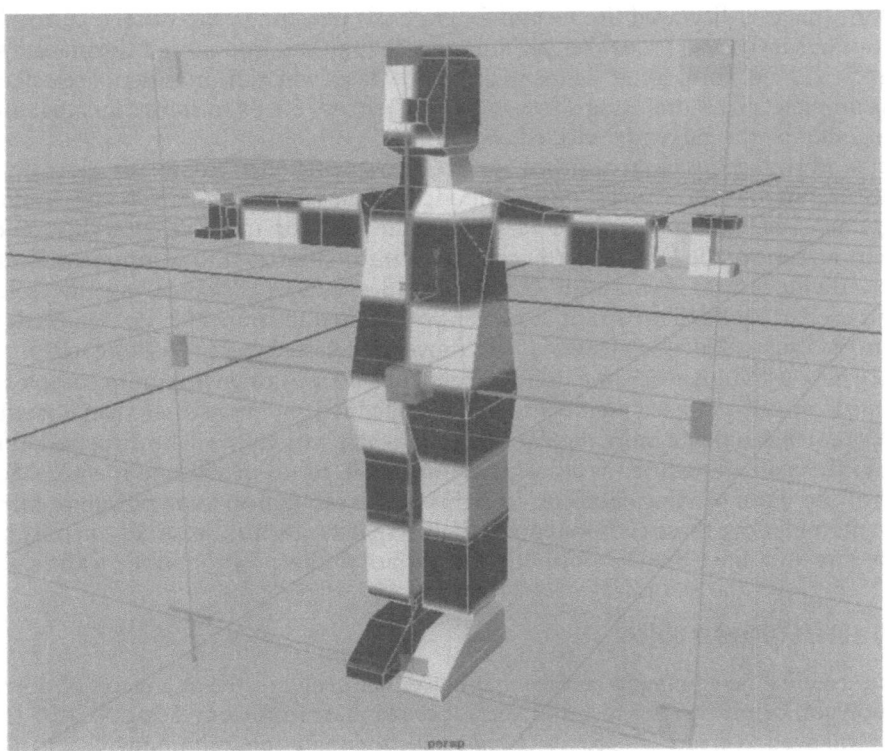

Figure 6.17 A Planar Projection on the Polygon Character.

to Into Square and Scale to Stretch into Square. The separate option will cut UVs if they are folded or overlapping and the rest deal with how the resultant UVs will be placed within the texture square.

Now your character can be edited so that any relevant pieces can be connected using the Sew functions and any remaining pieces can be moved onto the important texture areas. Other surface may well require other types of mapping, but they all need to be easy to texture shapes in the UV Texture Editor. UVs can also be moved for editing using Edit Polygons|Texture|Flip UVs and Edit Polygons|Texture|Rotate UVs – this will transform the selected components (faces and UVs respectively) depending on the options set. You can make your job even easier if you know where the UVs are going to be positioned, before you apply a texture map to them. This can be achieved by rendering the UV Texture Editor view of your surface once the UVs have been edited and clearly positioned. In the UV Texture View, use Polygons|UV Snapshot... to open up an options box detailing how and where the image file(s) will be created. This can then be imported into a paint package and used as a template for the creation of accurate texture maps. This new texture map can then be imported as a file texture and connected to the surface shader.

If you need to texture a more complex piece of polygonal topology, different mapping styles may have to be used. For example, the teapot constructed earlier could be a good contender for a planar mapping to create UVs upon its surface, but the hole that the handle

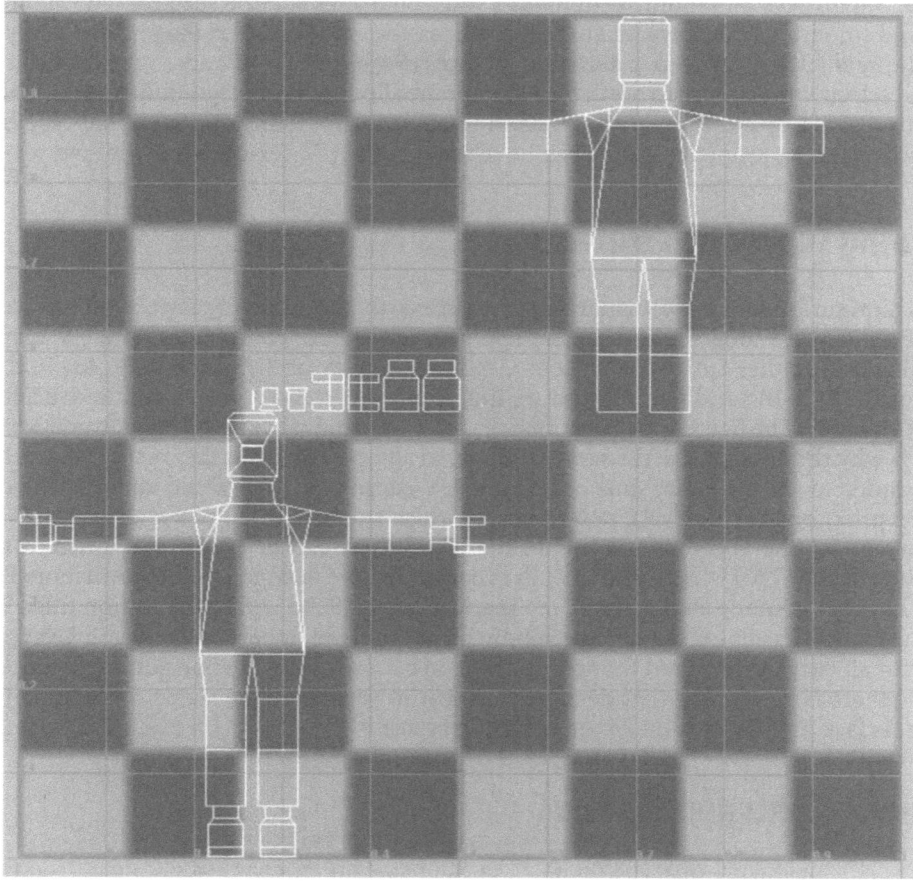

Figure 6.18 The Character after the Unwrapping Functions in the Texture View Window.

creates might well end up being distorted by the mapping. We have seen how these distortions can be "fixed" using Layout UVs, but what we want is to do less UV editing and more UV texturing. A spherical projection could give us the main body of the teapot with less work to do on the handle using the layout method, but as we move into far more complex shapes, regular projections will provide a UV layout that will require a lot of UV editing. A polygon model of a tree would have no real line of symmetry, so a good choice for a projection type would be "Automatic" which creates UV maps from several angles and combines these according to criteria in the options box. The UVs will require the use of the cutting and sewing tools, but they will be split up into regular, obvious sections so that the UV editing will be straightforward. A better method would be to map selected faces in order and to combine one texture map with another. This way, the same texture map could be used for continuity, while keeping the UV selections simpler to work with on a branch-by-branch basis. This workflow can be greatly sped up if a set for each branch is created; placing the sets into their own partition would also mean that the same face could not be selected for different shaders. So although texturing polygons requires you to create and edit the actual texture mapping co-ordinates for the surface, you do have a lot more freedom than you would with NURBS surfaces. The more complex (and smoother) the polygonal model becomes, the more complex the process of applying and editing the UVs will be as the number of faces climbs into thousands, but use of selection sets and selective mapping can break this task into smaller and more digestible chunks. This can be further aided by creating new UV sets in the options for whichever mapping type that is used, so that the appropriate UV set can be selected in the UV Texture View window.

Texturing Subdivision Surfaces

Subdivision surfaces have UVs applied to them in exactly the same way as polygon surfaces but there are a few less tools for editing and applying the texture coordinates. The UV mapping is applied using either `Subdiv Surfaces|Texture|Planar` or `Subdiv Surfaces|Texture| Automatic Mapping` and the UV Texture Editor allows us to cut, layout and move and sew subdiv Uvs only. The usage and operation is exactly the same as for texturing polygon surfaces, which is why they both share the same window, so all operations on the images are the same. If we wanted to use the entire suite of polygon UV editing tools, we could edit the UVs of the polygon proxy object (the level 0 polygon cage) which would allow us to use all of the UV editing tools under the Polygons heading in the UV Texture Editor and all the different menu items under `Edit Polygons|Texture`. In order to this, we need to open the Attribute Editor whilst in polygon mode and open the tab marked `polyToSubdivn`. In the section titled "Uvs" is a foldout that lets us either keep the subdiv Uvs as they are, inherit the polygon Uvs or have no Uvs at all (which can speed the scene). If we do choose to use the polygon cages' UV coordinates, there is the danger that detail will be lost if we change the shape of the underlying subdiv surface past the bounds of the polygon surface.

Texturing Lights and Shadows

In addition to texturing materials, lights and shadows can also have their colours controlled by textures. This gives a lot of creative control when determining how scenes will look and feel. To create a textured shadow or light, just LMB click the `Map Texture` button at the side of the attribute and create the texture and effect that is required. Great light and shadow effects can be created from the use of a ramp texture, so that you can subtly alter the colour of a shadow as it falls across a wall without changing any of the lighting within a scene. Because the V values for each colour entry in the ramp appear as keyable/connectable attributes, these can be connected to driven keys so that the shadow colour can be changed swiftly. Using a simple black and white ramp in the shadow colour also means that you can change the fade-off of a shadow map for a more convincing faked soft shadow. You can create the effect of light caustics from a transparent sphere by changing the ramp type to "circular". This allows you to edit the effect of transparency on shadow casting and the "hotspots" can be moved around within the shadow area by changing the `Translate Frame` attributes in the `place2Dtexture` node for the ramp.

Utilities

As you start to create shading networks in the Hypershade window you may find that you need additional information from your scene or that you need to convert or control the data flowing from one node to another node. At this point you will need to use another part of the Hypershade toolkit: Utilities. These nodes are responsible for any operations that you need that do not involve the creation of shaders or textures. We have already seen several utilities at work when creating and editing textures: the place2Dtexture node is a utility that allows you to map the UV value from a texture to the UV value on a NURBS or polygon surface.

Utilities let you edit and extend your shading tree so that you can create detailed shaders for specialized use, which will generally be every production, plus you can also export shaders to your own library for further use using the File menu in the Hypershade. When creating specialist shaders, remember to save out any custom networks so that if a particular effect or tool is required, you don't have to re-invent the wheel. Utilities come in six types: General, Colour, Switch, Particle, Image Planes and Glows, each of them able to manipulate data in different manners. One way that you can use a utility is to modulate the amount of data that reaches the displacement shader of a shading group. In a displacement map, the luminance (or alpha) value of a texture will determine the actual amount of displacement that will be applied to a surface, so any changes to this value must be done at the texture level. If you want to keep the relative values of your texture in terms of contrast and tonality then you should use a utility to interpret and change the data that flows from the fractal texture node to the displacement shader.

- Create a NURBS sphere with a Phong shader, light and render it.
- Attach a 2D fractal texture to the shading group's Displacement attribute.
- Render.

You can see that the fractal texture has exploded the surface. The following process explains how to use a utility to scale this effect so that the displacement is smoother and less violent.

- Switch the Create bar to Create Utilities and from the General Utilities select the Multiply/Divide node.
- Break the connection that the Fractal texture has with the Displacement utility, noting what the connection is.
- MMB drag and drop the Fractal texture onto the Multiply/Divide node and connect out alpha to Input 1X.
- MMB drag and drop the Multiply/Divide node onto the Displacement utility and connect outputX to displacement.

The Multiply/Divide node can take up to two sets of three inputs (input1X, input 1Y, input 1Z and input 2X, input 2Y, input 2Z) and will return up to three outputs (outputX, outputY, outputZ), whose value will be determined by the operation of the node (no operation, multiply, divide or power). In this case, you want to multiply a single input by a floating point and return that output to the displacement shader. Double-click the Multiply/Divide node to bring up the Attribute Editor, set the operation to multiply and in the input2X, type 0.2. Render the scene again and the effect of the displacement shader will be scaled down, while retaining the intrinsic values of the original fractal texture. This node could also be used to invert the value of the displacement, but this could start to become confusing, so use a Reverse utility instead.

You can also control the amount of texture or colour that a shader receives by using any of the colour utilities, allowing you to build complex layered attributes before you even start to

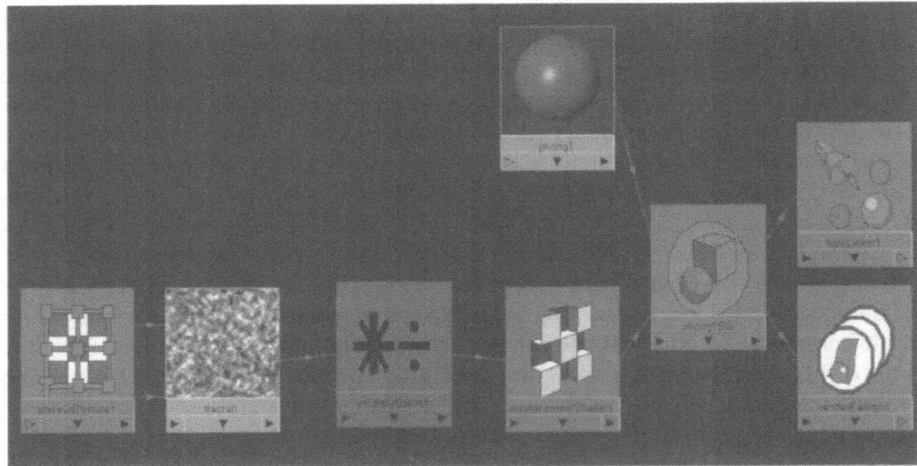

Figure 6.19 The Shading Network to Control Displacement Values.

create layered textures. This gives you almost infinite complexity when it comes to creating multi-layered colour attributes.

- Delete the Displacement shader that feeds into the Phong shading group and IPR render the sphere.
- Create a 2D Noise texture and a 2D Ramp texture.

To mix portions of one texture with portions of another texture, possibly through the use of another texture or controllable attribute:

- Create a Blend utility from the Colour Utilities section.
- Connect the outColour of the noise texture to the colour1 attribute of the Blend utility.
- Connect the outColour of the ramp texture to the colour2 attribute of the Blend utility.
- Connect the output of the Blend utility to the colour attribute of the Phong shader.

The surface of the sphere should now be a blend of the ramp colours and the noise colours. Bringing up the Attribute Editor and changing the value for the Blender attribute can control this blending, but a more interesting effect can be achieved by attaching another utility or texture to this blender attribute.

- MMB drag and drop the noise texture onto the Blend utility.
- Connect outAlpha to Blender.

We can now use this self-contained shading network to create new effects, the look (albeit basic) of clouds moving across a planet can be created easily by animating the noise texture's attributes and the place2Dtexture node to give rotation. Further improvements can be made by adding utilities to interpret the data from the noise function before it is passed to the blender node.

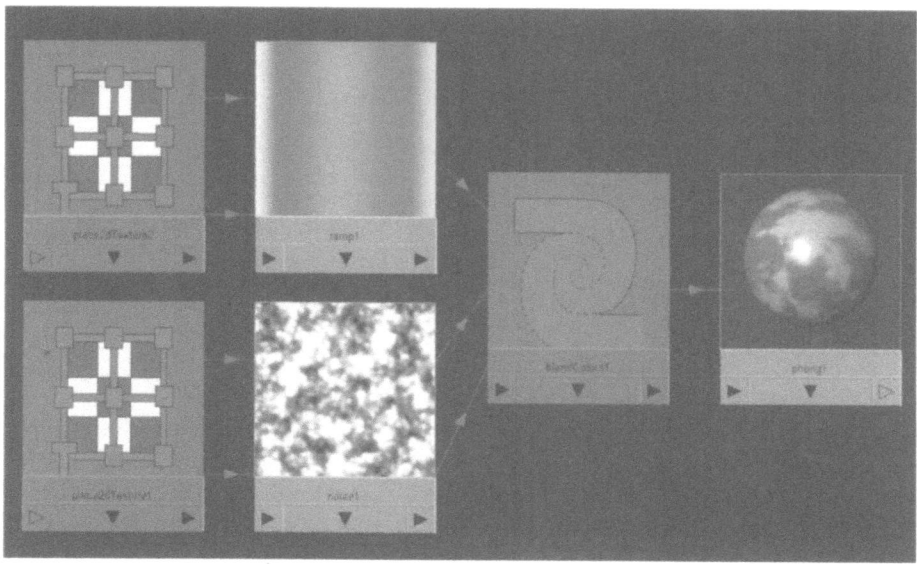

Figure 6.20 Blending Colour Values.

Building a Basic Shader

We're going to explain how to use a combination of utilities and build up a simple iridescence shader which can be saved to disk for inclusion into other projects. Iridescence can be found on feathers and insect shells, so the first thing you need to do is to determine the base material type that the shading network will feed into. The Anisotropic material will suit our purposes here, due to the fact that it simulates the changing specularity of a surface when the angle of view changes and an iridescent surface changes its colour values as the angle of view changes as well.

- Create a NURBS sphere, set the end sweep to 180 degrees and set the number of sections to 15.
- Rotate and scale the surface until it lies flat on the XZ plane and has an oval shape to it.
- Select every other hull that runs along the length of the surface.
- Scale and translate these hulls so that there is a ripple running over the width of the surface.
- Freeze transformations and delete the history.

Open the Hypershade and create an Anisotropic shader, rename it Irid, rename the shading group Iri_SG and attach the shader to the NURBS surface. Set up a few lights about the surface and IPR render the scene. You can now set up the specular highlights, so change the Angle, SpreadX and Y, Roughness, Fresnel Index and Specular Colour until you get a good effect across the surface. To provide better feedback for the specular highlights, set the Diffuse to zero and the Colour to black. Once the specular highlights have been roughed in (you can fine-tune them later, but it is always better to start from somewhere), you should

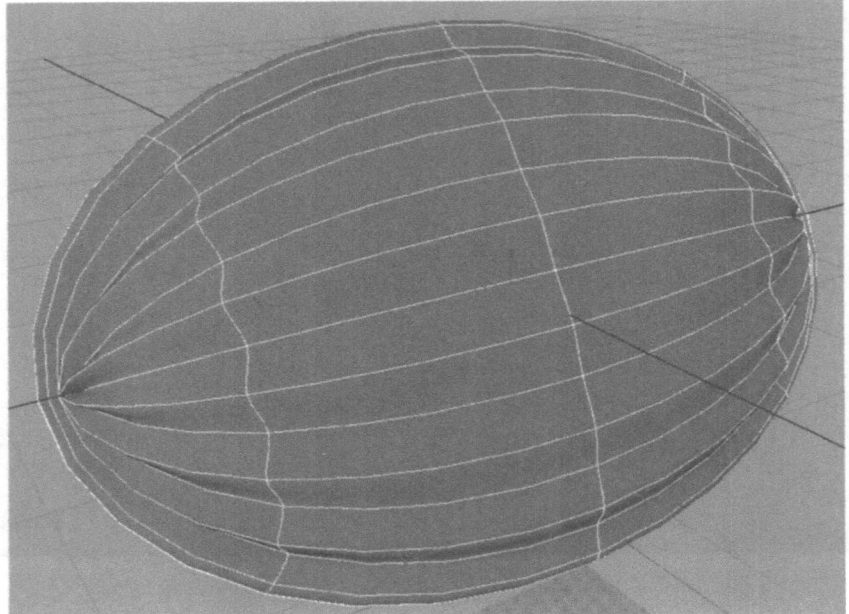

Figure 6.21 The NURBS Surface for the Iridescence Effect.

determine the rest of the effects that the shader will exhibit. An iridescent material will change its colour depending on the viewer's position relative to the surface and the brightness of the colour may also change relative to the viewpoint. You can use a utility to find out the ratio between the point being sampled and its orientation to the camera. The utility in question is the samplerInfo node – this allows you to inquire about each sampled point on a surface that is being rendered and to provide information that can be extracted and used. In this case, you need to use the facingRatio, which returns a zero to one value, describing whether a point is facing the camera (value of one) or not. We now want the surface colour to change depending on the value of this facing ratio, so to give the greatest control over the surface colour, use the facingRatio to select colours from a ramp. A ramp is a two-dimensional texture defined in terms of the parametrics U and V, so you can take the facing ratio of the samplerInfo node and drive the V position of the ramp that is used to return a colour value for the point being sampled. Set the diffuse value of the Irid shader back to 0.8 before you start connecting values to the colour attribute.

- Create a ramp texture and a samplerInfo utility.
- Connect the facingRatio of the samplerInfo node to the vCoord of the ramp texture.
- Connect the outColour of the ramp to the colour attribute of the Irid shader.

If you double-click on the ramp texture, you can now change the colour values and their positions to suit your requirements for the iridescent colours, allowing you to interactively change these values with the IPR renderer. The surface is quite bright now, as a result of the original

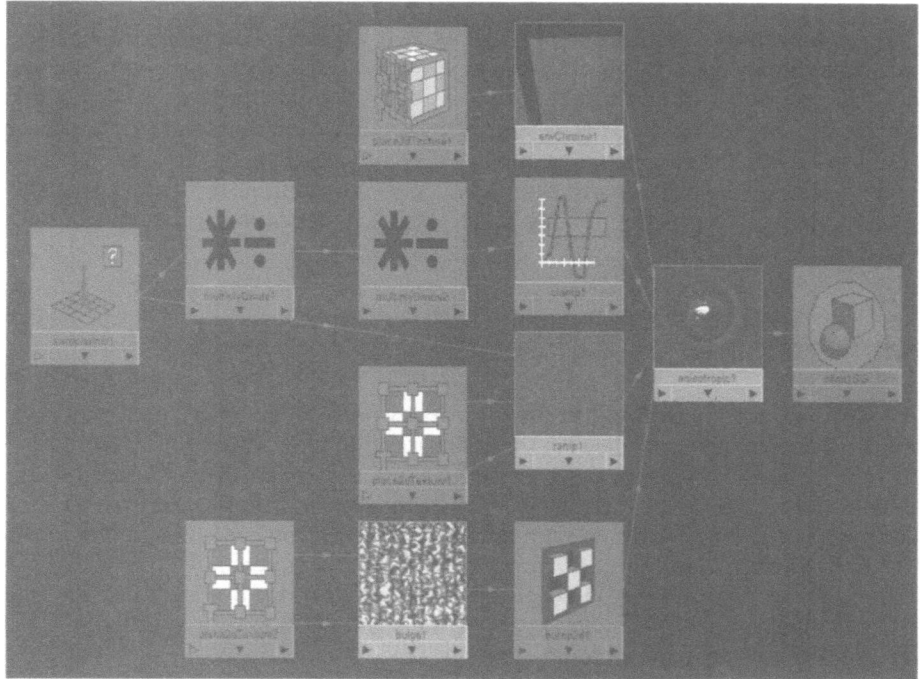

Figure 6.22 The Final Shader Network.

diffuse value, but again, you should modulate the diffuse value by the facing ratio so that the surface luminance can also be as a result of the viewing angle.

• Connect the facingRatio to the Diffuse attribute.

The surface is starting to burn out at the points facing forwards and provides little contrast to those surfaces that face away, so create a multiply/divide utility and connect the facingRatio to the input1X and connect the outputX to the Diffuse attribute instead. Now set the mode to Multiply and set the input2X value to 0.6 to scale the whole diffuse effect down. This still doesn't change too much in terms of the position of the point being sampled and the viewpoint; all that has been achieved is the scaling of the original effect.

• Disconnect the multiply/divide node from the Irid shader.
• Create a surfaceLuminance utility and attach the outValue to the input2X of the multiply/divide node.
• Create another multiply/divide utility, connect the output1X from the first multiply/divide node to the input1X of the new multiply/divide node.
• Connect the outputX of the new multiply/divide node to the Diffuse attribute.
• Set the value of the input2X of the new multiply/divide node to 0.75.
• Change the mode of the old multiply/divide node to Power.

The surfaceLuminance node gives the luminance value of each point being sampled, which is a result of all lighting calculations but excluding specular highlights, so combining this with another `multiply/divide` node allows you to control the final scaling of the diffuse effect. The clamp utility comes in handy here as well, allowing you to set upper and lower limits for any colour value in your shading network. Create a clamp utility and connect it between the output of the last `multiply/divide` node and the `Irid` shader, setting the clamping range between 0.1 and 1.0 so your diffuse values won't burn out or under expose. Select the top of the shading network and use `File|Export Selected Network` to save this current shading network to a project folder. Now you can import this shader at any time using `File|Import...` and manipulate it or extend it depending on the scene and the circumstances.

Environments

So far, we have looked at how to colour the surface or volume of an object, how to provide surface detail and how to create shaders for these surfaces that reflect the lighting conditions that surround them. For a closer representation of the natural properties of some materials we need to look at the other visual cues that we (sometimes unconsciously) use to determine how realistic an object is. This becomes extremely important if you are going to be placing the object into a live action photograph or film. The first cue that is generally used is that of shadows, the second cue that is used is that of reflection. Any surface that exhibits shininess will reflect its surrounding environment as part of the shading. How you choose to reflect this environment depends on a few factors:

1. What is the environment that we are reflecting?
2. How close do we get to the reflecting object?
3. How sharp are the reflections?
4. How much time do we have to render these reflections?

Using raytracing to accurately reflect the environment on the surface is the most straightforward method of reflection creation that Maya offers. Raytraced reflections have a couple of advantages:

1. Accurate reflection and refraction of light.
2. Easy to set up and to control.

Create a NURBS sphere and a NURBS torus and place them on a lit ground plane. We shall explain how to use raytracing to create all of the reflections in the scene, so the IPR renderer will be of no use here. Attach a Phong material to the sphere, a Blinn material to the torus and a Lambert material to the ground plane. Texture the various materials as desired, turn on raytracing in the `Render Globals` and render the scene. As you can see, the raytracing takes care of all reflections in the scene at the expense of rendering speed. Reflections when using raytracing are controlled by the reflectivity attribute for each material, so set the reflectivity of the Blinn material to 1.0, and 0.0 for the Phong and re-render. This reflectivity can also be modulated through the use of textures and utilities as not many real world surfaces ever have a perfect reflective surface. You can easily see the reflections that fall onto a surface by setting the diffuse value to zero and re-rendering. This brings us to the next problem of integrating the objects with a live action environment.

If you have set the Phong material's colour to black with 100 per cent reflection and no diffuse value it will look like a chrome surface when raytraced. In this scene, as there is no sky this will look fairly dull, and will look even stranger if you were to try and integrate the sphere with a background photo. You need to get the sphere to reflect your live action environment. This can be done by using one of Maya's environment textures. These textures are used to create a reflected colour for a surface by either procedurally generating a pattern or using file textures to create a background colour for reflection. Click on the `Reflected Colour` attribute of the Phong material and choose `Env Chrome` from the Create Render Node window and re-render the scene. Those reflections on the surface of the sphere that are not a result of rays bouncing from other objects in the scene are taken from the colour values of the Env Chrome sphere that is now mapped to the reflected colour attribute. The Env Chrome texture creates a simple blue sky, brown floor environment that is attached to an infinitely large sphere, so that any rays that don't hit surfaces will hit this sphere instead, returning the chrome sky effect. If you hide the ground plane, only the sphere gets a floor colour mapped to its reflections and not the torus, as the environment texture is mapped only to the sphere. Again, you can modulate the reflectivity of a surface using textures.

The other environment textures allow you to create different methods of creating a reflected environment upon your surfaces, so that when you set up a realistic effect, all you have to do is to attach it to your objects and they will all reflect the same background. The Env Ball texture is specifically for integrating CG objects with live action footage, by using images taken from an onset chrome sphere and recreating them in the CG scene. The Env Cube texture lets you map six faces of a cube with six orthogonal textures or photos so that reflections can be received from all directions. The cube can be scaled in terms of scene size, thereby allowing you to move your objects through the reflections. Single photos or textures can be mapped onto an Env Sphere texture, which places the texture on the inside of an infinitely large sphere. Massive sky backdrops can be used on these or even created quickly from ramps mapped to the colour attribute of the Env Sphere instead (a 3D leather texture can be easily turned into a starfield and mapped to one of the colour entries of the ramp).

Just as surrounding surfaces can be reflected using raytracing, you can also use this technique to accurately trace refraction of transparent objects as well.

- Create a NURBS sphere and a polygon cube.
- Scale the sphere so that it is elliptical in shape and scale the cube so that it covers three quarters of the sphere.
- Attach a Phong material to the cube and a Lambert material to the sphere.
- Map a grid texture to the colour attribute of the Lambert and set the transparency of the Phong material to 0.7 in red, green and blue.
- Open the fold-out titled `Raytrace Options` and turn on `Refractions`.
- Render the scene.

The refractive index will need to be changed before the cube exhibits any refractive properties, so set it to 0.7 and then 1.4, rendering each time to see the effect. The quality of the refraction effect can be altered using the various attributes here, such as the simulation of translucence and the thickness of the surface, but the most important is the `Refractive Limit` which determines how many times the light rays can be refracted inside the material. Setting this limit correctly can allow you to rigidly control how many times the renderer will bounce rays into the scene, so if you just want to roughly create the appearance of refraction, then the limit can be kept low and the render sped up.

Reflection Mapping

Although raytracing can be extremely useful for the creation of accurate reflections on surfaces, it may prove time consuming if all you need is a more general reflection that will not
have an impact upon rendering time like raytracing. The maxims for using raytracing will
generally be whether you need to represent physically accurate reflections and refractions that
will be noticed by the viewer. If not, then you can use scanline rendering and environment textures. Environment textures are utilized in the same way here as when they were used in conjunction with raytracing. If you turn off raytracing in the Render Globals and re-render the
scene, all of the effects that were achieved with raytracing instantly disappear, apart from the
effect of any environment textures that feed into the material's reflected colour attributes. It is
now up to you to create convincing pictures of an environment that can be used for the faked
reflections, a process known as "reflection mapping".

You can choose to use any of the environment textures available, but the most useful will be
the EnvCube because we can represent six rendered orthographic views of the scene can be
represented as file textures for each side of the environment cube.

In the scene in which your object is due to appear, create six cameras set to "orthographic"
and place them at the centre of the scene looking outwards along the six axes. Render a single
view from all of the cameras, naming the files plusX, minusX etc., and then reload them in as
file textures mapped to the Env Cube's six faces. Each orthographic camera should be placed

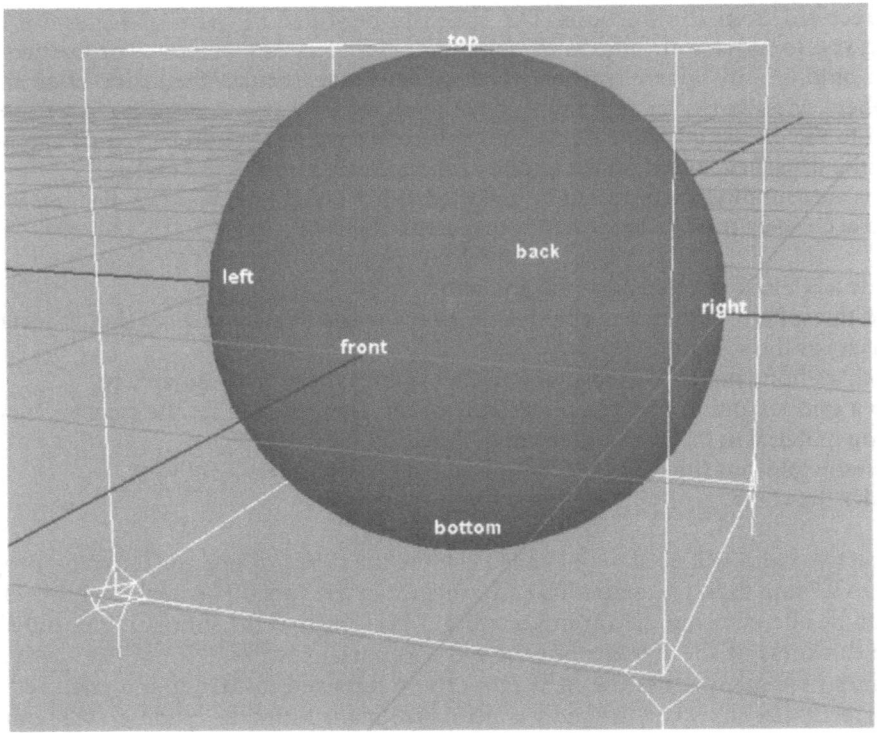

Figure 6.23 The Different Sides of an Env Cube Placement Node.

and scaled so that the views can be seamlessly rendered from face to face, with no obvious edges or splits. This Env Cube can now be scaled up in the workspace to fit the scene size (each face has its relevant name in the placement icon) or the Infinite Size attribute can be turned on.

Backgrounds and Integration

You can also integrate CG objects into background scenes within Maya, instead of using any form of paint or compositing software, through the use of *image planes* and the *use background shader*. As previously mentioned, the use background shader allows you to match the background colours from your current rendered view to your surface, irrespective of changes in shape or orientation of the object.

Delete all of the items in your scene and create a sphere, a ground plane and some lights. First, you need to create a background picture in perspective view, so open the Attribute Editor for the perspective view and open the fold-out titled Environment where you can set the background colour of your rendered view or create an image plane. An image plane is a texture (usually a file texture) that is aligned to the camera and can either move with it or stay in a fixed position, so LMB click on the Create button.

Create an image plane and add a file texture to it. Image files can be loaded in and can either be single files, a series of files or a movie file. If you wish to use a sequence of frames, then you need to turn on Use Frame Extension and keyframe the start and end frame numbers in the timeline. You can choose to display it in several modes in hardware view depending on the speed of the graphics card and the relative speed of interaction that you wish to have in your scene. If you render the scene now, you can see that the image plane is now created as the background. If you attach a use background shader to the ground plane and render again, the ground plane will take on the colour values of the background while still receiving shadows and reflections from the sphere. You can now align the ground plane to the alignment of any surface in the background image, so that you can integrate the sphere's shadows and reflections. Because you have an image file for the background, you can also use it as the colour attribute for an Env Sphere which can then be mapped to the reflectivity of your original sphere, further "fixing" it into the scene.

Volumes

Maya has a set of primitives known as *volume primitives* that allow you to create fast volume effects for areas in scenes and also for lighting effects. The fog primitives exhibit a semi-volumetric effect, so that if you were to move the camera through the volume, we would not appear to move through it and lights won't cast light through the volume, only onto its surface. The appearance of the volume primitives can be further altered using textures to control transparency, colour, incandescence, density and glow. The volume primitives also have attributes to control the more fog-like attributes, such as how the density of the material changes at the edges of the volume material and how light is scattered by the material.

- Create a volume cube from Create|Volume Primitives|Cube.
- Scale the cube so that it is broad and flat, then create a cylinder and place it at the centre of the volume primitive.
- Light the scene and render.

You can see that the volume primitive gives the effect of a translucent block, through which the cylinder can be seen. Other than that, there are no real volume effects being exhibited, so map a 3D cloud texture to the transparency attribute of the volume cube and scale the `place3dTexture` node so that it is larger than the volume cube. The volume can be made to look less "object" like by changing the way the volume drops off at the edges.

Set the `Dropoff Shape` to `Cube` and the `Edge Dropoff` to `0.4` and re-render the scene. Altering the density of the volume and the Dropoff method can offset the dropoff changes (`Subtract Density` will scale the amount of edge dropoff by the density of the volume, whereas `Scale Opacity` will scale the dropoff uniformly across the volume). One of the main uses of the volume primitives is to create a fast rendering volumetric light effect such as the glowing spheres around streetlights or cones of light around a searchlight as it illuminates particles in the air or under the water.

- Create a spotlight, volume cone and volume sphere.
- Scale the volume sphere so that it is elliptical and scale and position the volume cone so that it is extending from the sphere.
- Position and scale the spotlight so that it is pointing in the same direction as the volume cone.
- Group all three objects and open the Attribute Editor with the volume sphere selected.
- Map a 3D cloud texture to the transparency attribute and open the Hypershade.
- Select the volume cone and MMB drag and drop the cloud texture from the Hypershade onto the transparency attribute of the volume cone.
- Scale the `place3DTexture` placement node by 100 units in all axes.
- Render the scene.

Because the two volume primitives both share the same 3D texture for their transparency attributes, they will both appear to illuminate the same medium when rendered and when they move. To add the final touch to the effect, select the spotlight and add a light glow node to it, so that you can see a halo about the light when it is facing the camera.

The Renderer

Although we have been using the renderer via the render view to see how our materials, lights and textures are looking, we haven't looked at the renderer in terms of the final process of our work in Maya: a series of rendered frames. How the renderer behaves is controlled by the Render Globals, which we have seen previously when we have needed to use raytracing, but how objects render in terms of their surface description and visibility is controlled by a surface's shape node.

Surface Rendering

If we create a NURBS sphere we see that it is displayed as a smooth, round surface and that when we render it, the isoparms are interpolated mathematically to create a smooth shape and a smooth edge. During the shading process, the surface of the sphere is turned into polygon triangles (this is called "tessellation") to enable the various rendering algorithms to work. The number of triangles that the renderer splits the surface into is determined by the tessellation criteria in the shape node for a surface, and changes to these criteria determine how accurately the smooth surface is represented.

Select the NURBS sphere and display its shape node in the Attribute Editor. Open the fold-out titled `Tessellation` and turn on `Display Render Tessellation`. This will show how many triangles the surface will be split up into. If you know that your surfaces will constantly be in the foreground and under heavy audience scrutiny, then you should increase the `Curvature Tolerance` and the `Divisions Factor` attributes and vice versa if your objects are always going to be in the background. This tessellation is also important for the way that a displacement map will render; if the number of triangles that the surface will be turned into is too low, the displacement effect will be rough and faceted (this is the only reason that there are tessellation criteria for polygon surfaces). However, there is also a section in the shape node for each surface that allows you to change how a displacement map will be rendered using the `Feature Displacement` attribute which asks Maya to attain the highest possible quality. Other factors governing the criteria will be at the edges of NURBS surfaces, whether they are trimmed, stitched or filleted (too low a curvature tolerance and the edges will have holes between them), and whether you need to use `Advanced tessellation`. Advanced tessellation gives much more freedom in choosing the criteria for surfaces and can let you define the rules in terms of object size in 3D, in screen size or in terms of local surface definition. If you keep `Display tessellation` on, then you can see the effects of changes to the tessellation criteria directly.

You can also use the attributes in the shape node for NURBS surfaces to determine how textures are interpolated across the UV parameters. Open the fold-out titled `Texture Map` and there is a checkbox titled `Fix Texture Warp` which allows you to keep texture parameterization constant across a NURBS surface. This means that any changes to the surface at a

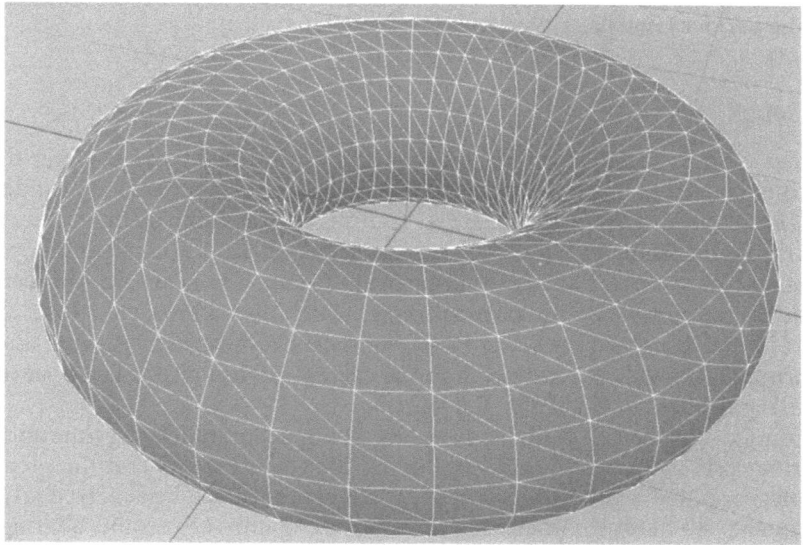

Figure 6.24 Tessellation of a Standard NURBS Torus.

component level (i.e. moving CVs or unequally spaced isoparms) will not unevenly stretch UV textures. If you open the fold-out titled Render Stats you can now control what rendering effects each object contributes to the final scene. You can turn on or off the creation of shadows, control reflection and refraction, motion blur and whether an object is double-sided or not (by default, all surfaces are double-sided, but this can cause longer rendering times). This allows you to fine tune scenes in terms of whether all of the objects will appear in reflections and cast shadows, or just foreground objects, optimizing the scene drastically. Additionally, you can also turn off objects' primary visibility so that you cannot see them but they can still appear in reflection, refractions and cast shadows.

The Camera

The camera in Maya comes in several different forms; as we've seen, we can have an orthographic camera and a perspective camera and as we will generally be rendering from a perspective camera, we will discuss its attributes. A perspective camera comes in three forms (camera, camera and aim, camera and aim and up) which all describe how the camera is controlled. You can change between these types in the Attribute Editor for a selected camera, but if keys have been set then this may adversely affect their interpolation. The perspective camera will render a frame whose resolution is determined in the Render Globals and you can see this resolution in the view by turning on Resolution Gate under View|Camera Settings where you can also display other guides such as Safe Title and Safe Action. These and other guides can also be displayed from the Attribute Editor from the Display Options fold-out. What happens within this frame will be largely controlled by real world camera attributes such as focal length and angle of view, whose ratio is controlled by the Film Gate, an attribute that also determines how the image is formatted within the Resolution Gate. If the focal length and angle of view need to be set individually then the Film Back will be set to User, but the resolution of the final frame can only be set in the Render Globals. In the Output Settings fold-out, you can also decide what channels will be rendered when you select the camera in the Render Globals.

Rendering Setup

In the Render Globals window, we will be changing attributes for the renderer that have an effect over the rendering of the entire scene. The first set of attributes in the window concern the actual file output of the rendered frame. You can set the name of the frame, the type of frame, what is being rendered (all objects or just active objects), which camera you are rendering from and what channels the output file will contain. The next fold-out section is concerned with the resolution of the output frame, which also allows you to set the Device Aspect Ratio and Pixel Aspect Ratio for consistent results when viewing the frames on different formats. Files will be rendered into the current project directory, so set this prior to rendering using File|Project|Edit Current.

Anti-aliasing quality settings will have the largest impact on rendering time and it is worth experimenting with the settings here, combining the requirements and final format of the rendered images so that a good ratio of quality against speed can be achieved. The default is the lowest quality, so gradually increase values for the quality of the anti-aliasing, sampling and filtering of the scene until a usable speed/quality ratio is achieved. Several settings will just not be necessary for some scenes, so don't create extra work for the renderer if it's not going to be seen. Try rendering with the Presets set to Intermediate Quality and work from there. You can also check to see if the rendering set-up will be inefficient or wasteful by using Render|Render Diagnostics, which will run through the scene and the Render Globals to report its findings in the Script Editor, which can really help keep wasteful settings to a minimum.

Under Render Options you can also create environment fog to give a sense of depth fading to the scene or create depth passes. Clicking the map button will create an EnvFog material that is applied to the scene upon rendering. You can then either set up the fog to behave as a real physically based fog with layering and lumpiness or as a standard CGI fog effect which becomes denser over distance (determined by the near and far clipping planes for the camera in the Attribute Editor).

Render Layers and Render Passes

Render passes let you break up the render into separate shading contributions (diffuse, specular, colour or shadow) to give maximum flexibility when compositing (the default pass is the beauty pass, which includes all shading calculations). Render layers allow you to break the scene up into different layers, which you can then render individually. These render layers are created in exactly the same way as normal display layers are created, except you can now tell the renderer via the Render Layer/Pass Control section in the Render Globals window which layers to render and also what portion of the shading contributions for each layer to render. This section is set out in a similar fashion to the Attribute Spreadsheet and you can cross index layers against passes. If layers are used, then make sure that objects that interact with shadows, reflections or refractions are all put into the same layer, otherwise all the time that was spent creating these masterpieces will be wasted by rendering out in layers. If you decide to use this option then it can be quite handy, logistically, to turn on the Output to Subdirectories option, so that you can clearly see what frames are what by their directory headings and locations.

Rendering and Reviewing an Animation

If you need to just quickly preview animation without any rendering effects, you can use the Playblast function. Playblast takes a screen grab from the currently selected window. It is invoked from Window|Playblast where the options concerning playback, number of frames reviewed, aspect ratio and how the frames are played back, are worth setting before using. Rendering multiple frames is just a question of changing the Frame/Animation Ext. attribute in the Render Globals window from name.ext (Single Frame) to any of the other options, depending on where the frame number is to be inserted. After that, the Start Frame, End Frame, By Frame and Frame Padding can be set to whatever is required by the production environment and the output names of the files will be displayed at the top of the Render Globals window. Always check the naming and numbering formats that the output device or compositing/image manipulation software that you will be using will accept, otherwise it can be a real pain to rename and renumber the rendered frames. Once these have been set, the batch renderer can be invoked using Render|(Save) Batch Render. This will open an options box to save a temporary file that the batch renderer will use to render the frames from. Once the batch renderer has been invoked, it will sit in the background allowing the continued use of Maya. You can view the state of the rendering process by looking in the Script Editor, which will show the frames completed and the percentage completion of the current frame. You can also use `Render|Show Batch Render...` to view the currently rendering frame and `Render|Cancel Batch Render` to stop the current rendering task.

Renderer Effects

So far, we have been using lighting, shadows and surface detail to create the illusion of scenes existing in three dimensions. All of these cues go to making up an image that, when viewed as a two-dimensional image, is perceived by our brains as having depth and dimension, whether the scene is photoreal or complete fantasy. All of this has been created by our application of detail to our scene in terms of the items that we can directly manipulate and view as part of that manipulation process, from texture networks in the Hypershade to light position in the perspective view. We can also create further cues that our scene exists by using the artefacts that we are used to seeing when watching films. When we use a camera to take a picture of the world, we can introduce several effects into our composition and picture using the mechanisms of the shutter and of the lens itself. However, these mechanisms do not exist in our CG camera, but we can simulate them in order to add more realism to our still images and make moving images more cohesive. All of these effects are created using the renderer via attributes that we can use in the camera shape node. We only get to see the outcome once we have rendered a frame, which in a way brings us full circle to the act of photographing a scene.

Depth of Field

The first of these camera mechanisms that we can simulate is depth of field, which determines how much of a frame is in sharp focus, from near to far from the camera. Depth of field is a time-consuming process to render in computer graphics and should only be used if other techniques will not create the same effect, such as rendering in layers and blurring them in a paint package. You can also fake this effect by rendering a depth pass and using the colour values to successively blur the original frame.

* Create a scene with five primitives spaced equally apart down one axis and position a new perspective camera so that it is looking down this axis, but at a slant so that you can see all five objects.
* Activate the distance measuring tool from `Create|Measure Tool|Distance Tool` and in the top view measure from the centre of the new camera to the central object (which should be at the centre of the frame).
* This distance will be the "Focus Distance" and sets the start point for the depth of field, which will extend forward and behind of this point.
* Measure the distance from the camera to the closest object and the distance to the farthest object. These measuring items will stay in the workspace unless deleted, which allows you to see these values.
* Open the Attribute Editor for the camera, render the current view and save the frame.

You can also obtain information about distances from camera to objects by turning on the HUD (Heads Up Display) for objects using `Display|Heads Up Display|Object Details`. You can now select an object in the camera view and this particular HUD will show its distance to the camera. On opening the `Depth of Field` fold-out in the Attribute Editor, the attributes which allow you to control the depth of field can be found. First and foremost is the

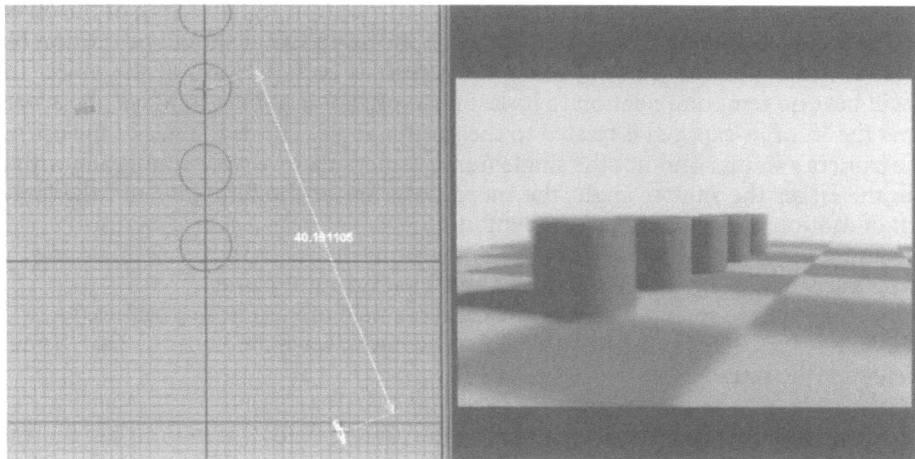

Figure 6.25 Depth of Field and the Measuring Icon for the Camera within the Scene.

Depth of Field checkbox, which should be turned on. Set the Focus Distance to the distance of the centre object and re-render the scene. As expected, the central object will be in focus and the surrounding objects will be blurred as a result of their distance from the plane perpendicular to the focus distance point. What we really want to control is the actual depth of the focus, the amount of the frame that is in focus, because we are now simulating the behaviour of a real camera. F-stop and Focal Length will affect the depth of field and for those of us who have experimented with cameras and photography, this next section will be academic. F-stop determines the size of the aperture in your camera and ranges from 1.0 (large aperture) to 64.0 (small aperture); this means that a small f-stop will have a small depth of field and increasing the f-stop will increase the depth of field. Render and save frames at different aperture settings for comparison. One real life camera process that we don't have to worry about will be available light for the film, so changing f-stops won't have an effect on the graininess or exposure.

Focal length will also affect the depth of field by increasing the depth of field as the focal length decreases for a given f-stop setting. The optical reasons for this are a little beyond the scope of this book, but it is worth remembering these rules of thumb. Focal length and its effect on the frame being rendered is controlled as a ratio determined by the film gate of the camera. By default, the Film Gate is set to User but can also be set to many different camera types. These camera types will control the size of the aperture (film back size) which determines the ratio between the focal length and the angle of view that is rendered – set the focal length to 50 (this is measured in millimetres) and change the film gates. Choose a film gate and stick with it because later changes to the camera will have a knock-on effect for attributes like depth of field and angle of view that could severely disrupt the composition of the camera view.

Motion Blur

The second artefact that attempts to reproduce the effect of a real world camera is that of motion blur. Motion blur occurs when the shutter speed of a camera is relatively slow and an object travels across the film during the time of the exposure. Thus the amount of blur is

a combination of shutter speed, speed of the object in question and direction of the object relative to the plane of the film gate. When an object moves in CG, it should be motion blurred
otherwise it will appear to "stutter" across the screen as each position of the object in each
frame will bear no temporal relation to its last position. For a camera in Maya, the amount of
time that the "film" is exposed is related to the shutter angle. This is the size of the opening in
a movie camera's shutter and not the single frame camera that we were simulating with depth
of field; the larger the shutter angle, the more exposure of the film gate and the larger the
amount of motion blur moving objects exhibit.

- Create a scene with a few lights, a sphere and a background plane.
- Animate the sphere so that it crosses the camera's field of view in five frames.
- Turn on Motion Blur in the Render Globals window, leave the Motion Blur Type as 3D
  and render the scene.

The sphere should now be blurred as it crosses the camera field of view. You can increase the
amount of blur in two ways: shutter angle and blur by frame. The former is an attribute
local to the camera from which you are rendering and will control the general "footprint" that
the moving object will make across the frame as it is "exposed". The latter attribute is in the
Render Globals and tells the renderer how many frames prior to the currently rendering frame
to consider when sampling the motion of the object(s). For example, render frames with
different shutter angle values and then re-render with a different Blur by Frame value.
Increasing Blur by Frame will generally smooth the motion blur and the length of the blur
can be attenuated by a smaller shutter angle.

   You can change the type of motion blur to 2D, which will help keep down render times, by
applying the blur as a post-process effect. The speed and direction of a moving object are
stored as motion vectors in each frame, with the blurring being applied as a result of various
factors such as shutter angle and the 2D motion blur attributes.

   Switch the Motion Blur Type to 2D and render again. You can now see that the motion
blur is applied once the scene has been rendered and it has also rendered faster. You can
change the appearance of the 2D motion blur by using Blur Length, Blur Sharpness and
Smooth Value to alter the way that Maya uses the post-process blurring. You can also speed
up rendering by dealing with the motion blur in two passes. Turning on Keep Motion
Vectors will cause Maya to store motion vectors with each frame but not to apply them for
motion blurring; you can then invoke the 2D motion blurring from the command line (DOS
or UNIX) which will then apply the post-process blurring. When rendering a large number of
frames, this can break up the number of tasks the renderer has to accomplish and can speed
up the total time taken to render animation. Do note, however, that motion blur does not
blur shadows, so it may well be necessary to blur the objects and then to render the shadows
using different render passes in the Render Globals and blur them in a paint or compositing
package.

Summary

We have seen how to colour surfaces, light scenes and render frames. Because frame output is
the reason that we use a piece of animation software like Maya and not just to display rendered
pictures on the monitor, being able to render these frames before the deadline will be an
important aspect when considering a timeline for a project. At all points during the project,

set off test renders so that you can keep an eye on total render time, and sit and do the calculations for the entire project. What can create a faster turnaround from rendering the scene to delivering the final output is the "divide and conquer" method of rendering. Sometimes a compositing solution will be required to integrate different rendered layers and other elements. If you take this to be a given, then you can swiftly look at your scene and start splitting up your rendering requirements into layers. Maya provides a user-friendly way of achieving this with the Render Layers technique, so all you have to do is to sort your scene into groups of reciprocal objects and render these layers for compositing into the background images. You can optimize the renderer further by tuning the surface attributes for each object so that they are only as complex as you need them to be for the amount of space that they take up on the screen. This is also true of textures; use bump maps for distant objects (if you can see this effect) and only use displacement maps when silhouettes and shadows get closer to the camera.

Particle Systems

7

Introduction

Particle systems are used to model objects that do not have a definite edge or surface but are instead composed of many sub-objects (particles) such as smoke or dust clouds. This means that the look and behaviour of the system is a result of the properties of the underlying particles. A general particle system consists of two objects: an *emitter* object and a *particle* object. Both of these contain various attributes that help to change the way that the item interacts with the scene and how it is represented visually. An emitter can exist as a point in space, a surface, a volume or a curve and controls all of the starting aspects of the particle object's behaviour, such as initial direction, speed and the number of particles that are emitted per second from it. A particle object is a group of particles that are emitted and controls attributes of the individual particles such as appearance, how this may change over time and how external forces can affect the particle positions.

Because particle systems are used to mimic naturally occurring phenomena and use physical laws to achieve the effects, observation of any source material will be important so that details such as density, interaction and behaviour can be noted down. Sparks and fire continually change their colour and it is these changes which go to adding to the effect, so other details should be noted when observing any source material: colour can be as dynamic a process as movement. A third object can be included into a particle system: a *field*. Field objects can influence the frame-to-frame position of each particle, subject to various mechanisms such as attenuation over distance and strength. Last of all, particles can be made to interact with surfaces by way of *collisions*. Collisions will create collision events, which allow you to create effects such as splashes or shrapnel and let you govern how the interaction is carried.

Emitters, Particle Objects and Fields

Maya's dynamics use natural physical laws to control the transforms of objects or particles, allowing you to simulate naturally occurring phenomena such as fire or water. Once you start to use a dynamic system to simulate these phenomena, you hand over all control of the transformation to the dynamics solver. The dynamics solver operates in much the same way as an IK solver does, in that it works out how the position of a particle or surface should be evaluated and then moved. All dynamic solvers work on an incremented frame forwards basis, so that positions are assessed and changed when the frame advances. This method has been used before in the form of the Jiggle deformer, which could only be implemented as soft body dynamics prior to Maya 4.0, but has kept a lot of the original mechanisms such as caching data to disk. When a dynamic system is used, the scene has to be set up differently, because a dynamic solver needs to be able to play each frame in order to accurately calculate the positions of dynamic objects.

Open the Animation Preferences window (click on its icon beside the timeline) and set the Playback Speed to Play Every Frame so that each frame is played and can be evaluated by each dynamics solver, regardless of how much time it will take. You also need to make sure that playback begins from frame zero. All of this has an impact on scenes if you want to integrate dynamics systems with normal animation, so extract any useful animated surfaces or items (or create dummy objects) so that dynamics can be created in a new scene and then re-imported to the main scene later on. Due to the inherent non-real time playback of dynamic systems, it will always be worth Playblasting the work to get a better feel for how dynamics will work when imported into non-dynamic scenes.

Creating an Emitter

Emitters are the items that create particles and can be divided into two types: *position* and *object* emitters. Position emitters create particles from one point in space and can emit in all directions (an "omni" emitter) or emit in a direction (a "directional" emitter). Object emitters emit particles from evenly distributed positions over the surface of an object or a curve's length. The distinction between emitter types can be blurred, however, when point emitters are attached to surface components. You can explore how Maya controls and manages these systems by creating a fountain of particles. When you create an emitter, Maya will automatically create the particle object that is emitted, so you can quickly get the fundamental parts of the fountain working without further ado.

- Create a new scene, set the timeline to 200 frames and change the menu set to Dynamics (F4).
- Open the options box for Particles|Create Emitter.

This options box contains numerous options that are used to define the initial settings for the emitter, some of which are passed onto the particle, such as speed of ejection. Most of these options can be changed in the Channels Box or Attribute Editor afterwards so that you can tune the action of the particle system. For now, we want to set out the rough effect of the emitter, so you should set the Emitter Type to Directional and the Rate to 200 (per second). Because we have chosen a directional emitter, you should set out the attributes in regard to this, so open the fold-out titled Distance/Direction Attributes, set the direction to one in Y and zero in the rest and set Spread to 0.35. Spread is the fraction of 180 degrees from the plane that is perpendicular to the emission direction, so 0.35 will create a cone of 63 degrees. Click the Create button and the emitter should appear at the origin and start emitting particles upon playback. There is also a particle object in the Outliner as well as the emitter and selecting this will bring up the relevant attributes for it.

- Select the emitter to display its attributes in the Channels Box.
- Set Speed to 5 and Rate to 200.
- Rewind and play back.

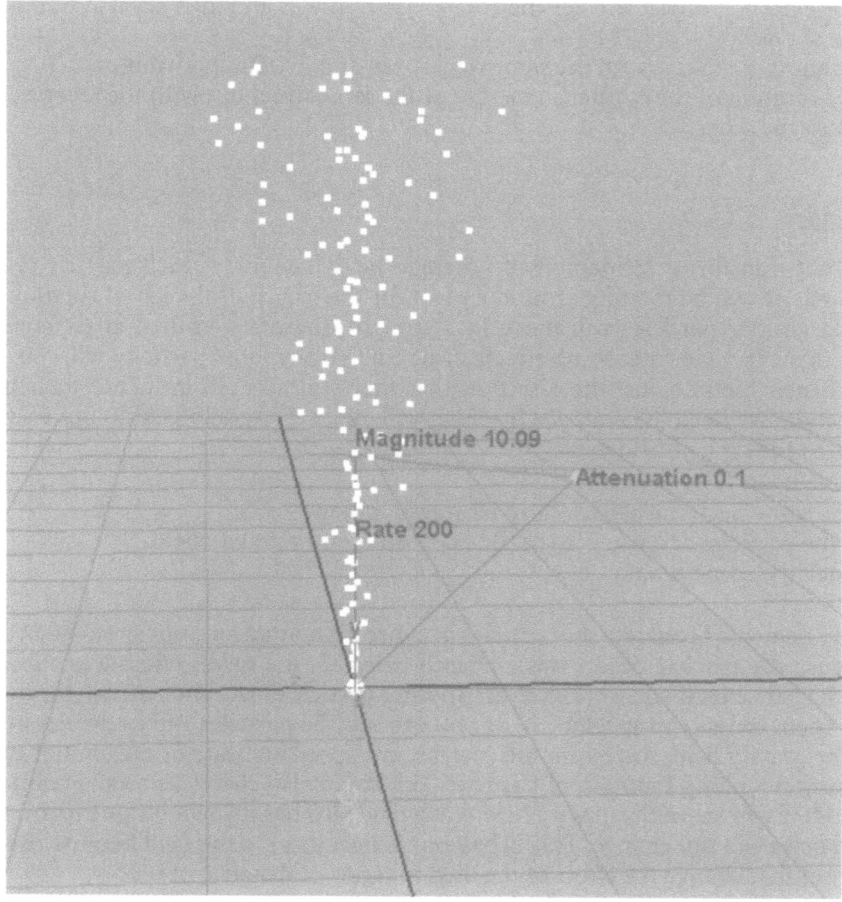

Figure 7.1 The Basic Particle Spray.

You can also change some of the attributes for the emitter with the Show Manipulator tool, which lets you change speed, direction, spread, rate and min and max distance. Min and max distance allow you to tightly define an area in which the particles will be born. If you want to create the exhaust from an F16 jet engine, you can use an animated min and max distance to change the area that the particles start in, in relation to how fast gases are being burnt. So far, particles are being emitted in an upward stream and will continue to move until the current time wraps round to zero, so although the particles are being born with a velocity and direction, any other forces do not affect them. Note that the emitter and the particle object both have transforms, either as separate nodes or built into their top node. This will be useful for the emitter so that you can have the particle object either follow the character or object that is emitting. Keying the transform values for the particle object will have a slightly different effect because although the particles move through 3D space, they will only be born at the emitter's position.

- Select the particle object and key the rotateX at frame 25 and then key it at frame 100 with a value of 180.
- Create another emitter with the same rate, speed and direction attributes.
- Key the rotation of the emitter's rotateX at the same times but with the reverse rotation.
- Play back the scene.

Adding Fields

The different transforms fundamentally change the behaviour of each particle system: the rotated particles will be rotating around a pivot for the length of the keyed rotation whereas the rotated emitter particles will move in a straight line once emitted at different angles. Although this can yield interesting effects, it doesn't govern how particles will move during the rest of their lifetime, just the direction that they will take. To influence their frame-to-frame position, we need to create *fields*, which will effect changes to position of each particle in relation to the type of field used.

- Play the scene until the particles can be seen in a view.
- Select the particles and use Fields|Gravity to create a gravity field.
- Play back the scene again.

The gravity field will accelerate the particles in a direction by an amount specified in its attributes. Because the particle object was currently selected, the field's effect was automatically linked to the particles. If you were to create another particle object and emitter, the field would not affect them unless you specified it. As you can see, the particles will be accelerated downward by the gravity field, so you should increase the speed and rate of the emitter to provide a more normal looking fountain of particles. You could also change several attributes of the gravity field; if you move the gravity field (each field also has its own unique icon), the effect on the particles will not change. This behaviour is non-local to the field because there are no attributes set that change the effect of the field in terms of distance in space.

Because we are going to be using the Attribute Editor more than the Channels Box, you should set the Attribute Editor to be your default editor at the right-hand side of the Maya window. Bring up the Hotbox and with the LMB, click and hold in the east zone until a marking menu appears. Select Attributes and then when the next sub-menu appears select Attribute Editor.

- Select the gravity field and translate it back to the origin.
- Set the Attenuation to 0.1, 0.3 and 0.5, playing back each setting.

Attenuation works as an exponent on distance and because distance from the gravity field is now involved, there will be a point when the particles are not affected by the field whatsoever. You can further modify how the effect of the gravity field propagates itself through space by using the Max Distance attribute. This will set a limit on the distance over which the field can have an effect. Used in conjunction with Attenuation, you can now fine tune the field, but remember that all of these values are relative and if you were to animate the emitter position then the particles might well fall outside of the field's effect. For now, set the Attenuation to 0.1 and turn off Max Distance. All fields use these common attributes of Magnitude, Attenuation and Max Distance, but their effects will depend on their individual nature and any attributes that help to create the effect.

As more fields are added to the particle object, you may need to create new fields in order to counter the effects of other fields. If you want to add some rotation to the particles as they reach the apex of their travel, you can use a vortex field which will create a tornado-like effect.

- Select the particle object.
- Create a Vortex field, translate it 4.0 units upwards in the Y axis.
- Set the Attenuation to 2.0.

Playing back the scene, you can see that the vortex field is adding a rotational amount to each particle in a similar fashion to setting keys for the rotate channels. Changing the axis of the vortex field can also have some interesting effects; try setting the axis to one in X and zero in Y and Z to create a solar flare effect. However, this tends to spread the particles out even though the field has a large amount of attenuation, so another field can be added to counter some of these effects. A *radial* field either pulls particles to it or pushes particles away from it depending on the magnitude (a positive will push away) so a radial field with a negative magnitude can be used to pull particles towards it while retaining their vortex-like spin about the Y axis.

- Select the particle object and add a radial field.
- Translate it upwards 2.5 units in the Y axis.
- Set the Attenuation to 1.0 and the Magnitude to -2.0.

We can use attributes of the particle object to change the way that the particles move and play back. Select the particle object and in the Attribute Editor, change the Dynamics Weight to zero and play back the scene. The gravity field won't slow the particles down any more as the Dynamics Weight attribute scales the effect of any dynamic forces upon the particle object. The Conserve attribute determines how much of a particle's velocity is retained from the previous frame. This can drastically change how the particle object works in a scene and will almost destroy the effect of movement if set to anything below 0.9; a setting of 0.98 will still have a pronounced effect on the system. If the emitter is moving then the Inherit Factor setting will determine the amount of the emitter's movement that will pass onto the particle's movement – zero will inherit none of the emitter's movement. You can also change how dynamic forces affect a particle object by changing the Forces in World attribute and the Expressions before Dynamics attribute. Forces in World mean that any dynamic forces will act using the global axis as opposed to the particle's own local axis. You can also change the start time for the particle system, as it will be inconvenient if particles have to start at frame zero, so open the Time Attributes fold-out and change the Start Frame.

As we start increasing the complexity of our particle systems we will need to begin optimizing the display of the actual particles themselves as the hundreds of thousands of particles that go into making up a sandstorm may not be required until we need to finally render the whole scene.

Open the fold-out titled Emission Attributes and change the Max Count to 200. Now all emission will stop after 200 particles have been emitted allowing you to quickly see the effect of all items in the particle system interacting, without cluttering the scene. However, if you have a long running simulation, then you should set Max Count to -1 (this states that the value is set to infinity or "none") and change the Level of Detail attribute. This attribute only displays a fraction of the particles emitted, so setting this to 0.1 will display every tenth particle – this can dramatically speed up playback while still showing what the particle systems will look like.

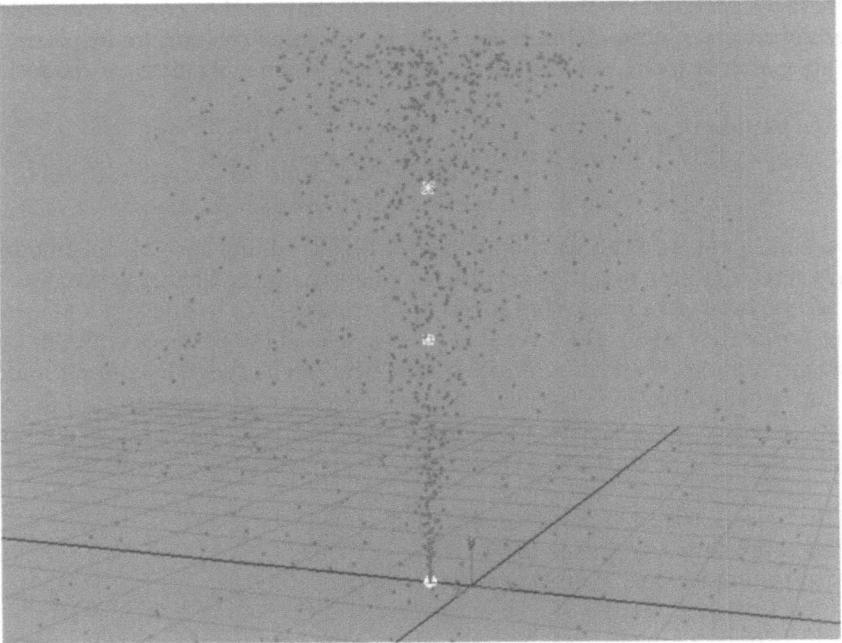

Figure 7.2 The Final Fountain Effect.

Now that we have a working fountain effect, we can cover our scene in fountains. The quickest way to duplicate a particle system is to save the scene. If the scene is solely the particle system, use File|Save as... and then use File|Import to merge a selected file with the current scene. Another way to do this if the scene consists of multiple objects is to group the particle system and all associated fields, use File|Export Selected to save the selected group and then import this scene into the current file. This will now give multiple copies of the same particle system, so you can alter the start times and any expressions or keys that you wish to save on the emitters, fields or particles. If your scene has a field such as a gravity field or an air field that provides an overall global effect, then you need to be able to connect your new particle object to it.

- Save this scene once as Fountain2.
- Select the particle object, create an air field and translate it 10.0 units upward.
- Set Type to Wind, Attenuation to 0.0, Direction to 1.0, 0.0, 1.0 and Speed to 2.0.
- Import Fountain2 so that there are two fountain particle systems.
- Move the emitters and field apart so that they can clearly be seen.

There is only one fountain particle system connected to the global air field, so any new particle systems will require connection. This can be achieved through the use of the Dynamic Relationships window which can be found under the Windows|Relationship Editors menu heading. This editor lets you choose an item or items in the left-hand side and depending upon the Selection Mode (Fields, Collisions, Emitters, All) will display any dynamic objects that can be or are connected to the selected item(s); connections are displayed as highlighted names, similar to light linking.

- Select the newly imported particle object and set the mode to Fields.
- Select and highlight the Air field that appears in the right-hand side of the editor.
- Replay the scene.

Now you can change any aspect of the emitter and particles while being able to connect to any field of your choice. One attribute that is important with emitters is the randomness of emission. If you have two identical particle systems, you can change the way that the particles are emitted by changing the seed number that the emitter uses to generate their random positioning. This allows you to create particle systems that act the same and have the same forces working on them but will look different in terms of particle placement. Each particle object has an Emission Random Stream Seeds fold-out and the seed number here can be changed to create different particle positions at birth.

Collisions

Collisions can be added to the particle system so that when the water falls down it can rebound off other surfaces that lie in the scene. Collisions can be easily integrated into scenes and they utilize the same set of rules as all dynamic systems. All you have to make sure of is that the surfaces that the particles will be interacting with are set up correctly and that you create an appropriate event for each collision.

- Delete the scene and open up the saved Fountain2 scene.
- Create a polygon plane and scale it by 30 units in all axes.
- Select the particle object and the polygon plane then select Particles|Make Collide.
- Play the scene back.

You now have the particles colliding with the surface and bouncing high into the air where the fields will influence them again. The first thing to do will be to edit the surface collision effect so that the bounce can be set to a more realistic level and you will probably have to re-edit the effect of the fields so that they don't contribute once the particles have hit the floor. Then you can define any new events because these collisions can create new events, such as splashes from water particles, which will be represented by new particle objects.

- Select the particle object and open the fold-out titled Collision Attributes.
- Hold the RMB over Resilience to bring up a marking menu for the selected attribute and select geoConnector*n*. Resilience.
- Set the Resilience (bounciness) to 0.1 and the Friction to 0.5.
- Replay the scene.

The geoConnector is a node that holds data for each collision created between a particle object and a surface. This means that you can create multiple collisions with multiple surfaces and the particle object will hold all the relevant data for these interactions. However, the fields are still affecting the particles, causing them to be gathered into the central axis of the fields, so you need to use the Max Distance attribute for the radial and vortex field so that they won't affect the particles past a certain point. So that you aren't using guesswork when setting this attribute, you should use a measuring tool in the side view so that you can decide the farthest reach for each field.

- Pop the side view to the foreground and rewind the timeline so that no particles are evident.
- Use Create|Measure Tools|Distance Tool, LMB click on the vortex field and then LMB click on the furthest distance that you want it to affect the particles.
- Do the same for the radial field.

The distance tool creates two locators with a measurement icon between them and the beauty of this is that if you move any locator, the measurement updates. If you look in the Attribute Editor, this measurement is the Distance attribute and could even be connected to the Max Distance attribute for the field through an expression. These locators can now provide useful distances that you can plug into fields, although you may still need to increase the magnitudes of the fields to balance the changes made so that the fountain keeps its shape. Playing the scene back now shows a fountain of particles that react when they encounter the surface. The fountain looks like it is emitting marbles, however, because water does not continue bouncing around when it hits a surface and so you need to edit what occurs at the point of collision, known as a "collision event". Open the Collision Event Editor from Particles|Particle Collision Events... and select the Particle object in the top left-hand side. You now have the choice of when the event will occur and what will occur at each event.

Tick All Collisions so that any time the particle object collides while it exists this event will occur, although you can create an event for each bounce of the particle object by setting the collision number instead. You should then set the Event Type to Split because the other option will cause the original particle to stay alive, whereas we want the particle to split into sub-particles and disappear when this happens. Tick Random # particles and set this to 5, meaning that between one and five particles will be created when the original particle splits and dies. Spread has the same effect as it has for emitters so set this to 0.5 so that you get a rounded emission from the point of impact, and set Inherit Velocity to 0.7 so that the splashes don't zoom off too far upon creation. Click Create Event and play the scene back to see the new collision event in action. Now you have another particle system in your scene, which means that you can create new events for when these particles collide. But first you need to connect the new particles to your existing fields and to collide with the polygon plane.

- Open the Dynamic Relationships Editor and select the new particle object.
- Set the mode to Fields and highlight the gravity field.
- Set the mode to Collisions and select the polygon plane.
- Play the scene back.

Because you are killing the original particles when they collide, you can change the resilience and friction of the geoConnector to only affect the newly born particles. But you will probably want to kill these particles when they collide with the polygon plane, so open the Collision Event Editor again. Turn off Split and Emit and you can see that at the bottom of the window, the Original Particle Dies attribute has been activated, because you are defining an event that neither splits or emits.

Now that you can rebound particles from surfaces, you can use them to precisely guide your particle systems through space by creating surfaces, making your particle systems collide

Figure 7.3 The Original Particle Object Splitting on Impact with the Plane.

with them and then hiding the surfaces. If you want the wind to suddenly whip up a section of blizzard across the camera for a wipe and reveal, you can model a tube and then emit particles inside it at speed. Using Friction can also dramatically alter how particles will interact. If you set the Resilience to 0.0 and the Friction to 0.1, you can have the particles creep across the hidden surface. What this does mean is that particle collision events need to be turned off, because the particles will be constantly interacting with the hidden surface, unless you want emissions to continually occur.

Volume Fields and Volume Emitters

It can become difficult to keep in mind the combined spatial effects of fields if all we have to deal with is a position and attributes. This is especially true when we wanted to define the effect of the vortex and radial field; measuring locators had to be created and then we had to input these values into the Max Distance attributes. Thankfully, Maya can create fields as volumes so that we can control the behaviour and effect of a field in terms of its spatial volume. There is also a specialized field called a "Volume Axis" that governs the position of particles within its volume by using its axis to control movement.

- Open the options box for Particles|Create Emitter and set the Emitter Type to Volume.
- Open the fold-out titled Volume Emitter Attributes and set the Volume Shape to Sphere.
- Click the Create button and play back the scene.

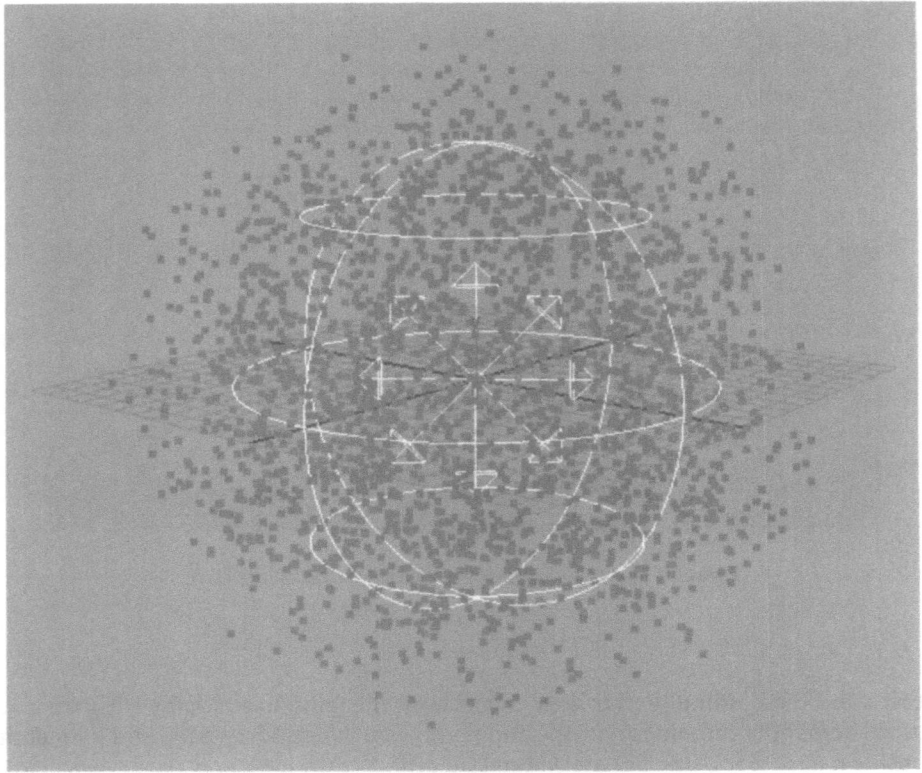

Figure 7.4 Spherical Volume Emission.

The particles are now emitted from the sphere's volume, instead of from a point in space, creating a more natural emission effect from a surface. All volume emitters have an axis around which they are made and about which the direction of particle emission can be determined. The emitted particles will roughly keep to the original shape of the volume emitter unless affected by fields. In the Attribute Editor for the sphere emitter you have just created, open the fold-outs titled Basic Emitter Attributes, Volume Emitter Attributes and Volume Speed Attributes. These fold-outs will present all of the attributes you require to shape the direction and initial velocities of your emitted particles. A fundamental attribute for volume emitters is whether the particles will die upon leaving the volume or not, which can be set in the Attribute Editor for the particle object. You can affect the speed and rate in a more intuitive manner by leaving Scale Speed by Size and Scale Rate by Object Size turned on, so you can just scale the volume emitter and these attributes will update automatically. You can also change the shape of the emitter which is controlled by the Sweep attribute (apart from if the emitter is a cube volume) and if a torus volume is used as an emitter, Section Radius. Now that you can control the emission shape, how the particles move in relation to the volume's axis is important.

- Create a Cube volume emitter and scale it 6 units in the X axis.
- In the Basic Emitter Attributes section, turn on Scale Rate by Object Size.

- The particles will be emitted along the axis lines at the centre of the volume.
- Set `Away from Center` to `0.0` and `Along Axis` to `5.0`.
- Play back the scene.

This will now create a more regular emission of particles suitable for steam rising from a vent and will also provide a useful curtain of particles with which to examine the effect of fields as volumes. Select the particle object, open the options box for `Fields|Turbulence` and set the volume shape to be a sphere. Move the sphere to the centre of the particle system and set the magnitude to 20.0 with no attenuation. You can now use volumes to tightly control where disturbances to particle objects occur; for instance, eddies in gas can be easily created and controlled visually in the workspace. This technique can be used to model particle systems that need a particular start shape, such as clouds or galaxies, and you can choose whether to affect the currently selected dynamic object or all dynamic objects in the scene.

- Create a volume emitter in the shape of a sphere, scale it and set the rate to 400.
- Set the `Away from Centre` attribute to `0.0`.
- Play for a few frames and then pause playback so that the sphere is full of non-moving particles.
- Select the particle object and use `Solvers|Initial State|Set for Selected`.
- Delete the emitter and rewind the scene.

Using this `Initial State` menu item will set the positions of any selected dynamic objects similar to freezing the transformations of an object, but any initial velocity and direction will be retained. Because you set `Away from Centre` to `0.0` the particles were just created in the volume without any velocity. You can connect new fields to particle objects by selecting the field and then the particle object you wish to connect to and using `Fields|Affect Selected Object(s)`.

Emitting from Surfaces and Curves

It is also possible to emit particles from surfaces and curves and use them as sources for fields, giving as much flexibility for the creation of particle systems as is needed. Just select the surface or curve and use `Particles|Emit from Object` which will then parent an emitter to the object and emit particles from evenly distributed points over the surface. The particle emission speed and direction will also be controlled by several additional attributes that relate to the surface or curve, tangent speed and normal speed. You can even narrow this down to emitting from the selected components of a surface or curve.

- Create a NURBS curve and a NURBS sphere.
- Select the curve and open the options box for `Particles|Emit from Object`.
- Set the `Emitter Type` to `Curve` and click Create.
- Play back the scene.

The curve is now emitting particles evenly along its length in the default direction (upward in Y). The curve will continue to emit particles no matter what is happening to it in terms of shape, so you can not only transform the curve but also deform it while emission continues. It will be worth animating the deformations in another scene because playback will be

Figure 7.5 The Curve Emitter.

extremely slow while Maya calculates the particle emission speeds and directions, so animation feedback will be limited. In the Attribute Editor for the curve emitter, changing the Normal speed and Tangent speed attributes will affect the direction in which the particles will be emitted, by multiplying the direction and speed of the particles by the tangency or normal direction. If the direction attributes are all set to zero so that the particles are emitted omni-directionally, then it is easier to see the effect of these attributes. You can create a curve emitter as a curve on surface so particles can appear while the underlying surface is being deformed by a skeleton and other deformers.

You can now extend the emission effects and indeed the field effects to objects, so that you can have a surface emit particles from its component positions and also be the source of fields. For instance, you can set your animated bouncing ball on fire by adding particles which resemble fire and smoke to it. You can also have surfaces emit fields, so you can have a flaming ball emit a weak radial field to move the flames away from its own surface.

- Create a NURBS sphere, open the Emit from Surface options box and set the Emitter Type to Surface and click Create.

The particles will now emit from each CV on the sphere (and each vertex if a polygon surface), so the more CVs, the denser the emission. The particles can be created in a more cloud-like fashion about the sphere by increasing the Max Distance attribute and possibly the Min Distance as well. The emissions are quite regularly spaced but several adjustments can be made to break it up. One is to increase the tangent speed so that the particles will cross the regular isoparm spacing; the other is to increase the tessellation in the geoConnector (created to provide surface information for collisions and for surface emission). Tessellation will break up the surface into smaller discreet sections to spread the emission between the CVs. You can change your surface emitter to a directional or omni-directional emitter so that the particles will be governed by emitter attributes more than surface attributes.

If you do change the emitter type from "surface" to "directional" or "omni" then you also have the option to alter the rates of particle emission, but because the particles will come from each component, the even positioning that surface emitters provide is lost. Normally, particles will be emitted at an even rate from each component position but you can vary emissions from each CV or vertex by selecting the item in question and using the Particles|

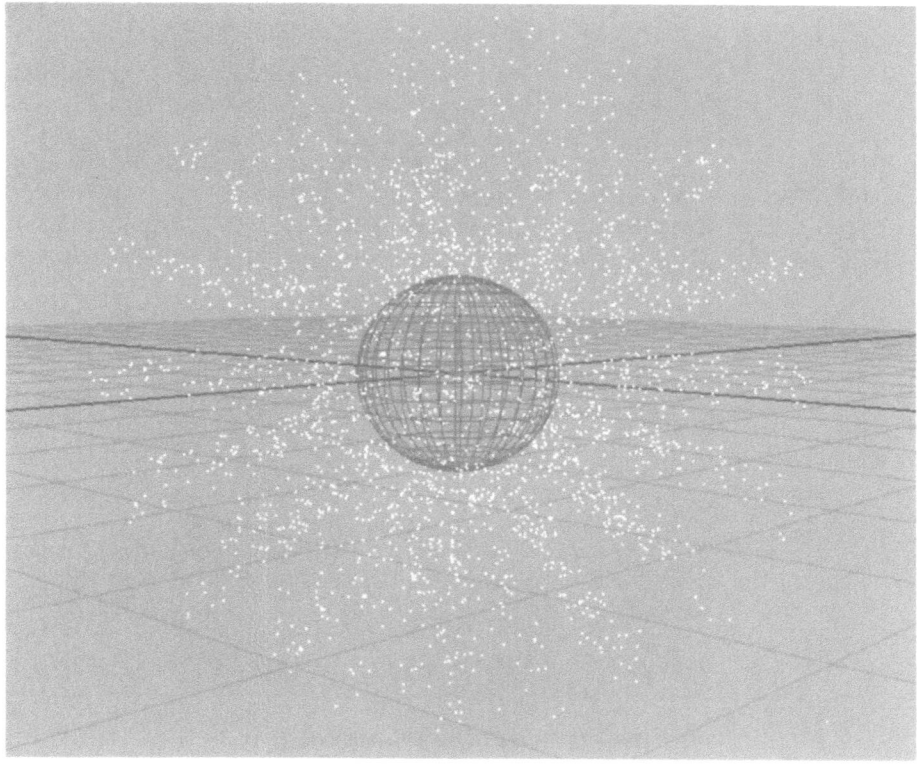

Figure 7.6 The Surface Emitter on a NURBS Sphere.

Per-Point Emission Rates menu item. The Attribute Editor or Channels Box will then reflect this option displaying a list of vertex or CV numbers and the associated particle rate beside it. In the Attribute Editor, particle rates are found in the surface shape node under Extra Attributes and are named Emitter*n* Rate *n* PP. The Channels Box will display these automatically in the side and access to these rates may be a little easier. If you want to have emission coming from only one section of the surface then it will be easier to select the CVs or vertices from which emission is required and then use Particles|Emit from Object and set the Emitter Type to Omni or Directional.

You can also have surfaces become the source of fields, which is useful when you require objects and characters to interact with particles and when the field shape cannot be easily represented by any of the volume fields. For example, a car moving through mist or a dolphin swimming through the particles in water will need this type of field emission if it is to appear close to camera, otherwise a simpler and faster way to calculate volume field should be used and parented to the character.

- Create a NURBS plane and deform it so that it has an undulating surface.
- Select the plane and create a surface emitter with a rate of 10,000 particles and all speed attributes set to zero.
- Play back the scene for three frames so a dense cloud of mobile particles builds up.

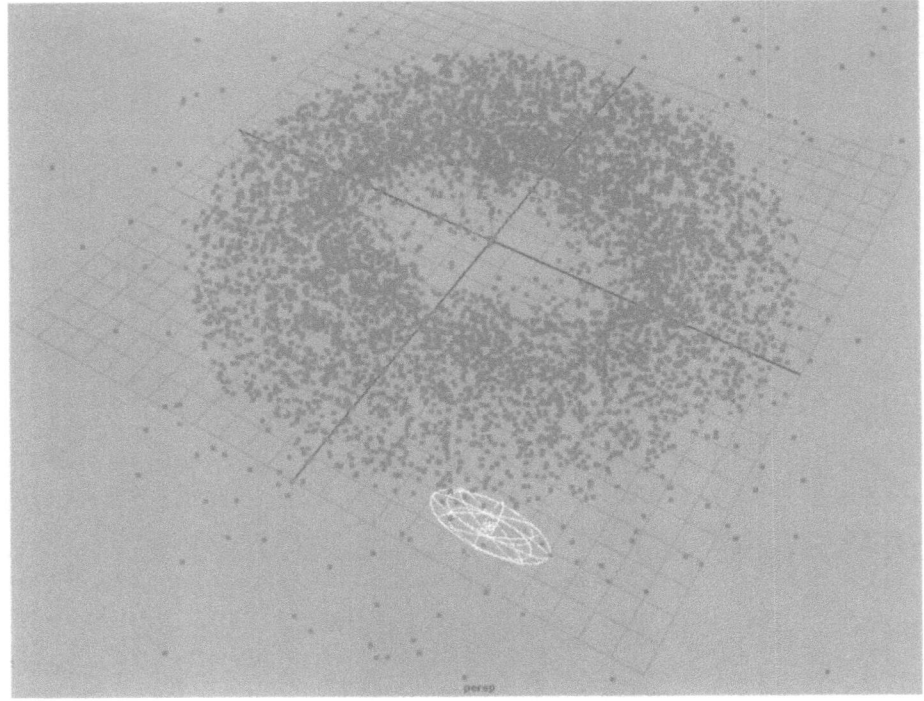

Figure 7.7 The Hole Created in the Particle Cloud.

- Select the particle object and use Solvers|Initial State|Set for Selected, then delete the surface and the emitter.
- Create a NURBS sphere and position it ten units above the particle cloud and set a key for translate Y at frame zero.
- Move the sphere 20 units down and set a key for this at frame 10, so that it passes through the cloud at speed.
- Select the particle object and create a radial field.
- With the radial field still selected, shift-select the sphere and use Fields|Use Selected as Source of Field, which will now place the field icon inside the object.
- In the Attribute Editor for the field, set the Magnitude to 50.0, Attenuation to 0.0 and turn on Max Distance and set that to 1.0.

If you now play the scene back, the sphere should punch a neat hole through the particles. However, this hole is just the max distance of the radial field's effect and nothing to do with the sphere itself apart from the transformation. If you scale the sphere so that it is an oval shape, the hole that is punched in the particle cloud will not change. In the Attribute Editor for the field, open the fold-out labeled Special Effects, turn on Apply per Vertex and play the scene back. This attribute now has the field emanating at equal strength at each CV of the sphere, so any shape changes will now affect the shape of the field. Because the field is applied equally to the components and not averaged across them, changing the max distance and magnitude will have dramatic effects. Set the Max Distance attribute to 2.0 for a much larger impact.

Figure 7.8 Field Emitting Particles Punching through a Particle Cloud.

By extension, you can also have curves emit fields but for some very interesting effects, you can have particles emit fields as well.

- Delete the animated sphere, but not the radial field, and select the particle cloud.
- Create a directional emitter, place it below the particle cloud and set the rate to 100.0 and the speed to 30.0.
- Animate the emitter's rotation over 30 frames so that the particles will move through the cloud.
- Select the radial field, shift-select the new particles and use Fields|Use Selected as Source of Field to attach the radial field to each particle (the field will only attach to each particle if Apply per Vertex is on).
- Playblast the scene to see the emitted particles saw through the particle cloud.

Because you have now created a field effect from each emitted particle, the playback of the scene will be a lot slower and it will almost always be worth Playblasting the scene.

Controlling Emission with Textures

When emitting particles from NURBS surfaces, you can control the rate of emission and the particle colour with a texture (2D only for emission rates).

- Create a NURBS plane and attach a new Lambert shader to it.
- Map a 2D chequer texture to the new Lambert shader's colour attribute and use the "6" hotkey to change to hardware texture mode.
- Select the NURBS plane and attach a surface emitter to it.
- Open the Attribute Editor for the emitter and open the fold-out titled Texture Emission Attributes.

This section allows you to control the rate and colour of the emitted particles by mapping the texture on the plane to the texture button in the Attribute Editor. Use the Textures tab in the Hypershade to display the chequer texture and MMB drag the chequer texture node onto the map button beside Texture Rate. Turn on the textured emission by checking the Enable Texture Rate; playing the scene back now should show the particles only emitting from the white squares on the plane, which you can reverse using the Emit from Dark attribute. The texture that controls the emission rate does not have to be attached to the surface at all, but surface texture will often give a good guide as to where emission will occur from, especially if they have been created as painted bitmaps for a specific effect.

The particles can also be coloured using a mapped texture (again, not necessarily from the texture that is applied to the emitting surface) but you first need to allow each particle to be separately coloured. This is done by attaching a dynamic Per Particle colour attribute to the particle object, meaning that colour can be applied on a per particle basis.

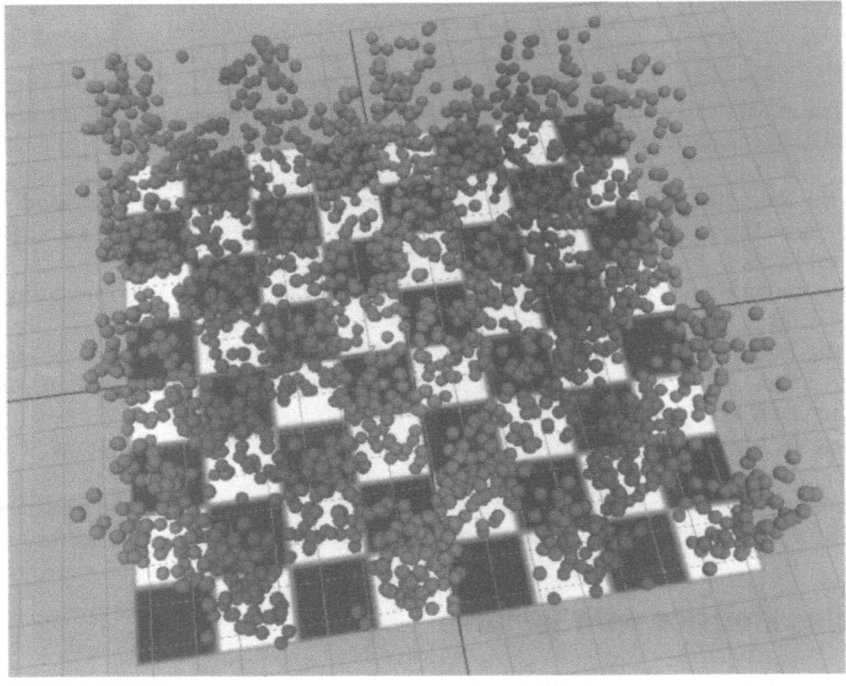

Figure 7.9 Particle Emission Using a Chequer Texture.

Select the particle object and in the Attribute Editor click the Colour button in the Add Dynamic Attributes section. This will bring up a small option box allowing you to check the Add Per Particle Attribute and click the Add Attribute button. Now you can return to the Emitter section of the Attribute Editor and MMB drag and drop the chequer texture onto the Particle Colour attribute. Turn on Inherit Colour and play the scene back. Because you are using the same texture to affect the colour and rate of the particles, only the particles that are emitted from the white sections will be coloured and that will be white. Instead, use the RMB beside the Particle Colour attribute, select Break Connection, map a ramp texture to it and play the scene back.

Particle Goals

One final way to control a particle's position is to introduce goals. A goal is an attractor object that influenced particles will head towards. Because goals have goal strengths, these can be animated or changed to affect where the particles will move, similar to animating different constraint weights. The goal strengths indicate how much of the particle's movement will be directed towards a goal object, so a strength of 0.1 will only move a particle 10 per cent of the way towards a goal object which, when combined with its velocity, may not move it towards the goal whatsoever.

- Create a directional emitter that will spray particles upwards into the scene.
- Create two spheres and place them 10 units either side of the emitter.
- Select the particle object, then the first sphere and use Particles|Goal to create a goal relationship.
- Repeat for the second sphere.
- Open the Attribute Editor for the particle object and fold out Goal Weights and Objects.
- Set one goal to 0.3 and the other to 0.5 and play the scene back.
- While the scene is playing back change the weights on the sliders to see the effect that this has on the particles.

The Goal Smoothness attribute will control the way that the transition between goal forces is handled; a higher setting will result in a smoother transition. Animating goal objects along with the goal weights can create fascinating dynamic animations.

Particle Replacement

If you want to create dynamic movement, but don't want objects to be represented as clouds of particles, then you can take advantage of Maya's particle instancer node. This will allow you to place a piece of geometry or several pieces of geometry onto the positions of the particles so you can use the movement of the particles to drive the positions of geometry.

- Create a polygonal leaf model.
- Create a directional emitter, position it at the top of the scene and have it emit downwards into the scene.
- Create a gravity field and an air field (set it to wind) and have them influence the particles.
- Set the rate to 20.0 and the spread to 0.8 so that particles are gently drifting downwards.

- Select the leaf model, shift-select the particle object and use `Particles|Instancer (Replacement)`.

There should be a new item in the Outliner that represents the particle `instancer` node and the leaf geometry should be copied to each particle. You can now affect how the instantiated geometry will react to its position or velocity in terms of orientation, so the leaves can aim and rotate depending on what they are doing. These options in the `instancer` fold-out allow you to set variations in the geometry's movements and appearance although the actual geometry cannot differ from shape to shape. The original model can be rotated and scaled while the `instancer` is working and these transformations will be passed onto the instances. It is also worthwhile hiding the original geometry.

- Select the `instancer` node and in the Attribute Editor set the `Rotation Angle Units` to `Radians`.
- Select the particle object and in its shape node open the fold-out titled `Instancer(Geometry Replacement)`.
- Set the `Rotation` to `worldPosition`.

You can add different pieces of geometry to the `instancer`, so different looking pieces of geometry can be included into the instancer using its cycling function. Normally you would cycle objects in the particle instancer to provide simple animation by changing the positioned shape. For example, you could create a cloud of snapping false teeth by providing geometry in

Figure 7.10 The Particle Replacer Placing Leaf Geometry at Particle Positions.

closed, open and mid shapes and then use the cycling function to cycle between these shapes and thus create the illusion of movement. You can use part of this function to provide the method to place a random piece of geometry from a provided list at each particle position. The more pieces of geometry, the less the similarity between shapes and colours. To do this you will need to give your particles some new attributes.

- Create a sphere, cone and a cube and scale them so that they are the same dimensions as the leaf model.
- Select all of these new objects and then shift-select the `instancer` node so that it is available for editing in the Attribute Editor.
- Click the Add Selection button so that the new pieces of geometry are now in the list.

It can be seen that each object in the list has an ID number beside it. If you set the `Cycle` attribute to `sequential`, the `Cycle Step Unit` to `Frames` and play the scene back, the `instancer` will cycle through the list of IDs, changing for every frame that each particle has been alive. Every particle has its own ID number and carries with it a list of dynamic attributes such as when it was born, how long it has been alive and how long it will live for. These attributes are known as `Per Particle` attributes or "PP" and later we shall be writing expressions that can access and change these attributes because PP attributes cannot be keyed. For now, we need to use the list of geometry that the `instancer` has but assign only one piece to each particle.

Turn off the cycling and open up the Attribute Editor for the particle object. In the `General Options` for the `Instancer` section, there is an attribute named `Object Index` and this allows you to assign an object to a particle by some indexing method other than sequentially. What we want to do is give each particle a number when it is born that will look up the object index ID and have the relevant piece of geometry assigned to it.

- Open the `Per Particle (Array) Attributes` fold-out and the `Add Dynamic Attributes` fold-out.
- Click the General button and in the `Add Attribute` window select the particle tab.
- Select `userScalar1PP` and click OK.

You have just created a custom per particle attribute whose value (which we are going to vary) will be applied to every particle created. Use the RMB in the text field beside `userScalar1PP` to bring up a sub-menu and select `Creation Expression` from this, which will bring up the Expression Editor. We shall show you how to write a small expression that will assign a random number to each particle and because we want this attribute to be set upon the birth of each particle and not to change during the particle's life, a creation expression will be used.

- Type `particleShape1.userScalar1PP = clamp(0, 3, trunc (rand(0,4)));` and click Create.
- Close the Expression Editor and scroll up in the Attribute Editor so the `Instancer` attributes are visible.
- Select `userScalar1PP` from the list of inputs for the `ObjectIndex` attribute.
- Rewind and play the scene back.

Creating per particle and per object attributes will become important as you start working on different particle effects. When you use the Attribute Editor to create dynamic attributes for particle objects, you are effectively creating custom attributes that are applied to the particle object, but because the attribute is a PP attribute, it has a different value for each particle.

Figure 7.11 The Particle Replacer now Placing Additional Geometry at Particle Positions.

Caching the Scene for Improved Feedback

When particle systems are created, you may well want to integrate them with other scenes so that you can see how they work with your normally animated characters and environments. You may also have a surface animating which will also be the source of fields and particle emission, so you will probably want to see how the whole scene works together. The methods for integration aren't a problem though, but the feedback is. You can always create a Playblast of your scene, which will provide exact real-time playback and the facility to scrub the animation back and forth, but if you wish to change your viewpoint or zoom in closer, you have to recreate the Playblast from scratch.

In the same way that you created a cache for the Jiggle deformer, you can create a disk cache for your particle systems. This cache works in exactly the same way as the jiggle disk cache and works to the same set of rules. If you create a disk cache, Maya will use that when you change the current time instead of recalculating the dynamics, so you can scrub backwards or forwards and play particle effects in real time, giving a reasonable feedback loop for integrating dynamic scenes with non-dynamic scenes. If you change anything that influences the dynamics, then you will have to create the cache all over again. Maya also provides an alternative to disk caching called "memory caching" – this creates the cache in memory not on the disk. This can be faster to implement and while it will save disk space, it will depend on how much memory the computer has.

- Create a new particle system or open a saved particle system file.
- Turn on memory caching using `Solvers|Memory Caching|Enable`.
- Play the scene once.
- Scrub the timeline back and forth.

Now that a memory cache has been created, you can have your dynamic objects act as if they were keyed. You will need to delete and recreate a memory cache if you change any attributes that will affect your particle – this can be done using `Solvers|Memory Caching|Delete Memory Cache` and then playing the scene back again. Playing the scene back again will automatically create a new cache because the memory cache option is still enabled. If you need to free up memory or wish to make changes to the scene and not to create a new cache every time the scene is played back, use `Solvers|Memory Caching|Disable`. You can also create memory caches for individual particle objects by setting the `Cache Data` attribute on or off in the Attribute Editor under the `General Control Attributes` heading. This lets you selectively control which particles are played back and allows you some freedom in what you wish to save in memory at each current playback.

Disk caching is activated in the same way that it was when caching the movements for the Jiggle deformer. Open the options box for `Solvers|Create Particle Disk Cache` so that you can name the directory that you will be creating or using for overwriting. Maya will create a directory called `particles` and then the named cache directories will be created here. These directories will be filled with a series of files describing the state of all particles in the scene, which will be read back by Maya the next time the scene is played back. The other options let you specify whether you want to create a cache whose length is specified by the time line or in the Render Globals and whether you wish to only update particles.

- Create a particle volume emitter in the shape of a sphere, set `Speed` to `10.0` and set `Away from Axis` and `Away from Centre` to `5.0`.
- Open the options for `Solvers|Create Particle Disk Cache` and set the name of the cache directory to `SP_1`.
- Make sure the timeline is rewound to zero and click Create.
- Once the disk cache has been created, scrub the timeline back and forth.

You can save multiple disk caches and turn off the use of disk caches through `Solvers|Edit Oversampling` or `Cache Settings`. These settings are controlled though a node named `dynGlobalsn`. You can turn off the use of disk caches, so that you can see any changes you make to the dynamic systems, otherwise Maya will always play back the currently selected disk cache. You can change the name of the cache directory used when playing back cached data, so you can switch different disk caches when playing back the scene. This can be useful when testing or presenting different dynamic effects when you wish to see how they integrate with non-dynamic scenes.

- Select the volume emitter and set `Away from Centre` to `0.0` and `Away from Axis` to `5.0`.
- Rewind the scene and open the options box for `Solvers|Create Particle Disk Cache` and set the name of the cache directory to `SP_2`.
- Make sure the timeline is rewound to zero and click Create.

Scrubbing the timeline back and forth will now play back the most recent disk cache. In the Attribute Editor for the `dynGlobalsn` node (either through `Solvers|Edit Oversampling` or

Cache Settings or by changing the focus of the Attribute Editor), you can now change the name of the disk cache directory and instantly have different particle playback. You don't have to put in a full pathname to the disk cache because Maya will always store these caches inside the particles directory it creates in the current project.

There is one other type of cache that is useful whenever you save and then open scenes containing dynamics, called a "startup cache". Having a startup cache allows you to save a scene at a non-zero frame and when the scene is re-opened, the particles will have their attributes and influences pre-calculated and will appear at the correct positions. If you saved scenes without a startup cache, you would have to rewind and play the scene to get the correct dynamic positions. This doesn't appear to be much of a real problem, in that you can always play the scene back, but if you have an extremely data-heavy scene and you wish to begin work from the position in time at which the scene was saved, using a startup cache can minimize having to wait for all the calculations to be made before you can work. The startup cache is also important if you wish to render particles without starting from frame zero.

Rendering Particles

We have looked at all of the ways that we can shape a particle object through the use of emission attributes, particle attributes, emitter types, fields, collisions and goals. These all work together to form the shape and volume of the particle system so that each point moves in a manner representative of the dynamic phenomenon that we are trying to model. If you look at the simple fountain you created, the movement was there but the dynamic system you created didn't look like water, only the positions of particles were moving like water. A fountain looks like a fountain for two reasons: the way it moves and the way it looks. This section is about creating the look of the particle system. Unlike most characters who are given surface colour and texture after animation, the appearance of a particle system is a combination of its movement and colour attributes.

So far, we have been looking at particles as points in space, but it would be hard to create the look of an explosion using just points, so Maya provides ten different types of particle shape.

Create a new particle emitter and pause playback so that you can see the particles clearly, select the particle object and in the Attribute Editor open the fold-out titled Render Attributes. This determines how the particles will look in terms of shape; currently they are set to Point which is the default particle type. Opening the pull-down menu for Particle Render Type will show what is available; what you want your particles to represent will often determine what particle type you will use. All of the different particle types have their own render attributes which can be displayed by clicking the Current Render Type button, so for the fountain you might want to use a MultiPoint render type, possibly combined with several other particle systems to create the final look. Each type of particle comes with its own attributes that help to affect the look of the particle either as fixed or driven attributes. On top of the look of a particular effect will come expressions, keyframes and driven keys driving channels responsible for the colour, opacity, lifespan for each particle or for the particle object as a whole.

- Open the Fountain scene, change the rate to 5000 and play back the scene.
- In the Render Attributes section, change the point size to 2.

- Create a new particle emitter and move it to the side of the fountain.
- Play back the scene so that all three particle objects can be seen.
- Delete the second emitter and open the Dynamic Relationships window.
- Connect the second particle object to the original emitter and gravity field.
- Change the second particle type to `MultiPoint` with a size setting of 1 and a `MultiCount` of 3.
- Replay the scene.

Because you connected a new particle object to your old emitter, you have twice the flexibility when trying to create your look, while retaining all of the emission attributes such as speed and spread. The fountain has the right amount of mist, which is now combined with the larger original particles that can now represent the heavier droplets raining down. Several things could be added here to increase the realism of the scene – a sideways wind that peels the finer misty particles away from the top and changing the min/max distance from which the emitter emits so that the multipoint particles don't start from under the floor. The finer spray particles also need to disappear after a certain time, as they just continue to fly off into the distance, which is a distraction and creates needless calculations.

- Open the `Lifespan Attributes` fold-out and set the `Lifespan Mode` to `Constant`.
- Set this length in seconds so that the particles die after they have been blown a small distance from the top of the fountain.

The particles now disappear gracefully as the dynamic simulation carries on. The particles die after the same length of time, but not at the same time because each particle carries an attribute called "age" which holds the length of time that each particle has been alive for. If the current age of a particle is greater or equal to the lifespan then the particle dies. This `Lifespan` attribute can be created as a `Per Particle` attribute – this allows you to create more randomness in the appearance of the particle object. Generally, the age of a particle will tend to drive most of the other attributes that will go to creating the look; the age of the fine spray particles would drive their opacity so that they don't just disappear but fade out gently. Your requirements will guide your choices as to the type of particle you will require and you will find that the type of particle you use will mean that you will have to make some further adjustments to the ways that you integrate your particles with your scene.

Three of the particle types in the `Render Attributes` have "s/w" after their names. This stands for "software" and means that Maya can only render these using the Software Renderer. This renderer is the normal renderer that is used to render out scenes and, as such, means that you can render the scene and particles together in one pass, if so required, with no limitations set on what will render. All of the other particles can only be rendered using the Hardware Renderer which means that the rendered particles will also be subject to a few caveats:

1. The particles will have to be composited with the software rendering of the scene.
2. The rendering can only take place as a hardware screen render, so the scene cannot be rendered in the background or from the command line.
3. The results will depend upon the graphics hardware available to you.

Although the method of compositing the hardware rendered particles is beyond the scope of this book, you do have a wide choice when it comes to providing the rendered frames with an alpha channel.

Hardware Rendered Particles

Hardware rendered particles come in several varieties: points, streaks, spheres, sprites, numerics, multi-points and multi-streaks. *Points* we have already seen and *multi-points* create a cloud of points around the position of the original point particles. *Streaks* will create a point particle with a faded tail whose length increases with velocity (*multi-streaks* do the same as multi-points), *spheres* are non-deformable polygonal spheres and *sprites* allows you to place bitmaps onto the particles to create a textured effect. *Numerics* simply place the particle ID number at the position of each particle or each selected particle. All of these particle types can be extremely useful in the correct situation and can be even more useful when combined, as we saw with the simple fountain. Sprites can be used in conjunction with the Sprite Wizard (Particles|Sprite Wizard) so that you can assign an animated bitmap to each particle, which means that you can use filmed dust clouds or explosions instead of trying to simulate these phenomena purely with dynamic particle colour and movement.

To examine these particle types, create an emitter, select the particles and in the Attribute Editor just change the Particle Render Type. Clicking the Current Render Type button will bring up attributes responsible for altering each particle type's appearance. One useful thing about hardware rendered particles is that we can easily see how they are going to look by turning on smooth shading in any of the views. You can quickly Playblast your scenes prior to final hardware rendering, giving a quick feedback loop for fine tuning the effect.

Creating Sparks

The following example uses hardware particles to create sparks from a circular cutting saw and examines how they can be integrated with a scene.

Create a ground plane and an emitter. Sparks will generally streak as they move through space and will exhibit several other properties in terms of lifespan and colour. Set the emitter to be directional, so that the sparks can fly off in the direction of the cutting saw's rotation and set the direction to be 1.0 in Y. It will be far easier and more intuitive to have the emission occur in a single direction and just rotate the emitter than to control the sparks' direction through the direction attribute. Set the rate to 300, speed to 15.0 and change the particle type to streaks, clicking the Current Render Type button so that you can start changing the look of the sparks. Several particle attributes will need to be changed in order for the sparks to look like the real thing:

- Spark shape
- Lifespan
- Colour

Spark shape will be a combination of the Render Attributes scaled by the speed of the particles, so it is important to get the movement right first. Rotate the emitter so that the particles are being emitted at a 45-degree slant to the ground plane and add a gravity field with a low magnitude but no attenuation so that the particles want to return to the ground. Once the speed is correct, set the Tail Size and Line Width attributes so that the sparks begin to take shape. Because the tails extend backwards from the spark position, you will need to change the min/max distance for the emitter so that the spark tails appear from the emitter and not before it.

Possibly the most important attribute for the sparks will be the lifespan. This will drive all of the other attributes that go to making up the look since the colour and glow of the particles will need to change as the sparks age and cool down. In the `Lifespan Attribute` section, set the `Lifespan Mode` to `lifespanPP only` and open the `Per Particle (Array) Attributes` section. The lifespan needs to be a `Per Particle` attribute because sparks don't live and die in a uniform manner, one after the other, but tend towards a more individual, random existence. Fortunately, there is a very direct way of infusing the particles with a random existence by setting the `Lifespan Mode` attribute to `lifespanPP only`. The other mode choices allow you to set the particle object's lifespan as infinite, a constant value or a random range that is centred about a constant value. Setting the mode to `lifespanPP` means that you have to scroll down the Attribute Editor and use the `lifespanPP` entry field in the `Per Particle (Array) Attributes` and define your values using an expression.

Particle expressions are written as either *creation* or *runtime expressions*, so that you can set and then alter (if required) the values created during the particle's lifetime. Writing a creation expression means that the expression will be evaluated for each particle as it is born. Use the RMB in the `lifespanPP` field to select `Creation Expression` to bring up the Expression Editor (notice that the editor now shows whether this particular expression is creation or runtime). Type `particleShapen.lifespanPP=gauss(0.5)+0.5`; and click Create. Now each particle will have a random age that will tend to centre about 0.5 due to the use of the `gauss()` function.

Now the particles are moving correctly and have the correct lifespan so that they burn out and die in a fashion similar to real world sparks, you need to create the colour changes that will complete and complement the particle system, a change from white hot to orange. Click the

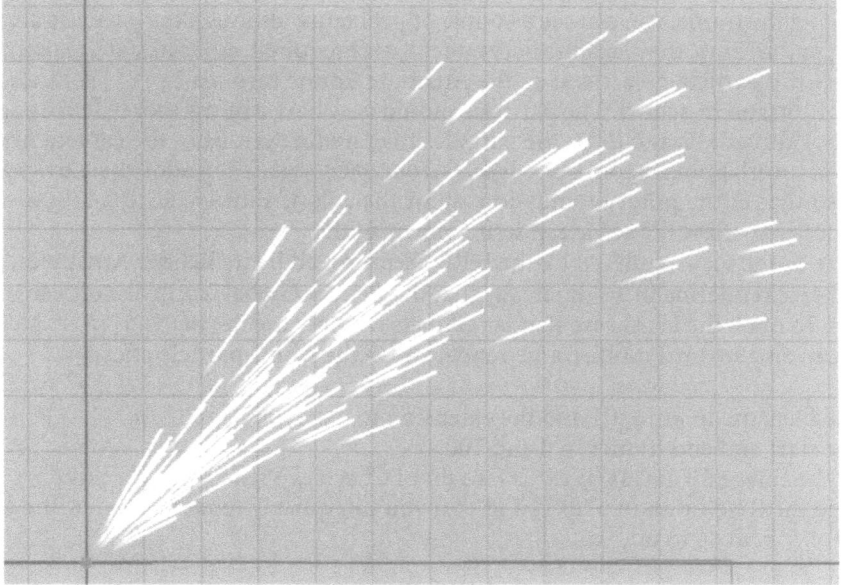

Figure 7.12 A Stream of Spark Particles.

Colour button in the Add Dynamic Attributes section, check the Add per particle check-box and click Add Attribute. This will update the Per Particle attributes section with a new entry field, allowing you to make a link. On top of using expressions, you can also use colour textures to drive attributes, which is especially useful as you have to drive a colour value. Use the RMB in this new entry field and select the options box icon for Create Ramp, which will open the Create Ramp options box. You need to provide some form of particle data for the Array Mapper node to interpret (created automatically by Maya to act as the middleman), so that it can return a colour value for each particle. The Ramp is defined in U and V with the V attribute being the vertical position on the ramp. Set the Input V fold-out to Particle's Age so that the vertical position on the ramp will be driven by the normalized age of each particle (particle age has to be normalized between zero and one so that it fits into the zero to one parameter space of the ramp). Clicking OK will create a new ramp (or you can map age to an existing ramp if required) and an Array Mapper node. Use the RMB in the entry field (which will now have arrayMapper*n*.outValuePP in it) and select Edit Ramp to change the Attribute Editor focus to the ramp in question. Change the values on the ramp so that there is a colour change from white to orange to red, with the white portion only taking up a very small seg-ment of the ramp.

In order to see these colour changes, you can either switch to the shaded mode or use the Hardware Render Buffer (HRB) to view how the final rendered frames will appear. This renderer takes screen grabs of the currently selected camera and can be invoked using Window|Rendering Editors|Hardware Render Buffer. Because you are going to be using this renderer so many times, either assign a hotkey, marking menu position or shelf item to this. When the HRB appears, it mimics the current view and you can actually change the cam-era position using the camera manipulation keys inside the HRB window and can change the camera using the Cameras menu item. The HRB also has a timeline and transport controls so that you can play the scene back as well – the clapperboard in the centre lets you test render the current frame.

Rendering the frame, you can see a couple of problems: although the particles are coloured according to the ramp, they lack the fiery effect that is required, especially at the point of emis-sion. Select the particle object and in the Attribute Editor turn on Depth Sort and Colour Accumulation and re-render. The particles should now have a much more lifelike appearance; Depth Sort forces Maya to draw the particles that are furthest from the camera first, so that there are no overlapping colours or edges. Colour accumulation adds the particles' colours together so that at the point of emission, all of the colour values add to a bright white, but both of these may slow the scene rendering down a little.

The size of the view rendered by the HRB is controlled by its Render Attributes, and con-trols hardware rendering in a similar way that the Render Globals controls software rendering attributes. To open the Hardware Render Globals window use Rendering|Attributes... so that you can also set up a multi-frame render to see the whole particle effect.

- Set the filename to Weld_01 and the extension to name.0001.ext.
- Set the start and end frames to 0 and 100.
- Leave the Image format as Maya IFF so that FCheck can read them quickly.
- Change the Resolution to 320x240 so that you can quickly render and view the frames.
- Set Alpha Source to off.

Close or minimize this window, return to the HRB and invoke the multi-frame rendering from Render|Render Sequence. Once the sequence has finished rendering, it can be played

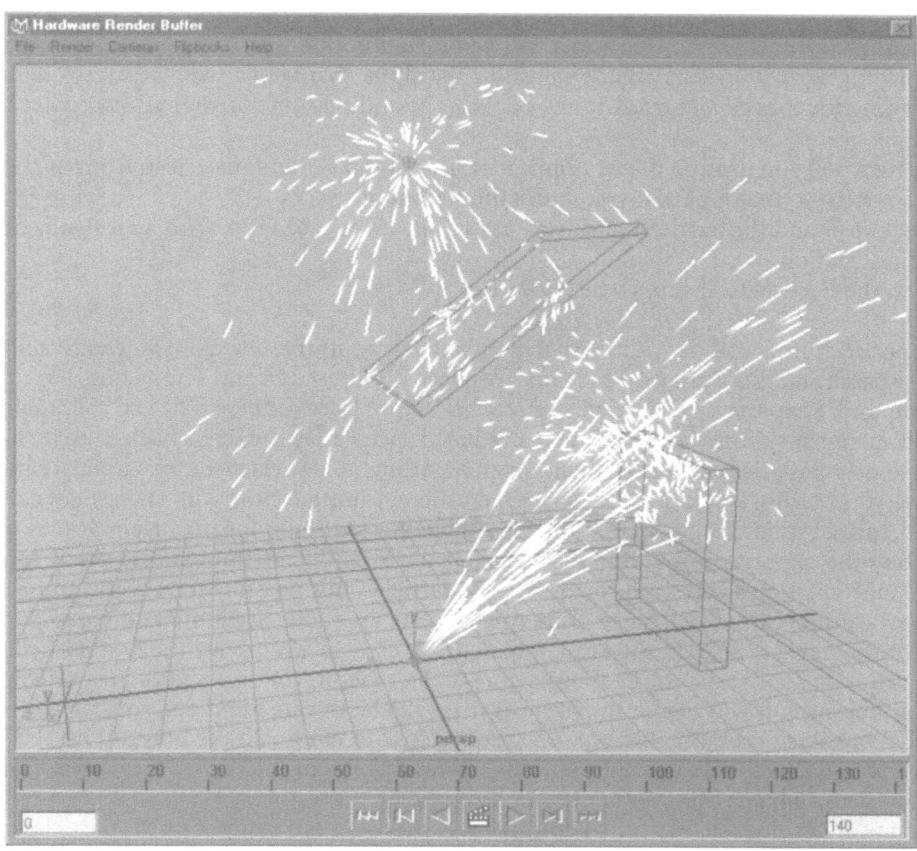

Figure 7.13 The Sparks as They Appear in the Hardware Render Buffer.

back by selecting the name from the Flipbooks menu – this will store each differently named sequence that you render while the HRB window is open. If you close the HRB window or use the Flipbooks|Options|Clear Flipbook menu to remove sequences, these frames will still reside on the hard drive, so remember to delete them afterwards. In the Hardware Render Globals, turn on Line Smoothing and Full Image Resolution to set the final smoothing for streak particles and render the sequence again. If you want to composite this sequence, then set the alpha source to a setting that either is supported by the graphics board or one that is representative of the particle effect (luminance would be useful here).

If you were using the multi-point or multi-streak particles, you could take advantage of the multi-pass option in the HRB. Multi-pass rendering jitters each particle a set number of times per frame and then averages the result to produce a smoother and successively more blurred result, simulating motion blur. You can get around this for your particles by setting the particle type to multi-streak, but limiting the number of particles to one. In the HRB, turn on Multi-Pass Rendering, set Edge Smoothing and Motion Blur to 0.0 and set the number of passes to the minimum of 3. Render this new sequence to get a smoother, motion-blurred effect at little extra cost to the rendering; if the particles require further blurring, then set the

Render Passes to a higher number. Because the alpha source comes from the look of the particle (luminance in this case) the alpha will be blurred in line with the particles (pressing "a" while playing back frames in Fcheck will show the alpha channel, "c" will return to colour).

Finishing touches can be made to the particles by adding some further effects to the scene.

- Create a polygon ground plane, duplicate this, call it Wall and place it in front of the particle system so that it partially occludes the stream of sparks.
- Select Wall and the particles and use Particles|Make Collide, with a resiliency of 0.17 and no friction.
- Open the Particle Collision Events Editor.

As the particles now collide with the polygon wall, we want them to do two things: split into smaller sparks and die. Turn on Split and Random # Particles and set the Num Particles attribute to 5. Keep the spread small and set the Inherit Velocity to 0.9 so that the particles will spring back from the wall but at a reduced speed. Play the scene back so that you can see these new particles and select them. In the Outliner, Ctrl-select the gravity field and use Fields|Affect Selected Object(s). Open the Attribute Editor with these new particles selected and set its attributes so that they resemble the attributes for the original spark particles. Copy the expression for the first particle's lifespanPP attribute and paste it into the lifespanPP creation expression for these new particles, but possibly reduce the amounts so that they are short lived but more numerous. Create an rgbPP attribute and corresponding ramp for the new particles in the same way that you created a ramp for the first particles, but set the ramp up so that the start colour is orange but fades into a dark red as the particles lose more of their heat. If you render the scene again in the Hardware Renderer, you can clearly see the polygon collision object. Turn on Geometry Mask to eliminate the polygon objects from being rendered and to also cut out the alpha channel of the particles that they are in front of, similar to using a black hole matte object.

If you want a whole factory full of cutting machines, you can easily copy the particles across to other emitters, allowing you to change all of the emission attributes such as spread and timing without having to worry about recreating the same particles.

- Create a new omni emitter and place it high up in the scene.
- Delete the new particle object that was created with the new emitter and open the Dynamic Relationships window.
- Set the mode to Emitter and select the original spark's particle object.
- Highlight the new emitter and close the window.

Creating new collision objects and collision events won't slow you down because you have Maya's collision events creating the second collision sparks whenever the first sparks collide with anything. Playing the scene back will now give a new spark emitter, but from a different emitter type. This method of selectively creating particles allows you to quickly populate a scene once you have identified what the scene requirements will be; you can even create three variants of the particle spark object for near, mid ground and far emitters. All you would need to do is to key frame the sparks being emitted from each emitter in an easy to use manner. This can be done by creating a locator which will hold a series of on/off attributes for each emitter created and using either driven keys to connect the on and off (1/0) values to the rates, or an expression multiplying the rates by the on/off value. You can also retime the emission of the particles by changing the value of the Start Frame attribute in the Time Attributes fold-out.

Figure 7.14 Multiple Collisions from Different Emitters.

For point, multi-point, streak and multi-streak, there is also an attribute called Normal Dir that allows you to change how light reflects from them, depending on how the particles are moving relative to the lights. If the particles aren't moving or are just in front of the scene lights (this is also depending on whether the All Lights or Selected Lights options in the Hardware Render Buffer are used), such as an underwater sequence, then the Normal Dir attribute should be set to 2. If the particles are moving towards the light, then use 1 and if they are moving away from the light, use 3. These options give a little bit more flexibility on how particles will be lit in the scene, especially if you are using local pools of light that will illuminate parts of the scene and the particles.

Software Rendered Particles

There are three types of software (s/w) rendered particles available in Maya: clouds, tubes and blobs. All of these particles have to be rendered in software because their surfaces and inner regions are defined as volumes and the edges defined by a shader. All of these software particles have render attributes that control how distinct each particle is from the other particle, called threshold, which determines the amount of blending between adjacent particles. In the case of blobby surfaces, this threshold can create a smooth surface that is interpolated across the particle object and is useful for creating liquid effects. For clouds, threshold will determine a blending effect which is also modulated with the Surface Shading attribute to produce clear edges to each particle or a more blurry edged cloud mass.

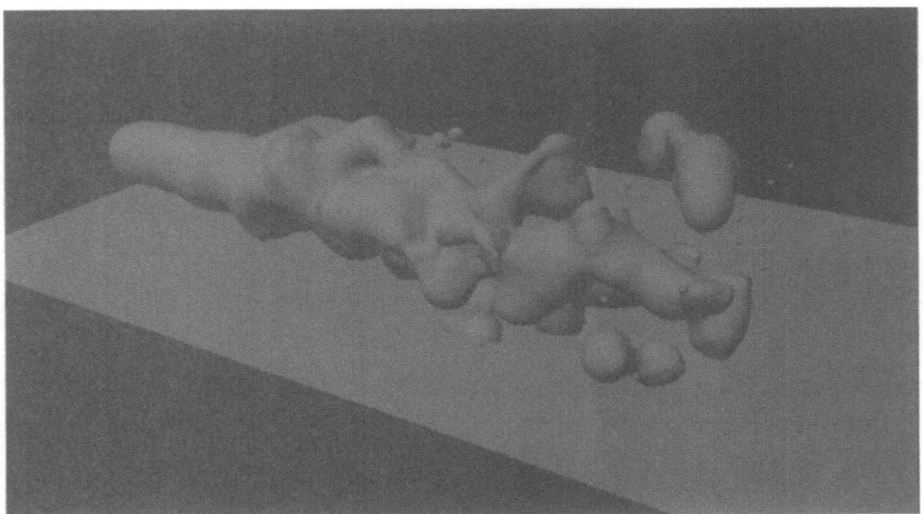

Figure 7.15 Blobby Particles Rendered in Software.

- Create a directional emitter that is emitting upwards and set the particle type to Blobby Surface.
- Create a few lights and software render the scene once a large mass of particles have been emitted.
- Set the threshold to 0.2, 0.8, 1.0 and 1.5, rendering each time.

Creating Dust Clouds

The radius attribute will also have an effect over the particle mass, as the edge of each particle will be blended in relation to the size and distance from its neighbouring particles. Colour, reflection and transparency will also heavily affect the final look of the blobby surface; a red Phong shader and a transparent blue Phong shader will make the change from blood to water. Blobby particles ably demonstrate the effect that threshold and radius will have without any other per object or per particle attributes. Cloud particles will be affected by the radius and threshold attributes, but a particle cloud shader and an associated particle sampler info node will create the real changes to the final look. The particle sampler info node is used by a particle cloud shader to interpret changes in colour over time, which Maya creates automatically.

- Select the particles in the scene and change their render type to Clouds.
- Open the Hypershade and create a new particle cloud shader from the Volumetric menu at the left.
- Attach it to the selected particles using the RMB menu item Assign material to selection.
- Open the Attribute Editor with the focus on the new cloud shader.

If you render now, the clouds will be coloured the default blue cloud colour. Changes to the particle colour can be made in two ways: over the particle's lifetime or as a constant colour.

- LMB click the texture button at the side of the colour attribute in the cloud shader and map a ramp texture to it.
- Render the scene.

The ramp texture has been applied to each particle giving it a strange quality. If you delete the attribute in the Attribute Editor using the RMB menu item `Break Connection` and then MMB drag and drop the ramp from the Hypershade onto the `Life Colour` attribute and re-render, the particle's age will now be mapped to the V attribute of the ramp. Looking in the Hypershade, it can now be seen that Maya has created a particle sampler node to map age to the V attribute. This sampler node won't be created for any 3D textures because they are not defined in U and V, but you can cheat a little and create a 3D texture at each colour entry position instead. If you decide to use 3D textures, then these will be applied to the particles in terms of their position in relation to the 3D texture space.

- Delete the colour at the centre of the ramp and select the first colour at the bottom of the ramp.
- LMB click the texture button beside the ramp colour and create a 3D crater texture and create a 3D cloud texture for the other colour entry in the ramp.
- Re-render the scene.

Now the two textures can be coloured so that they are complementary to each other. 2D ramp textures can also be used to affect the overall life transparency and incandescence of a particle object. The next major fold-out for the Particle Cloud shader is the `Transparency` section that lets you change overall characteristics of the rendered volume. This contains attributes such as `Density` and `Translucence` (which scale the overall particle transparency) plus `Roundness` and `Blob Map` that lets you change the shape of each cloud particle and any local transparency scaling respectively. `Incandescence` can be used to "light" particles so that you can have glowing particles emanating from the source. The shape and silhouette of the particle cloud can also be further affected using the attributes in the `Built-in Noise` section, which control how evenly the particle cloud appears to be across its surface. If you want the particle system to interact with scene lighting, then you can use the attributes within the Surface Shading Properties which let you control how much light from the light sources in the scene is diffused and scattered.

Because so many of these shading properties are affected by the particle cloud shape, it is important to have this set up first so that the particle shader can then be applied and tuned. All of the shader attributes can also be animated so that the colour and transparency do not appear to be in a uniform position through space, as can the shape, position, rotation and scaling of the 3D texture placement nodes. Emitter properties such as rate, speed and direction should also be animated so that you can begin to shape the particle object. You can look at creating a dust cloud to examine how all of these attributes work together and where to start tuning the particle system.

- Create a new scene and create an emitter, a ground plane and a few lights.
- Change the emitter to a volume sphere and scale it so that it resembles a flattened oval.
- In the `Volume Speed Attributes` section, set `Away from Centre` to `20.0` and `Along Axis` to `0.9`, leaving the other attributes at `0.0`.
- Change the particles to `Cloud` and set the `Lifespan Mode` to `Constant` and `5.0`.
- Raise the emitter above the ground plane and play the scene back.

You can see that the particles are being emitted in a roughly even distribution about the volume, but the particles need to be confined to an area about the impact site. The speed is correct though, because the dust should be kicked up quickly, but after the impact it should just hang there.

- Select the particle object and the ground plane, use `Particles|Make Collide` and set the resilience to 0.3 and the friction to 0.1.
- Select the particle object and create a drag field to slow the particles down smoothly in space.
- Select the drag field and make it a volume cylinder field.
- Scale the cylinder so that it is a little larger than the volume emitter.
- Set the magnitude to 10.0 and the attenuation to 0.3.
- In the `Volume Control Attributes` section, turn on `Volume Exclusion`.

Playing the scene back now should have the particles being emitted and suddenly slowing as soon as they have exited the volume of the drag field (this should be made a little larger than the emitter so that the particles have some time to move away from the impact site). However, the scene really slows down as more and more particles are created. Key the rate of the emitter so that it is zero at frame 20, 500 or so at frame 22 and zero again at frame 24. Now the particles will be emitted in a burst and you can start working on the visual characteristics of the particle cloud. The only attribute that you need to change for the particle object is the radius, so that the clouds slowly expand as they move away from the emitter. This effect can be produced easily with the `radiusPP` attribute, created by clicking the General button in the `Add Dynamic Attributes` section and opening the `Particle` section. Once this attribute has been added, use the RMB in the entry field, select `Creation Expression` and type `particleShape1.radiusPP=1.5+rand(-0.3,0.3);` into the Expression Editor. You have now set the start conditions for each particle so you can switch the Expression Editor to `Runtime` and type `particleShape1.radiusPP+=0.05;` which will increase the size of the particle radius by 0.05 each frame.

Now that the particles' shape and movement is set up, we can now concentrate on getting the particle cloud shader looking right.

- In the Hypershade, create a new particle cloud shader from the `Volumetric Materials`.
- Assign it to the particle object and open the Attribute Editor on the particle cloud shader.
- Click the Texture button beside the `Colour` attribute and assign a 3D cloud texture to it.

Because the dust colour won't actually be changing during the course of the animation, you can safely use a 3D texture, so try rendering it with different scaling values for the texture placement node. The cloud texture should have light colours for the `Colour1` and `Colour2` attributes and the higher the amplitude, the lighter the cloud will appear. If you render the dust cloud, you will get a very thick cotton wool look for the dust clouds, so the next attribute to change will be the transparency of the dust clouds. This will be changing over time to simulate the effect of the dust becoming less densely packed, so click the Texture button beside the `Life Transparency` attribute. Create a ramp for this attribute starting at mid to dark grey and finishing at black for the transparency. Although the particles themselves are now fairly transparent, when they are packed closely together, this does not render so well, so the density attribute should be brought down to somewhere near 0.2. You can increase the `Diffuse Coefficient` so that the dust cloud begins to scatter light correctly, while turning on `Surface`

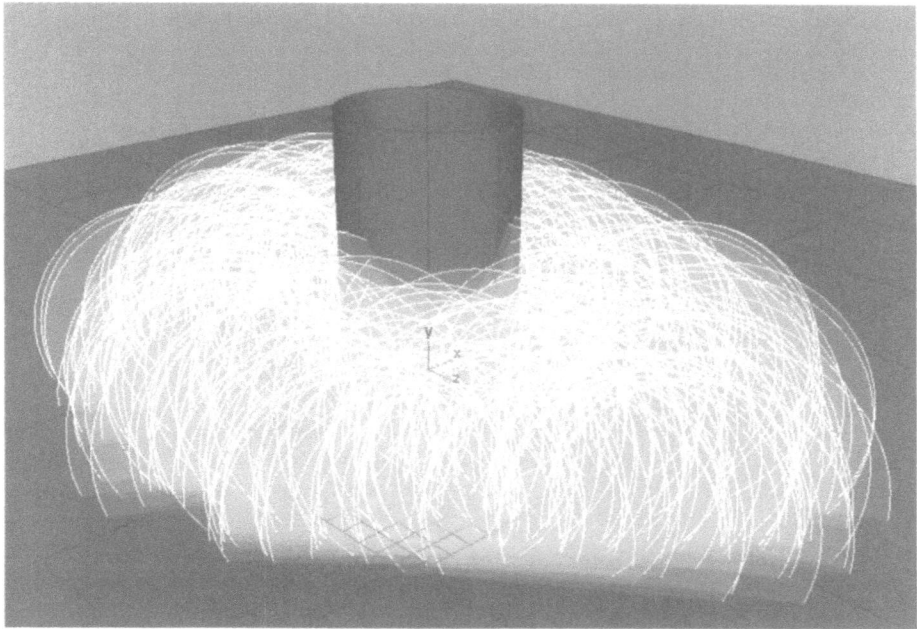

Figure 7.16 The Cloud Particle Sizes after Emission.

Shading Shadow can also add to the feeling of volume as the dust is affected by the scene lighting. If you decide to have the dust cloud casting shadows, look at the difference between depth mapped or raytraced shadows.

Summary

The whole of this chapter has been about describing movement and colour that simulates physical interactions via Newtonian physics. One important thing to remember when dealing with particle effects is how the system functions and how any required changes are implemented. Adding fields to a particle system should be done in a stepwise manner so that it is easy to see what changes have to be made if the effect needs to be changed. It is worth creating a framework that contains a set of basic assumptions, such as the gravity is x and the bounciness of all surfaces is y. Particle systems can either be included with a scene if they are software particles and possibly rendered in a separate layer or will have to be composited into the scene at a later date. Keeping these factors in mind will avoid any problems that may crop up when trying to integrate a particle system into an animated scene.

Dynamic Objects

Introduction

Dynamic objects take the implementation of movement, fields and collisions for particle systems and apply them to an object as a whole (rigid body dynamics) or to a surface (soft body dynamics). We have already seen dynamic forces in effect while working with particle system movement and collisions, so all of the guidelines that we had to follow for using particles in Maya scenes are still relevant to this form of animation, such as playback and memory caching. Rigid body dynamics let you create collisions between surfaces (and particles) creating dynamic movement; soft body dynamics will let you apply dynamic forces to the underlying components of an object creating dynamic deformation.

Rigid Body Dynamics

Rigid body dynamics use all of the physical laws and rules that govern particle movement, such as momentum, field effects and collisions and apply them to moving objects. The objects won't deform due to any movement, which is why they are called rigid bodies, but they will have dynamic forces applied to them and their outer surfaces when colliding with other rigid bodies. Rigid bodies can become a very useful way of animating physical interaction between objects and can also be a great way of creating little interacting worlds such as a pinball table.

Bouncing Bodies

Creation of rigid bodies is a simple process and there are two types that can be created and used within Maya. One type is an "active" rigid body, meaning that the object will participate in the scene with other objects and fields, the other type is a "passive" rigid body, which just contributes to the dynamic scene. The passive rigid body just provides a surface for collisions to be calculated from and will not be moved by fields or other dynamic forces.

- Create a polygon sphere and a polygon plane.
- Scale the plane 10 units in all axes and place the sphere 10 units above the plane.
- Select the sphere and use Soft/Rigid Bodies|Create Active Rigid Body.
- Select the plane and use Soft/Rigid Bodies|Create Passive Rigid Body.
- Select the sphere and create a gravity field with no attenuation.
- Play back the scene.

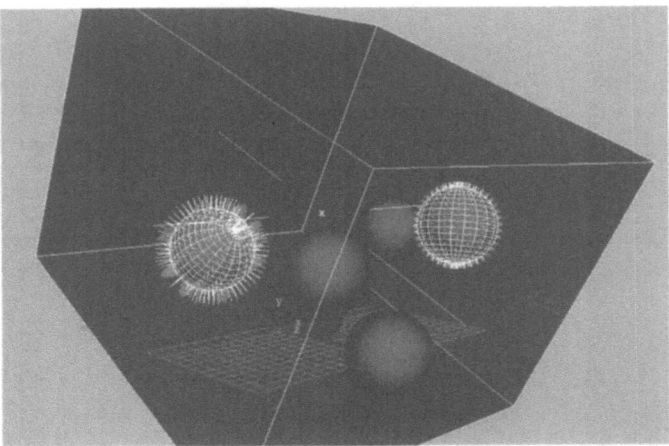

Figure 8.1 Colliding Bodies and Surface Normals.

The ball should be affected by gravity and collide with the plane, rebounding until it comes to rest. If you look closely at each rigid body, you should notice that each object has an "x" at its centre, which marks the position of its centre of mass, and moving this will affect how the object is subjected to forces. If the centre of mass is moved to the right of the sphere, the movement will change upon collision (the centre of mass is usually placed at the centre of an object and like a local axis has a start position of 0,0,0).

Making sure that the rigid bodies and their surfaces are ready for collisions will be an important part of the scene set up.

- Delete all of the objects in the scene and create a polygon cube.
- Scale the cube by 20 units and make the polygon cube a passive rigid body.
- Rotate the cube by 45 degrees so that one edge is pointing downwards.
- Create a polygon sphere, cube, cylinder and torus.
- Make all of these active rigid bodies and position them inside the cube.
- Select the active bodies and create a gravity field.
- Play the scene back.

The objects will drop through the cube and carry on accelerating towards negative infinity until the scene playback reaches zero again. This occurs because the components that are used to calculate collisions are not aligned correctly. Maya uses surface normals to calculate all collision dynamics, so making sure that surfaces are correctly aligned will be extremely important. Although we saw that all surfaces are created double-sided, this is purely for shading calculations, so display the polygon normals of the cube using Display|Polygon Components| Normals and you can see that the normals are facing the wrong way for our purposes. Invert the polygon normals using Edit Polygons|Normals|Reverse (this is under the Modeling menu set and might be worth placing this action and the display normals action to a shelf) and then play the scene back; the objects should now bounce around within the cube.

We have used polygons so far because they represent the faster of the two surface types to calculate collision boundaries with, but NURBS surface will work just as accurately, so create a few NURBS primitives and add them to the dynamic scene. Once the rigid body simulations have been set up, the playback can be paused and the passive bodies can be transformed into any position and the dynamics will adapt to these changes. If any of the active bodies are moved at any point during playback, they will now be recomputed from this new position.

Now you have a colliding set of bodies, you can change attributes to change the way that the bodies interact with the various surfaces. Increasing the strength of the gravity field will obviously change one effect, but each rigid body has its own set of attributes which are stored in the rigidBody*n* node, which is displayed in the Channels Box or Attribute Editor. The first attribute that can be changed to alter events is Mass – this determines a relative value for collisions between rigid bodies.

Set up the scene so that at least two rigid bodies will collide after the first bounce and then change the mass of one object to ten and the other to a half. The collision should now work in favour of the "heavier" object. As we saw, changing the centre of mass will also have a very important effect upon these collisions. Static Friction will affect an object while it is at rest, so as a table top is tilted, an object with a high static friction value will be less prone to sliding along the surface. The next two attributes that can change the collision and rebound are Dynamic Friction and Bounciness. Bounciness is similar to resilience and can make an object move like a cannonball (plus a high mass) or like a rubber ball. Dynamic Friction allows you to define how resistant a moving body is to another moving body when they meet, for example Teflon will have a dynamic friction of near zero whereas rubber will have a dynamic friction nearer one. Damping can be used to deaden an object's movement at each bounce or if set to a negative number will accelerate an object after each bounce. If you select the passive rigid object, you will see that in the Attribute Editor, all of the attributes are blanked out apart from Static Friction, Dynamic Friction and Bounciness because the other attributes are concerned with active collisions and movement.

All active rigid bodies allow you to influence their movement either initially or at each frame by applying an impulse force. Impulses can be in terms of spin where the object will rotate about a specified axis or in terms of speed in any of the axes. These can be applied to active rigid bodies as initial impulse values that will start the objects moving and rotating. They can be found under the Initial Settings fold-out. In this Initial Settings section, there are also two additional attributes showing the position and orientation of the object at frame zero. Otherwise, impulse can be set as a constant which is applied to an object at every frame, with impulse position determining at what point the impulse is applied, having the same sort of effect as moving the centre of mass away from an object's centre. The impulse settings can be very useful when setting up a rigid body simulation that involves more than just reacting to several fields; a scene that starts with spinning and bouncing debris could have a large initial spin added, which will then be applied to each shard. There are also additional attributes in the Attribute Editor, which are read-only and contain values such as torque and force that cannot be edited. These read-only attributes can provide useful information when combined with expressions to drive other animation channels. As expected, rigid body simulations drive the rotation and translation channels of the rigid bodies, but the scaling is not controlled at all. When a rigid body is created, the outer shape of the surface is taken into account once. Any changes to an object's scaling channels will result in unpredictable effects and is not recommended. If the scaling of an object is incorrect after creating a rigid body, then it will be easier to create a new rigid body object.

Rigid Body Keyframes

One facility that is at hand with rigid body dynamics is the ability to set keys before, during and after rigid body dynamics are computed. This means that you can keyframe a car speeding along a road and then switch over to rigid body dynamics when it is time to calculate a more physically accurate crash than you could otherwise keyframe. Another thing that you can do is to parent or constrain objects to rigid bodies, so for the above car example, you could animate a rough car shape and then use it in the crash simulation, parenting the high resolution car model to the dummy surface later. Any keyframes that have been set will add to an object's velocity in the same way that using initial impulse settings will. However, looking at the Channels Box for a rigid body's transform node will show that the rigid body solver controls the transform channels. If you want to set keys, you have to use a set of special keying commands in a fashion similar to when you were setting keys for switching between IK and FK keys.

- Create a sphere, a large ground plane and two tall cylinders.
- Make the ground plane a passive rigid body and the rest active rigid bodies.
- Place the sphere at one end of the plane and the cylinders in the middle of the plane.
- Create a gravity field and connect the cylinders and the ball to it.
- Move the centres of mass for each cylinder down to the bottoms of each object.

We also want the cylinders to be resting on the plane without moving, so that they don't settle as the simulation occurs. If the cylinders have been placed at frame zero so that their undersides are below the plane then they will fall through the plane. You can make sure that the cylinders are stood still at the start of the simulation by setting their static friction settings to one. Then play the scene through (don't worry about the sphere for now) until the cylinders have settled in place and still, select both of them and use Solvers|Initial State|Set for Selected. This can be useful for setting up the position and orientation for any dynamic objects before playback has occurred, such as the flying debris from an explosion that occurred in a previous scene. Now you can play the scene through and change their static friction settings so they will be more likely to move when hit by the sphere.

There would be two ways that you could have the ball bounce and hit the cylinders:

1. By creating an initial impulse setting for the sphere so that it looks like a thrown ball arcing in to hit the cylinders.
2. By keying the position motion of the ball prior to letting the rigid body solver take over.

If the ball was being thrown by a character or was a ball with a mind of its own then the keyframed method will need to be chosen, but the last few keys must be moving the ball towards the cylinders to provide velocity.

- Rewind the playback to frame zero and move the ball to a new starting place.
- Use Soft/Rigid Bodies|Set Passive Key to place a key for the ball's start position.
- Set passive keys for the ball so that it "buzzes" around the end of the ground plane.
- Set the last two keys using Soft/Rigid Bodies|Set Passive Key so that the ball moves swiftly towards the cylinders.
- One frame after the last passive key, use Soft/Rigid Bodies|Set Active Key to return positional control back to the rigid body solver.
- Rewind and play the scene back.

Any keys set using this method can be manipulated in the same way that all keys can be, so it is possible to use the functions of the Timeline, Dopesheet and Graph Editor so that the objects move exactly as you wish. One thing that you cannot do is to parent, constrain or otherwise control the position and rotation channels of the rigid bodies (other than using the active/passive keys method). So you wouldn't be able to constrain a ball to a character's hand as it picked up the sphere and threw it at our cylinders. The best method would be to find the frame where the ball leaves the character's hand and hide it, then unhide the rigid body and commence with the dynamic simulation. However, you need to be able to define when the dynamic simulation begins because starting at frame zero is never usually convenient.

Editing the Rigid Body Solver

If you want to begin the dynamics at a different time, then you need to edit the rigid body solver which is controlling the simulation. This can be accessed from the Solvers|Rigid Body Solver... menu item and will open the Attribute Editor displaying the editable attributes. The Start Time attribute will define when the solver will begin calculating events, so any objects under the solver's control will only start moving at this time. The other attributes available here allow you to optimize how the simulation will be calculated. You may want to optimize the simulation because these effects are for background objects, which don't need as much accuracy, or you simply don't have the time to process the calculations before rendering the scene for a deadline.

Accuracy

The first set of optimizations is to define how accurate the calculations are for collision events between rigid bodies. Step Size will tell Maya how many times per second to sample the scene; Collision Tolerance will allow you to set the accuracy of collisions between surfaces. Decreasing these two attributes will increase the overall accuracy of the scene when complex collisions occur at the expense of calculation time. If the scene has relatively few and/or simple collisions, then these two attributes should be increased so that calculations are faster. You can also change the mathematics employed for the solver and the effects that are calculated by the solver by opening the fold-outs titled Rigid Solver Methods and Rigid Solver States. There are three methods that the rigid body solver can employ to solve collisions and each method has a varying ratio between accuracy and speed, with Runge-Kutta Adaptive being the slower but more accurate. Several states can be turned off for the solver so that the playback is quicker or the calculations that aren't needed are removed. Of these, State will turn the dynamics calculations on or off so that other things happening in the scene can be looked at without the solver working. Turning off Bounciness and Friction will remove these from calculations and turning off Contact Motion will mean that the only things that will move the rigid bodies will be fields. Having Contact Data turned on will save data that can be read later but this will slow scene playback down, and turning on Allow Disconnection means that you can remove rigid bodies from the control of the solver. You can also display the velocities and whether an object is active or passive using the relevant checkboxes in the Rigid Solver Display Options fold-out.

You can optimize the collision accuracy and collision time for each rigid body using the attributes in the rigidBody*n* node in the Performance Attributes fold-out. When there isn't sufficient collision accuracy between two or more colliding surfaces, Maya will pause playback and display an error message about interpenetration while highlighting the offending surfaces. Interpenetration errors can greatly slow down or even stop playback and they occur due to inaccuracies over whether a surface is colliding or not. If the accuracy of calculation is too low, then in one frame Maya may not see a collision, but the next frame Maya may see that surfaces are penetrating each other, which sets up an error loop. You can set up the calculation speeds for each object, which will be relevant to where the rigid bodies are in the scene, how important they are in the scene and how complex the collisions will be. Turing on Ignore will remove the object from all dynamics – this can be useful when trying to tune the movement of other objects. Turning off Collisions will stop any dynamic collisions being calculated for the object and Stand In will use a sphere or a cube to apply collisions to, instead of the object itself (if set to none) and can greatly increase calculation time. Forces can be applied to an object in three different ways: at the Centre of Mass, to the Bounding Box corners and to each Vertex/CV and increase the calculation times respectively. If you are using NURBS surfaces, then the solver will tessellate them so that a polygonal face and its normal can be used for collisions (in the same way that tessellation occurs when rendering). If the tessellation is low then the accuracy will be low but if the NURBS surface isn't complex then you can lower this value to speed up the dynamic process. A further troubleshooting method is to turn collisions off between selected objects using Solvers|Set Rigid Body Interpenetration (turn them on using Solvers|Set Rigid Body Collision).

Collision Layers

The last performance attribute to be examined is the Collision Layer attribute. There are 12 collision layers available to use and objects that are in the same layer will collide and objects that are in different layers will not. Select one of the cylinders and place it in Collision Layer 1 and play the scene back. Not only does the sphere not collide with the cylinder but the cylinder also falls through the plane due to lack of collisions. Select the plane and place it in Collision Layer -1 and play the scene back. Collision layer -1 is used to place objects so that they will collide with all rigid bodies in the scene irrespective of their collision layer. Breaking objects up into collision layers can really speed up a scene if there are a lot of rigid bodies colliding which you may not want to collide with each other owing to possible interpenetration errors. If you were simulating a car window shattering and exploding as a result of an impact, you will be creating many small pieces of glass and some large "hero" pieces of glass. The large hero pieces of glass and the car body could be placed in Layer -1 so that everything collides with them and their performance attributes could be set high. However, you will not need to see each tiny piece of glass collide with each other tiny piece of glass, so you can separate them up with collision layers which will stop interpenetration errors. If you do want certain pieces colliding, then place them in the same layer.

Multiple Solvers

You can go one step further if you want to use a divide and conquer method for the rigid bodies by creating multiple solvers. This means that you could create one solver for each rigid body event that occurs in the scene, as long as they do not have to interact – this is different to using collision layers because you cannot use Layer -1. Each solver will affect only the objects that are created with it, but fields will affect all objects regardless of solvers (they do not affect collisions only forces within the scene).

- Create a cube and position it above the cylinders.
- Create a new solver using `Solvers|Create Rigid Body Solver`.
- Change to the new solver using `Solvers|Current Rigid Solver` and selecting the new solver.
- Select the cube and make it an active rigid body using `Soft/Rigid Bodies|Create Active Rigid Body`.
- Connect the cube to the gravity field through either the Dynamic Relationships Editor or selecting the cube and the field and using `Fields|Affect Selected Object(s)`.
- Play the scene back.

The currently selected rigid body solver will affect any objects which are created as active or passive rigid bodies, which is why you had to change the scene focus to the new solver prior to making the cube an active rigid body. Solver optimizations are made for the solver not for each object, but overall calculations will be faster if you have a very complex scene, because there will be a lighter mathematical and data load on the solvers used. It also means that you can set different start times for each solver and each object controlled by it. It is often worth changing the name of the solver in the Attribute Editor so that when you change the current solver in the scene, the name is more meaningful. Different solvers should always be used for different levels of detail within a scene, so background and far off objects should utilize a low accuracy solver and foreground objects should use a high accuracy solver with multiple collision layers if required.

If you want to move objects from one layer to another (especially if you forgot to switch the current solver before creating rigid bodies) you have to use the command line which is in the bottom left-hand side of the Maya window (if it is turned on). We will be looking at the command line in the next chapter, but sometimes we need to use typed commands to access features of Maya, such as placing rigid bodies into different solvers. Select a rigid body and type `rigidBody -edit -solver <name>`; where <name> is the name of the solver into which you wish to place the rigid body, and press the numerical Enter key.

Rigid Body Constraints

So far, all of the effects that we have been achieving have been to do with fields and collisions. This is fine for simulating free objects in space with no other mechanics affecting their movement. However, if you wish to create the effect of a wrecking ball smashing its way through a wall then you will need to use rigid body constraints. These allow you to add mechanical constraints onto the movement of a rigid body, such as the position of a pivot for a seesaw.

- Create a polygon plane and make it an active rigid body.
- Select the plane and open up the options box for `Soft/Rigid Bodies|Create Constraint`.
- Change the constraint type to `Nail` and click Create.
- Move the nail constraint upwards and the polygon plane to the left.
- Play the scene back.

The *nail constraint* creates a pivot or if moved, a pendulum for the rigid body, which will now swing around under the influence of the gravity field (a seesaw can be created by placing the nail constraint at the centre of the object). This type of constraint is perfect for items such as

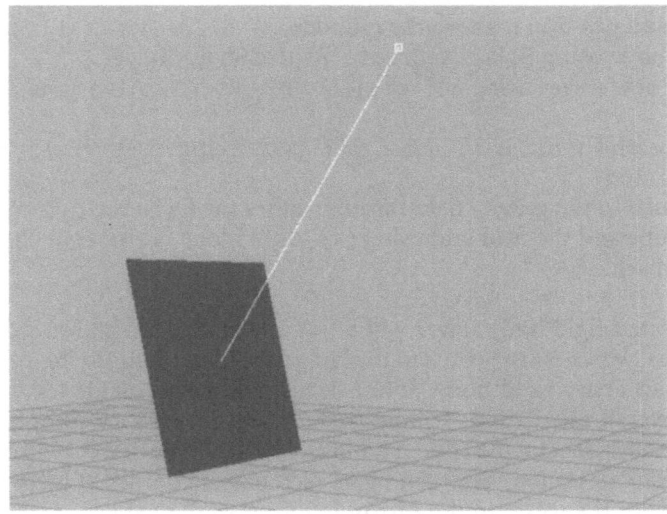

Figure 8.2 A Single Nail Constraint.

wrecking balls swinging or simulating Newton's Cradles. You can change the position of the nail constraint and the constrained object at the start of the playback but after that you cannot control them. Now you can start to use the dynamic and collision properties of rigid bodies with constraints for a more varied effect.

- Create another polygon plane and make it an active rigid body.
- Connect it to the gravity field and position it at frame zero so that it lies a few units under the first plane.
- Select both polygon planes and open the Create Constraint dialogue.
- Change the constraint type to Pin and click Create.
- Play the scene back.

A *pin constraint* creates a positional relationship between the two objects to form a point of rotation. Each plane will affect the other via the pin constraint while taking into account all the dynamic forces that are acting on the active rigid bodies (try increasing the mass of the second plane to 20). If you want to have the rotation of the objects constrained to just one axis, like the spheres in a Newton's Cradle, then you should use a *hinge constraint* instead. The hinge's orientation can be changed by rotating it with the normal Rotate tool, so that it lies parallel with the desired rotation axis. However, in the Attribute Editor we can have either the normal Hinge constraint or a Directional Hinge constraint. The Directional Hinge always maintains it's direction no matter what, whereas the normal Hinge constraint can be rotated by outside forces, for example a twisting applied by the objects that are constrained will also apply a rotation to the axis that the hinge lies on. The movement of active rigid bodies can be further constrained by using a *barrier constraint* which creates an infinite plane that the rigid body cannot move past. This method is cheaper in terms of processing power because you don't have to create collision objects, but the barrier constraint does not have any bounciness or friction attributes, so the rigid body will not bounce when it meets the constraint, just stop

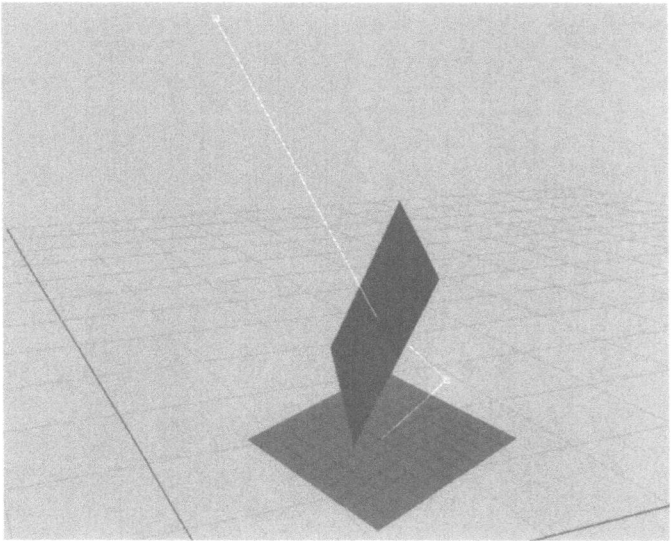

Figure 8.3 Two Planes Connected by a Hinge Constraint.

moving. If you want one rigid body to appear to rotate around the other rigid body, simply move the hinge or pin constraint to the centre of the rigid body at frame zero.

The final rigid body constraint that can be used is the *spring constraint* which creates a spring effect between the selected objects or a position in space if only one rigid body is selected. When this constraint is used, various attributes can be changed creating different effects between the constrained rigid bodies. Rest Length will set the length that the spring will attempt to return to and is set at creation as the distance between the two objects, so setting this to a smaller value will mean that the spring will draw the two object together. Stiffness determines the spring's resistance to being stretched and Damping will slow down the motion of the spring if set to a positive number and accentuate the motion if set to a negative number.

- Create four polygon cylinders, making them all active rigid bodies.
- Create a gravity field and connect the cylinders to it.
- Select each cylinder individually and create a spring constraint for each one.
- Move the end of the spring constraints so that they are 5 units above the objects.
- Change the rest lengths for all of them to 4.5.
- Set different damping and stiffness attributes for each spring and play the scene back to see the different effects.

For the pin, hinge and spring constraints, there is an Interpenetration attribute. This attribute sets whether mutually constrained rigid bodies will collide or not, again a useful optimization when calculating rigid body animation. Because we are using Maya's dynamics engine to solve rigid body dynamics, we can connect one type of dynamics to another.

- Create two polygon planes and position one a couple of units above the other.
- Turn both planes into active rigid bodies.

Figure 8.4 Cylinders with the Same Mass Held by Different Strength Springs.

- Create a directional particle emitter beneath the polygon planes.
- Select the particle object, the two polygon planes and create a gravity field.
- Create a nail constraint for the topmost polygon plane and move it up by 10 units so you have a pendulum.
- Create a pin constraint between the two polygon planes.
- Play the scene back a few frames.
- Select the Particle object then the lower polygon plane and use Particles|Make Collide.
- Repeat for the other polygon plane.
- Play the scene back.

The planes should swing around in the particle stream deflecting them off their surfaces. A more violent effect can be created by moving the pin constraint so that the polygon planes swing faster through the particles and giving the lower plane a higher mass than the other one. Both surfaces can also be affected by the particles as well as just deflecting them, by turning on Particle Collision in the Attribute Editor for the rigid body. Playing the scene back now will show the polygon planes being spun and tossed about by the particle system.

Baking out Rigid Body Motion

You will generally be creating rigid body dynamics for inclusion within your scenes, not just as the only part of your scenes. You can integrate these rigid bodies into keyframed scenes by "baking" the position and rotation of the dynamic objects into keyframes. Baking a dynamic object will create a full set of keys so that you can delete all of the dynamic controls on the

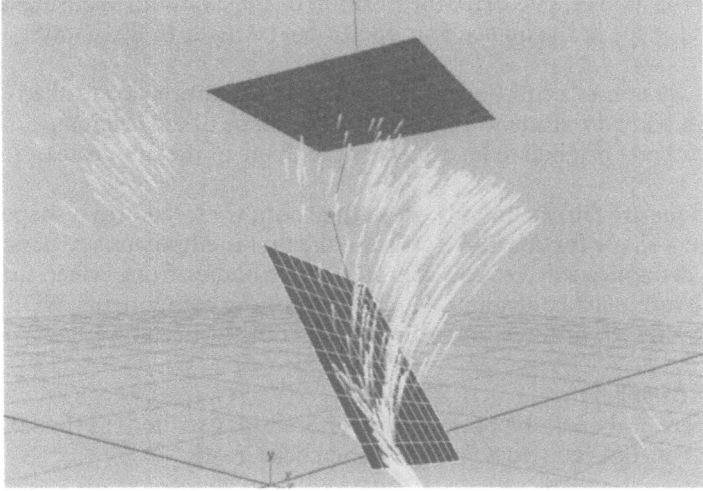

Figure 8.5 Planes Deflecting and Deflected by a Particle System.

object (fields, constraints and solvers), then integrate them into your normally animated scene with no impact on playback (i.e. you can play the scene back using the "real-time" setting). You can then manipulate the object's position and rotation using the familiar keyframe methods in the Dopesheet and Graph Editor.

- Select the lower polygon plane.
- Open the options box for Edit|Keys|Bake Simulation.

The important settings for this operation are the channels that you will be controlling as keyframed animation, the length of time the baking will happen and how much information is sampled. If you set the Channels to All Keyable then an animation curve will be created for every channel you can see in the Channels Box. It is more efficient to select From Channel Box and highlight the relevant channels, such as translation and rotation. The sample range will determine how accurately the keyframes represent the motion of the object by creating a key for each channel at the sample rate. A sample rate of 1.0 will create a very dense curve, as there will be a key each frame, but this can be solved later by using the Simplify Curves function from within the Graph Editor. Now that the movement and rotation for an object has been baked out, you don't need the rigid body node any more, so open the Hypergraph and delete the useless node. You can now change the movement of the object as you wish, so you can edit and replace keys at points to fit in with your animated scene.

Soft Body Dynamics

In sharp contrast to rigid body dynamics, soft body dynamics are concerned with changing the shape of surfaces using dynamic forces. Because all surfaces are composed of components, when you create soft bodies, you drive the position of the components using dynamic forces and so change the shape of the object. Soft bodies can be made in three ways:

1. Complete conversion to a soft body so that the shape is entirely controlled.
2. Creating a soft body duplicate to be driven by the shape of the original.
3. Creating a soft body original to be driven by the shape of the duplicate.

The last two options are fairly similar because they both try to deform a shape using a reference to the original shape for control; if you use the first method you are passing shape control over to the dynamics solvers. You can create soft bodies from either surface type, but because dynamic forces are controlling the position of the components, NURBS soft bodies will tend towards smooth surfaces, and polygons can quickly become angular.

- Create a NURBS sphere.
- Select the sphere and open the options box for Soft/Rigid Bodies|Create Soft Body.
- Set the Creation Options to Make Soft and click Create.

In the Outliner, you can now see that there is a new node under the sphere's transform node which is a particle object that, when selected, shows the particles at the component positions. Select the particle object, create a turbulence field and play the scene back. The shape of the NURBS sphere is now altered by the particles driving the component positions. This relationship can be seen by selecting the particle object and displaying the Input and Output connections in the Hypergraph, so that you can see how the output geometry from the makeNurbsSphere node is passed into the particle object. You can key the transform node of the sphere so that it can be animated through the scene while various fields change its shape.

A Dynamic Curtain

A more useful feature of soft bodies is using the technique to create a dynamic surface that corresponds to a real surface within a scene, for example, curtains in a breeze. This will use the second method of soft body creation where the soft body is a duplicate of the original. This option is used because the original surface can be used as a goal for the soft body particles. You need to be able to control part of the dynamic curtain surface so that dynamic forces don't completely destroy the shape in the places that shouldn't move, such as near the curtain rail. This method also provides a lot more control because you can define the goal weighting that the surface has and thus define the amount that the dynamic forces control the soft body shape.

- Create a NURBS plane, rotate it so that it is standing vertically and scale it so that it has an oblong shape.
- Make sure that there are more vertical isoparms than there are horizontal; however, the total number of isoparms will define the smoothness of the surface.
- Freeze the transformations and delete the history.
- Open the options box for Soft/Rigid Bodies|Create Soft Body.
- Set the Creation Options to Duplicate, Make Copy Soft, turn off Duplicate Input Graph, leave the others on and click Create.

The difference in this type of soft body is that the original object is left as it is and hidden, whereas the soft body now becomes the surface that you wish to see and manipulate, with the appropriate underlying particles. What you do have is the original surface that will act as a target for the soft body particles giving a new way to control the soft bodies in addition to the dynamic forces. In the options box, the target weight for the particles is set to 1.0 and this is the target weight for every particle and its corresponding CV. The following process shows how to change the weights for some of the particles so that the edge of the curtain that is to be fixed to the wall won't move.

- Select the duplicate object.
- Open the options box for the Paint Dynamic Weights tool, found under Soft/Rigid Bodies|Paint Soft Body Weights Tool.
- Set the Value to zero, the Paint Operation to Replace and click the Flood button so that the entire surface is black.
- Set the Value to one and paint the top edge of the surface so that there is an unbroken white line.

You have just set the target weights of all of the soft body particles to zero apart from the top row, so that when you apply any fields to the soft body, the top of the surface won't move. You can use the Paint Dynamic Weights tool to add small random areas of target weight to the surface in order to break up the field effect. You can see these weightings and edit them more precisely by selecting the particles as components and opening the Particles tab in the Component Editor. Once the weights have been set up (you can keep editing and painting the weights until the effect is right for the scene), you can apply some fields to create the effect of the surface blowing in a breeze.

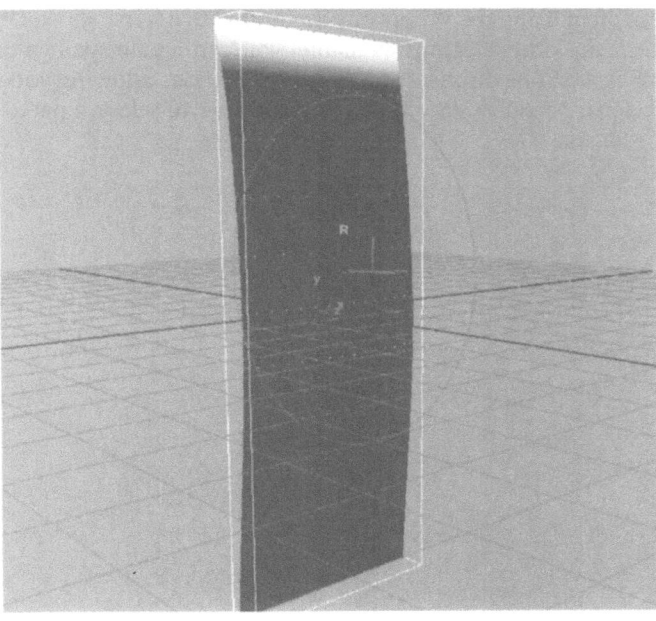

Figure 8.6 Painting Dynamic Goal Weights.

- Select the soft body particles.
- Create a gravity field with no attenuation.
- Play the scene back.

Springs

The effect of the target weighting is quite obvious here as most of the surface drops away to minus infinity. Because we are trying to simulate a coherent surface and not a loosely connected series of points, we need to introduce some form of tension between the particles. This tension is provided in the form of springs, whose effect we have already seen when using rigid body constraints.

- Select the particle object.
- Select Soft/Rigid Bodies|Springs and open the options box for this action.

There are three ways to create springs onto a particle object and these describe the relationship each particle has with its neighbouring particles.

1. Min/Max will create springs between particles if they fall within the minimum and maximum specified distance.
2. All will create springs between all particles that can result in a very dense spring object but is a good way to keep the volume of a soft body consistent.
3. Wireframe will create a set number of springs between each particle – a good way to keep a shape as the springs have a more local effect.

Springs should be created using the Wireframe method with a Wire Walk Length setting of 3. As can be seen from the other options available, you can create springs on top of existing springs or so that they won't be duplicated if they already exist, allowing you to slowly add layers of springs to selected particles. You can also add springs to selected particles giving further

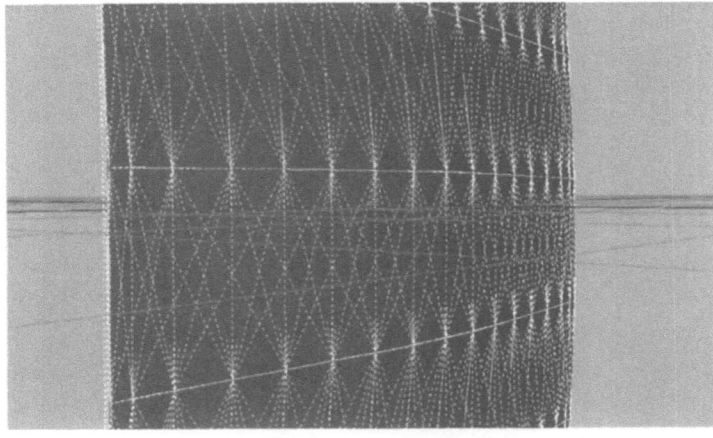

Figure 8.7 Wirewalk Springs across the Dynamic NURBS Curtain Surface.

sophistication when creating tension in soft bodies. Click the Create button and the spring object will appear in the Outliner and on the surface of the soft body, which allows you to review how the springs connect each particle.

Hide the springs for now as they can slow down playback and tend to get in the way when watching a Playblast. Now you need to add an air field to the particles so that they are moved by a gentle breeze.

- Select the particle object.
- Open the options box for Fields|Air, click the Wind button and then the Create button.
- Open the Attribute Editor and set the Attenuation to zero and use the RMB menu in the magnitude field to select Create New Expression...
- In the Expressions Editor set the air field magnitude to equal cos(time)*5.
- Make sure that the air field is blowing along the correct axis.
- Play the scene back.

Playing the scene back, you can see that the springs add a "boingy" effect to the surface as the particles drop due to gravity and move due to the air field blowing back and forth, which is fine if simulating a rubber sheet but not for a cotton one.

Set the rest length to a value that is just shorter than the distance between the rows of particles (use the Distance tool under Create|Measure Tools), set the Stiffness to around 100.0 and the Damping attribute to 20.0 and play the scene back. The soft body may explode after wildly oscillating for a few frames. This is happening because you are now asking Maya to calculate a lot of physics and the solver cannot calculate the actions accurately enough on a frame-to-frame basis. Use Solvers|Edit Oversampling or Cache Settings to bring up the attributes for the soft body solver and change the Over Samples value to 10. Now Maya can calculate the dynamics ten times a frame, giving greater accuracy and correct results; if this problem persists then the oversampling can always be increased. If you play the scene back, the soft body will tend to move into a rest position before the springs take effect, so you should set the sheet up so that it appears to be at rest before any of the dynamics take an effect.

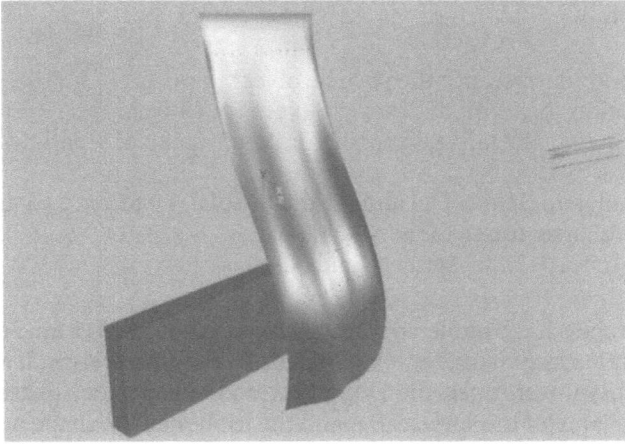

Figure 8.8 Curtains in a Breeze.

- Open the Dynamic Relationships Editor and disconnect the particle object from the air field.
- Play the scene again and wait until the surface is still and pause playback.
- Select the particle object and use `Solvers|Initial State|Set for Selected`.
- Reconnect the air field to the particle object and play the scene back again.

A turbulence field can be added to the soft body simulation so that you can begin to create subtle (or not) ripples in the surface of the soft body. Create a turbulence field, connect it to the particle object and set the attenuation to zero. For the magnitude, create an expression that sets the value to `sin(time*5)*2` so that you get a smoothly oscillating magnitude but is out of phase with the air field due to the use of the `sin()` function. You can further play with the soft body by painting dynamic weights to increase the weight by a fraction at the edges to accentuate the effect at the centre of the surface.

Baking the Motion of the Soft Body

Because the shape of the soft body is defined by particles, the particles can also collide with other surfaces using the normal method of creating particle collisions so that dummy windowsills can be created around the soft body or any other objects can be used to create these collisions.

Create a series of polygon cubes around the edges of the soft body to act as the window frames. These can be used purely for collision purposes and can have their primary and shadow visibility render attributes turned off. Select the particle object and then each polygon object in turn and use `Particles|Make Collide`, setting the resiliency to a low value and the friction to a low value so that the soft body doesn't bounce from the surfaces when it collides. If you are to integrate it into your keyframed animation scenes, you will come up against the problem of the slow playback of the dynamic systems slowing down the feedback for the keyframed animation. You can either render the two scenes separately and composite them together later, import the dynamics scene into your animation scene when you are sure that they are both finished and render them together with the correct interaction occurring, or you could bake the animation of the dynamic surface out. Then you could integrate it into your keyframed scene with no feedback problems and the ability to further manipulate and edit the surface's movement.

- Select the soft body surface, not the particle object.
- Open up the options box for `Edit|Keys|Bake Simulation`.
- Set Channels to `All Keyable`, turn off `Driven Channels` and `Shapes` and turn on `Control Points`.
- Set the `Time Range` to `Start/End` and set the `Sample By` to `0.25` so that you can sample the shape every quarter frame for accuracy.
- Turn off `Disable Implicit Control` and bake.

Once the baking process has completed, you can delete all of the dynamic objects (apart from the actual soft body surface) and then play back the scene in real time. If you want to retime the animation then you can open the Dopesheet and expand the square with the cross in it which lies by the name of the surface. Expand the list beside the shape node name and a list of all the animated CVs will appear, so shift-select all of them and then use the Scale tool to expand or contract the timing. `Bake Simulation` also places keys for the transform node, so if you want to animate the transformations of the surface, break the connections and re-key the channels.

Further Uses of Soft Body Dynamics

Using soft body dynamics in this way allows you to take advantage of Maya's particle dynamics to drive the shapes of surfaces. This can be employed to add any kind of dynamic motion to any surface such as a character's cape, and by using dummy objects to provide collisions with, the realism of the effect is increased. Because of the nature of the dynamic simulation and the different way of working that it involves, it is usually best to create soft body effects after keyframed animation has been done so that the dynamic simulation is the last stage before rendering a scene. However, there are some times when the dynamics in the scene will end up driving the animation of the character.

- Create a new scene and draw a ten-joint bone chain.
- Place an IK spline handle through all of the bones.
- Select the IK spline and open the options box for Soft/Rigid Bodies|Create Soft Body.
- Set the Creation Options to Duplicate, Make Original Soft.
- Turn on Hide Non-Soft Object, Make Non-Soft a Goal and turn off Duplicate Input Graph.
- Set Weight to 1.0 and click Create.

What we have done is to recreate the original IK spline as a soft body so that it can still pass controls via the IK handle to rotation of the joint chain. The new curve that has appeared in the scene, that isn't soft, will now act as a goal object for the soft body to move towards, letting you animate the goal curve using clusters, while the dynamics adds its own animation.

- Select the particle object that has been created and create a turbulence field.
- Play the scene back.

The joint chain should jiggle as the turbulence field affects the CVs, but it stays completely still. This is because the goal weight of the particles was set to 1.0, so select the particle components and open the Particle tab in the Component Editor and set all the weights to 0.3 and play the scene back. You can now add your own keyframed animation to the dynamic curve so that you have further control of your character, or you can import an animated spline IK system and use the above soft body options to add the dynamic movement afterwards.

- Select one of the CVs of the non-soft curve.
- Create a cluster for it and animate its position over 30 frames.
- Play the scene back.

Now the goal object is moving, the soft body particles controlling the curve will try to reach its goal in addition to the turbulence field and the rotations for the joints in the hierarchy can be baked out as required. This method is a very useful way to add dynamic details to movement such as for trees in a wind or strands of seaweed in the water, with or without additional keyframed animation.

Clip FX

In addition to the dynamics section, Maya also ships with seven "Clip FX" which let you create quick dynamics affects, found under the Effects menu heading. These can be extremely useful as they supply a functionality that would otherwise be difficult to implement and for the simpler effects, provide an insight into the mechanics needed to create such an effect from scratch. All of the Clip FX are dynamics apart from one, which is a modeling aid that can be incorporated into rigid body and soft body dynamics. Some of the Clip FX may require some item or items to be selected, and it is always worth setting the behaviour of the effects in the relative options box, especially for the Shatter effect.

Curve Flow and Surface Flow

Curve flow and surface flow concern the creation of particles as flowing systems. Curve flow requires a curve to be created, either in 3D or as a curve on surface, which will then provide a path on which particles can flow from one end to another. The particles are continually emitted from the start and will die when they reach the end of the defined flow. The flow curve system consists of several rings placed around the selected curve, which help define the width of the particle flow, and which can be altered by scaling the rings and the speed between the rings. The group that is created will contain all of the necessary attributes to create a flow path animation and lifespan will determine how quickly the particles flow from one end to another. Surface flow will require a NURBS surface to be selected before the action can take place, but will create a group (that holds all of the attributes necessary for controlling the effect) containing several emission manipulators along the length of the NURBS surface. The manipulators for this particle effect cannot be selected and scaled like the flow curve rings, so you need to use attributes in the Channels Box or the Attribute Editor (found under the Extra

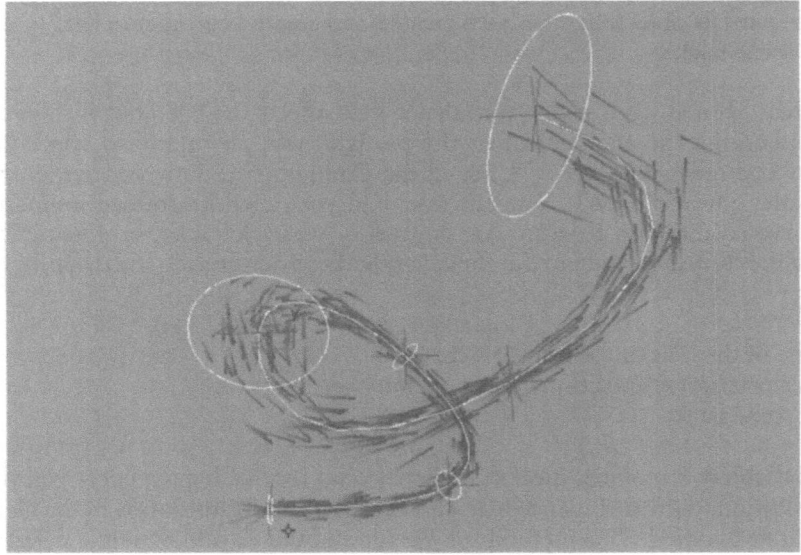

Figure 8.9 Curve Flow Particles.

`Attributes` section) to move and scale the flow manipulators. For both of these effects, you need to set the start conditions, such as the number of manipulators and what direction the particles will flow in (for surface flow) in the options box before creating them.

Fire, Smoke and Fireworks

Fire, smoke and fireworks create pure particle effects whose operation must be set in the Creation options box. Fire creates a point, surface or curve emitter that emits software rendered cloud particles along with corresponding fields to create the movement effect, so be careful if integrating this effect into a scene with any global fields. Smoke will create a column of smoke from a point or from a selected surface, but will require the use of the Hardware Renderer as it utilizes sprite particles with an animated texture applied to each sprite. Maya is shipped with a default animated texture which needs to be applied in the Creation options box, but other animated textures can also be supplied if available. Fireworks provide a firework rocket airburst effect by instancing different coloured cones onto a particle system via the particle instancer. What these effects additionally provide is a good starting point to investigate the creation and implementation of more sophisticated particle effects.

Lightning and Shatter

The lightning effect lets you create a lightning bolt between two objects and the shatter effect lets you break a surface into shards. The lightning effect creates an animated extrusion between the two supplied objects, which can be manipulated using the provided locators and the position of the objects between which the bolts are stretched. The important attributes to set in the Creation options are how the lightning bolt propagates between more than two objects; the rest can be changed either as attributes, such as intensity and glow, and tangency direction in the 3D view.

Shatter lets you crack a surface into polygon shards, with rules governing how the shards are formed and what they will be able to do afterwards. Because of this, it is vital to use the Creation options for this effect. The effects of the shatter operation create polygon shards

Figure 8.10 A Shattered NURBS Sphere.

which can either be surfaces, rigid bodies or soft bodies and comes in three varieties: surface, solid and crack shattering. *Surface shatter* lets you break up a NURBS or polygon surface into polygon shards that represent only the surface; you can extrude these shards to provide a measure of solidity to the resultant pieces, like breaking up a thick surface. *Solid shatter* will break up the selected object into solid shards that are made from the volume of the surface, not just the edge. Because of this, the interior surface can be assigned a different shader making the process of texturing the interiors easier via the Texture View window. *Crack shattering* requires that you pick a CV or a vertex, which is used as the originating point for the propagation of cracks across the surface. This crack effect is extremely useful when combined with rigid body dynamics, so you can realistically simulate not only the movement and collisions of surfaces but also their breaking and shattering upon impact.

Summary

An issue raised in this chapter (and the previous chapter) is the re-integration of any dynamic systems back into non-dynamic scenes, rigid body dynamics can be baked out as can soft body dynamics. Keeping this in mind will allow you to make the correct choices about the way that the effect will be handled using Maya and what resources will be needed in terms of time and processing power when the integration of dynamics into keyframed scenes will occur. Because of the nature of the calculations required for rigid bodies, optimizing their use is of paramount importance. Often, a low-resolution stand-in object can be used to provide the physical interactions required in a scene, removing the need for expensive computation times. It is also worth bearing in mind that the motion of a rigid body or soft body may only provide the starting point for the completed motion. Often, a production will require that additional subtle motion be added using keyframes, a method that would be impractical if only dynamic simulation was used. Once baked out, you are free to manipulate all aspects of a dynamic body.

MEL Scripting　9

Introduction

MEL is an acronym standing for Maya Embedded Language and it is the language that Maya uses to run and create all of the actions, tools and system commands that we have been using to create scenes. Everything that we have done so far can be represented in MEL, but this wouldn't be particularly user-friendly, so this chapter will show when and why you would want to use written code instead of the Maya interface. The whole of the Maya interface and the way that you access the commands and actions that make up the software package are created using MEL scripts. You can also utilize interface commands to create your own custom user interfaces for complex scripts and could extend this idea further to rewrite the actual front end of Maya if required. Because we will be using MEL as a high level scripting language, some familiarity with programming and scripting concepts is required. All of the available MEL commands are in the Maya online documentation.

Simple Commands

Everything that occurs in Maya will be represented by a MEL command that we can examine by looking in the Script Editor. The Script Editor can be opened using `Window|General Editors|Script Editor` or by LMB clicking on the Script Editor icon in the bottom right-hand side of the Maya interface under the Animation Preferences icon. The Script Editor is split into two sections, the upper section is the history section and displays any MEL commands that Maya has generated or any MEL commands or scripts that have been compiled. The bottom half is the input section where you can enter commands or entire scripts. If you create a NURBS sphere using the menu, this action is printed out in the history section of the Script Editor as the "sphere" command combined with a series of modifying flags which determine the shape node attributes of the sphere and the axis positioning and orientation. Looking in the documentation for the sphere command will display the meanings and possible values for the flags, any other flags that can be added to modify the MEL command and the return value (in this case, the return value is the name of the sphere). You can easily examine the flags for the sphere command by LMB highlighting the sphere command and using the MMB to drag and drop the command into the input section. If you are using commands with which you are familiar, you can also write them in the Command Line, which is in the bottom left-hand side of the main Maya window, opposite the Feedback Line that Maya uses to print any errors, warnings or MEL command results.

Once the command is in the input section you can edit it and then enter it into Maya. Change the value of the `-esw` flag to 180 and then enter the command using the Enter key in the numeric keypad. As long as the command is sound, Maya will interpret it and create the NURBS sphere. You can use the Script Editor in this way to examine any actions and commands; it also lets you create custom commands and create and enter multiple commands (the basis of a script).

We shall explain how to create a small two-command script that creates half a NURBS sphere and deletes its history. First, we should clean up the Script Editor to give us a clean slate. Use `Edit|Clear History` to clear the upper half and `Edit|Clear Input` to clear the lower half, or use `Edit|Clear All` to remove any text from both halves of the Script Editor.

Create a NURBS sphere and delete its history. You will note that the delete history action hasn't generated a MEL command. When Maya does things, the generated MEL script might be too low level for the Script Editor to display unless you use `Script|Echo All Commands`, which will suddenly create a brand new line of MEL that is quite abstract. As enabling this option means that all commands that go on in Maya will be echoed, everything will now be displayed in the Script Editor. The Maya interface that you use to access commands and actions is also generated in MEL, so any changes to the interface will now be displayed in the upper half of the Script Editor. For example, open the `Preferences` window from `Window|Settings Preferences|Preferences...` and look at how much MEL is generated; typing `PreferencesWindow;` will do just the same. But all of this does mean that the delete history MEL command will now be displayed in the Script Editor. Clear the upper and lower half of the window, create a NURBS sphere and delete its history. You can now create a two-line script that reads:

```
sphere -p 0 0 0 -ax 0 1 0 -ssw 0 -esw 180 -r 1 -d 3 -ut 0 -tol 0.01 -s 6 -nsp
    4 -ch 1;
DeleteHistory;
```

If you highlight the two lines and then press the numeric Enter key, you can enter these commands into Maya without placing the script into the upper half of the Script Editor – this means that you can keep editing the lines. If you come across a script that you want to use again and again, you can easily store it by MMB dragging and dropping the highlighted lines onto the shelf. The action will now be represented as a MEL icon on the shelf, whose appearance can be edited using the Shelf Editor. You can also store this script for further use by placing it into a Marking Menu or map a hotkey to it. These methods can be used because every action or command is just a MEL script, so whether you use an icon that holds the script or the raw script itself is immaterial. If you edit the lights marking menu that you created in Chapter 6, you can see that each menu item is internally represented as a MEL command.

There are also some actions and commands that can only be used by writing them as MEL commands, not accessed via the user interface. These hidden commands will be found in the online documentation for MEL commands or within the chapters themselves. One command which is extremely useful moves rigid bodies from one rigid body solver to another. Normally, you would have to create a new solver, switch context to it and then any new rigid bodies created would be controlled by this current solver. What we don't have is a menu item to switch existing rigid bodies to newly created solvers. However, this action can be done using a MEL command.

- Select the rigid body that you wish to move
- Type `rigidBody -edit -solver <solverName>;` and as long as the solver that has been named exists, the selected rigid body will be switched over to it.

You have to use the `-edit` flag to tell Maya that you wish to change the current solver. The documentation for all the MEL commands will show how certain flags can be used: Edit, Query, Create or More than once. So we use the `rigidBody` command with the flag `-edit` followed by `-layer` to change the layer that the currently selected rigid body belongs to, or use the `-query` command instead of the `-edit` command to find the layer that the currently selected rigid body belongs to.

Changing Attributes

Similar to the attributes that you have changed using the Expression Editor, you will find that MEL commands are different from expressions in two ways:

1. MEL commands do not execute every frame, only when they are entered into the command line or Script Editor in Maya.
2. Expressions have an "=" at their heart, driving channels of items whereas MEL scripts may not even drive a channel at all.

If you create a sphere and rename it `ball`, you can use written instructions to change the values of the sphere's attributes through the Script Editor or the Expressions Editor. Open the Expressions Editor and turn off `Always Evaluate` so that the expression only has an effect once. Type in `ball.translateY=5;` and click Create. The ball will move five units up in Y and the `translateY` channel will now be driven by the expression. Use the RMB to break the connection in the Channels Box and set the `translateY` attribute to 0. In the Command Line, write `setAttr ball.ty 5;` and press the numeric Enter key. The ball should now move up by five units but there will be no connection driving the attribute, which you would also see if you wrote this in the Expression Editor. Because of this, you should avoid using MEL commands in the Expression Editor because Maya is unable to make the correct node attachment using this command, instead of passing the value of a statement via an expression node.

Using this `setAttr` command allows you to change attribute values without driving them, so you can use this to change the attributes of items without driving their values. This means that you can connect animation curves, driven keys etc. to them, without having to freeze or disconnect anything. Appropriately, you can also use the `getAttr` command to query the value of any attribute that you know the selected item contains, but further to this you can also list the attributes of a selected node using `listAttr`. This means that if you know what attributes a surface has, you can query them and set them very easily, such as randomly perturbing the surface of a polygon plane.

Writing Scripts

At its simplest, a MEL script is a collection of commands that are evaluated one after the other to create a composite action, such as creating half a NURBS sphere and deleting its history. However, we can take this further, because the MEL language is also comprised of a set of programming control functions so that you can start directing how your MEL script executes, depending on various conditions. You can now write a MEL script to accomplish tasks that would be otherwise tedious and overly repetitive, plus you can introduce mathematical expressions and functions into the script if necessary. As stated at the beginning of the chapter, some basic familiarity with programming/scripting concepts and the construction of programs/scripts is required for the rest of the chapter, as explanation of the methods of script construction will be beyond the scope of this book.

Random Cylinder Distribution

We shall explain how to construct a script that will create a random number of cylinders, scale them randomly and place them randomly in a scene. This technique can be extremely useful for the task of placing debris, litter, rocks or people around scenes without driving you crazy. Although this might be a little daunting, it can be carried out in a simple manner as long as you know what each step will be. The first thing that you need to do, is to create a NURBS cylinder, scale, translate and rotate it and see what MEL commands are generated. If you do this, you can see that the script will be composed of five commands (where *x y z* are the three floating point values for the relevant axis), which can be seen if you first perform the actions and then look in the Script Editor:

- Create the NURBS cylinder: `cylinder...`
- Translate the cylinder: `move -r x y z;`
- Scale the cylinder: `scale -r x y z;`
- Rotate the cylinder about its Y axis: `rotate -r -eu x y z;`
- Delete the history: `DeleteHistory;`

You can now place all five of these commands into a five-line script, but replacing the *x*, *y* and *z* values with a random number generation function. This function can be ably represented by the `rand()` function that returns a random number between the supplied upper and lower values. Because the function is being used to return a value, you will need to encapsulate it in a set of brackets, but the simple script will now look like this:

```
cylinder -p 0 0 0 -ax 0 1 0 -ssw 0 -esw 360 -r 1 -hr 2 -d 3 -ut 0 -tol 0.01
    -s 8 -nsp 1 -ch 1;
move -r (rand(-20.0, 20.0)) 0 (rand(-20.0, 20.0));
scale -r (rand(1, 3)) (rand(2, 10.0)) (rand(1, 3));
rotate -r -eu 0 (rand(-360.0, 360.0)) 0;
DeleteHistory;
```

If you highlight the script and keep pressing the numeric Enter key, you will soon build up a large number of randomly placed, randomly scaled cylinders. You could even create this as a shelf item, to aid the repetition of this task (the shelf can be a good temporary storage point for scripts). However, you should have done one other thing to the cylinder prior to moving and scaling it – move the pivot to the bottom of the cylinder and set the *y* value to zero. This means that the bottom of every cylinder you create will be set to zero, which makes the manipulation of the cylinders easier if placing them onto surfaces. This just involves changing `-p 0 0 0` to `-p 0 1 0` so that the pivot creation position is changed.

Procedures

Although the shelf is a very useful place to store scripts and you can even MMB drag and drop shelf items into the input part of the Script Editor to examine them, it may make your work easier if you write the script as a procedure. This can then be saved to a directory in the hard drive, so you just have to call the procedure name instead. Save the current script to the shelf, clear the input section of the Script Editor and write

```
global proc cy_rand()
{
}
```

MMB drag and drop the saved shelf item into the middle of the global procedure body so the script now looks like this:

```
global proc cy_rand()
{
cylinder -p 0 1 0 -ax 0 1 0 -ssw 0 -esw 360 -r 1 -hr 2 -d 3 -ut 0 -tol 0.01
  -s 8 -nsp 1 -ch 1;
move -r (rand(-20.0, 20.0)) 0 (rand(-20.0, 20.0));
scale -r (rand(1, 3)) (rand(2, 10.0)) (rand(1, 3));
rotate -r -eu 0 (rand(-360.0, 360.0)) 0;
DeleteHistory;
}
```

Highlight this entire procedure and use File|Save Selected... to save the script as a .mel file. You can save this file anywhere that you wish, but there are two directories (script paths) that Maya will automatically search, so check the online documentation for these locations which vary depending on the operating system used (for example, C:/WINNT/profiles/ <login-name>/maya on Windows NT). If scripts are saved in these locations, you can just call the procedure by its name instead of having to load it into memory using the File|Open Script command from the Script Editor menu. Save this procedure under its own name cy_rand.mel in one of the script path locations and close Maya down. Re-start Maya and once the interface has loaded, open the Script Editor and type cy_rand; to call the procedure – this call can be created as a shelf button in itself. Any changes you now want to make to this script can be done in a Text Editor which is a far more flexible writing environment than the Script Editor. If you use a Text Editor to edit and save your scripts while Maya is open, you will need to use File|Source Script... to reload the procedures into memory so saved changes will be updated.

You may need to debug your code when errors creep in (as they usually will) and this will become even more imperative when your scripts start gaining size and weight. Turning on Show Line Numbers and Show Stack Trace from the Scripts menu will make it a little easier, but if you are going to be using a Text Editor, then it is worth finding one that supports line numbering as well.

All work which follows involves a Text Editor, Maya and the Script Editor, so open cy_rand.mel in a Text Editor. We are now going to change the script so that it creates a random number of cylinders every time it is executed, by using a For loop. This will entail setting up two variables to hold the control test for the number of cylinders and to hold the current iterated value. In the Text Editor, write the following lines after the procedure declaration:

```
int $rnum=rand(2,20);
int $i;
for($i=1;$i<$rnum;$i++)
  {
  }
print "finished\n";
```

The original four-line procedure can now be placed inside the brackets that start and finish the For loop, then save the file. In Maya, source the script, save the procedure name as a shelf item and execute it. Every time the cy_rand procedure is called, a random number of NURBS cylinders will be created.

Random Polygon Creation

If you wanted to do the same with polygon primitives, you will have a small problem, because looking in the documentation for the polyCube, it is not possible to specify where the pivot point will be placed.

- Clear the Script Editor.
- Create a polygon cube and move it 0.5 units up in the Y axis so that its bottom is at 0.
- Manually move the pivot to 0, 0, 0.

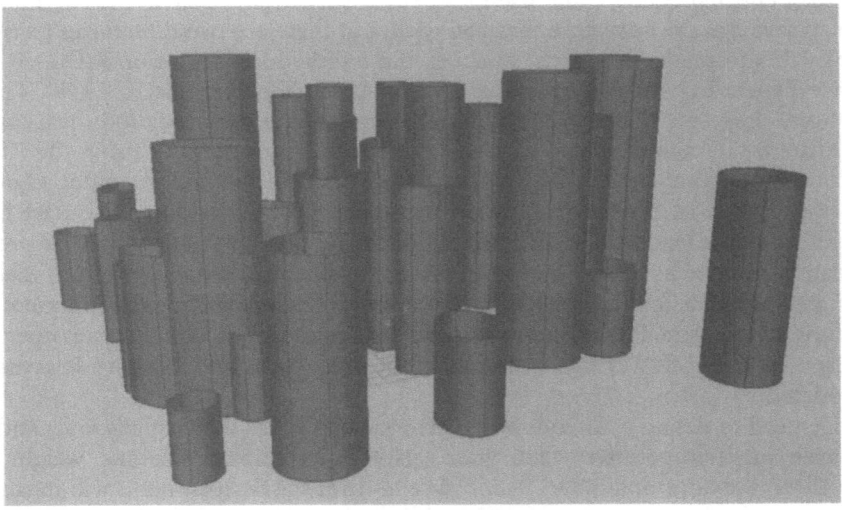

Figure 9.1 Randomly Scaled and Placed Cylinders Using the cy_rand Procedure.

You can see from the generated MEL commands in the Script Editor that this operation will be a little more tricky to automate, because the move command associated with the pivot position requires the object's two pivot names: <objectname>.scalePivot and <objectname>.rotatePivot. As you don't know what each object will be called, moving the pivots will require a little more work. Thankfully, the return value for the polyCube command is the name of the transform and shape node of the cube. These can be stored and used later in conjunction with MEL's flexible string operators that will provide the correct name for every polygon cube created and its associated pivots. You can start small and then add the new lines of MEL script into your existing MEL script, as all of the original transformation commands work on the currently selected objects. Clear the Script Editor and type the following into the input section and execute it:

```
$Polyname=`polyCube -w 1 -h 1 -d 1 -sx 1 -sy 1 -sz 1 -ax 0 1 0 -tx 1
  -ch 1`;
print $Polyname;
```

This should create a polygon cube and print the names of the transform and input nodes in the Script Editor. This is because we are enclosing the polyCube command in left-slanting apostrophes (`) which will evaluate the command and then return the value to the variable on the left-hand side. The variable $Polyname has been internally converted by Maya into the required data type needed, which in this case would be a string array as there are two strings returned. The following MEL code would accomplish the same thing:

```
string $Play[]=`polyCube -w 1 -h 1 -d 1 -sx 1 -sy 1 -sz 1 -ax 0 1 0 -tx 1
  -ch 1`;
print ($Play[0]+"\n");
print ($Play[1]+"\n");
```

Now that you can trap the name of the polygon cube in the string array, you can change the pivot position of each cube by concatenating a series of predefined strings that describe the operations you wish to perform with the polygon cube name. This will create a string that holds the entire command required, then the eval command can be used to execute the string. These are the strings:

```
string $P_name=".scalePivot";
string $P_name=".rotatePivot";
string $M_Comm="move -a 0 0 0";
```

The lines that you will insert after trapping the returned value of the create polygon cube command are:

```
$FComm=($M_Comm+$Polyname[0]+$SP_name+" "+$Polyname[0]+$RP_name);
eval ($FComm);
```

These lines can now be integrated into your script so that it looks like this:

```
global proc poly_ran()
{
int $rnum=rand(2,15);
int $i;

string $SP_name=".scalePivot";
string $RP_name=".rotatePivot";
string $M_Comm="move -a 0 0 0";

for($i=1;$I<$rnum;$i++)
{
$Polyname=`polyCube -w 1 -h 1 -d 1 -sx 1 -sy 1 -sz 1 -ax 0 1 0 -tx 1
   -ch 1`;
move -r 0 0.5 0;
$FComm=($M_Comm+$Polyname[0]+$SP_name+" "+$Polyname[0]+$RP_name);

eval ($FComm);
DeleteHistory;

move -r (rand(-10,10)) 0 (rand(-10,10));
scale -r (rand(1,10)) (rand(1,10)) (rand(1,10));
rotate -r -eu 0 (rand(-360.0, 360.0)) 0;
}
print "finished\n";
};
```

The above MEL script can now serve as a useful template for most basic item manipulation, especially as you know that $Polyname[1] contains the name for the shape input node, granting access to the other attributes that go to make up the polygon cube. You can even edit the values for each attribute, if you know the names of the attribute, by creating a set of string variables with the attribute names in, then they can be appended to the string containing the relevant node name. MEL's ability to add together large strings make it very flexible when trying to change or access attributes, especially when combined with some of the list commands.

Perturbing a Polygon Surface

First, you need to know something about the makeup of the polygon surface, which can be found from the attributes in the shape node. These can either be displayed in the Channels Box or using MEL, as we know from the last example script how to access the shape node name from a created polygon object:

```
$nodes=`polyPlane -sx 10 -sy 10`;
listAttr $nodes[1];
```

This should list a series of node attributes. The attributes we are interested in are subdivisions Width and subdivisions Height (which may be a little moot as we set these in the

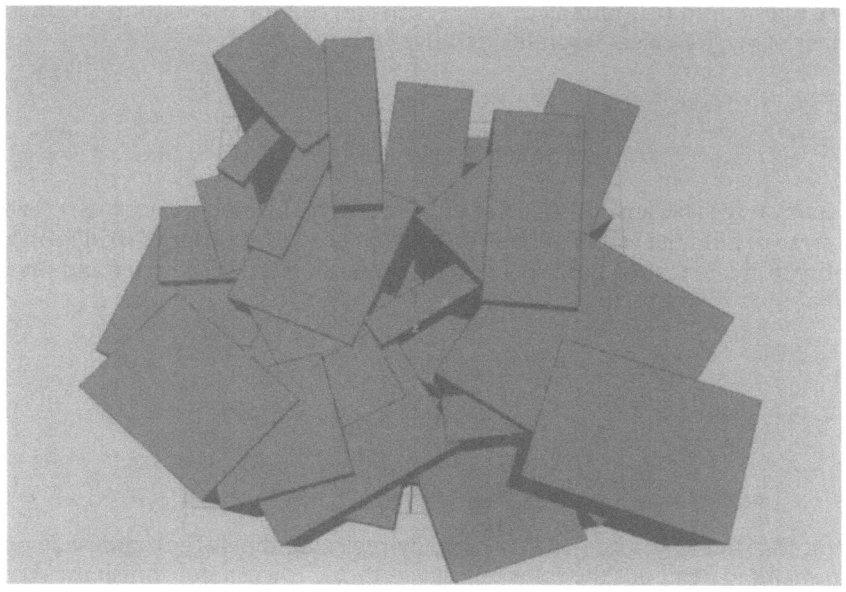

Figure 9.2 The Results of the poly ran Procedure.

polyPlane line). The values for these attributes will give the number of vertices that make up the polygon plane; just add one to each attribute and multiply, because a subdivision is a split in an edge not a line of vertices. So, type

```
$nodes=`polyPlane -sx 10 -sy 10`;
int $num_W_verts=getAttr (($nodes[1]+".subdivisionsWidth")+1);
int $num_H_verts=getAttr (($nodes[1]+".subdivisionsHeight")+1);
int $total_verts=($num_W_verts*$num_H_verts);
print ("total number of vertices is :"+$total_verts+"\n");
```

This is useful if every time you want to query the total number of vertices in a polygon plane, you want to create one as well. However, you can look at the values of these attributes by selecting the plane and typing:

```
$whom=`ls -sl`;
int $num_W_verts=(`polyPlane -query -subdivisionsWidth $whom`)+1;
int $num_H_verts=(`polyPlane -query -subdivisionsHeight $whom`)+1;
```

The ls -sl command is the list command with the "currently selected" modifying flag added to it. Now that you can inquire about the number of vertices that make up your polygon plane, you can create a loop that will run through all of the vertices and move them. First insert the above three lines into the beginning of your script and add the summation line that gives the total number of vertices. Next begin the iterative loop:

```
for($i=0;$i<$total_verts;$i++)
```

The loop starts at zero because the first vertex of the polygon plane is vertex zero (owing to the use of an array to hold the vertex numbers). You will need to use Maya's string concatenation functionality to create the required string so that you can select each vertex and then move it:

```
{
$current_cv=($whom[0]+".vtx["+$i+"]");
select -r $current_cv;
move -r 0 (rand(-0.2, 0.2)) 0;
}
```

You can test that this is working at any time, by replacing the `select` and `move` commands with a command to print out the value of `$current_cv`. You can now finish the script with:

```
print "all done\n";
select -r $whom;
```

so that you return Maya to its original state, ready to operate on the polygon again if required. Place all of this inside a global procedure and the entire script will be ready for use at any time. If you were to do this to a NURBS plane, you would have to change the way that you iterated through the CVs because they are stored as a double subscripted array `[u][v]` instead of the single subscript array for polygon surfaces `[vertex]`.

Figure 9.3 The Perturbed Polygon Plane.

The MEL User Interface

We have so far explained how to create MEL scripts that use Maya commands in a manner that is most useful for you, either by being able to access "hidden" functions, being able to repeat commands or by using maths functions to change the results. One area that we haven't covered that comprises part of the internal MEL scripts and commands that Maya utilizes, are the interface commands. Being able to wrap MEL scripts in a user interface lets people use MEL procedures and scripts via the familiar set of controls that comprise the Maya interface, such as sliders and text input fields, instead of getting caught up in compiling MEL scripts. If, for example, a MEL script is created that forms an important part of a production environment, then it would make sense to wrap this script in an interface so that non-programmers can utilize it. This means you can extend your toolset into the hands of those who may not necessarily want to run functions. It also allows you to enter varying amounts into the parameters for MEL scripts that would otherwise need the script to be resourced.

A Simple Interface

At the top of the user interface (UI) structure is the window. A window will hold all of the various interface objects that you will use to enter data and activate commands and will nominally consist of a border, a title and a set of the usual windowing buttons to minimize, maximize and close the window. This can also be seen as the top of the interface hierarchy, so that the window will contain various children who can in turn contain various children. Maya will need to keep a name for each interface object in memory so that it knows who belongs to what, so that if you resize or close a window, Maya can take care of the general interface housekeeping. You can quickly create a window by typing the following into the Script Editor:

```
window -widthHeight 200 100 -title "Title" -iconName "Icon Name" -rtf true
   Win1;
showWindow;
```

Once this has been typed into the input area, you can either compile it by using Script|Execute and pressing the numeric Enter button, or by highlighting the script and pressing the numeric Enter key, which keeps the script in the input area and allows you to re-edit it. The last word in the window command names the window for Maya's internal purposes, giving the system a "handle" with which it can access the window. If you try and create the window again with the current window still active you will get an error message saying that the name of the window is not unique. You can either create a window with a new name or you could add the following lines at the start of the MEL script:

```
if(`window -exists Win1`)
   deleteUI Win1;
```

These lines will check to see if anything named Win1 exists and if it does, delete it. Now you can create the same named window again and again, thus allowing you to recompile the same script without worrying about whether the name or identity of the window has been already used. It does mean that you will need to carefully examine the names of other custom interfaces, as using one name and meaning another can recreate old windows as completely new windows instead.

Layouts

Once you have created your window, you can place interface objects inside it and then link the interface objects to commands and actions. When you create child objects within a window, these have to be ordered into some form of plan known as a "layout" that defines how these children are to be placed within the window. Add these lines to your script:

```
rowLayout -nc 3 row_1;
   button -label "button 1";
   button -label "button 2";
   button -label "button 3";
setParent...;
```

The first line here creates a layout, which has its own name, that will hold three columns (using the -nc flag or "number of children") side by side. The next three buttons are created as children of the layout, and the layout itself must define itself as a child of the window by using the setParent...; command, which says that it is a child of the interface object that is directly above it. We could have the rowLayout specify a name that it will be parented to, but it is more usual to specify the interface object that it is nested inside of. Now you can begin nesting interface layouts within each other for a more ordered way of working, but first you need to create an overall layout that will contain all children of the window itself. Therefore, before the rowLayout line, type the following:

```
columnLayout all_kids;
```

Now you can nest any layouts inside this one, so after the setParent command of the layout containing the buttons, you can add:

```
columnLayout col_2;
radioButtonGrp -cat 1 left 0 -numberOfRadioButtons 3 -label "Buttons"
   -labelArray3 "Yes" "No" "Maybe";
setParent...;
```

Compile and run the script. You now have a series of nested layouts that attach themselves to the window that you have created. Notice that each UI element that controls a sub-set of items has to be named. Now that you are creating interface controls and can add these in at any stage of your UI creation, you can begin to tie these buttons to commands so that you can actually use the interface for something. Delete all of the button, radioButton and layout commands in the script so that you are left with just the bare bones of the interface. You need to start placing the different aspects of your MEL scripts into different procedures, so that you have a main procedure for the UI creation and other procedures for the actual commands and actions being called from the UI elements. Place the window checking lines, column layout line and window creation line into a procedure called `create_win` so that you have a bare procedure – all of the scripting will now be done after the initial `columnLayout` line:

```
proc create_win()
{
if(`window -exists Win5`)
  deleteUI Win5;

  window -widthHeight 100 25 -title "My_Win" -iconName "MWin" -rtf true Win5;

    columnLayout allkids;
showWindow;
}
```

Buttons

The first thing to do will be to create a child layout that will be parented to the main layout `allKids`, then a few lines of MEL will be placed inside the layout that will create the button and map the command called by the button to another procedure. The first line:

```
string $print_text=`button -label "print : hello world"`;
```

defines the string variable `$print_text` as a command that will create a button with the label `print : hello world` on it and trap the returned name, similar to the way that you trapped the names of the polygon nodes in an earlier example. You can do this through the use of the left slanting apostrophe that enables you to create a command for evaluation, either at once or for later use (as in this example). The next line will create a procedure call:

```
button -edit -command ("printtext()") $print_text;
```

The use of the `-edit` flag means that you are going to change the value that is supplied to the `-command` flag. The `-command` flag will execute the following procedure call `printtext()`, but the whole line requires a button to map all of this to, which is where the variable `$print_text` is used. This variable has trapped the name of the created button, which is supplied to the `button -edit` command. You could bypass this way of doing things by hardwiring the button name into the script so that you could have the name at the end of the button creation line, so that the command line is simplified as well:

```
button -label "print : hello world" button_1;
button -edit -command ("printtext()") button_1;
```

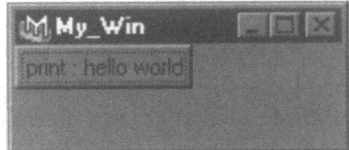

Figure 9.4 The Window and Button.

but using a variable in this way you can forget about the names of the buttons and let Maya take care of it. All you need to do now is to write the printtext() procedure:

```
proc printtext()
{
print "Hello World\n";
}
```

Now you can compile both at the same time, type in create_win; and have a small UI appear that will print a line of text. The entire script should look like this:

```
proc create_win()
{
if(`window -exists Win5`)
  deleteUI Win5;
  window -widthHeight 100 25 -title "My_Win" -iconName "MWin" -rtf true Win5;
    columnLayout allkids;
    string $print_text=`button -label "print : hello world"`;
    button -edit -command ("printtext()") $print_text;
showWindow;
}
Proc printtext()
{
print "Hello World\n";
}
```

Implementing a More Complex Interface

All of the above scripting has given you sufficient practice to enable you to create and implement an interface into your random cube maker so that upper and lower limits can be imposed upon the scaling, translation and numbers of cubes. You should have the actual cube creation and randomization placed in a separate procedure and the UI creation in the main procedure. All you need to do is create and pass 12 parameters to the cube creation procedure (upper/lower X and Z translation limits, upper/lower X, Y and Z scaling limits and minimum/

maximum number of cubes to make). You should first start with the interface and then create the bare bones of the window. To help you set up the "look", you can use text where the final interface objects will lie, but one large thing that has changed is the use of alignment flags for the layouts, so that labels can be positioned correctly.

```
proc mwin()
{
  if(`window -exists mwn`)
    deleteUI mwn;
window -rtf true -width 300 -title "rando_cuberiser" mwn;
//set up the main layout
columnLayout -columnAttach "both" 5 -rowSpacing 10 -columnWidth 285 -adj true
  mcol_1;

//sub layout to main columnLayout mcol_1
frameLayout -label "Min/Max Translate and Scale settings" -cll true frame_1;
  columnLayout -adj true fr_col1;
    separator -height 10 -style "in";

//sub layout to frameLayout frame_1
rowLayout -nc 3 -cw 1 100 -cw 2 100 -cw 3 100 -ct3 "both" "left" "left" -co3
  15 15 15 sRow;
    text -label "scale X";
    text -label "scale Y";
    text -label "scale Z";
  setParent...;

//sub layout to frameLayout frame_1
rowLayout -nc 3 -cw 1 100 -cw 2 100 -cw 3 100 sfRow;
    text "input X values here";
    text "input Y values here";
    text "input Z values here";
  setParent...;

separator -height 5 -style "out";

//sub layout to frameLayout frame_1
rowLayout -nc 2 -cw 1 150 -cw 2 150 -ct2 "both" "left" -co2 40 20 tRow;
    text -label "translate X";
    text -label "translate Z";
  setParent...;

//sub layout to frameLayout frame_1
rowLayout -nc 2 -cw 1 150 -cw 2 150 tfRow;
    text "input X values here";
    text "input Z values here";
  setParent...;
 setParent...;

setParent...;
```

```
//sub layout to columnLayout mcol_1
frameLayout -label "Min/Max Cubes" -cll true frame_2;

//sub layout to frameLayout frame_2
  columnLayout -adj true fr_col2;
    separator -height 10 -style "in";
    text -label "minimum number of cubes" -align "left";
    text "input lower cube values here";

separator -height 5 -style "out";
    text -label "maximum number of cubes"-align "left";
    text "input upper cube values here";
  setParent...;
setParent...;

//sub layout to columnLayout mcol_1
columnLayout bc_01;
button -label "create" -align "center" -width 300;
setParent...;

showWindow;
}
```

If you enter this into the Script Editor you should get a reasonable facsimile of the interface that you wish to use. Notice the use of comments which are preceded by a "//", although you can also use "/*" as well.

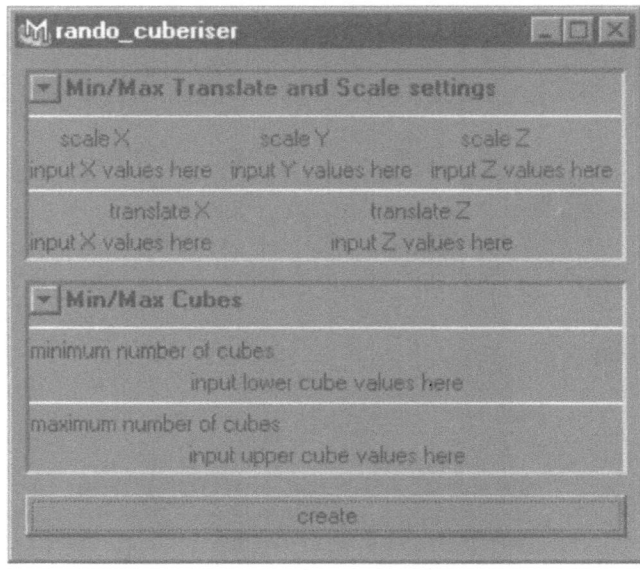

Figure 9.5 The Interface So Far.

All that remains is to plug in your UI elements that will set the parameters, and a means to collect and pass these parameters to your cube creation procedure. You can control your input for the first ten (upper and lower scale and translate) parameters using integer fields and the min/max number of cubes can be controlled by a set of integer sliders with input fields that should sit nicely under the aligned text labels. Replace the first set of dummy text labels with:

```
intFieldGrp -numberOfFields 2 -cw2 35 35 -ct2 "both" "both" -value1 1 -value2
   10 sXfld;
intFieldGrp -numberOfFields 2 -cw2 35 35 -ct2 "both" "both" -value1 2 -value2
   12 sYfld;
intFieldGrp -numberOfFields 2 -cw2 35 35 -ct2 "both" "both" -value1 3 -value2
   13 sZfld;
```

This should create upper and lower scaling fields under each label.
    Replace the second set of dummy text labels with:

```
intFieldGrp -numberOfFields 2 -cw2 100 50 -ct2 "left" "left" -co2 20 -30
   -value1 8 -value2 10 tXfld;
intFieldGrp -numberOfFields 2 -cw2 50 50 -ct2 "right" "right" -co2 0 0 -value1
   2 -value2 12 tZfld;
```

These lines should now create the necessary fields that you require for each translate axis. Make a note of the names of each of the `intFieldGrps`, as you will need these names in order to access the values held in each of the numeric fields. The minimum and maximum number of cubes can be set using a slider for each, so change the last set of dummy text fields to:

```
intSliderGrp -field true -minValue 1 -maxValue 20 -fieldMinValue 1
   -fieldMaxValue 20 -value 1 cMin;
```

and

```
intSliderGrp -field true -minValue 2 -maxValue 20 -fieldMinValue 2
   -fieldMaxValue 20 -value 10 cMax;
```

When you recompile the program, you now have a reasonable interface that will let you create a series of randomly scaled and translated cubes. All you have to do is to access the values held in each of the integer and slider fields and pass them to the procedure to create the cubes. You should write the procedure for the cubes first, so that you know the order in which the parameters will be required, but the procedure heading should look like this:

```
proc make_random_cubes(int $LSX, int $USX,
                       int $LSY, int $USY,
                       int $LSZ, int $USZ,
```

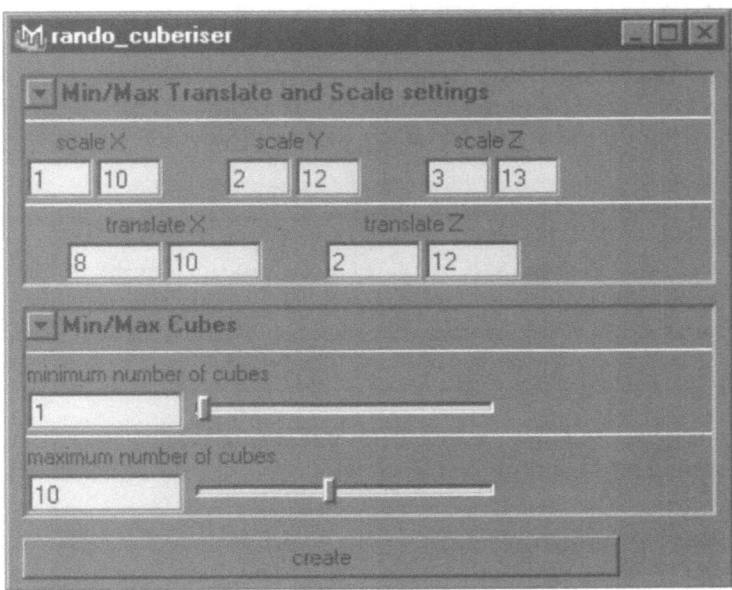

Figure 9.6 The Finished Interface.

```
                       int $LTX, int $UTX,
                       int $LTZ, int $UTZ,
                       int $lower, int $upper)
```

We are going to use the same technique to create, trap and pass the command through a button as we did in the MEL script we used to print "Hello World", but we will be using a much larger list of parameters. The button creation line can now be changed to this:

```
string $createButton=`button -label "create" -align "center" -width 300`;
```

and we can trap access the values for each UI object through their names and the names of the object's items. For example, if you wanted trap the value of the first field (the minimum scale X value) you would write:

```
button -edit -command ("create_random_cubes(`intFieldGrp -query -value1
   sXfld`)") $createButton;
```

By using the -query flag, you can access the value held in the -value1 field for the sXfld UI object. All that remains is to fill out the rest of the parameter field so that the make_random_cubes procedure receives the correct parameters in the correct order. Then you need to make the relevant adjustments to the cube creator script so that it can utilize these variables. The procedure call when the button is pressed should look like this:

```
button -edit -command
("create_random_cubes(`intFieldGrp -query -value1 sXfld`,
                      `intFieldGrp -query -value2 sXfld`,
                      `intFieldGrp -query -value1 sYfld`,
                      `intFieldGrp -query -value2 sYfld`,
                      `intFieldGrp -query -value1 sZfld`,
                      `intFieldGrp -query -value2 sZfld`,
                      `intFieldGrp -query -value1 tXfld`,
                      `intFieldGrp -query -value2 tXfld`,
                      `intFieldGrp -query -value1 tZfld`,
                      `intFieldGrp -query -value2 tZfld`,
                      `intSliderGrp -query -value cMin`,
                      `intSliderGrp -query -value cMax`)") $createButton;
```

Finally, replace the numbers that are hardwired into the cubes procedure with the correct variable names and you should be able to create random numbers of randomly scaled, translated and rotated cubes. Make sure that a new variable is created to hold the value that the "i" count will be checking against; or you could always change the iterative loop so that "i" starts at the lower cube value and iterates through to the upper cube value. You don't have to perform any error checking because you are using random number generators, which don't make much of a fuss if one number is higher than another, even though it's supposed to be lower. Both procedures can now be created as global procedures and placed in the /maya/scripts directory for use later.

Summary

We have seen in this chapter how we can utilize the language that Maya uses to create and change the state of any item within scenes. MEL can be used not only to create short one-line commands, but can be put together to form massively complex scripts or to access special commands not available through the standard interface. Knowing how and when to use MEL effectively can be as important as knowing how to model effectively, as it can be used for custom effects or to speed up highly repetitive jobs and introduce mathematical randomness or periodic functions into scenes. One example of this is the Particle Replacer that started life as a script and is now a "normal" part of the Maya Dynamics interface, as are the Clip Effects. The Script Editor can also be used to debug or examine Maya as it works, so if anything goes wrong, you can quickly examine the state of the system. All scripts are held local to the installation of Maya and due to the nature of scripting, many more are available at various Internet resources, which when combined with the online documentation can provide a great jumping point for MEL script writing.

Custom user interfaces can now be created for collections of normal tools and actions, or collections of custom actions. These gather up the important things that you (or your colleagues) will be using on a day-to-day basis through the course of a production, which in turn can condense the required knowledge of where required tools are into a small window. Anyone who is new to the software or new to the production can quickly come on board when presented with the custom interface. Interface creation can become a very time-consuming process, getting the layouts of buttons and sliders correct while at the same time actually getting the functionality correct. Of importance is to make sure that you aren't held back by the actual interface design itself, so drawing interfaces first, avoids coding a headache of an interface.

Paint Effects 10

Introduction

Paint Effects is a tool unique to Maya that allows you to literally paint 3D detail into scenes. The tool uses a combination of curves, procedural rules and tube rendering techniques to create plants, hair, trees and even popcorn according to interpretations or simple rules. What this means for us, as users, is that we can now create detail and filler in our scenes, such as forests and the forest flora, that would otherwise have been time consuming to build and texture and extremely geometry heavy. Because Paint Effects uses a brush-like interface and a painting paradigm, we can create and use many different brushes (which hold the actual rules for the creation of the paint effect objects) and customize the large set of supplied brushes.

Painting in 2D

We will look at the general effect that Paint Effects can give us by first painting into a window called the "Canvas" which allows us to paint in 2D. Because we are going to be using and creating brushes, it will be easiest to store them on the shelf, so create a new shelf labeled `Brushes`. Pop an orthographic view to the foreground and open the Canvas by pressing the hotkey "8" or using `Panel|Paint Effects`. The window will now clear to the default background colour (which can be changed using the options in `Canvas|Clear`) and present a new set of Paint Effects menus. Additionally, the menu set should be changed to Rendering so that you can access the Paint Effects menu items.

The first thing you need to do is to paint something, so use `Brush|Get Brush` to open up Visor, which lets you browse the Paint Effects brushes that Maya contains. Open the `Airbrush` directory and MMB drag and drop the `mediumAir.mel` brush onto the new Brushes shelf and close Visor. Click on the new brush icon on the shelf, use the LMB to paint and, as expected, the brush leaves a painted trail across the canvas. You can alter the two colour attributes that the brush is made from by changing the colours for the "C" (colour) attribute and the "T" (transparency) attribute via the slider or by using the colour chooser, activated by an LMB click on the colour swatch.

So this is all quite straightforward, but doesn't really do much that a normal paint package can do (although it does mean that you don't need a paint package in order to paint textures;

Figure 10.1 A Paint Effect Dahlia in the Perspective View.

just press the camera icon in the Canvas to save a snapshot to disk). Open Visor again and select the Flowers directory. MMB drag and drop the dahliaRed.mel brush onto the shelf, select the brush and begin painting. You should now have quite realistic red dahlias growing before your eyes as you paint in the canvas. These flowers (and all Paint Effects brushes) are rendered in colour and have an alpha channel, which can be viewed by clicking the Display alpha channel button. These flowers are using exactly the same mechanisms that the Airbrush Paint Effects brush uses and both are written using the same MEL script interfaces. There are large selections of different brushes, all of which have their own unique look, but there may be times when you need to create something new. There are a lot of plants in the world and Paint Effects doesn't have them all, or you may need to create some completely alien effect with your brushes. What makes these brushes different are their attributes and how basic paint effects rules are used.

With a series of flowers drawn in the canvas window, select the mediumAir brush and open the Brush menu heading. The first basic settings that a brush has are Paint, Smear, Blur and Erase. The mediumAir brush is set to "Paint", naturally, but if you change the brush type to "Smear" and then paint across the dahlias, you can now smear them, and if you set the type to "Erase" you can erase dahlia-shaped sections from the canvas. When you set the mediumAir to "Smear" notice that the airbrush path was divided into circular components so that you don't get a smooth smearing effect. These circular cross-sections are called *stamps* and stamps are placed along the path that you draw according to the brush attributes (each path that you draw is known as a *stroke*). At each stamp position, you create the paint effect according to the brush, such as a colour for the mediumAir or a grown flower in the case of the redDahlia brush – varying the stamp size and frequency you can start changing the effect of each brush.

Brush Attributes

Select the mediumAir brush and open its attributes using the Brush|Edit Template Brush... (or Ctrl+b) which will bring up a Paint Effects style Attribute Editor called the Paint Effects Brush Settings window. The first attribute is the paint type, which we have already looked at; the next is "Global Scale" – this will change the size of the stamp radius. You can paint colour, alpha values and depth values so that your strokes will be painted in front or behind other strokes using a Paint Effects brush and can be set in the Channels fold-out.

- Clear the canvas and select the dahliaRed brush.
- Open the attributes for the brush, set the Global Scale to 0.7 and turn on Depth.
- Paint a few flowers onto the canvas.
- Use Paint|Save Depth as Greyscale to save a depth map of the canvas to disk.

You have been using both of the available types of stroke so far, *simple strokes* and *tube strokes*. A simple stroke means that colour or texture will be applied at the position of the actual stamp like the mediumAir brush. A tube stroke means that a series of tubes will be created (and possibly grown) at the stamp position. You can alter the appearance of simple strokes by changing not only the way that the stamps appear at the strokes but also what the actual stamps look like.

- Select the mediumAir brush and open the Paint Effects Brush Settings window.
- Turn on Depth and change the Brush Width attribute to 0.75 and the Softness attribute to 0.2.

Painting in the window will now reveal how many stamps you get along the strokes that you draw, so increase the Stroke Density to 10.0 and then set the Brush Width to 0.3. You can change the colour of the brush using the Shading attributes, so changing Colour 1 will change the colour of the brush stamps.

- Open the Texturing fold-out and turn on Map Colour.
- Change Texture Type to checker.
- Paint in the canvas window.

You now have a chequer texture associated with the stamp colour and you can change how the chequer is evaluated along the path by changing the Tex Uniformity value. Set this to 0.0 and the chequer pattern will be created in relation to the speed that the stroke is drawn at; set it to 1.0 and the chequer texture will be uniform across the entire stroke length. However, much more interesting results can be had from mapping a file texture to the stamp.

- Set the Texture Type to File and scroll down until the Image Name attribute is visible, along with the file browser button.
- LMB click the browser button and change to the directory that Paint Effects brush images are stored (\Maya4.0\brushImages\, though this will vary according to the operating system used).
- Select aluminiumFoil.iff and paint in the canvas again.

Now you have a much richer effect for your brush as the bitmap is applied to each stamp. You can change this effect by using custom created file textures and even have animated file

Figure 10.2 The Results of the Clover Textured Brush.

textures by turning on Frame Extension and keyframing the attribute. Textures can also supply an alpha channel so that the backgrounds are transparent, which helps when using non-square images.

- Change the file texture to clover.gif and paint in the canvas window.
- Turn on Map Opacity and set Tex Alpha1 to 1.0 and Tex Alpha2 to 0.0.
- Paint in the canvas window.

If you use Brush|Get Brush, open the Metals directory and MMB drag and drop the "duct.mel" brush to the shelf, you can see how the use of a good texture map can make an effective Paint Effects brush.

The other type of brush that you can create and edit is the tube brush, which grows tubes along strokes, such as the redDahlia brush used earlier. Select this brush and open the Paint Effects Brush Settings window – the biggest single change to this brush is the creation of tubes at the stroke. Open the Tubes fold-out so that you can start looking at the rules that go into making a brush like the redDahlia. Two attributes are at the head of this section: Tubes will turn on the creation of tubes along the stroke and Tube completion will create whole flowers along the stroke no matter when the stroke was drawn. The Creation fold-out has attributes that govern how many tubes are created along the stroke (increase the Tubes per Step to increase the density of dahlias created along the stroke), where the tubes end up pointing and how they will generally appear in terms of thickness and curvature. The Growth fold-out governs what will actually grow from the first tube and contains checkboxes turning on or off the creation of branches, twigs, leaves, flowers and buds.

Figure 10.3 Paint Effects Brushes on a Shelf.

All of these five items occur at different stages of growth (one usually follows on from the other) and the use of these different stages and their individual attributes will define the final paint effect. For example, the redDahlia brush has leaves, flowers and buds (which can also be texture mapped) but no branches or twigs. You can quickly deconstruct this brush by turning off leaves and flowers, so that only buds are grown at the top of the first tube. Turn on leaves and you can start to see how these new attributes work together to create the look of the dahlia.

The basics of this redDahlia brush can be used to create a completely new type of Paint Effects brush. Keep Flowers turned off and turn on Branches so that there are a set of tubes created before the main flowers are grown. Open the Buds fold-out, change the colour to white and the size to 0.04. The buds aren't changing to a white colour because the colour is still being controlled by the attributes in the Texturing section, so open the Texturing section and turn off Map Colour. Next you need to increase the number of leaves and decrease the lengths of the branches so that the new plants are more bunched. Open the Branches section and set Start Branches to 1.0 so that only one branch is placed at the start of the first tube (larger bunches can be created by setting this to 2 or higher) and set Num Branches to 5.0. When you use this brush, you should have a reasonable imitation of mistletoe, which you can save to the shelf (or the brushes directory). Use Paint Effects|Save Brush Preset... to open the save dialogue, change the name of the label to Mistletoe, click the Grab Icon button (which allows you to drag a box around a section of the canvas for the icon) and click Save Brush Preset to place the brush on the shelf for further use.

Painting in 3D

The Paint Effects brushes can be transferred to a 3D scene by closing the canvas window, selecting a NURBS surface (polygon surfaces cannot be painted onto) and using Paint Effects|Make Paintable. Then, making sure that Paint Effects|Paint on Paintable is turned on, select a brush and paint onto the target surface (or grid plane). What you will notice now is that the paintbrush leaves a curve that represents the stroke on the surface, similar to a curve on surface from a projection or duplication. This stroke defines the positioning of each stamp but is discarded in the canvas window once the painting has been completed. Because you can now see the strokes in your scene, you can further manipulate them to add more dynamism to your scenes. What you see in the perspective window is a cut-down version of the actual Paint Effects brush. You will only see the final result (the way that it looks in the Canvas window) when you use the software renderer. Paint Effects strokes are displayed in this rough wireframe version to keep the interactivity of your scenes as high as possible. You can change the representation of each stroke by selecting the stroke and then changing the Display Percent value in the Channels Box or in the shape node attributes in the Attribute Editor. Other attributes in the shape node for each stroke govern the number of tubes planted along each stroke (Sample Density), the order in which a stroke is rendered compared to other strokes (bigger numbers rendered first, smaller numbers are then overlaid), stroke smoothness and the offset from any surface on which the stroke lies. Because the stroke is created as a form of curve on surface (unless you actually use a curve on surface), any deformation to the parent surface will also deform the stroke shape, making Paint Effects perfect for creating fur or hair on an animated character.

If you paint across a surface and decide that you should have used a geranium brush instead of a dahlia brush, you can select the stroke, select the geranium brush either from the shelf or from Visor and use `Paint Effects|Apply Settings to Selected Stroke`. Conversely, using `Paint Effects|Get Settings from Selected Stroke` will make the current brush change to whatever brush was used on the current stroke. This makes sketching out Paint Effects scenes very easy, by roughly positioning strokes, and then once a quick render shows the general look, selecting the strokes, taking the brush from them and painting in the rest of the detail. You can make existing 3D curves into strokes by selecting them and a brush and then using `Paint Effects|Curve Utilities|Attach Brush to Curves`. If you wish to paint across the whole of a surface to create hair or grass, you can use the `Paint Effects|Auto Paint` menu item. It lets you create either an evenly ordered grid of strokes across the selected surface or a random arrangement of strokes using `Paint Grid` or `Paint Random` respectively.

The process of creating detail with Paint Effects brushes can be simplified through using the *share brushes* options in the Paint Effects menu. Share brushes means that you can draw many strokes in your scene, but only use one brush preset across them. Usually, Maya will create a new brush preset for each stroke, so that you can use a template for a Paint Effects brush and then change each stroke in the Attribute Editor (which is why the brushes are called templates). If you were to paint an entire grid of grass using the `Paint Effects|Auto Paint|Paint Grid` menu item, it would create a large amount of strokes, all with their own individual attributes giving individual control over each stroke. If you want to have each stroke created looking the same, with no real variation on the colours or tubes, then having this many individual strokes is a waste of space and time consuming to change for each stroke. You can share the attributes of a single stroke across a series of strokes by selecting all of the strokes, shift-selecting the stroke which has the attributes you wish to share, and using `Paint Effects|Share One Brush`. All strokes will now share the same attributes and any changes made to the last selected stroke will ripple down through all of the others, similar to making an instance. This method of keeping strokes uniform in terms of colour and look makes even

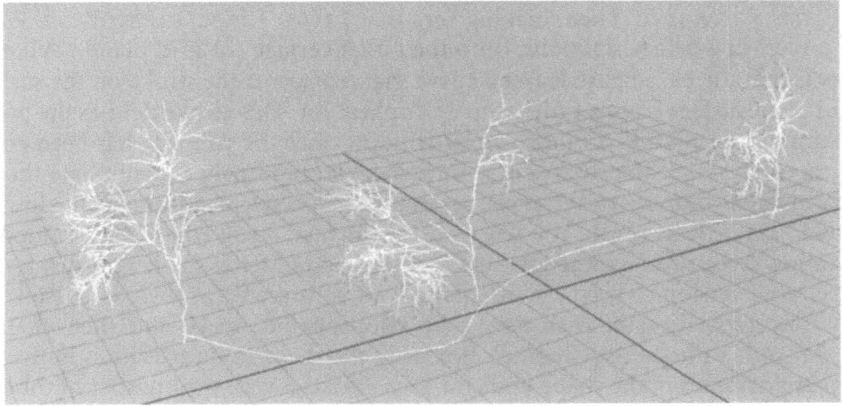

Figure 10.4 A 3D Stroke and Tree.

more sense when you come to animate the strokes, as that will involve keying only one stroke's attributes which can then be shared across the other strokes to create a whole field of gently blowing grasses.

Animating Paint Effects Objects

When you animate Paint Effects strokes, you can animate the strokes that you have created and animate the attributes for the strokes. Because 3D strokes are based on curves drawn in the scene, you can select the CVs of the curves and manipulate the strokes this way. This uses all of the tools and techniques with which you are familiar, such as soft body dynamics and deformers like clusters or blend shape deformation. If you want to create a unique motion for the actual Paint Effects itself, not just the position of the stroke, then you can create and animate guide curves.

- Select the `pineFast.mel` brush from the `Trees` directory in Visor and draw a very short stroke in the scene.
- Draw an EP curve beside the visible wireframe display of the Paint Effects brush.
- Position the curve so that it matches the shape of the Paint Effects item.
- Select the stroke and then the new curve and use `Paint Effects|Curve Utilities|Set Stroke Control Curves`.
- Animate the shape of the control curve.

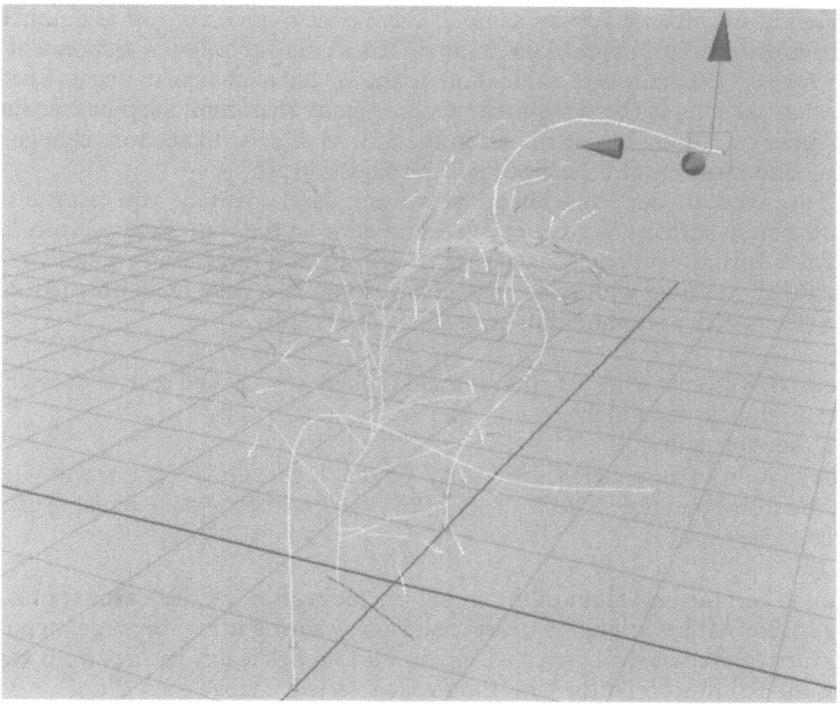

Figure 10.5 Guide Curves Bending the Tree Tubes.

If you want to add more control curves to the selected stroke, you have to start again. You just go through the selection process once more (but this time with the new curves included in the selection list) and use the same `Set Stroke Control Curves` menu item to create a new set of guide curves. You can replace guide curves, however, by opening up the Hypergraph, selecting the stroke and using `Input and Output Connections` to display how the control curves feed into the stroke. Draw a new curve and use shift-MMB to drag and drop it onto the stroke, which will invoke the Connection Editor. Now connect the `worldSpace out` attribute of the new curve to one of the `controlCurve[n]` attributes for the stroke.

Each Paint Effects stroke has its own attributes that allow you to create dynamic looking movement, as it would be no good creating forests where the trees and branches never moved. These effects come in two varieties: those that need to be keyed or driven and those that need to be set and which run themselves. All of these effects can be accessed from the `Behaviour` fold-out in the `Tubes` section of the brush attributes or templates. If you use the `pine1.mel` Paint Effects brush and paint a single pine tree into the scene, you can see these effects more clearly than using any of the other brushes we have already used. The attributes found in the `Displacement` section let you distort the paint effect along the length of the tubes. In fact, the pine brush has used a certain amount of noise to shape the branches so that they are less uniform. The `Forces` section will change the shape of the entire paint effect object in relation to the path such as the `Path Attract` attribute or will change the overall shape using effects such as `Gravity` or `Uniform Force`. These attributes can be useful for creating animation such as trees being knocked over (animate the `Path Follow` from `0.0` to `1.0`). Try using a `sin()` function to drive the `Path Attract` attribute to get the pine tree swaying and because you are using Paint Effects, you can set the playback to real time as all of the forces that you are creating are pseudo-dynamic. However, some of these effects can be set off as automatic forces without having to use any expressions, as attributes in the `Turbulence` section will be evaluated every frame. Delete any expressions and set the `Turbulence` type to `Grass Wind` and play the scene back. As long as the three attributes are greater than zero, the pine tree should now sway and move over time. The attributes in the `Spiral` and `Twist` sections change the shape of the tubes about the upwards axis of the Paint Effects brush.

If you have created your Paint Effects by painting onto a surface, you can use any movement of the parent surface to create reactive animation in the Paint Effects brush itself using springs. These springs will react to changes in velocity and direction in a similar fashion to the springs that you used with dynamics, plus you can also bake the animation out so that rendering effects such as motion blur are evaluated correctly.

- Create a NURBS sphere (or use the animated sphere you created several chapters ago).
- Select it and make it paintable.
- Paint a pine tree onto it.
- Key the motion of the sphere (if necessary) so that it changes direction swiftly.
- Select the stroke and use `Paint Effects|Brush Animation|Make Brush Spring`.
- Play the scene back.

If you want to edit the behaviour of the spring (including how far the spring travels and what frame the spring starts working on), just create a new spring using the same menu item and this will override the last spring created. If you want to delete any springs from your stroke, then open the Expression Editor with the stroke selected, change the `Select Filter` to `By Expression Name`, select the expression that appears and delete it. Baking the spring animation out is a case of selecting the stroke, setting the start and end frame in the options (under

`Paint Effects|Brush Animation|Bake Spring Animation`) and deleting the spring after the motion has been baked.

Animating the Growth

When you draw a stroke in the canvas window, you can see the entire brush grow in front of your eyes. This is because of the way that a Paint Effects brush is constructed, from branch to twig to flower, so you can exploit this construction method to create the illusion of Paint Effects brushes growing from and also growing along the painted stroke (if painted in 3D).

- With the `pineTree` brush, draw a stroke in 3D so that only a single tree appears.
- Select it and in the Attribute Editor open the fold-out titled `Flow Animation`.
- Turn on `Time Clip` and set the `Flow Speed` to `1.0`.
- Play the scene back.

The pine tree should now spring out of the ground, growing in the same manner as it would in the Canvas window. You can increase the speed with which it grows by increasing the `Flow Speed` attribute. What we are doing is specifying a lifespan for the tubes that we have grown using `Start Time` and `End Time` attributes. If you set the `End Time` to `2.0` seconds and expand the time range so that it goes further than the two seconds (frames per second*seconds) you should see the tubes disappear from the base upwards. So it is usually worth having the `End Time` attribute set to a value larger than the total time for the current scene. You can also have the plants shrink back into the ground by keyframing the `Flow Speed` from a positive value to a small negative value like 0.05 over time. You can also create the illusion of growth along the stroke itself, so that your brushes grow out of the ground in the order that they are drawn.

- Use `Paint Effects|Get Brush` and select the `Grass1.mel` brush from the `Grasses` directory.
- Paint a long stroke in the 3D view along the grid.
- Open the Attribute Editor for the stroke and turn on `Time Clip` and set the `Flow Speed` to `3.0`.
- Play the scene back.

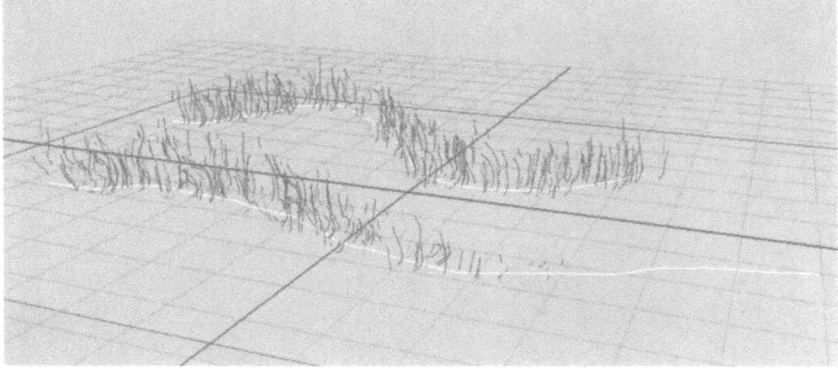

Figure 10.6 Fire Tubes Growing along Strokes.

The grasses should all grow out of the stroke in a uniform manner, but if you turn on Stroke Time and play the scene back, the grass should grow up and along the stroke. This effect is a lot more interesting if combined with a brush like the fire brushes, neon brushes or the sunrise brush.

Rendering

When rendering Paint Effects as part of a scene, you need to decide what part they play in the scene: are they detail or will they become a prominent part of the render? A few problems that might crop up when using Paint Effects are that they will start to look like collections of coloured tubes when viewed extremely closely and Paint Effects do not appear in raytraced reflections or refractions. However, Paint Effects will motion blur, be affected by depth of field and cast and receive shadows. Using the Attribute Editor for the selected brush, you can decide whether a stroke will be lit by the scene lights, by a faked light source or not lit at all. The Illumination fold-out will present two checkboxes, one titled Illuminated and when this is turned on, you have the choice of using the scene lights or a faked light from a 3D position if you choose to ignore the Real Lights checkbox. It is also possible to define the specularity of the Paint Effects brush (diffuse shading is controlled in the Shading section) and the colour of the specular highlight.

The next task is to define whether the Paint Effects strokes will cast shadows and what kind of shadows they will be. You can either fake the shadows cast in the scene by the Paint Effects stroke or you can use the shadows cast from the lights in the scene (you can only use depth mapped shadows with Paint Effects). Fake shadows are generated in the same rendering pass as the Paint Effects strokes themselves and as such cannot be pre-generated like depth mapped shadows can be.

Figure 10.7 Fake 2D Shadows.

- Create a NURBS plane and draw a long line of grass on it.
- Create a directional light and illuminate the grass and the plane.
- Render a frame and save it.
- Open the Attribute Editor for the stroke, open the fold-out titled Shadow Effects.
- Set Fake Shadow to 2D Offset and re-render the scene.

You will notice that the grass has been edged with a type of drop shadow that has been placed near the NURBS plane, which starts to give the impression of some sort of shadowing. This can be improved by setting the Back Shadow attribute to 0.2, which will darken the opposite edges of the grass blades, and set the Centre Shadow attribute to 0.7, which will darken those blades of grass in the centre of the clump. These two attributes will work even when the Fake Shadow attribute is turned off. However, if you set the Fake Shadows to 3D Cast and re-render the scene, you should get a more realistic shadowing effect as the Paint Effects render takes into account each light in the scene. The fake 3D shadows can be softened using the Shadow Diffusion and Shadow Transp. attributes, but you cannot change the colour of the shadows. If you want accurate depth map shadows cast from the strokes, then you need to turn on the depth map shadows for the lights in question, set the Fake Shadows to None and turn on Cast Shadows instead. You can now enjoy all the relative merits of depth map shadows such as shadow colour, separate shadow passes and constraining which lights are creating the shadows, but all at the cost of a longer rendering time. If it's a large Paint Effects scene then you may start running into problems concerning the size of the shadow map in relation to the brush complexity, so it may be more economical to use depth map shadows for more prominent singular items such as trees.

Generally, render any Paint Effects strokes with the rest of your scene for interaction purposes using the software renderer and the usual method of Batch Rendering. If you want to render the Paint Effects strokes independently of your scene so that you can composite them later, you need to set a few things up in the Render Globals and also for the Camera

Figure 10.8 Fake 3D Shadows.

Figure 10.9 Depth Mapped Shadows.

from which you are rendering. What you first need to do is to make sure that you are rendering the frames with a depth channel in them. You can then render the scene in software along with the shadowing interactions from the strokes. Once that has been completed, you will only render the Paint Effects strokes and Maya will use and interpret the depth channel values for the previously rendered non-strokes frames in order to place the Paint Effects strokes correctly.

In the Render Globals, turn on Depth Channel (Z Depth) and make sure that the camera from which you will be rendering also has Depth turned on in the Output Settings fold-out. Create a NURBS plane and a single pine tree with a directional light and set them up so that the stroke is casting a depth mapped shadow across the NURBS plane. Select the stroke and in the Channels fold-out, turn off Modify Colour and Modify Alpha – this has the same effect as turning off Primary Visibility for a surface. Set the filename for the single frame in the Render Globals and render the scene using the Render|Batch Render command. Once the background image has rendered, turn the Modify Colour and Modify Alpha for the stroke back on and open the Render Globals. Open the Paint Effects Rendering Options fold-out and turn on Only Render Strokes – this will activate the Read This Depth File text input field. This field is used to provide the full pathname to the frame with the required depth file which must be in the .iff file format. You can provide the filename as an animated series of frames by using a "#" where the frame number is, but make sure that the padding is correct. Maya will then composite the strokes into the frames that were provided for the depth passes. If you want to render the strokes without having them composited into any rendered images, then you will need to provide the path to an image of the same resolution that is completely empty (but doesn't need to be animated). Maya will just composite it into a black background; make sure that the black frame has an alpha channel for further compositing as Maya will not be able to create one.

Summary

Paint Effects is indeed a unique tool – its uses are only limited by user ingenuity and the varied selection of brushes already available, from plants to laser glares, pay testament to this. Paint Effects can be used as a novel alternative to creating hair and fur, will animate to a certain level of performance and even have reactions to velocity changes from the use of springs. Paint Effects can be integrated into most rendering jobs for little real cost in terms of time and speed and can be easily broken up into passes and composited (even by Maya's renderer). When considering making a brand new Paint Effects brush for a scene, it can be worthwhile starting with a brush that may resemble the desired effect either in terms of tube growth, colour use or both. The ability to texture all of the tubes independently of each stage of growth means that a lot of short cuts can be made in terms of look without having to model the effect with twigs and flowers.

Summary

Integration 11

Introduction

This chapter will look at creating a small piece of animation by integrating many of the techniques and tools that we have looked at in this book. This will demonstrate not only how you can cross between and utilize the different menu sets of Maya in harmony, but that you can also incorporate much of what you have learnt into one composite scene. The animation will be set in a wrecked corridor and focus upon a large security door. The body of the door is dented outwards several times as whatever is behind it attempts to break free; the door is broken off its hinges as several tentacles reach out around the doorframe and a much larger tentacle falls outwards from the darkened room onto the floor.

This chapter will not be a cookbook item saying "do this and do that and in forty minutes you will have a lovely piece of work to show" because this book (and chapter) is about using Maya to achieve desired results, not how particular scenes are created step by step. The final look of this piece will be left up to your imagination in terms of lighting, animation and texturing, as we will be looking at how to use Maya to solve the problems that arise.

After modeling the scenery and stars of the scene, you will be creating a piece of animation, which will involve changing attributes over time. How you achieve these changes in attributes will depend on the effect that you want to achieve; but we are looking at how to integrate all of the parts of Maya so you won't be creating a piece of fully hand-animated work. Because there will be many stages to this piece of work, you may well want to save each stage as you go, so open the options box for File|Save Scene and turn on Incremental save. This will add a number to the end of the scene title every time you use Save Scene, so that you can save the same filename, but never overwrite the last save made. All of these scenes are saved in a subdirectory that Maya creates in the scenes folder called incrementalSave/<scene_name.mb>/ <scene_01.mb>. The incremental save function is only set on a scene-by-scene basis, however, so if a new scene is started then this function will need to be turned on again.

The Corridor and Door

The corridor and door needs to be modeled first, to provide a working scale to which you can model all of the other objects, using layers to hold the many different sections and stages of your modeling. We will be looking at the door from almost around a corner, which should neatly provide a natural end to the model. You can quickly define the outline of the corridor

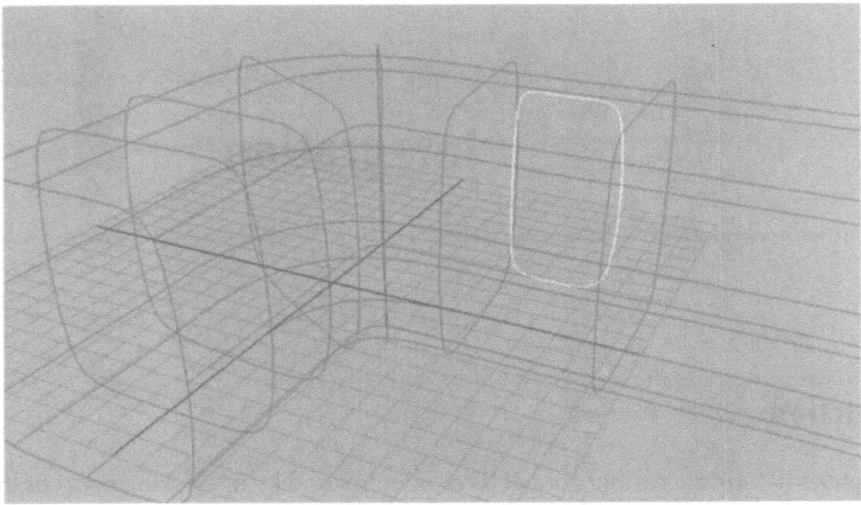

Figure 11.1 The NURBS Corridor with a Door Curve Ready for Trimming.

using a curve and then extrude a corridor cross-section along it, but make the end that we will be looking around longer so that you don't see an edge to the corridor. Because the corridor is made from a NURBS surface, you will need to trim a hole for the door, so duplicate the cross-section profile of the corridor and scale it so that it is more door shaped. Move the door in the side view so that it is in the correct position, select both the door and the corridor and use `Edit NURBS|Project Curve on Surface` to create a new trim curve. Delete the projected curve on the opposite side of the corridor wall as the remaining trim curve will provide the curves to create the door and doorframe. Keeping history on will let you change the trim curve on the corridor surface by transforming the original door curve, but delete when finished.

The doorframe will be constructed from the trim edge in the corridor, so select the trim edge using the RMB marking menu over the corridor, use `Edit Curves|Duplicate Surface Curves`, then hide the corridor and delete the history of the new curve. Because you are using a duplicated trim edge, the curve may have too many CVs, so delete enough that the curve keeps its shape but is less densely constructed. Duplicate and reshape three more curves so that they form the edges of the doorframe and loft them as a NURBS surface. Finally, create a polygon cube and position and scale it behind the doorframe to stand in as the room from which the tentacles will emerge. Invert the `Normals` using `Edit Polygons|Normals|Reverse` and in the `Render Stats` for the surface, turn off `double sided` so that only the interior of the polygon cube will be seen. For the door itself, duplicate the inner two curves of the doorway and then hide the doorframe, the other curves and the corridor. These two curves will form one edge of the door and if you duplicate them again and scale them down, you will have the inner edges. You can create another lofted (NURBS) surface from these to create the outer frame and for the actual deforming part of the door, create a NURBS plane with ten divisions in the U and V spans and scale and shape it so it fits into the outer frame. The new door should now fit flush into the doorway. All that remains is to build some detail in the form of handles onto the door and group it. Make sure any history is deleted and that the NURBS surfaces are rebuilt so that the parameterization is straight for texturing later on.

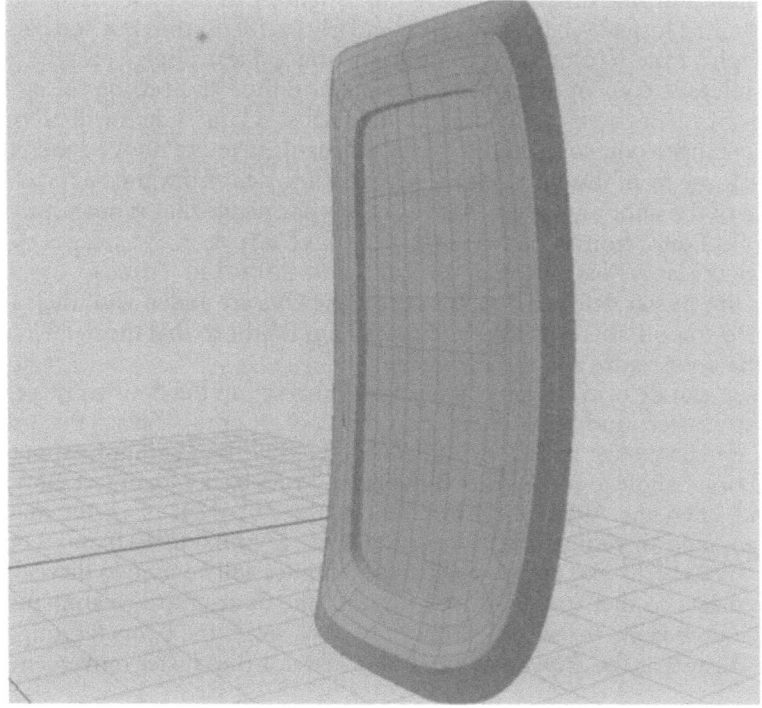

Figure 11.2 The NURBS Door in the DoorFrame Object.

Deformation Effects

Select the door centre and the door edge and group them together under the name Door_N. The group pivot doesn't need to be anywhere special, just at the centre of the door group, because you will be controlling its movement using another means. You can now set up the door for deformation so that when the tentacles decide to break out, you can create large dents in it. Select the plane that makes the centre of the door and cluster it three times, naming the clusters Minor_1, Minor_2 and Major (make sure that this naming is done for the actual deformer node as well as the transform node), ensuring that they are all in relative mode. The monster will be breaking the door down using its tentacles, which will first make large dents in the surface of the door. The clusters are going to be used to create these dents; two smaller dents followed by a much larger one which will eventually break the door off its hinges and across the corridor.

- Select the door surface and open the Paint Cluster Weights tool found under Deform.
- Select each cluster weight in turn (this is why you named the deformer nodes as well) and use Flood to set all of the values to zero.
- Move each cluster in turn a unit or so outwards from the door and paint the deformation back into the door.
- Make sure that the Major cluster makes a massive dent in comparison.

You can now test and fine tune the relative deformations of each cluster in turn using this method. The Paint Cluster Weights tool is particularly useful for this, but you can further trim any cluster weights to zero (especially so the door surface doesn't bulge past the door edge) by selecting the relevant CVs, opening the Component Editor and setting the weights to zero under the Weighted Deformers tab. Because the final and largest dent will precede knocking the door off its hinges, you could add some of this damage to the door edge so that the door starts to come loose from the frame. Make sure that the dent from the Major cluster extends out to the side of the door and select the CVs of the door edge that is nearest the dent. Open the Deformer Set Editor from Relationship Editors|Deformer Sets, select the Major cluster set and click the large Plus button or use Edit|Add Selected Items to add the select CVs of the edge to the cluster deformation. Because these CVs are added with their weight at 1.0, you may need to smooth this down in the Component Editor so that the deformation appears equal across the door centre and the door edge.

Now that you can deform the door, you should also set up the door so it is easily animatable. Select the clusters and move them into the Door_N group. Select this group and use Display|Object Components|Selection Handles, move into component mask mode and move the selection handle to somewhere convenient. Move back into object mask mode, select the group and open the Attribute Editor. Under the Attributes menu item, select Add Attributes and add three float attributes (with a range of 0.0 to 10.0 and a default of 0.0) named Bang_01, Bang_02 and Big_Bang. These attributes will be used to drive the movement of the three clusters so that you only need to select the door group to animate it. Open the driven keys window from Animate|Set Driven Key, select the Door_N group as the driver and the three clusters as the driven and set driven keys for the cluster movement and the new

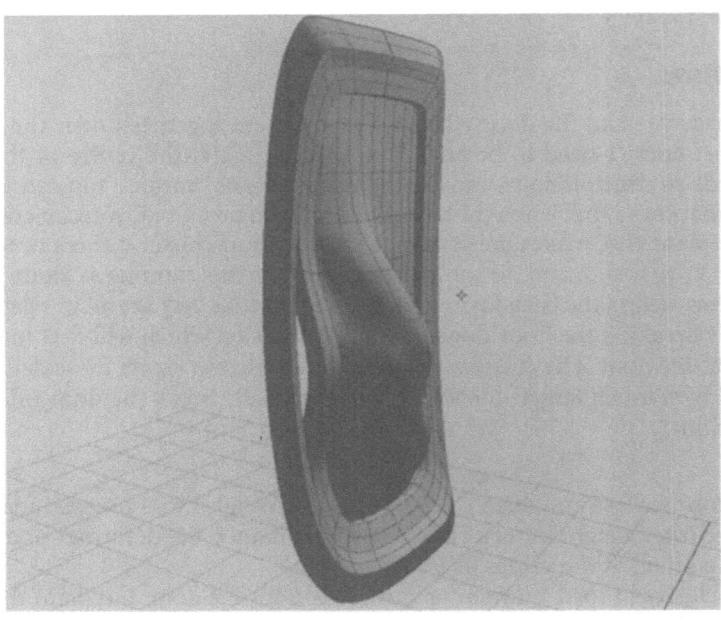

Figure 11.3 The Door with Dents.

attributes. You should now be able to select the Door_N group and animate the deformation from the Channels Box.

The Tentacles

There are two sets of tentacles in the scene, those that wrap around the doorframe and the large tentacle that falls out from the door after smashing it from its hinges. These will be animated in two different ways to give two separate effects, so the tentacles will be modeled in two different ways because of the effects. The tentacles that will snake around the doorframe should be made from polygons because we want to create a closed surface with a lot of detail, such as suckers. The tentacle that falls down across the floor should be made from NURBS because we will want to add some dynamics effects to the surface as it wobbles from the impact. The Polygon tentacle will be controlled by a series of bones, so the segmentation of the surface should be regular to give an even deformation when animated.

First of all, so that you can retain a working scale when you are modeling any objects, select the door curves and use File|Export selected, calling the file Door_Ref_Curves. Create a new scene, use File|Import to bring in the Door_Ref_Curves scene and template these curves. You can create the polygon tentacle from a series of face extrusions on a cube, followed by a smoothing operation and then some final tweaking. This cube will represent the rough cross-section of the tentacle, so create a polygon cube and scale it in relation to the doorframe curves. Select one of the faces and extrude it (Edit|Polygons|Extrude Face) until it is as long again as the original cube. In the Channels Box for this extrusion operation, look at the local distance for the extrusion and open the options box for Edit|Polygons|Extrude Face, putting this value into the relevant local distance attribute. Click Apply eleven times to create a long segmented polygon box and then set the attribute back to zero. Select the top faces of the first eleven sections and use Edit Polygons|Subdivide so that the faces are divided into four squares. Select each of the four squares and extrude them until you have created four suckers on every section apart from the last. Because you haven't deleted the history for the extrusions, you can now select the previous extrusion nodes in the Channels Box and use the Show Manipulator tool to taper the tentacle along its length.

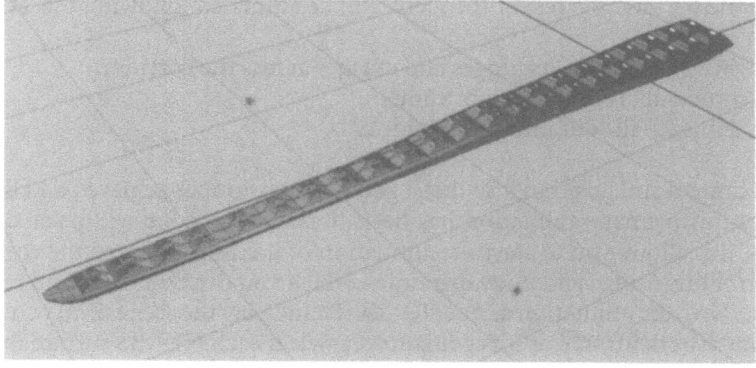

Figure 11.4 The Extruded Polygon Tentacle.

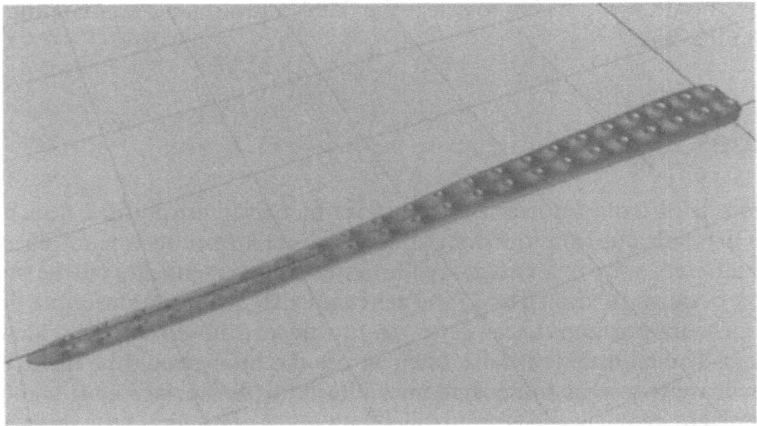

Figure 11.5 The Smoothed Polygon Tentacle.

Prior to smoothing the polygon tentacle, you should make sure that the sections of the tentacle are evenly built by using the Split Polygon tool and deleting redundant edges. Along the length in the side view, the splits towards the tapered end should also be evened out, as this tentacle end may well be used to "feel around" once in the corridor and should have enough surface detail to deform smoothly. Subdivide all of the faces along the side of the tentacle so that you can now begin building in some flatness and roundness to the cross-section. When this has been achieved, delete the history for the polygon surface and use Polygon|Smooth with a smoothness of one. Experiment with the continuity attribute until the correct shape is attained and, again, delete the history for the surface. It may well be worth smoothing the suckers once more and deleting any new triangular edges formed from the smoothing operations. Delete the history, delete the door curves and save the scene.

The Door Animation

Now that you have the "actors" ready for your scene, animate the door being dented. This needs to be done because the rest of the scene will be animated following this event:

• The door gets smashed off its hinges and crashes across the corridor.
• Tentacles come out around the doorframe.
• The main tentacle falls out into the corridor.

Create a new camera and position it so that a good composition is achieved and animate to the camera. Once this primary animation has been finished, the door will be as dented as it is going to get – this allows you to start the animation of it crashing across the corridor. We are going to control this using rigid body dynamics, which you can then bake and re-import into the final scene. Save the animation as doorDentAnim and play the scene until you get to a point where the door is as deformed as it is going to get. Select each NURBS surface that comprises the door, delete its history and convert it to a polygon surface using Modify|Convert|NURBS to Polygons. Set the method to General and open the Attribute Editor for the operation. You

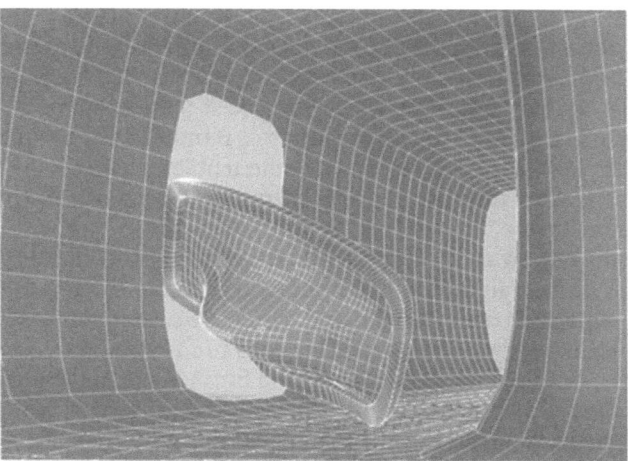

Figure 11.6 The Fully Dented Door in Dynamic Motion.

can now increase the samples at the curved portions using the U and V number values until you have a close representation of the door in polygons. Once that has been done, delete both histories and combine them so that you have one polygon model representing the door. Convert the corridor to a polygon mesh, make sure all the normals for both objects are facing the correct way and you are ready to set up the rigid body dynamics.

Turn the door object into an active rigid body and turn the corridor into a passive rigid body, delete everything else apart from the camera to which you are animating and then save the scene as rigidDoorAnim. You can now run some rigid body dynamics with the polygon door. This will provide a proxy surface that you can use to drive the animation of the NURBS door – this would have been too complex to use in an efficient rigid body simulation. Add a polygon cube as a battering ram to propel the door across the corridor, by making it a passive rigid body then animating its movement so that the door can be either flung spinning down the corridor or over the camera. Because you are going to be baking this simulation out (we are only interested in the transforms of this proxy object) you could further speed things up by using a polygon cube whose shape roughly mimics the original door. Once you have the desired piece of action, you can bake out the rigid body transforms, delete all of the solvers and the rest of the scene. Save this scene as rigidDoorAnim_Fin so that it just contains the moving proxy object; you can use the old scene to provide a testing ground to create additional shrapnel, such as door bolts flying off and rebounding through the scene. Open the animated deforming door scene (doorDentAnim) and constrain the NURBS door to the proxy object using a locator as an intermediary, so that you can move the locator to finish the animation of the NURBS door, so it rests or falls correctly. Now that you have the door being dented and flying out of the doorframe, you should set up the tentacles as they enter the scene from the darkened room.

The Side Tentacle Animation

The tentacles that slither around the side of the doorframe will need to be animated afterwards so that secondary animation can be added. You need to maintain flexibility in the methods used so that if changes need to be made, you can implement them with the minimum of re-wiring. You can use a path-like movement to move the tentacles around the doorframe so that they just burst out of the darkness and establish themselves in the scene. This, hopefully, can give a certain "stop-motion" feel to the sequence, harking back to the reverse filmed techniques used in some of the classic monster B movies. For the path-like movement, use an IK spline handle so that you can control the tentacles using joints for really smooth deformation, but at the same time use a "proxy technique" which will let you animate over the top of the IK spline control.

Create a new scene, import the polygon tentacle you made and change into the animation menu set. Draw a joint chain along the length of the skeleton, providing enough joints so that the tentacle can flex smoothly once skinned and then use a smooth bind. Import the door reference curves so you can see where the tentacles need to move to and in the top view draw a curve that would start inside the darkened room and finish at the point along the side wall that you want the tip of the tentacle to reach. This will be the IK spline curve, along which the joint chain will move. Open the options box for Skeleton|IK Spline Handle Tool and turn off all of the options apart from Auto Parent Curve and Root Twist Mode. Follow the instructions in the Help line and you should get the joint chain snap to the curve; by translating the start joint you can now move the tentacle down the curve. Changing the position and shape of the control curve can quickly implement any changes that you wish to make in terms of positioning for the tentacle, so it will be worth placing its pivot point at the start of the curve. This means that you can import the tentacle as many times as you like into the final scene and by changing where the IK curve appears (and texture of the tentacles) you can have multiple versions animated in your scene.

Using this technique, you cannot add any additional animation to the tentacle once it has moved into place, so you cannot add any waggling of the tips or other secondary motion. Delete the IK handle but retain the curve and duplicate the joint chain that the tentacle is bound to. Name the top of this new joint chain P_Chain, name the top of the original joint chain T_Chain and hide it and the polygon tentacle. Attach the proxy (P_Chain) joint chain to the curve using the same IK spline handle technique, so that you can move it in exactly the same way as you did with the tentacle chain. Select T_Chain and add a new attribute called IKcstr to it, making the attribute an integer with a maximum value of zero and a minimum value of zero (with the default value set to one). Show the original (T_Chain) joint chain and constrain each joint of the original to each corresponding joint of the new chain (P_Chain) so you can now move the smooth bound tentacle along the IK spline using the P_Chain to achieve this. Now open the Set Driven Keys option box from Animate|Driven Keys and select the top of T_Chain (with the new attribute) as the driver and select all of the joints in T_Chain as the driven. Use set driven keys to set the constraint weights for all of the joints to one when IKcstr is one and to set the constraint weights for all of the joints to zero when IKcstr is zero. Now you can animate the constraints of the T_Chain so you can have the P_Chain move the tentacle along the IK spline and then turn off all of the constraints and hand animate T_Chain afterwards. However, the movement of the joint chain appears to be in the direction of the curve only because the IK spline handle is snapping the nearest joints to it. You cannot key the position of the root joint in the normal manner because the IK spline handle is driving each joint's world position. You can group the joint chain though and keyframe the new group instead, so group P_Chain and call it PC_Group. Now the movement of PC_Group will drive the first movement of the tentacle(s), then the animated joints of T_Chain will drive the secondary animation once the constraints have been set to zero.

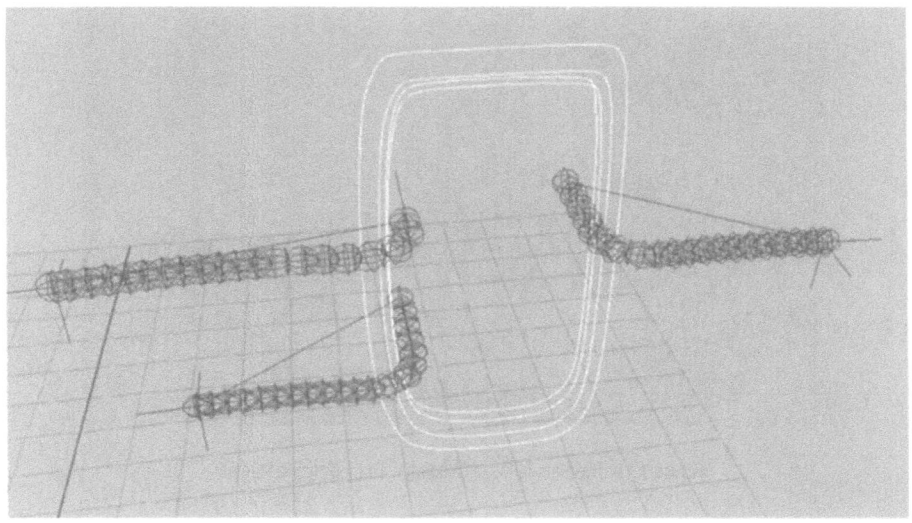

Figure 11.7 IK Spline Handles and Joint Chains about Reference Door Curves.

The Main Tentacle Animation

The main tentacle should be animated by hand using any selection of techniques, but owing to the type and construction of it, forward kinematics may well prove to be a better choice for total control. To improve the look of a fleshy tentacle bursting into the scene, soft body dynamics can be used to provide a flesh-like wobble when the tentacle impacts the floor.

Animate the tentacle so that it is timed to smash the door across the corridor, then save the scene. Change into the `Dynamics` menu set, select the tentacle and turn it into a soft body using the `Duplicate, make Copy Soft` option with a goal weighting of one. Now that the shape of the duplicate tentacle is being controlled by particles, you can take advantage of Maya's suite of particle tools and functions. Create a polygon plane with ten subdivisions in width and height and model the shape so that it roughly represents the curvature of the corridor. This will provide a surface that you can use in particle collisions, so move it so that it lies underneath the surface of the corridor because the particles that represent the NURBS object don't lie on the surface. Select the Particle object and then the polygon plane and use `Particles|Make Collide` and give the polygon plane a resiliency of `0.5` and a friction of `0.4` so that the particles will bounce but they won't bounce too far. Now select the tentacle surface and paint the weights for the particles until a correct fleshy bounce is achieved. Because the particles are now colliding with the polygon plane, you can animate the joints of the tentacle so that as the tentacle appears to sag and rest after the initial movement, the flesh will spread out around the joints as it comes to rest on the polygon plane. You can further influence the particles through the use of springs and fields. Create springs using the wireframe method so that the structure of the tentacle is held and create a cubic volume turbulence field that lies on the floor of the corridor. Now, as the tentacle falls into the field's volume, you can keyframe the magnitude from high to low so that the tentacle has additional wobble to it after the impact.

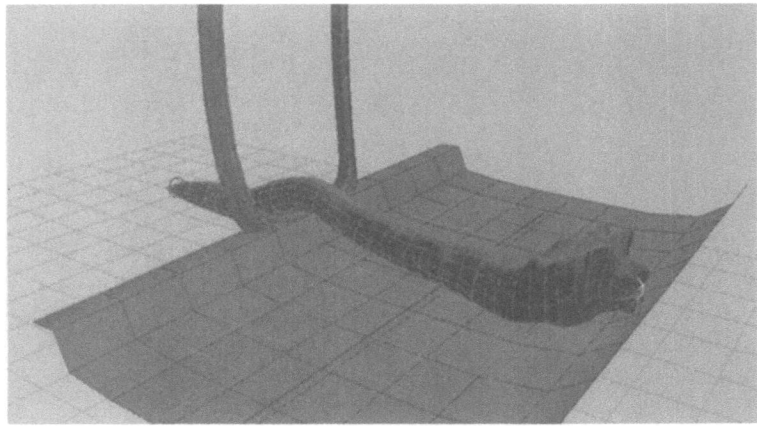

Figure 11.8 The Main Tentacle Colliding with the Polygon Stand in.

Finishing Touches

Now that the main animation work has been constructed, you can begin adding some finishing touches to the look of the piece. Pieces of door can use the same rigid body scene that you used for the main door to bake out more debris animation. The lights can be animated using an expression to control the intensity, but this will also have to be tied to the material properties of the surface that represents the light panel or bulb, such as the ambient colour on a semitranslucent material. Siren-type safety lighting can also be driven from a sin or cos expression, so that once these have been set up, they can be left alone during the course of the rendering. The shader for the door could also reflect the damage being sustained by using a layered shader to hold the diffuse Lambert paint on the door itself and the shiny Phong metal from which the door is constructed. You can then paint a texture map representing the areas where the door has been dented and use this combined with an animated `multiply/Divide utility` node in the Hypershade to increase the amount that the Phong material bleeds through by. Because we will be relating the amount of metalwork appearing to the deformation damage of the door from the clusters, you could create another driven key from the driven keys on the `Door_N` group to the shading node in the Hypershade.

Now all of these scenes have been built up, you can begin importing them to your master scene. Create a new scene and import the corridor and camera scene. Next import the animated door scene and verify that these both work together, deleting any doubled up items. The doorframe tentacle can now be imported as many times as is required until a sufficient number have been built up and animated. Finally import the main tentacle and again, delete any items that have been doubled up, such as cameras and corridors. If this scene is proving to be too heavy to render or would be better suited to dividing up for later compositing, then it is worth setting up the render layers or creating one copy of this scene for each element required and then turning the matte elements black (with the correct black hole alpha value). If these sub-scenes that have been imported need further work once the elements have been put in place, then it is worth using `File|Create Reference` instead of `File|Import`. Referencing a file creates a link to the file instead of fully importing it. This is extremely useful because every time the referencing scene file is opened, it will update the referenced files if the referenced files have been changed. If you have only animated the objects that you have referenced, when you texture them in their original files, this will update automatically in the scene that references them. It is not possible to delete referenced files, so there is no danger of accidentally destroying any imported work. The file referencing mechanisms mean that you can have different people working on scenes and use references to make sure that the work updates automatically each time the composite file is opened.

Summary

This section was created to show how to start combining the techniques in Maya together so that automatic effects can be created and how some attributes can be used to drive other effects and attributes. This all means that there are fewer levers to animate and can concentrate on creating the core animation or effects work. This tends to replicate the way that Maya organizes itself in terms of interconnected nodes all containing their own attributes that are then used to drive or pass messages to other attributes in other nodes. There really is no end to the amount of items that could be placed into this scene, but the amount of work and animation that would need to be done would start to increase exponentially, compared to the final effect in the rendered frames. This is where the ability to interlink and connect different nodes and effects comes in useful. All that is left to include in the scene is the actual monster that emerges from the darkened doorway.

Index